I'M ONLY IN THIS FOR ME

Other *Pearls Before Swine* Collections

King of the Comics
Breaking Stephan
Rat's Wars
Unsportsmanlike Conduct
Because Sometimes You Just Gotta Draw a Cover with Your Left Hand
Larry in Wonderland
When Pigs Fly
50,000,000 Pearls Fans Can't Be Wrong
The Saturday Evening Pearls
Macho Macho Animals
The Sopratos
Da Brudderhood of Zeeba Zeeba Eata
The Ratvolution Will Not Be Televised
Nighthogs
This Little Piggy Stayed Home
BLTs Taste So Darn Good

Treasuries

Pearls Gets Sacrificed
Pearls Falls Fast
Pearls Freaks the #%# Out*
Pearls Blows Up
Pearls Sells Out
The Crass Menagerie
Lions and Tigers and Crocs, Oh My!
Sgt. Piggy's Lonely Hearts Club Comic

Gift Books

Friends Should Know When They're Not Wanted
Da Crockydile Book o' Frendsheep

AMP! Comics for Kids

Skip School, Fly to Space
The Croc Ate My Homework
Beginning Pearls

I'M ONLY IN THIS FOR ME

A *Pearls Before Swine* Collection

By Stephan Pastis

Andrews McMeel
Publishing®

a division of Andrews McMeel Universal

Introduction

I really was in it only for myself.

It was some time in the 1990s (mercifully I have forgotten the exact year) and I decided I wanted to rule with an iron fist over a small American city.

So in my tiny little town of Albany, California, I ran for city council.

It was surprisingly easy to get my name on the ballot. I simply stood in a grocery store parking lot and got people to sign some petition-looking thingie. Most people just signed without asking any questions. (I was quite charming, or perhaps pathetic-looking.)

Others asked a slew of hard-hitting questions, like, "Do you live in the town?"

Then there was the grumpy, persistent woman who poked me in the chest and wanted to know exactly how much I knew about Albany. It was a fair question. So I did the wise thing and went to a different grocery store.

And when all was said and done, the good people of Albany, California had put me—a total loon—on the ballot.

Then things got more difficult.

The local newspaper decided to poke its nose where it didn't belong and do a feature on each of the four city council candidates. This was a problem.

It was a problem because I knew absolutely nothing about Albany, California. Other than the fact that my house was on its soil. I didn't even know why I was running, other than to initiate a coup and if possible, become emperor.

But I couldn't tell them that.

All I knew was that if they asked me one factual question about Albany, I was going to have to take a bathroom break. And if they asked me more than one, well, I was going to just stay in the bathroom. In fact, there was a good chance that the newspaper's only comment on me was going to be, "He should see a urologist."

So I met with my consultants (the other voices in my head) and did the honorable thing.

I hid.

No campaign. No signs. No interviews.

And thus, when the nosey newspaper ran their feature on the candidates, I was referred to simply as "mystery candidate Pastis."

And when the election occurred, I came in last. But I did get votes. If I remember right, I think I received something like 140 votes in an election where 600 or so votes would have put me on the city council.

Who those 140 people were, I have no idea. But it scares me that they're out there.

Because they almost facilitated my coup.

To rule a small American town in a way not unlike Kim Jong-un's North Korea.

In it only for me.

Stephan Pastis
May 2016

To the law school professor who told me that if I had to ask a dumb question like that, I probably shouldn't be in law school. Boy, were you right.

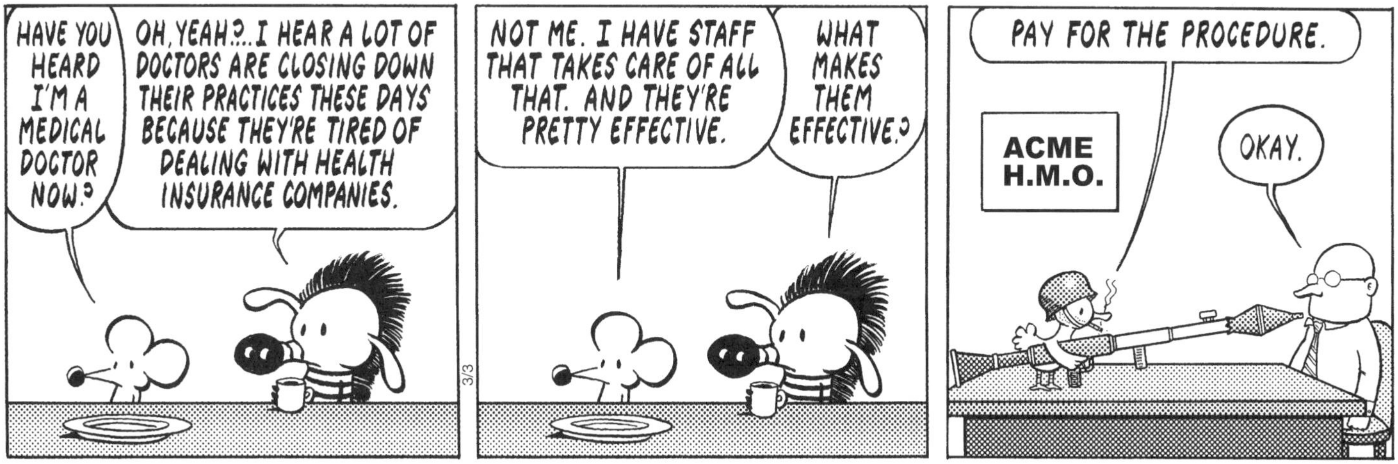
HAVE YOU HEARD I'M A MEDICAL DOCTOR NOW?
OH, YEAH?...I HEAR A LOT OF DOCTORS ARE CLOSING DOWN THEIR PRACTICES THESE DAYS BECAUSE THEY'RE TIRED OF DEALING WITH HEALTH INSURANCE COMPANIES.
3/3
NOT ME. I HAVE STAFF THAT TAKES CARE OF ALL THAT. AND THEY'RE PRETTY EFFECTIVE.
WHAT MAKES THEM EFFECTIVE?
PAY FOR THE PROCEDURE.
ACME H.M.O.
OKAY.

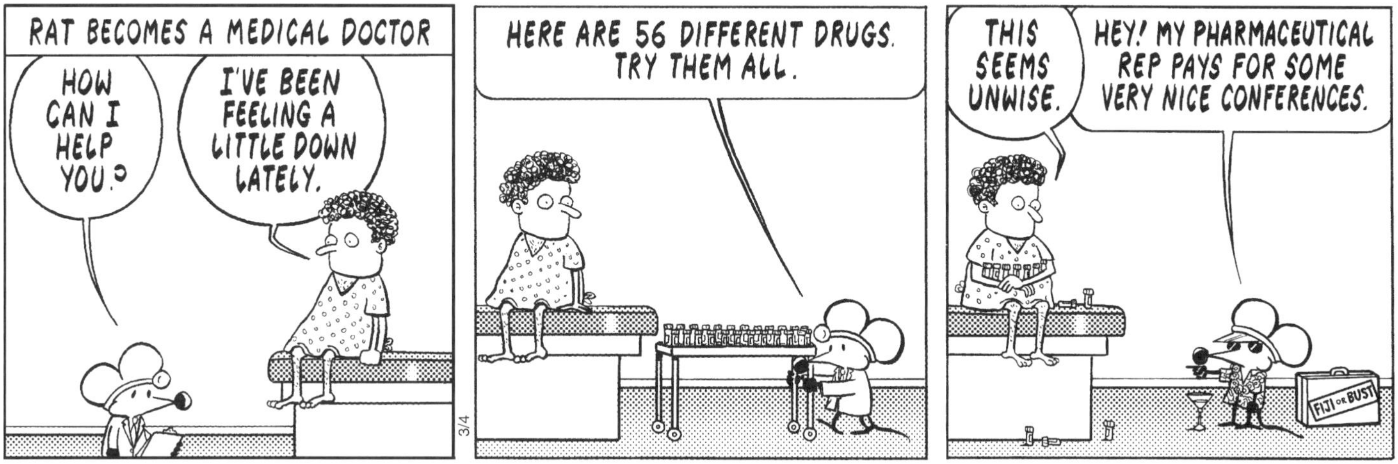
RAT BECOMES A MEDICAL DOCTOR
HOW CAN I HELP YOU?
I'VE BEEN FEELING A LITTLE DOWN LATELY.
3/4
HERE ARE 56 DIFFERENT DRUGS. TRY THEM ALL.
THIS SEEMS UNWISE.
HEY! MY PHARMACEUTICAL REP PAYS FOR SOME VERY NICE CONFERENCES.
FIJI OR BUST

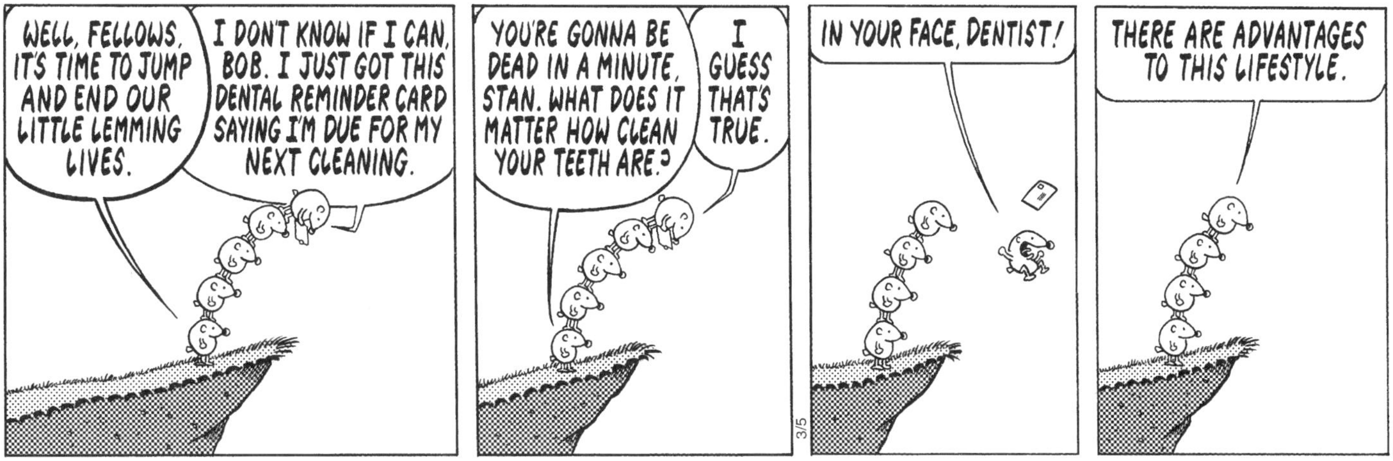
WELL, FELLOWS, IT'S TIME TO JUMP AND END OUR LITTLE LEMMING LIVES.
I DON'T KNOW IF I CAN, BOB. I JUST GOT THIS DENTAL REMINDER CARD SAYING I'M DUE FOR MY NEXT CLEANING.
YOU'RE GONNA BE DEAD IN A MINUTE, STAN. WHAT DOES IT MATTER HOW CLEAN YOUR TEETH ARE?
I GUESS THAT'S TRUE.
3/5
IN YOUR FACE, DENTIST!
THERE ARE ADVANTAGES TO THIS LIFESTYLE.

THAT POLAR BEAR'S FINALLY GONE, MORTY. TURNS OUT POLAR BEARS DON'T LIVE IN THE SOUTH POLE AFTER ALL.

SO WHAT DOES THAT MEAN?

IT MEANS WE'RE IN THE CLEAR, MORTY. NO MORE PREDATORS. NO MORE LIVING IN FEAR.

WOW, SAUL! THIS CALLS FOR A TOAST. WHAT SHOULD WE TOAST TO?

TO FAT, FLIGHTLESS BIRDS.

WELL, GUYS, THIS IS IT... THE END OF OUR LEMMING LIVES.... READY TO JUMP?

WHOA WHOA WHOA... BOB THERE OWES ME FIFTY BUCKS.

Lemmings' LEAP

YEAH, THAT'S TRUE. LET ME GET OUT MY CHECKBOOK AND ——

Lemmings' LEAP

SEE YOU IN HELL, SUCKERRRRRRR

Lemmings' LEAP

IT'S SO HARD TO COLLECT FROM A LEMMING.

HEY, I HEAR YOU WENT TO PARIS. HOW WAS IT?

OH, LOVELY! I WENT TO A BOULANGERIE, WHICH IS A PLACE THAT MAKES BREAD, AND A PATISSERIE, WHICH IS A PLACE THAT MAKES PASTRIES.

HOW WONDERFUL... AND DID YOU GO TO A WHOGIVESA@#☆☆#ERIE?

AND WHAT IS THAT?

NEVER MIND.

NOW SHOW ME 800 VACATION PHOTOS. BECAUSE FRIENDS LOVE THAT.

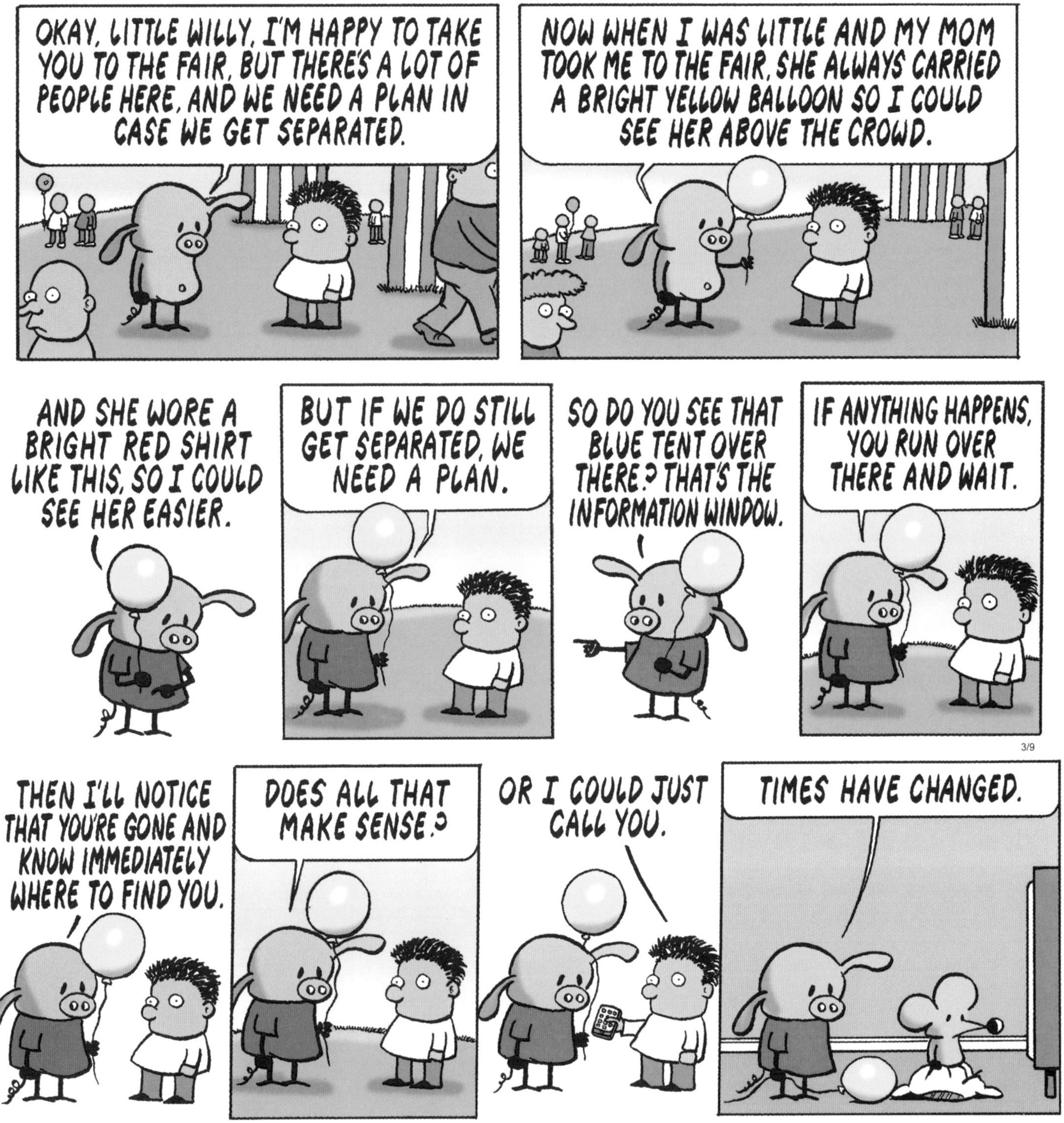
OKAY, LITTLE WILLY, I'M HAPPY TO TAKE YOU TO THE FAIR, BUT THERE'S A LOT OF PEOPLE HERE, AND WE NEED A PLAN IN CASE WE GET SEPARATED.
NOW WHEN I WAS LITTLE AND MY MOM TOOK ME TO THE FAIR, SHE ALWAYS CARRIED A BRIGHT YELLOW BALLOON SO I COULD SEE HER ABOVE THE CROWD.
AND SHE WORE A BRIGHT RED SHIRT LIKE THIS, SO I COULD SEE HER EASIER.
BUT IF WE DO STILL GET SEPARATED, WE NEED A PLAN.
SO DO YOU SEE THAT BLUE TENT OVER THERE? THAT'S THE INFORMATION WINDOW.
IF ANYTHING HAPPENS, YOU RUN OVER THERE AND WAIT.
3/9
THEN I'LL NOTICE THAT YOU'RE GONE AND KNOW IMMEDIATELY WHERE TO FIND YOU.
DOES ALL THAT MAKE SENSE?
OR I COULD JUST CALL YOU.
TIMES HAVE CHANGED.

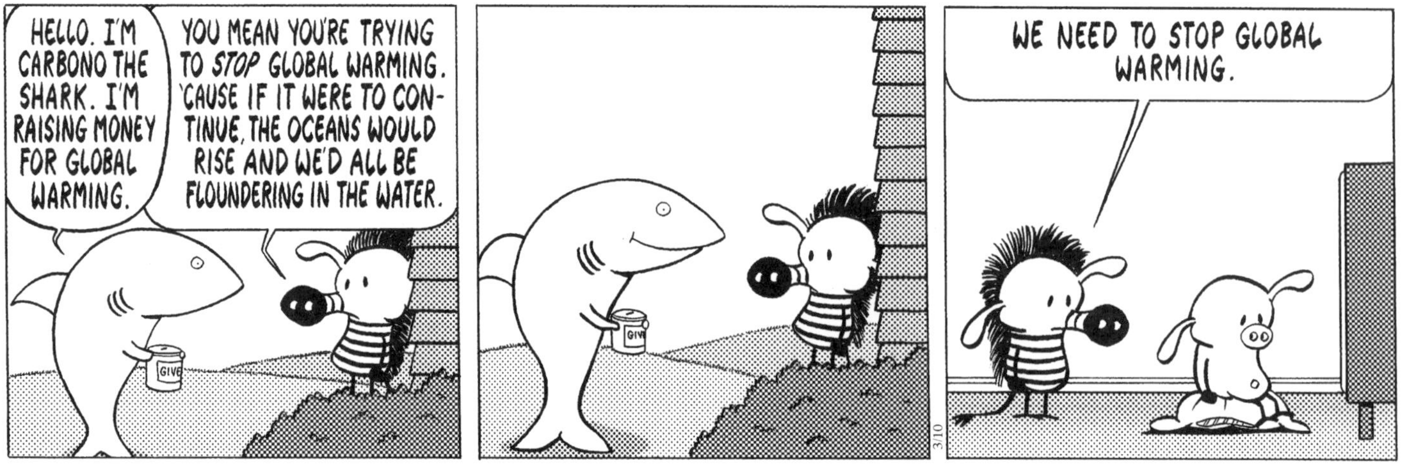
HELLO. I'M CARBONO THE SHARK. I'M RAISING MONEY FOR GLOBAL WARMING.
YOU MEAN YOU'RE TRYING TO *STOP* GLOBAL WARMING. 'CAUSE IF IT WERE TO CONTINUE, THE OCEANS WOULD RISE AND WE'D ALL BE FLOUNDERING IN THE WATER.
GIVE
GIVE
WE NEED TO STOP GLOBAL WARMING.
3/10

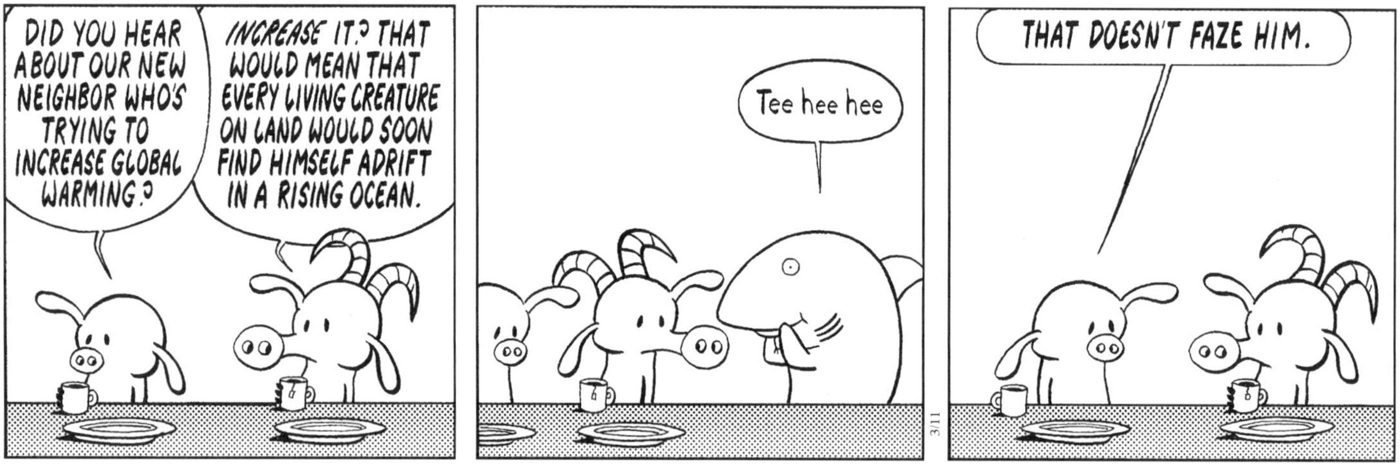
DID YOU HEAR ABOUT OUR NEW NEIGHBOR WHO'S TRYING TO INCREASE GLOBAL WARMING?
INCREASE IT? THAT WOULD MEAN THAT EVERY LIVING CREATURE ON LAND WOULD SOON FIND HIMSELF ADRIFT IN A RISING OCEAN.
Tee hee hee
THAT DOESN'T FAZE HIM.
3/11

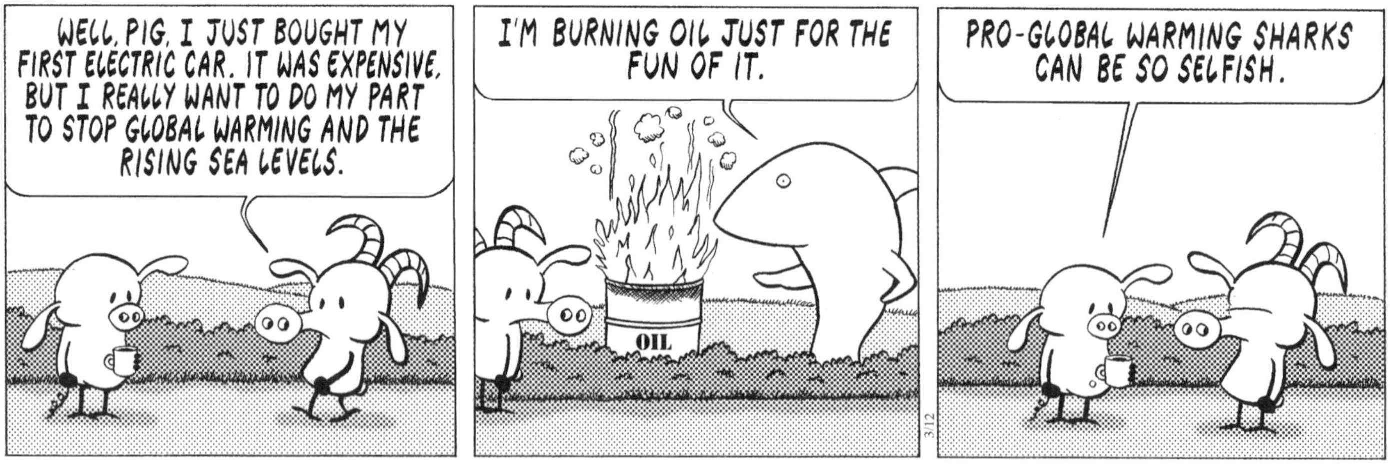
WELL, PIG, I JUST BOUGHT MY FIRST ELECTRIC CAR. IT WAS EXPENSIVE, BUT I REALLY WANT TO DO MY PART TO STOP GLOBAL WARMING AND THE RISING SEA LEVELS.
I'M BURNING OIL JUST FOR THE FUN OF IT.
OIL
PRO-GLOBAL WARMING SHARKS CAN BE SO SELFISH.
3/12

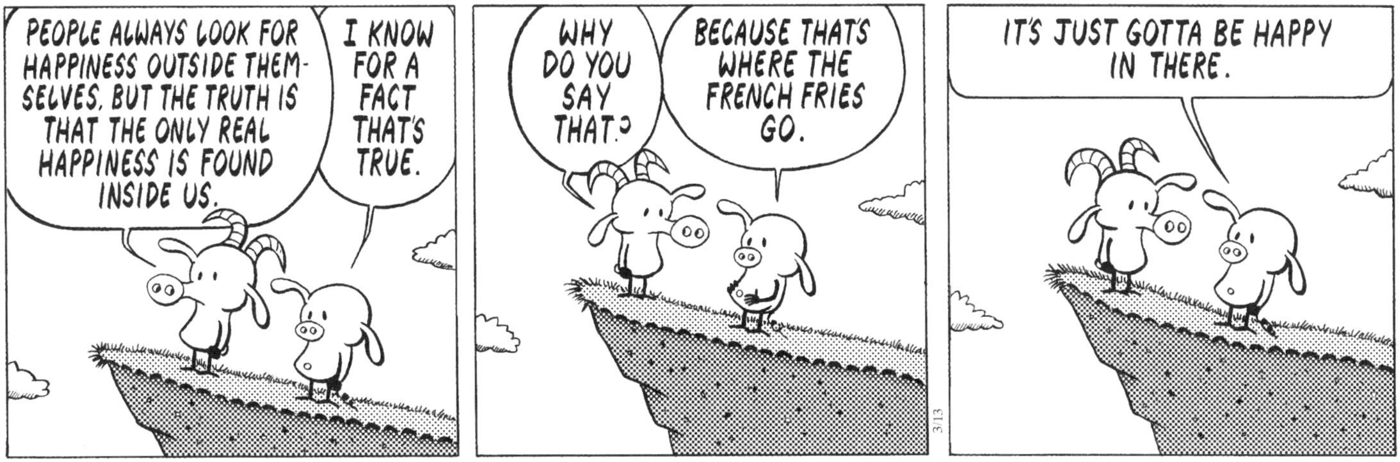
PEOPLE ALWAYS LOOK FOR HAPPINESS OUTSIDE THEMSELVES, BUT THE TRUTH IS THAT THE ONLY REAL HAPPINESS IS FOUND INSIDE US.
I KNOW FOR A FACT THAT'S TRUE.
WHY DO YOU SAY THAT?
BECAUSE THAT'S WHERE THE FRENCH FRIES GO.
IT'S JUST GOTTA BE HAPPY IN THERE.
3/13

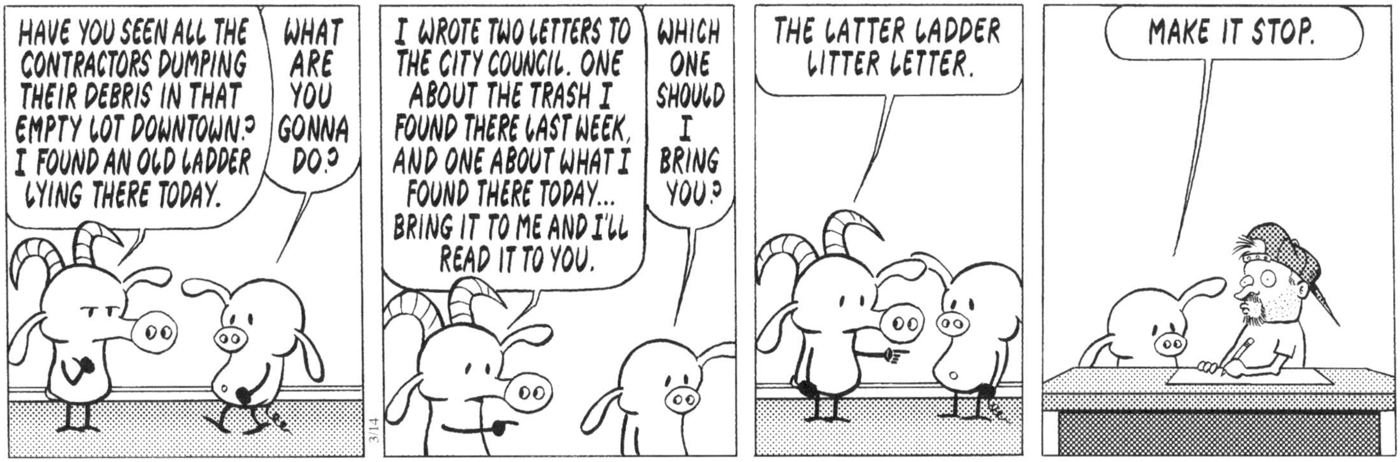
HAVE YOU SEEN ALL THE CONTRACTORS DUMPING THEIR DEBRIS IN THAT EMPTY LOT DOWNTOWN? I FOUND AN OLD LADDER LYING THERE TODAY.
WHAT ARE YOU GONNA DO?
I WROTE TWO LETTERS TO THE CITY COUNCIL. ONE ABOUT THE TRASH I FOUND THERE LAST WEEK, AND ONE ABOUT WHAT I FOUND THERE TODAY... BRING IT TO ME AND I'LL READ IT TO YOU.
WHICH ONE SHOULD I BRING YOU?
THE LATTER LADDER LITTER LETTER.
MAKE IT STOP.
3/14

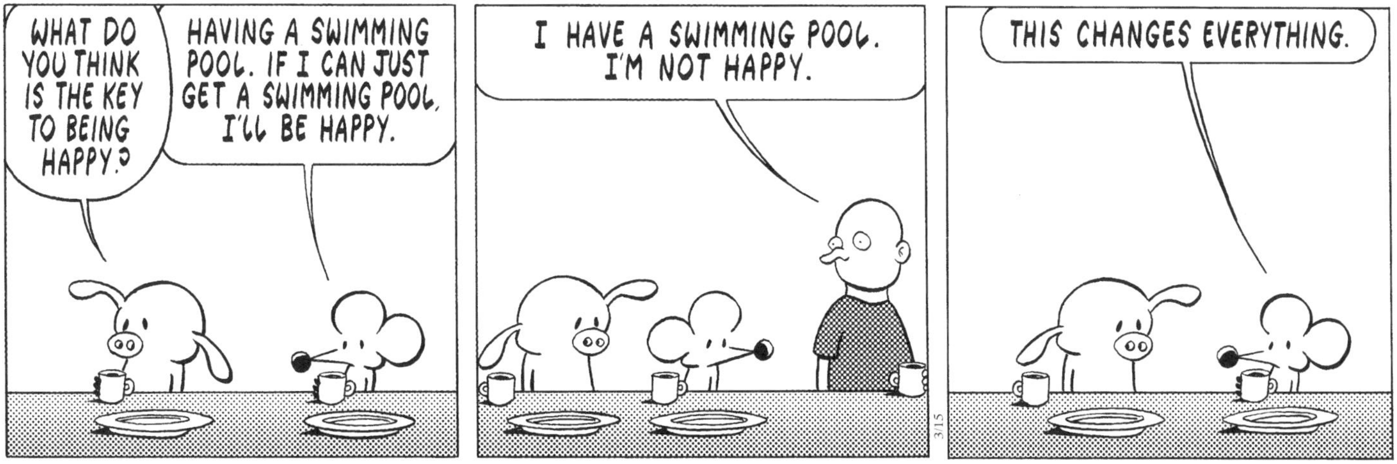
WHAT DO YOU THINK IS THE KEY TO BEING HAPPY?
HAVING A SWIMMING POOL. IF I CAN JUST GET A SWIMMING POOL, I'LL BE HAPPY.
I HAVE A SWIMMING POOL. I'M NOT HAPPY.
THIS CHANGES EVERYTHING.
3/15

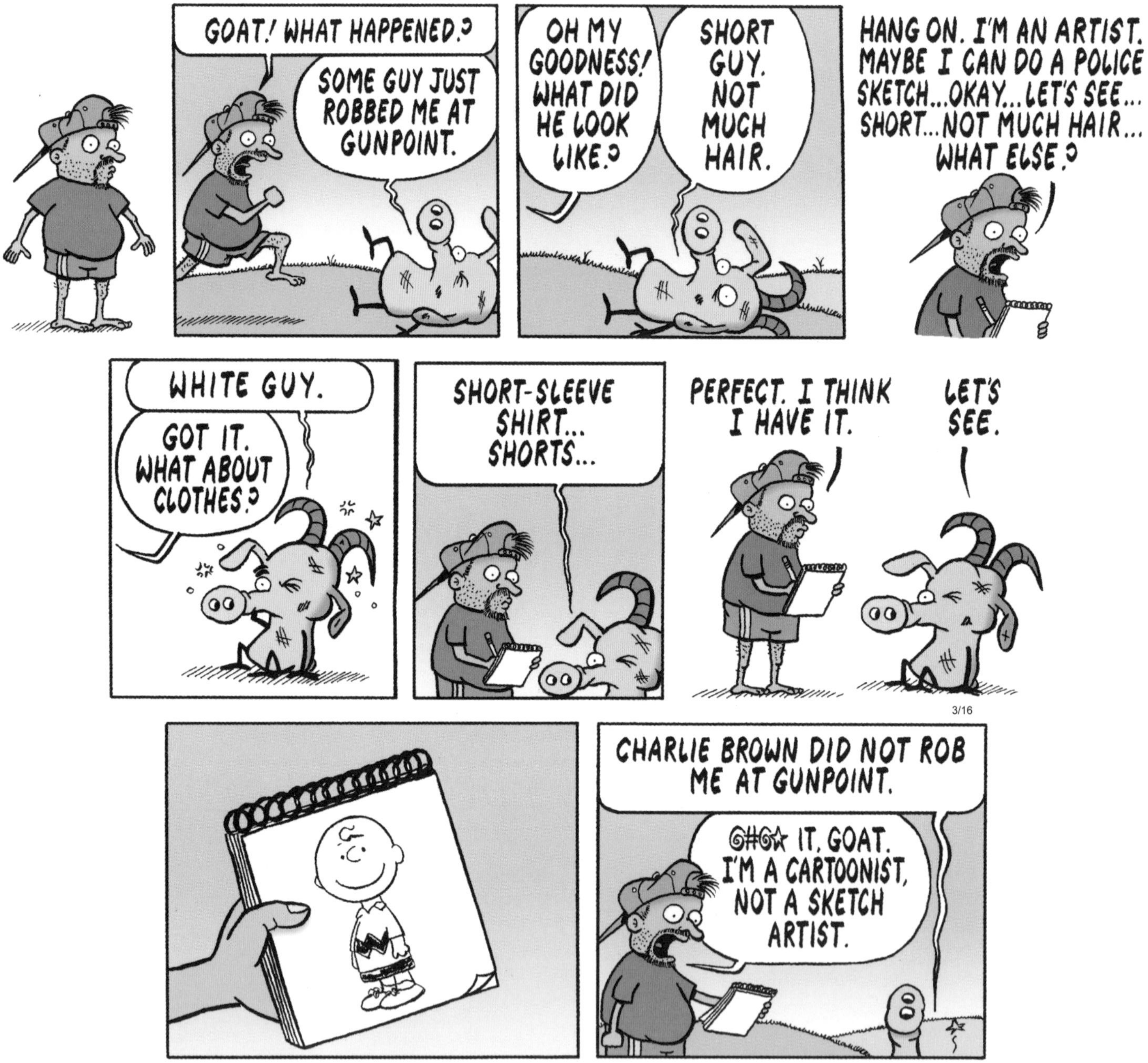
GOAT! WHAT HAPPENED?
SOME GUY JUST ROBBED ME AT GUNPOINT.
OH MY GOODNESS! WHAT DID HE LOOK LIKE?
SHORT GUY. NOT MUCH HAIR.
HANG ON. I'M AN ARTIST. MAYBE I CAN DO A POLICE SKETCH...OKAY...LET'S SEE... SHORT...NOT MUCH HAIR... WHAT ELSE?
WHITE GUY.
GOT IT. WHAT ABOUT CLOTHES?
SHORT-SLEEVE SHIRT... SHORTS...
PERFECT. I THINK I HAVE IT.
LET'S SEE.
3/16
CHARLIE BROWN DID NOT ROB ME AT GUNPOINT.
@#@☆ IT, GOAT. I'M A CARTOONIST, NOT A SKETCH ARTIST.

Panel 1:
OKAY, GUYS, I HAVE AN IDEA. INSTEAD OF ALL BLINDLY JUMPING OFF THIS CLIFF LIKE THE LEMMINGS THAT WE ARE, WHAT IF INSTEAD WE EACH CHOOSE TO THINK FOR OURSELVES?

BUT THAT'S SCARY.

Panel 2:
SURE, IT'S SCARY, PHIL. BUT THE ALTERNATIVE IS DEATH.

Panel 3:

Panel 4:
THAT'S DISCOURAGING.

Panel 5:
WHAT ARE YOU DOING, PIG?

BUILDING STUFF WITH MY NEW ERECTOR SET. NORMALLY, I DON'T LIKE THESE THINGS 'CAUSE IT'S SO HARD TO DISASSEMBLE WHAT YOU BUILD, BUT THIS ONE AUTOMATICALLY BREAKS APART AFTER YOU'RE FINISHED.

Panel 6:
IT'S THAT CONVENIENT?

YEAH. THOUGH IT DOES COME WITH A WARNING.

Panel 7:
WHAT'S THE WARNING?

'SEE DOCTOR FOR ERECTOR BUILDINGS LASTING MORE THAN FOUR HOURS.'

Panel 8:
PROUD OF YOURSELF?

HARDLY.

COMIC STRIP CENSOR

Panel 9:
Hey, zeeba neighba...Want play croquet wid us and lemmings?

YOU'RE ACTUALLY PARTICIPATING IN RECREATIONAL SPORTS WITH OTHER SPECIES?

Panel 10:
We use dem as balls.

Panel 11:
BEATS JUMPING OFF CLIFFS.

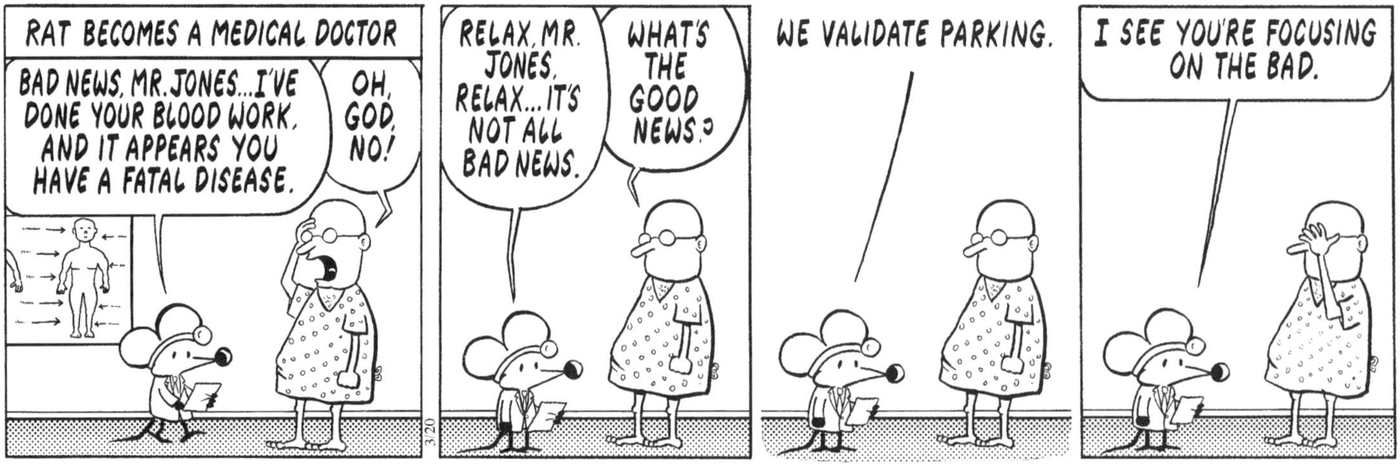
RAT BECOMES A MEDICAL DOCTOR
BAD NEWS, MR. JONES...I'VE DONE YOUR BLOOD WORK, AND IT APPEARS YOU HAVE A FATAL DISEASE.
OH, GOD, NO!
RELAX, MR. JONES, RELAX...IT'S NOT ALL BAD NEWS.
WHAT'S THE GOOD NEWS?
WE VALIDATE PARKING.
I SEE YOU'RE FOCUSING ON THE BAD.
3/20

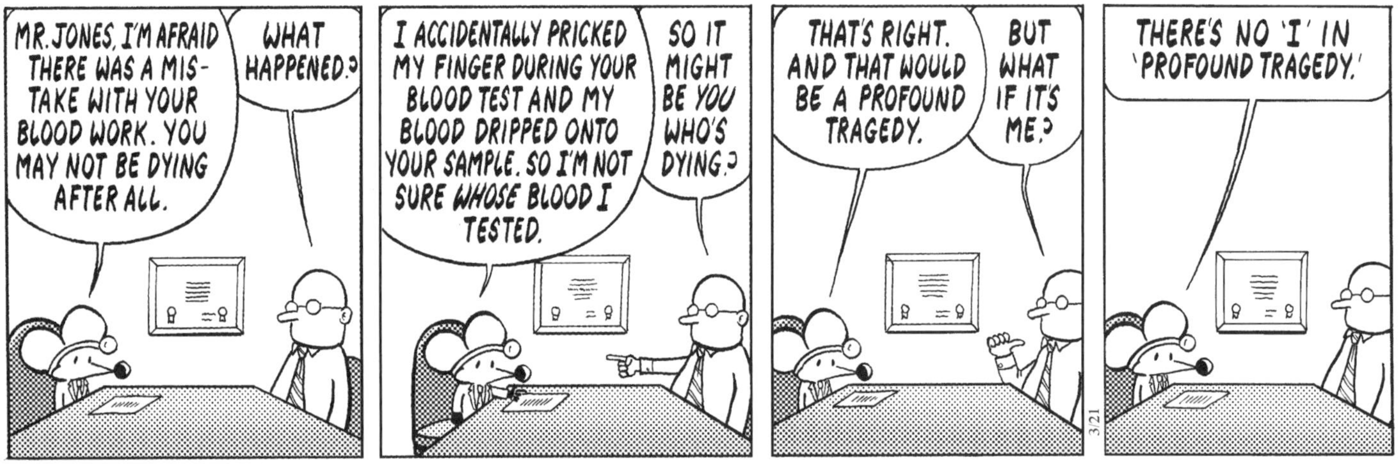
MR. JONES, I'M AFRAID THERE WAS A MISTAKE WITH YOUR BLOOD WORK. YOU MAY NOT BE DYING AFTER ALL.
WHAT HAPPENED?
I ACCIDENTALLY PRICKED MY FINGER DURING YOUR BLOOD TEST AND MY BLOOD DRIPPED ONTO YOUR SAMPLE. SO I'M NOT SURE WHOSE BLOOD I TESTED.
SO IT MIGHT BE YOU WHO'S DYING?
THAT'S RIGHT. AND THAT WOULD BE A PROFOUND TRAGEDY.
BUT WHAT IF IT'S ME?
THERE'S NO 'I' IN 'PROFOUND TRAGEDY.'
3/21

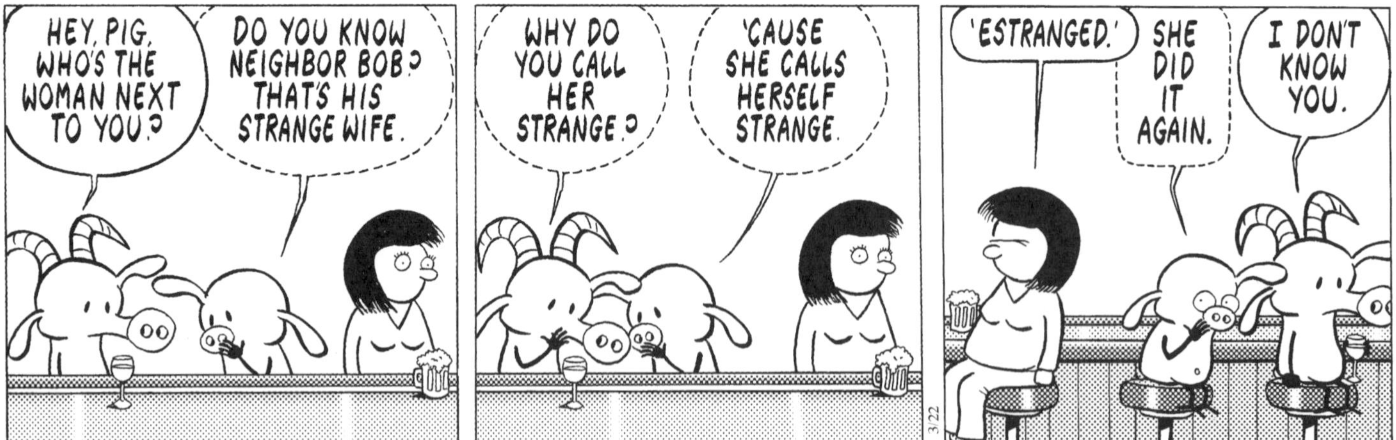
HEY, PIG, WHO'S THE WOMAN NEXT TO YOU?
DO YOU KNOW NEIGHBOR BOB? THAT'S HIS STRANGE WIFE.
WHY DO YOU CALL HER STRANGE?
'CAUSE SHE CALLS HERSELF STRANGE.
'ESTRANGED.'
SHE DID IT AGAIN.
I DON'T KNOW YOU.
3/22

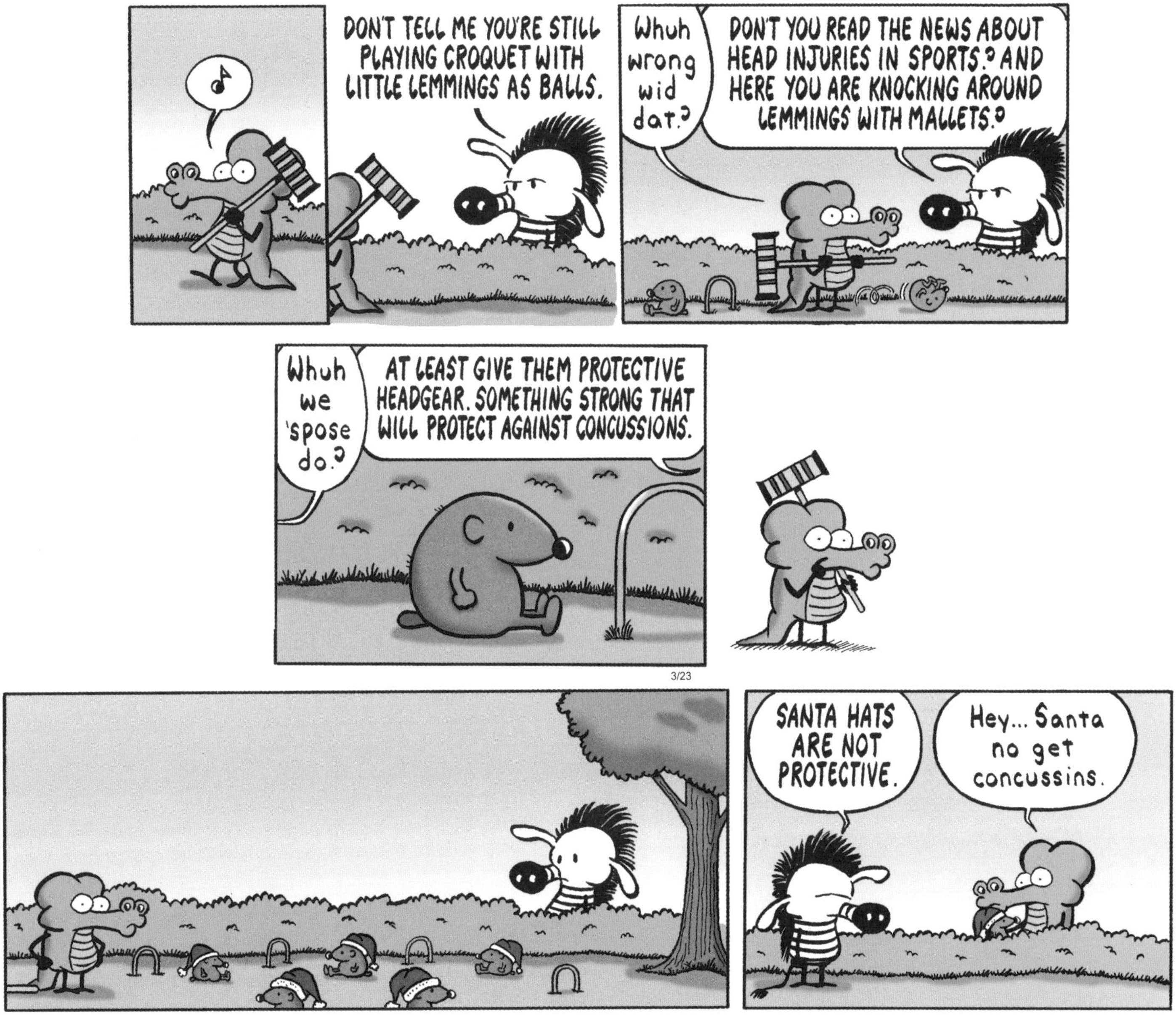
DON'T TELL ME YOU'RE STILL PLAYING CROQUET WITH LITTLE LEMMINGS AS BALLS.
Whuh wrong wid dat?
DON'T YOU READ THE NEWS ABOUT HEAD INJURIES IN SPORTS? AND HERE YOU ARE KNOCKING AROUND LEMMINGS WITH MALLETS?
Whuh we 'spose do?
AT LEAST GIVE THEM PROTECTIVE HEADGEAR. SOMETHING STRONG THAT WILL PROTECT AGAINST CONCUSSIONS.
3/23
SANTA HATS ARE NOT PROTECTIVE.
Hey... Santa no get concussins.

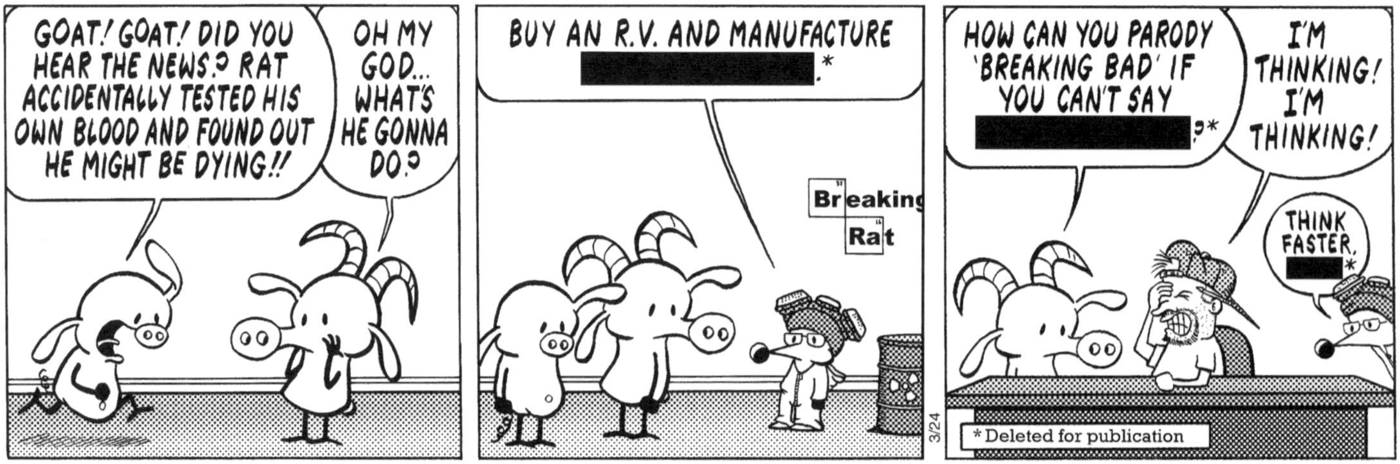
GOAT! GOAT! DID YOU HEAR THE NEWS? RAT ACCIDENTALLY TESTED HIS OWN BLOOD AND FOUND OUT HE MIGHT BE DYING!!
OH MY GOD... WHAT'S HE GONNA DO?
BUY AN R.V. AND MANUFACTURE [redacted].*
Breaking Rat
HOW CAN YOU PARODY 'BREAKING BAD' IF YOU CAN'T SAY [redacted]?*
I'M THINKING! I'M THINKING!
THINK FASTER, [redacted]*
3/24
*Deleted for publication

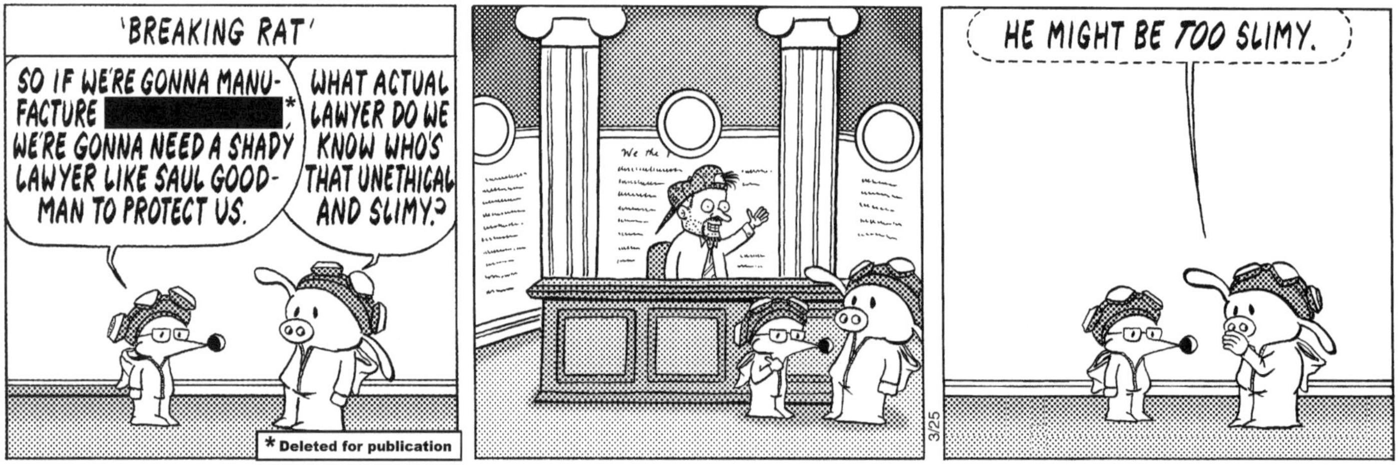
'BREAKING RAT'
SO IF WE'RE GONNA MANUFACTURE [redacted]*, WE'RE GONNA NEED A SHADY LAWYER LIKE SAUL GOODMAN TO PROTECT US.
WHAT ACTUAL LAWYER DO WE KNOW WHO'S THAT UNETHICAL AND SLIMY?
*Deleted for publication
3/25
HE MIGHT BE TOO SLIMY.

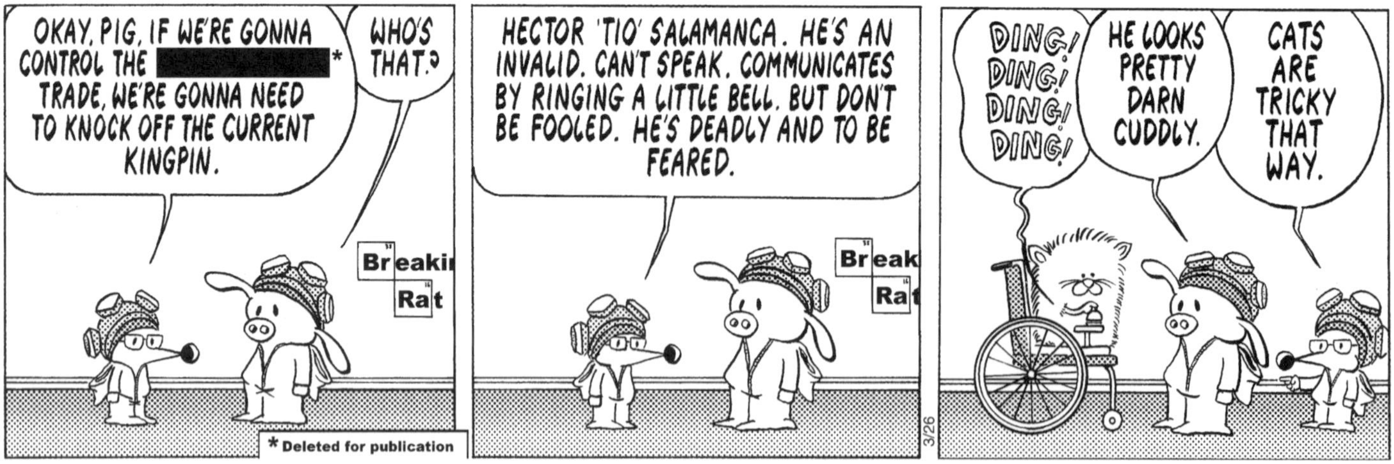
OKAY, PIG, IF WE'RE GONNA CONTROL THE [redacted]* TRADE, WE'RE GONNA NEED TO KNOCK OFF THE CURRENT KINGPIN.
WHO'S THAT?
*Deleted for publication
HECTOR 'TIO' SALAMANCA. HE'S AN INVALID. CAN'T SPEAK. COMMUNICATES BY RINGING A LITTLE BELL. BUT DON'T BE FOOLED. HE'S DEADLY AND TO BE FEARED.
3/26
DING! DING! DING! DING!
HE LOOKS PRETTY DARN CUDDLY.
CATS ARE TRICKY THAT WAY.

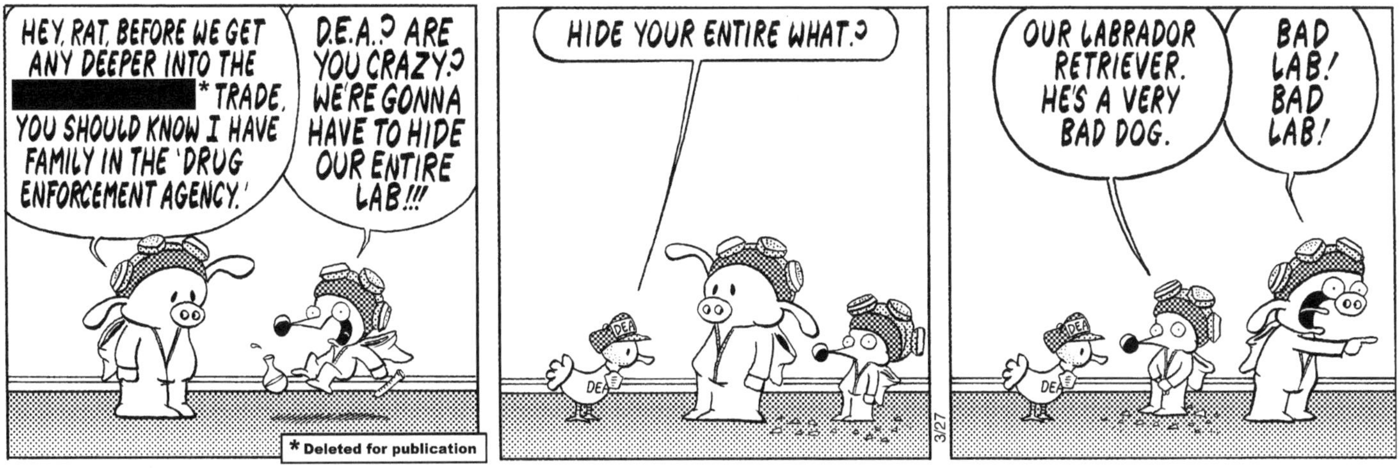
HEY, RAT, BEFORE WE GET ANY DEEPER INTO THE [redacted]* TRADE, YOU SHOULD KNOW I HAVE FAMILY IN THE 'DRUG ENFORCEMENT AGENCY.'
D.E.A.? ARE YOU CRAZY? WE'RE GONNA HAVE TO HIDE OUR ENTIRE LAB!!!
* Deleted for publication
HIDE YOUR ENTIRE WHAT?
DEA
DEA
3/27
OUR LABRADOR RETRIEVER. HE'S A VERY BAD DOG.
BAD LAB! BAD LAB!

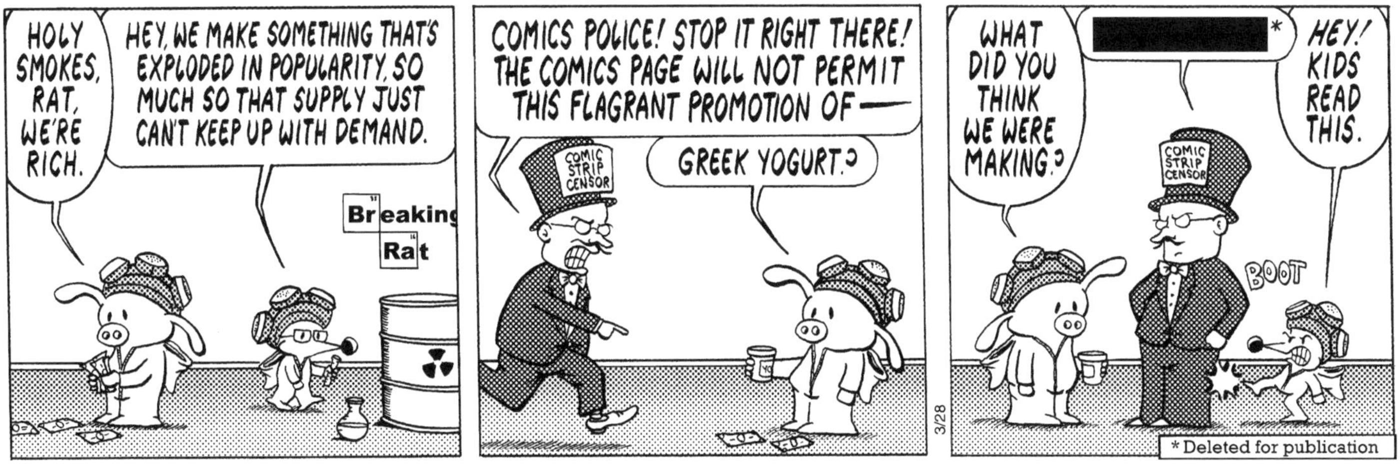
HOLY SMOKES, RAT, WE'RE RICH.
HEY, WE MAKE SOMETHING THAT'S EXPLODED IN POPULARITY, SO MUCH SO THAT SUPPLY JUST CAN'T KEEP UP WITH DEMAND.
Breaking
Rat
COMICS POLICE! STOP IT RIGHT THERE! THE COMICS PAGE WILL NOT PERMIT THIS FLAGRANT PROMOTION OF—
GREEK YOGURT?
COMIC STRIP CENSOR
3/28
WHAT DID YOU THINK WE WERE MAKING?
[redacted]*
HEY! KIDS READ THIS.
COMIC STRIP CENSOR
BOOT
* Deleted for publication

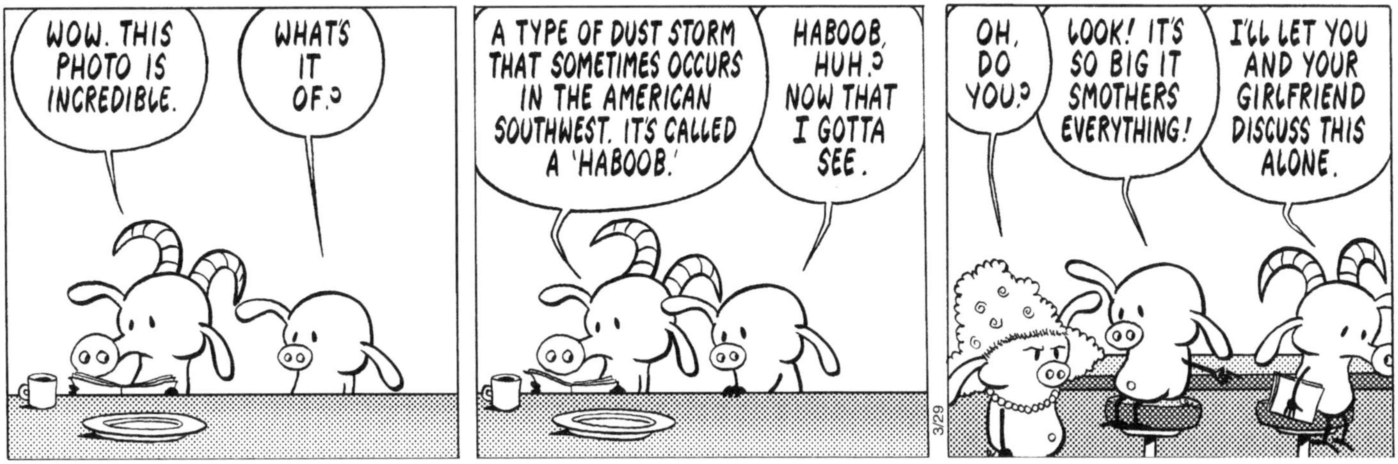
WOW. THIS PHOTO IS INCREDIBLE.
WHAT'S IT OF?
A TYPE OF DUST STORM THAT SOMETIMES OCCURS IN THE AMERICAN SOUTHWEST. IT'S CALLED A 'HABOOB.'
HABOOB, HUH? NOW THAT I GOTTA SEE.
3/29
OH, DO YOU?
LOOK! IT'S SO BIG IT SMOTHERS EVERYTHING!
I'LL LET YOU AND YOUR GIRLFRIEND DISCUSS THIS ALONE.

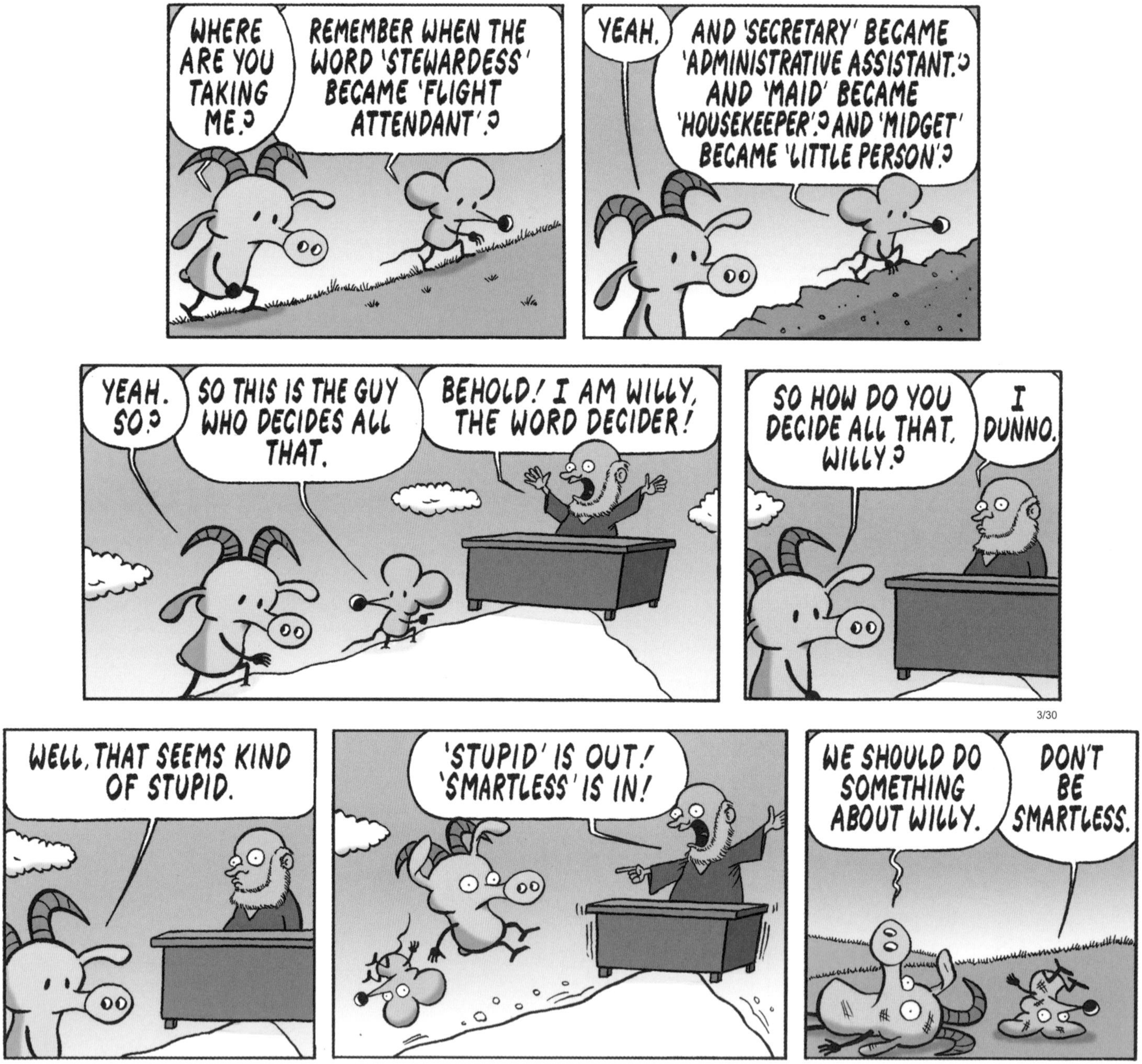
WHERE ARE YOU TAKING ME?
REMEMBER WHEN THE WORD 'STEWARDESS' BECAME 'FLIGHT ATTENDANT'?
YEAH.
AND 'SECRETARY' BECAME 'ADMINISTRATIVE ASSISTANT.' AND 'MAID' BECAME 'HOUSEKEEPER'? AND 'MIDGET' BECAME 'LITTLE PERSON'?
YEAH. SO?
SO THIS IS THE GUY WHO DECIDES ALL THAT.
BEHOLD! I AM WILLY, THE WORD DECIDER!
SO HOW DO YOU DECIDE ALL THAT, WILLY?
I DUNNO.
3/30
WELL, THAT SEEMS KIND OF STUPID.
'STUPID' IS OUT! 'SMARTLESS' IS IN!
WE SHOULD DO SOMETHING ABOUT WILLY.
DON'T BE SMARTLESS.

Panel 1: SO I'M DRIVING DOWN THE ROAD WHEN I SEE THIS PEDESTRIAN WHO WANTS TO CROSS THE ROAD IN FRONT OF ME. SO I SLOW DOWN TO LET HIM CROSS.

Panel 2: SO? / SO THE GUY FAILS TO GIVE THE HAND WAVE, THE UNIVERSAL ACKNOWLEDGEMENT THAT SOMEONE ON THE ROAD HAS DONE SOMETHING NICE FOR YOU.

3/31

Panel 3: WHO CARES? / HE DOES. I ACCELERATED AND RAN OVER HIS TOES.

Panel 4: YOU DIDN'T. / YOU GOTTA GIVE THE HAND WAVE.

Panel 5: HEY, RAT, I'D LIKE YOU TO MEET MY NEW FRIEND, DAWN. / I CAN'T SEE HER.

4/1

Panel 6: IT'S ALWAYS DARKEST BEFORE THE DAWN.

Panel 7: THERE'S SOME DARKNESS FOR YOU.

S. PASTIS

Panel 8: LOOK AT THAT PRETTY GIRL LISTENING TO HER iPOD. I SHOULD TALK TO HER, BUT SHE'S PROBABLY TOO HIP FOR ME. / OH, C'MON, DUDE. HOW CAN YOU HAVE SO LITTLE CONFIDENCE? GO OVER AND SAY SOMETHING TO HER.

Panel 9: HIYA... WHATCHA LISTENING TO? / CHUCK D.

Panel 10: CHARLES DARWIN HAS AUDIO RECORDINGS?

4/2

Panel 11: MAYBE YOU HAVE THE RIGHT AMOUNT OF CONFIDENCE.

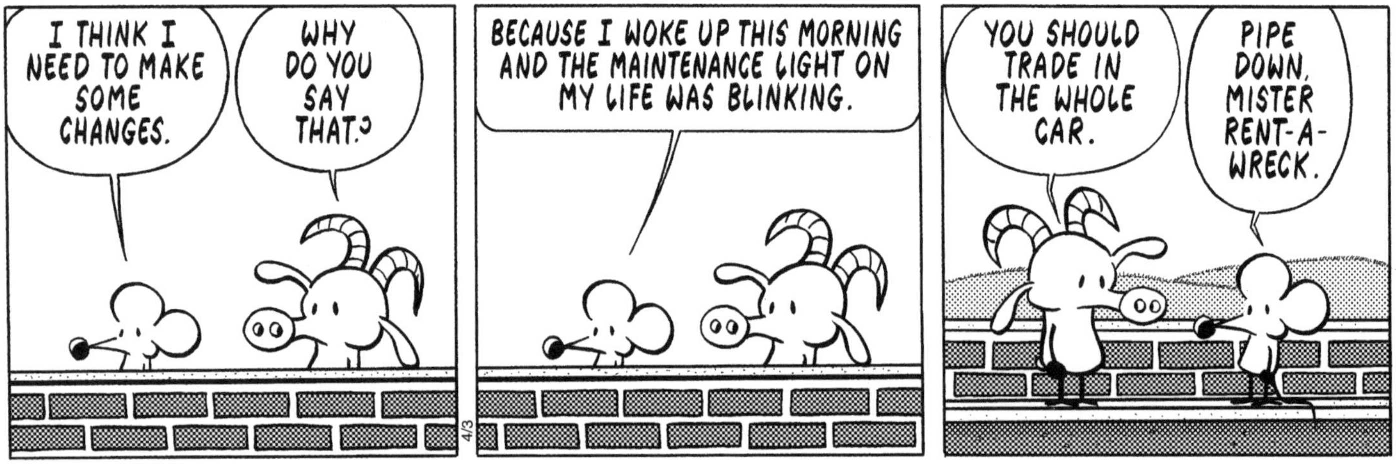
I THINK I NEED TO MAKE SOME CHANGES.
WHY DO YOU SAY THAT?
BECAUSE I WOKE UP THIS MORNING AND THE MAINTENANCE LIGHT ON MY LIFE WAS BLINKING.
YOU SHOULD TRADE IN THE WHOLE CAR.
PIPE DOWN, MISTER RENT-A-WRECK.
4/3

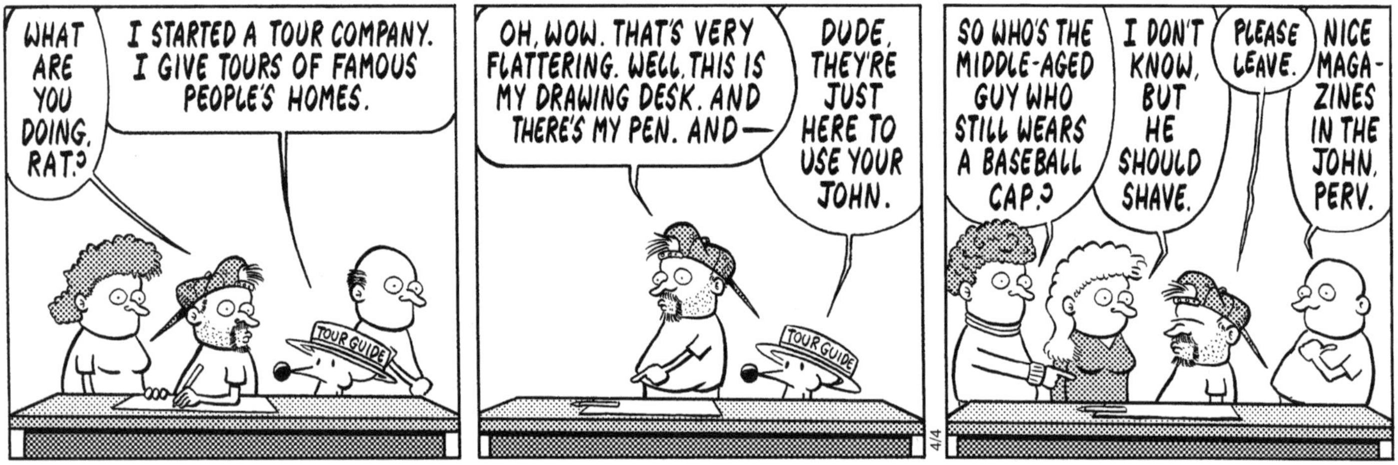
WHAT ARE YOU DOING, RAT?
I STARTED A TOUR COMPANY. I GIVE TOURS OF FAMOUS PEOPLE'S HOMES.
TOUR GUIDE
OH, WOW. THAT'S VERY FLATTERING. WELL, THIS IS MY DRAWING DESK. AND THERE'S MY PEN. AND—
DUDE, THEY'RE JUST HERE TO USE YOUR JOHN.
TOUR GUIDE
SO WHO'S THE MIDDLE-AGED GUY WHO STILL WEARS A BASEBALL CAP?
I DON'T KNOW, BUT HE SHOULD SHAVE.
PLEASE LEAVE.
NICE MAGAZINES IN THE JOHN, PERV.
4/4

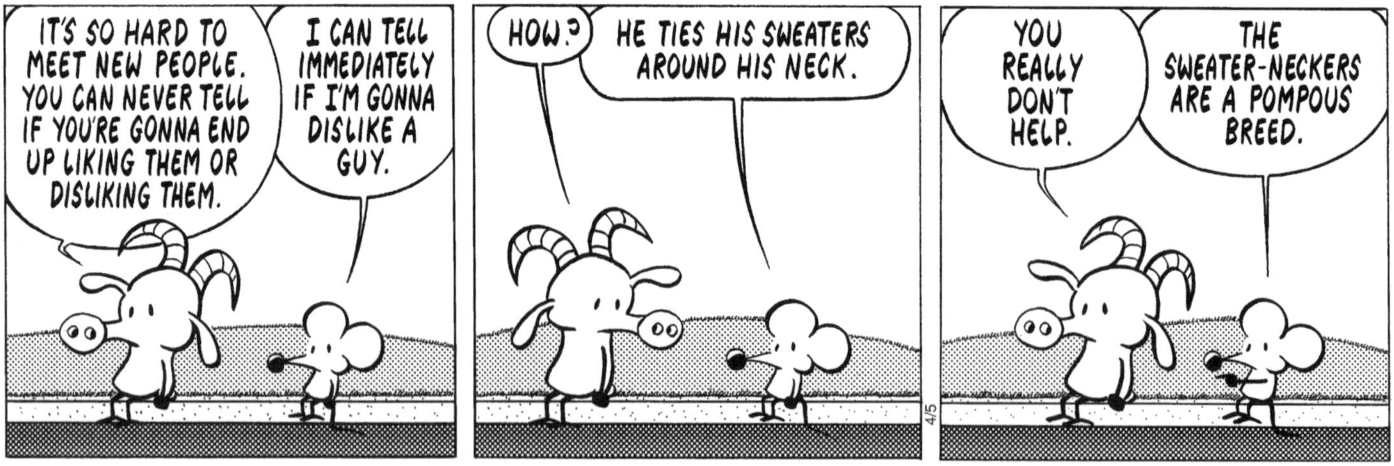
IT'S SO HARD TO MEET NEW PEOPLE. YOU CAN NEVER TELL IF YOU'RE GONNA END UP LIKING THEM OR DISLIKING THEM.
I CAN TELL IMMEDIATELY IF I'M GONNA DISLIKE A GUY.
HOW?
HE TIES HIS SWEATERS AROUND HIS NECK.
YOU REALLY DON'T HELP.
THE SWEATER-NECKERS ARE A POMPOUS BREED.
4/5

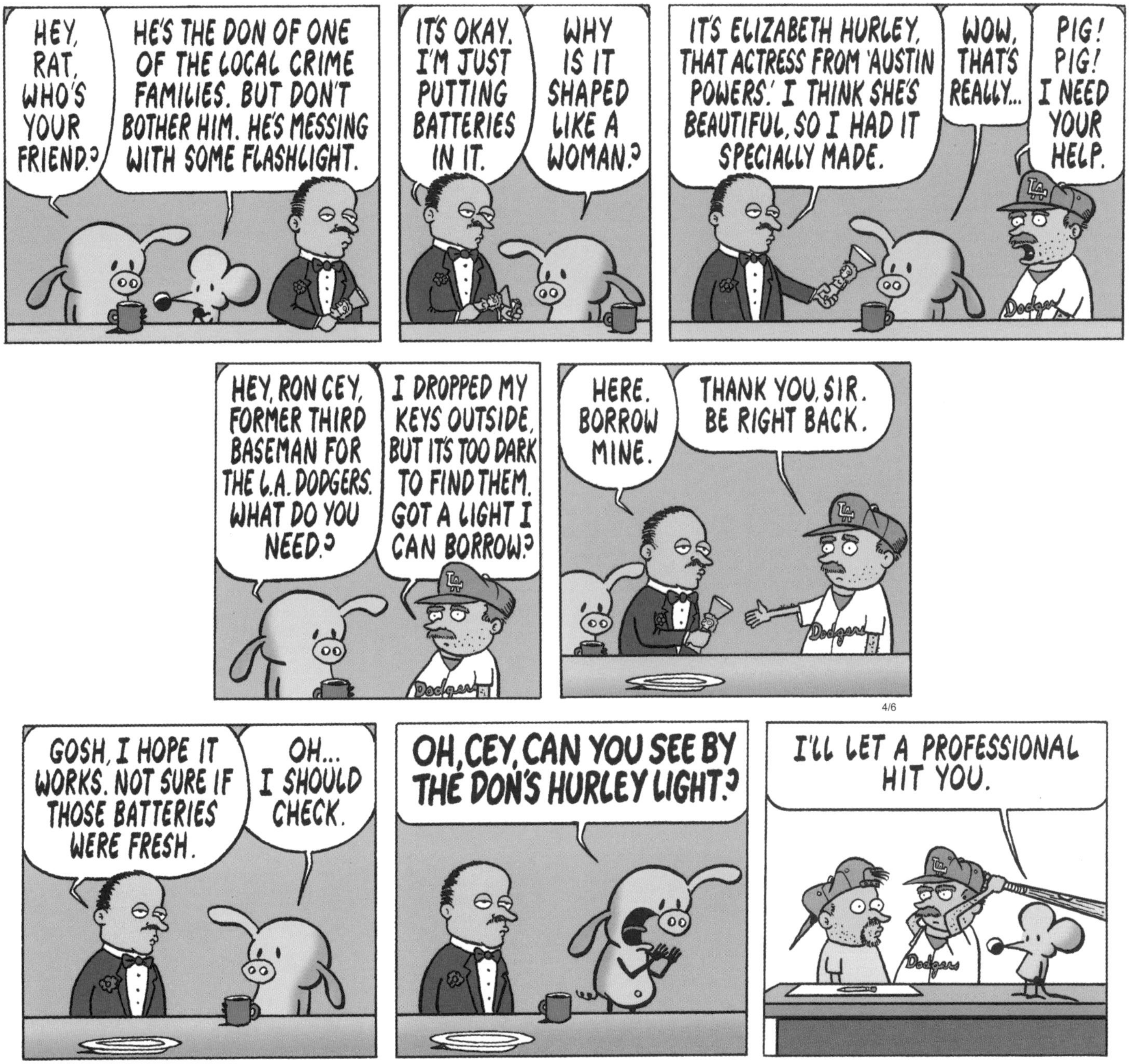
HEY, RAT, WHO'S YOUR FRIEND?
HE'S THE DON OF ONE OF THE LOCAL CRIME FAMILIES. BUT DON'T BOTHER HIM. HE'S MESSING WITH SOME FLASHLIGHT.
IT'S OKAY. I'M JUST PUTTING BATTERIES IN IT.
WHY IS IT SHAPED LIKE A WOMAN?
IT'S ELIZABETH HURLEY, THAT ACTRESS FROM 'AUSTIN POWERS.' I THINK SHE'S BEAUTIFUL, SO I HAD IT SPECIALLY MADE.
WOW, THAT'S REALLY...
PIG! PIG! I NEED YOUR HELP.
HEY, RON CEY, FORMER THIRD BASEMAN FOR THE L.A. DODGERS. WHAT DO YOU NEED?
I DROPPED MY KEYS OUTSIDE, BUT IT'S TOO DARK TO FIND THEM. GOT A LIGHT I CAN BORROW?
HERE. BORROW MINE.
THANK YOU, SIR. BE RIGHT BACK.
4/6
GOSH, I HOPE IT WORKS. NOT SURE IF THOSE BATTERIES WERE FRESH.
OH... I SHOULD CHECK.
OH, CEY, CAN YOU SEE BY THE DON'S HURLEY LIGHT?
I'LL LET A PROFESSIONAL HIT YOU.

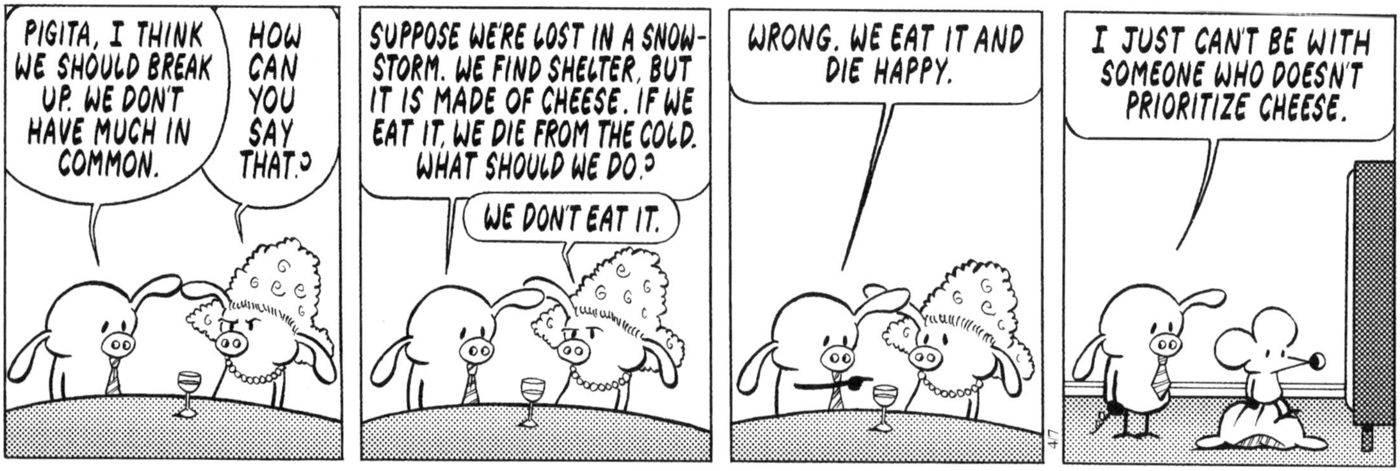
PIGITA, I THINK WE SHOULD BREAK UP. WE DON'T HAVE MUCH IN COMMON.
HOW CAN YOU SAY THAT?
SUPPOSE WE'RE LOST IN A SNOWSTORM. WE FIND SHELTER, BUT IT IS MADE OF CHEESE. IF WE EAT IT, WE DIE FROM THE COLD. WHAT SHOULD WE DO?
WE DON'T EAT IT.
WRONG. WE EAT IT AND DIE HAPPY.
I JUST CAN'T BE WITH SOMEONE WHO DOESN'T PRIORITIZE CHEESE.

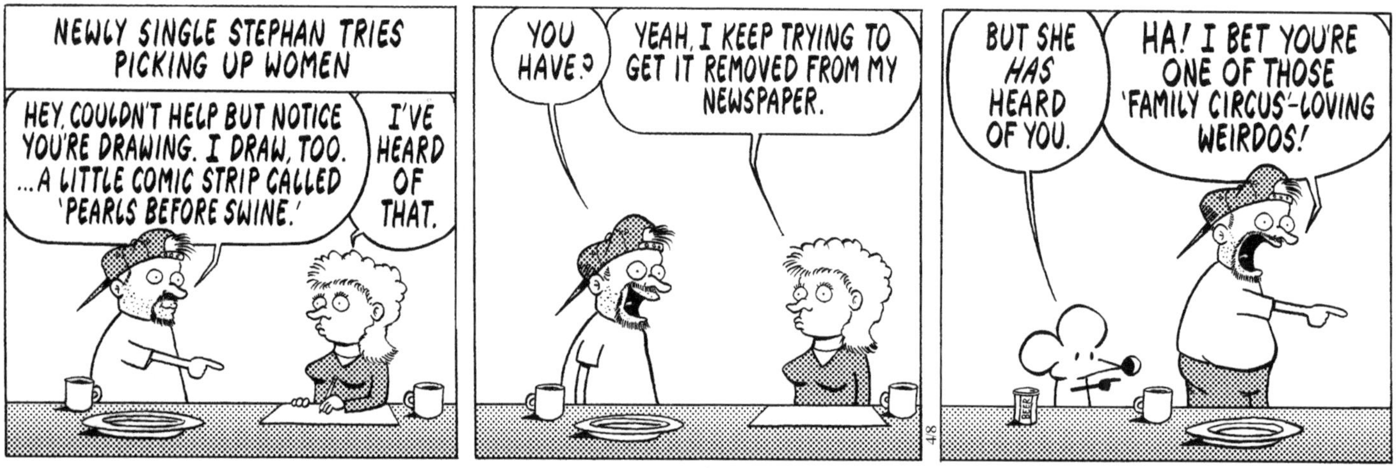
NEWLY SINGLE STEPHAN TRIES PICKING UP WOMEN
HEY, COULDN'T HELP BUT NOTICE YOU'RE DRAWING. I DRAW, TOO. ...A LITTLE COMIC STRIP CALLED 'PEARLS BEFORE SWINE.'
I'VE HEARD OF THAT.
YOU HAVE?
YEAH, I KEEP TRYING TO GET IT REMOVED FROM MY NEWSPAPER.
BUT SHE *HAS* HEARD OF YOU.
HA! I BET YOU'RE ONE OF THOSE 'FAMILY CIRCUS'-LOVING WEIRDOS!
BEER

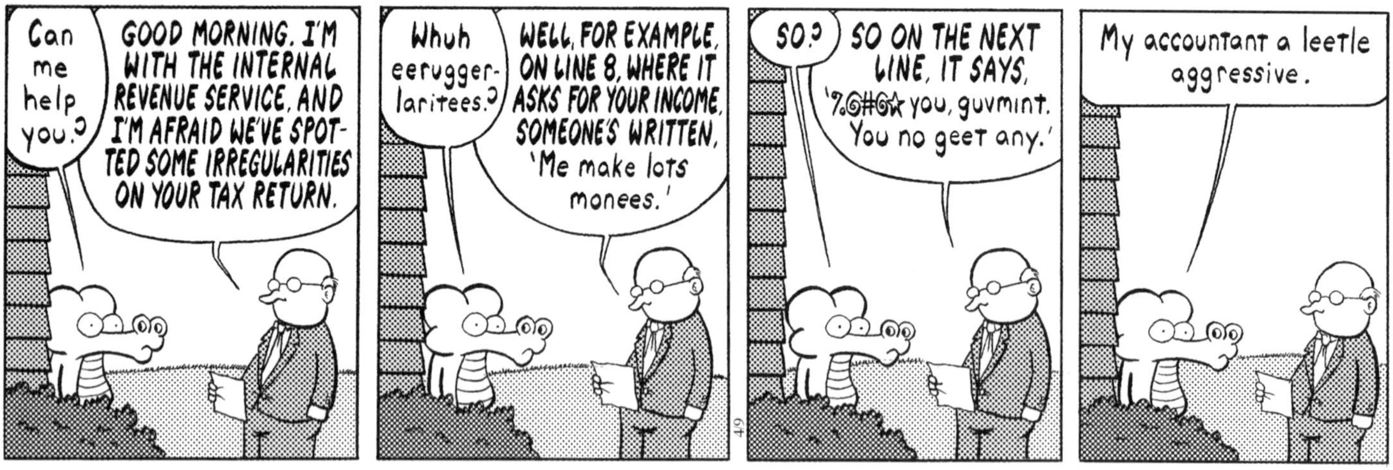
Can me help you?
GOOD MORNING. I'M WITH THE INTERNAL REVENUE SERVICE, AND I'M AFRAID WE'VE SPOTTED SOME IRREGULARITIES ON YOUR TAX RETURN.
Whuh eeruggerlaritees?
WELL, FOR EXAMPLE, ON LINE 8, WHERE IT ASKS FOR YOUR INCOME, SOMEONE'S WRITTEN, 'Me make lots monees.'
SO?
SO ON THE NEXT LINE, IT SAYS, '%@#☆ you, guvmint. You no geet any.'
My accountant a leetle aggressive.

Row 1, Panel 1:
NEWLY SINGLE STEPHAN TRIES PICKING UP WOMEN

I WANT TO TALK TO THAT WOMAN, BUT HOW? SHOULD I TELL HER WHO I AM? WHAT COMIC STRIP I DRAW? OFFER TO SKETCH HER SOMETHING?

Row 1, Panel 2:
PARDON ME, BUT ARE YOU STEPHAN PASTIS?

Row 1, Panel 3:
YES!! YES!! YOU RECOGNIZE ME! I'LL DRAW YOU SOMETHING! I'LL AUTOGRAPH SOMETHING! I'LL WRITE YOU SOMETHING!

Row 1, Panel 4:
UH... YOU DROPPED YOUR CREDIT CARD.

I'LL CRAWL INTO A HOLE.

Row 2, Panel 1:
NEWLY SINGLE STEPHAN TRIES PICKING UP WOMEN

I COULDN'T HELP BUT NOTICE YOU'RE READING THE COMICS PAGE... YOU KNOW, I DRAW A COMIC STRIP.

OH YEAH? WHICH ONE?

Row 2, Panel 3:
EVER HEARD OF 'CALVIN AND HOBBES'?

Row 2, Panel 4:
THAT WAS WRONG.

Row 3, Panel 1:
RAT'S DECIDED HE'S NO LONGER GONNA MAKE DIRECT EYE CONTACT WITH OTHERS. HE SAYS IT MAKES HIM TOO NERVOUS.

Row 3, Panel 2:
HOW STUPID. DOESN'T HE HAVE A DATE TONIGHT?

YEAH, BUT HE SAYS HE CAN STILL BE A GREAT CONVERSATIONALIST.

Row 3, Panel 3:
THEY REALLY NEED TO RE-PAINT THIS WALL.

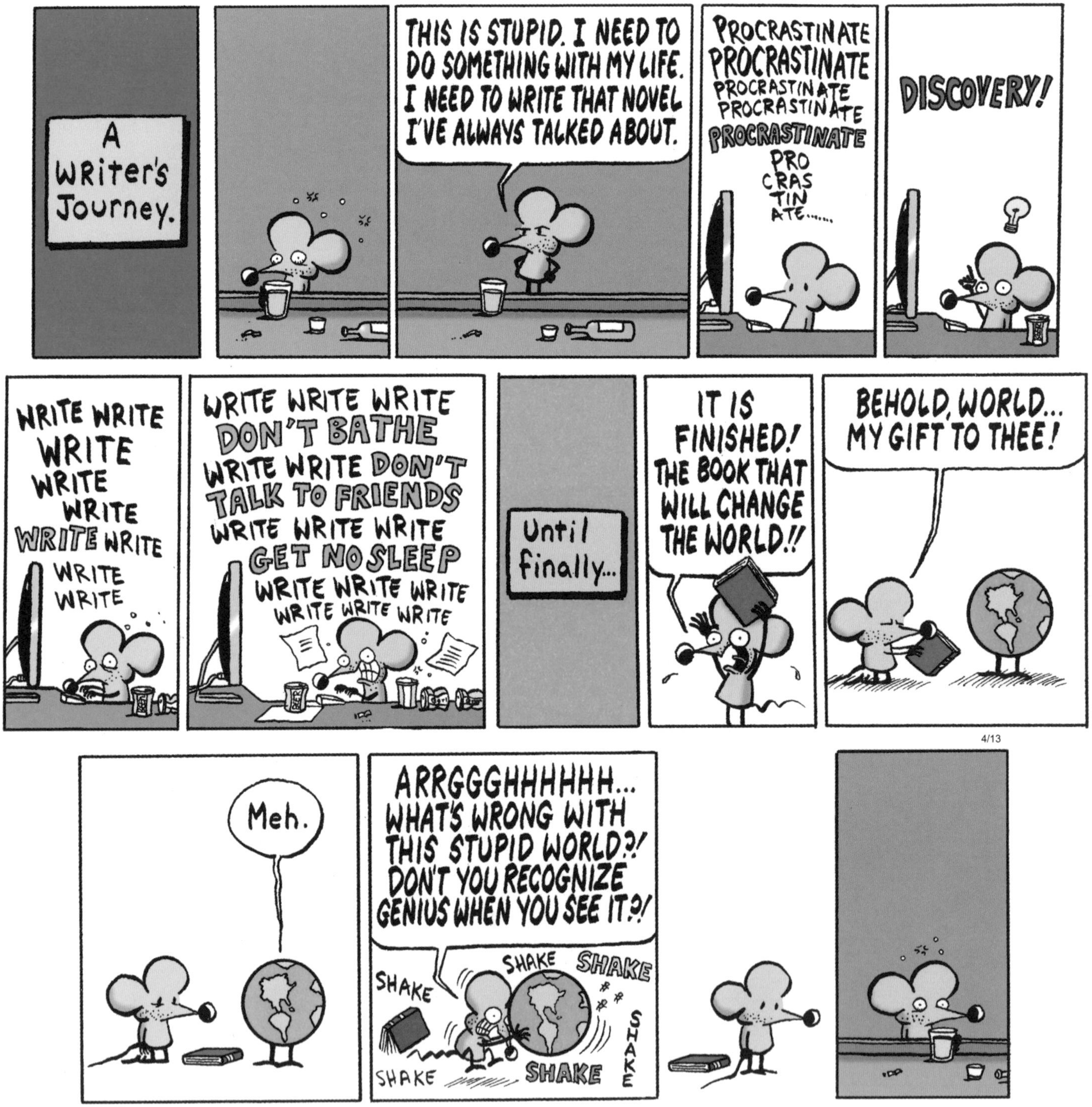
A Writer's Journey.
THIS IS STUPID. I NEED TO DO SOMETHING WITH MY LIFE. I NEED TO WRITE THAT NOVEL I'VE ALWAYS TALKED ABOUT.
PROCRASTINATE PROCRASTINATE PROCRASTINATE PROCRASTINATE PROCRASTINATE PRO CRAS TIN ATE......
DISCOVERY!
WRITE WRITE WRITE WRITE WRITE WRITE WRITE WRITE WRITE
WRITE WRITE WRITE DON'T BATHE WRITE WRITE DON'T TALK TO FRIENDS WRITE WRITE WRITE GET NO SLEEP WRITE WRITE WRITE WRITE WRITE WRITE
Until finally...
IT IS FINISHED! THE BOOK THAT WILL CHANGE THE WORLD!!
BEHOLD, WORLD... MY GIFT TO THEE!
4/13
Meh.
ARRGGGHHHHHH... WHAT'S WRONG WITH THIS STUPID WORLD?! DON'T YOU RECOGNIZE GENIUS WHEN YOU SEE IT?!
SHAKE
SHAKE
SHAKE
SHAKE
SHAKE
SHAKE
SHAKE

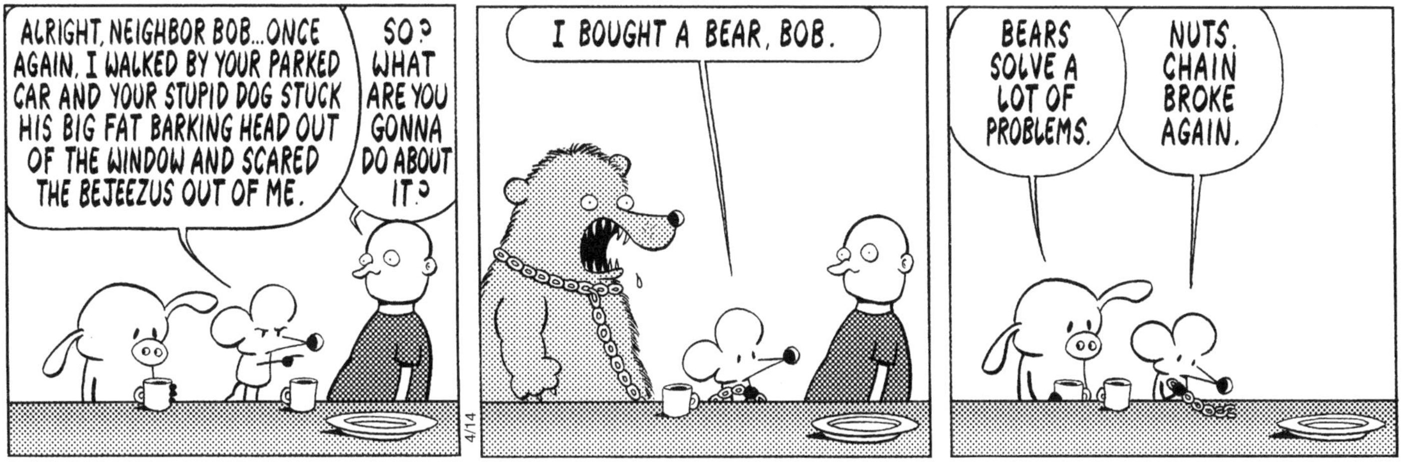
ALRIGHT, NEIGHBOR BOB...ONCE AGAIN, I WALKED BY YOUR PARKED CAR AND YOUR STUPID DOG STUCK HIS BIG FAT BARKING HEAD OUT OF THE WINDOW AND SCARED THE BEJEEZUS OUT OF ME.
SO? WHAT ARE YOU GONNA DO ABOUT IT?
4/14
I BOUGHT A BEAR, BOB.
BEARS SOLVE A LOT OF PROBLEMS.
NUTS. CHAIN BROKE AGAIN.

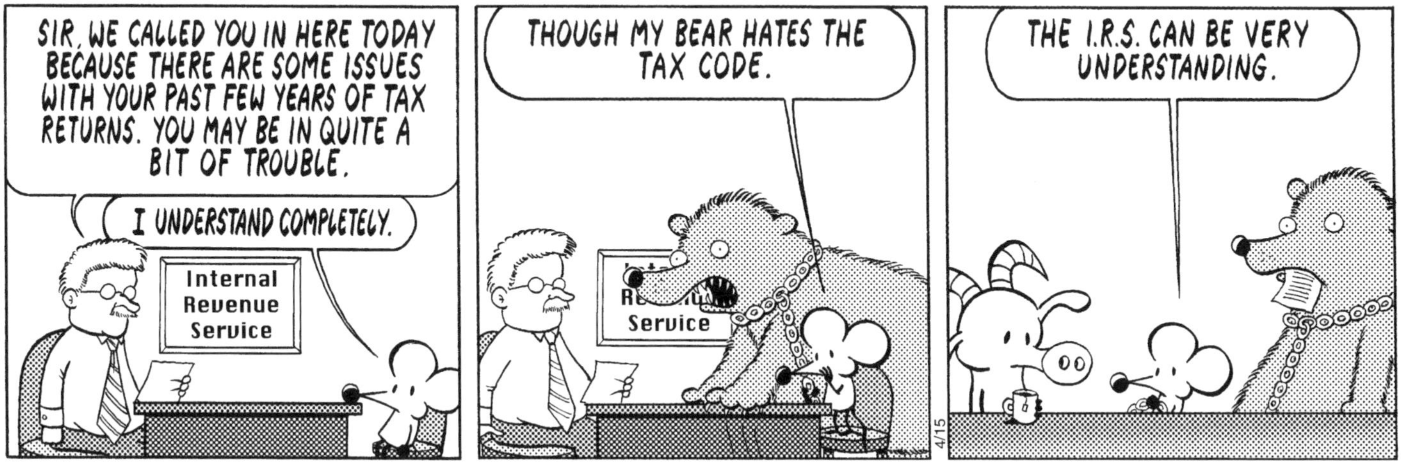
SIR, WE CALLED YOU IN HERE TODAY BECAUSE THERE ARE SOME ISSUES WITH YOUR PAST FEW YEARS OF TAX RETURNS. YOU MAY BE IN QUITE A BIT OF TROUBLE.
I UNDERSTAND COMPLETELY.
Internal Revenue Service
THOUGH MY BEAR HATES THE TAX CODE.
Service
4/15
THE I.R.S. CAN BE VERY UNDERSTANDING.

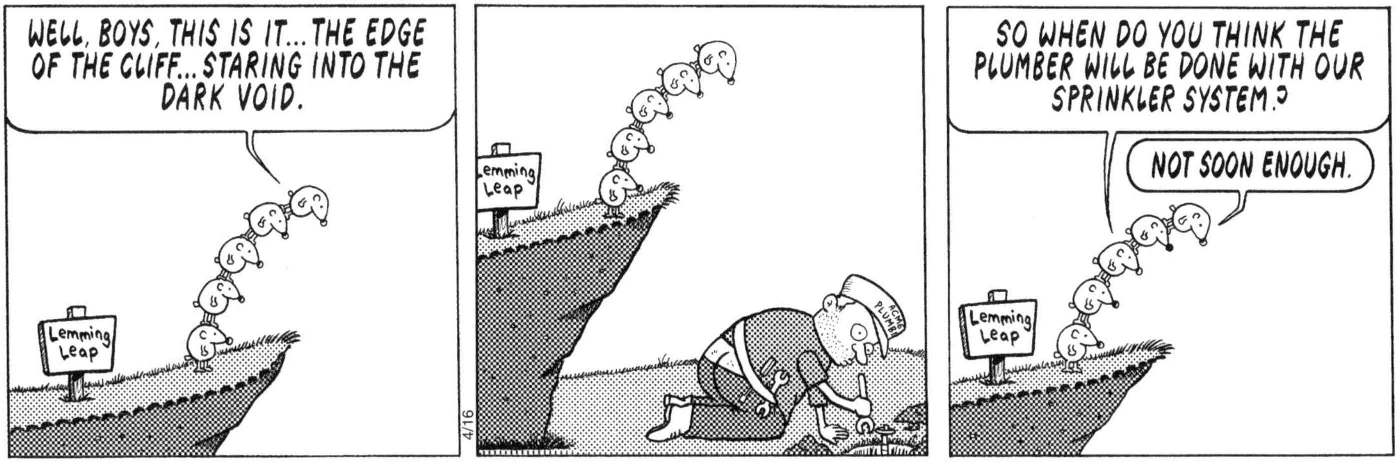
WELL, BOYS, THIS IS IT...THE EDGE OF THE CLIFF...STARING INTO THE DARK VOID.
Lemming Leap
4/16
Lemming Leap
SO WHEN DO YOU THINK THE PLUMBER WILL BE DONE WITH OUR SPRINKLER SYSTEM?
NOT SOON ENOUGH.
Lemming Leap

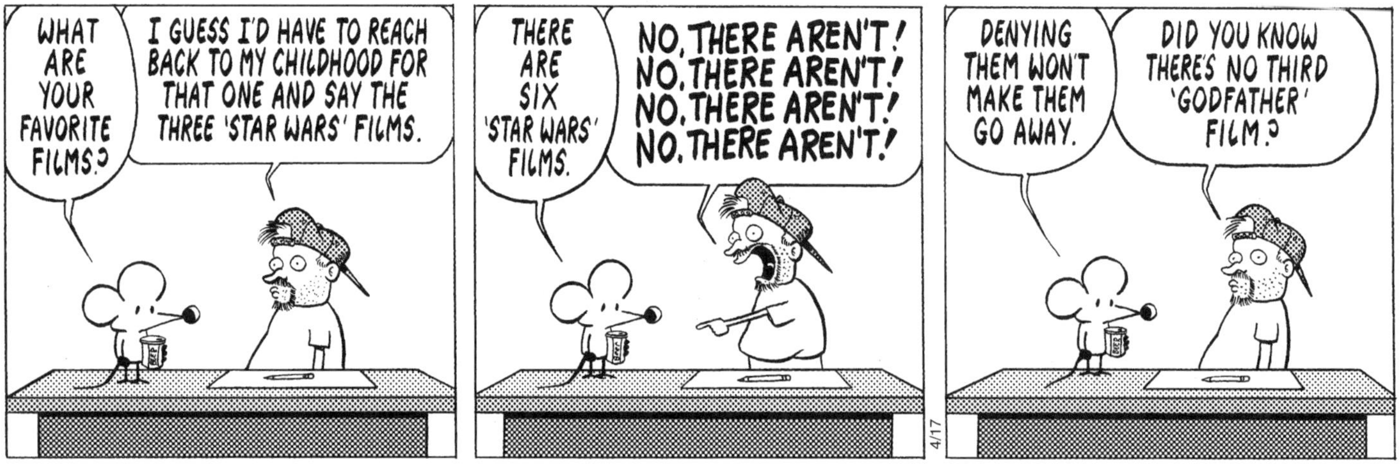
WHAT ARE YOUR FAVORITE FILMS?
I GUESS I'D HAVE TO REACH BACK TO MY CHILDHOOD FOR THAT ONE AND SAY THE THREE 'STAR WARS' FILMS.
THERE ARE SIX 'STAR WARS' FILMS.
NO, THERE AREN'T! NO, THERE AREN'T! NO, THERE AREN'T! NO, THERE AREN'T!
DENYING THEM WON'T MAKE THEM GO AWAY.
DID YOU KNOW THERE'S NO THIRD 'GODFATHER' FILM?
4/17

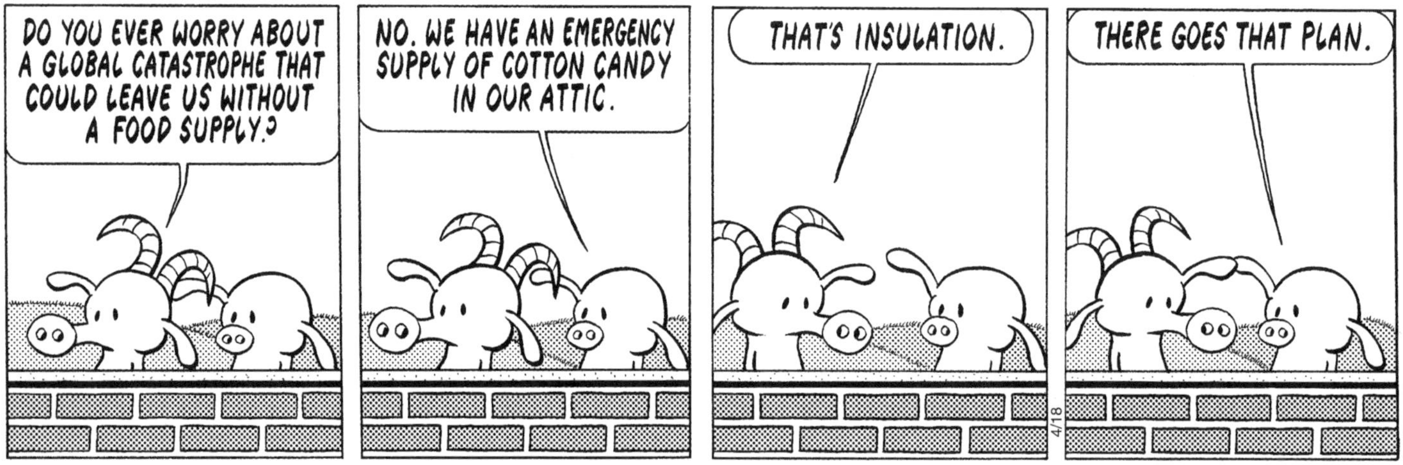
DO YOU EVER WORRY ABOUT A GLOBAL CATASTROPHE THAT COULD LEAVE US WITHOUT A FOOD SUPPLY?
NO. WE HAVE AN EMERGENCY SUPPLY OF COTTON CANDY IN OUR ATTIC.
THAT'S INSULATION.
THERE GOES THAT PLAN.
4/18

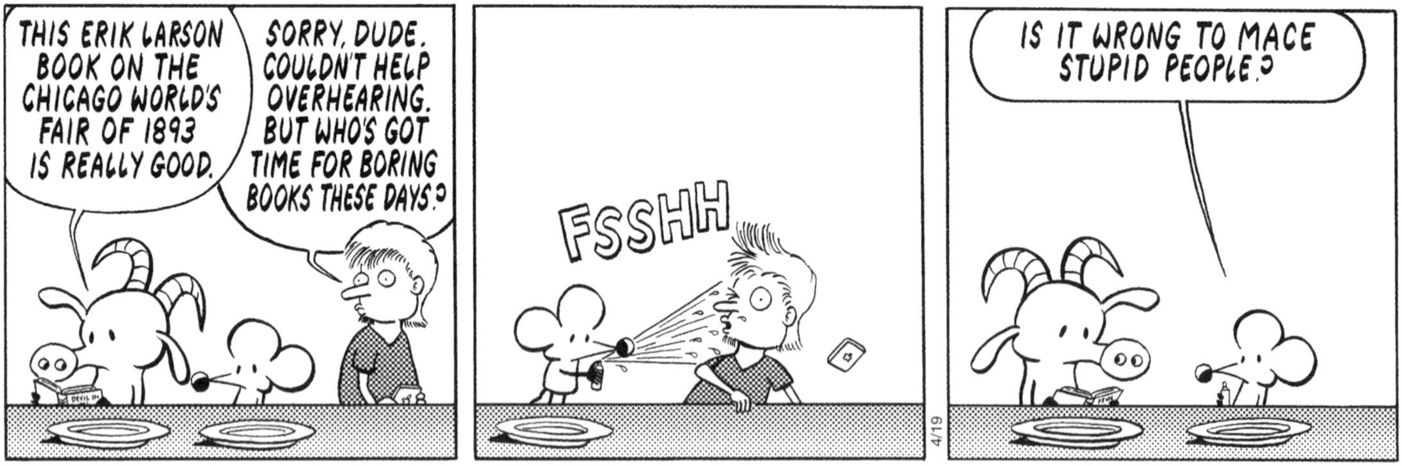
THIS ERIK LARSON BOOK ON THE CHICAGO WORLD'S FAIR OF 1893 IS REALLY GOOD.
SORRY, DUDE. COULDN'T HELP OVERHEARING. BUT WHO'S GOT TIME FOR BORING BOOKS THESE DAYS?
FSSHH
IS IT WRONG TO MACE STUPID PEOPLE?
4/19

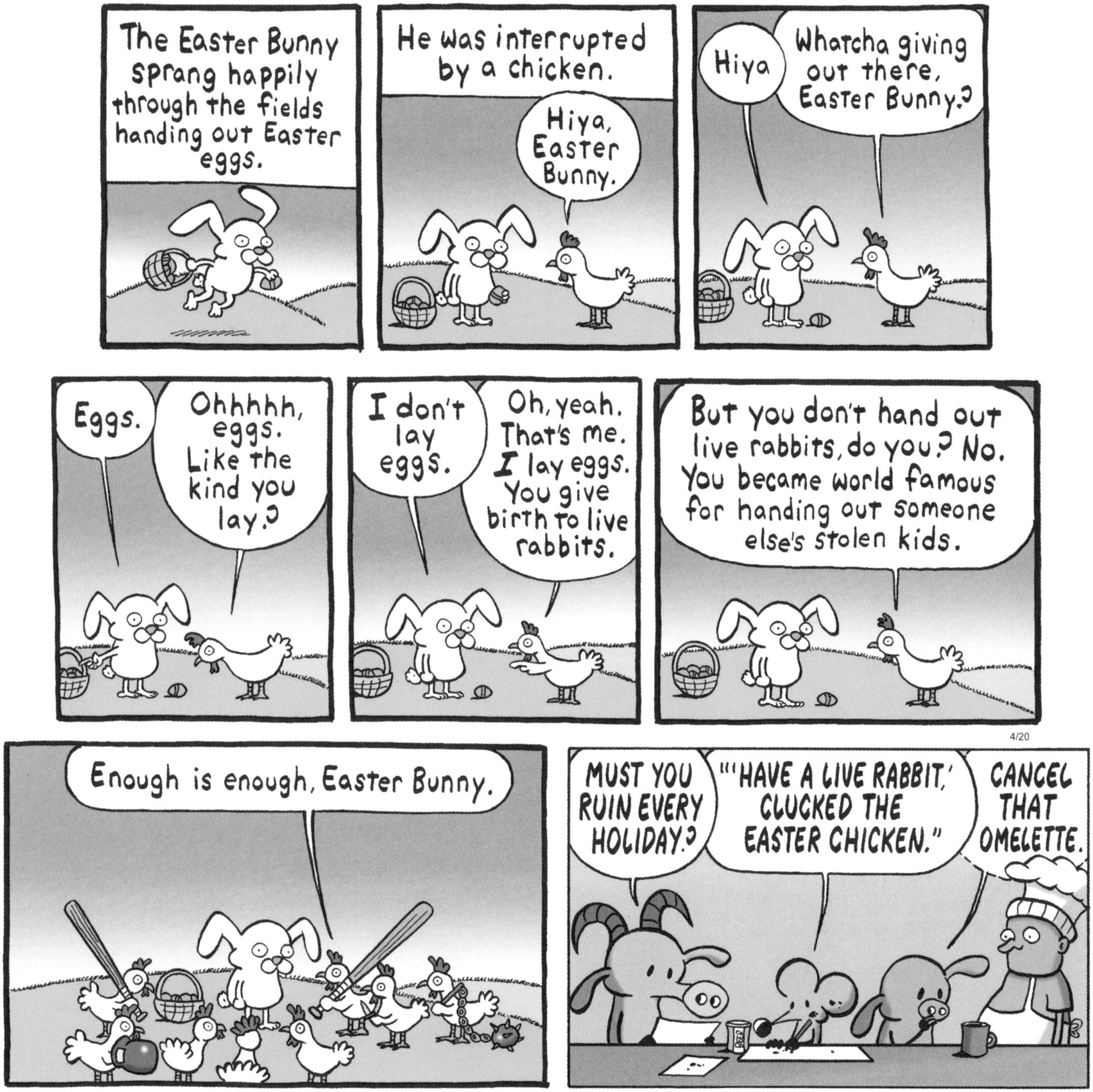

The Easter Bunny sprang happily through the fields handing out Easter eggs.
He was interrupted by a chicken.
Hiya, Easter Bunny.
Hiya
Whatcha giving out there, Easter Bunny?
Eggs.
Ohhhhh, eggs. Like the kind you lay?
I don't lay eggs.
Oh, yeah. That's me. I lay eggs. You give birth to live rabbits.
But you don't hand out live rabbits, do you? No. You became world famous for handing out someone else's stolen kids.
Enough is enough, Easter Bunny.
4/20
MUST YOU RUIN EVERY HOLIDAY?
"'HAVE A LIVE RABBIT,' CLUCKED THE EASTER CHICKEN."
CANCEL THAT OMELETTE.

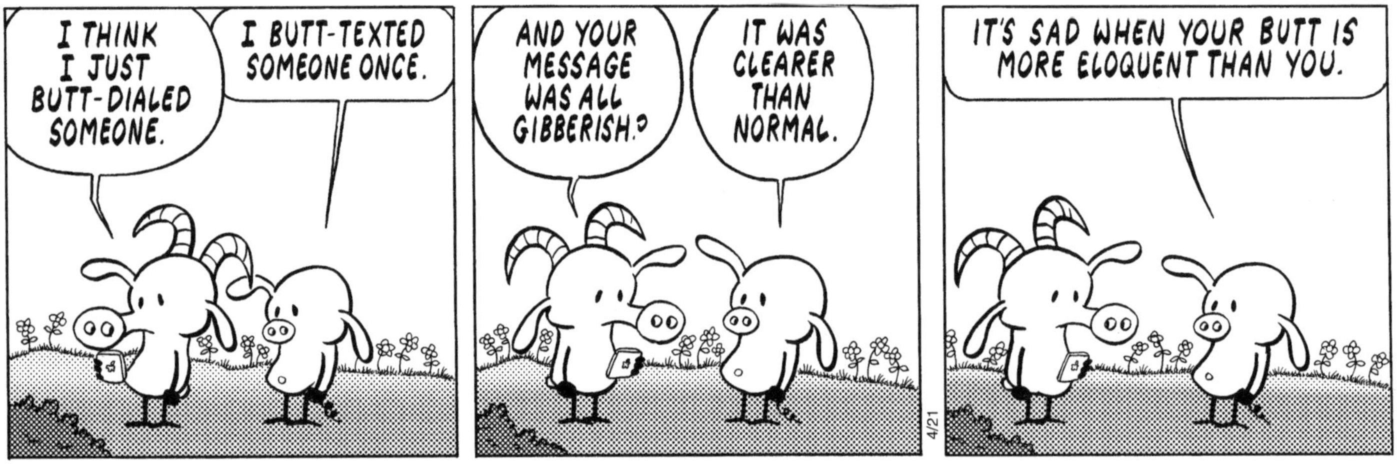
I THINK I JUST BUTT-DIALED SOMEONE.
I BUTT-TEXTED SOMEONE ONCE.
AND YOUR MESSAGE WAS ALL GIBBERISH?
IT WAS CLEARER THAN NORMAL.
IT'S SAD WHEN YOUR BUTT IS MORE ELOQUENT THAN YOU.
4/21

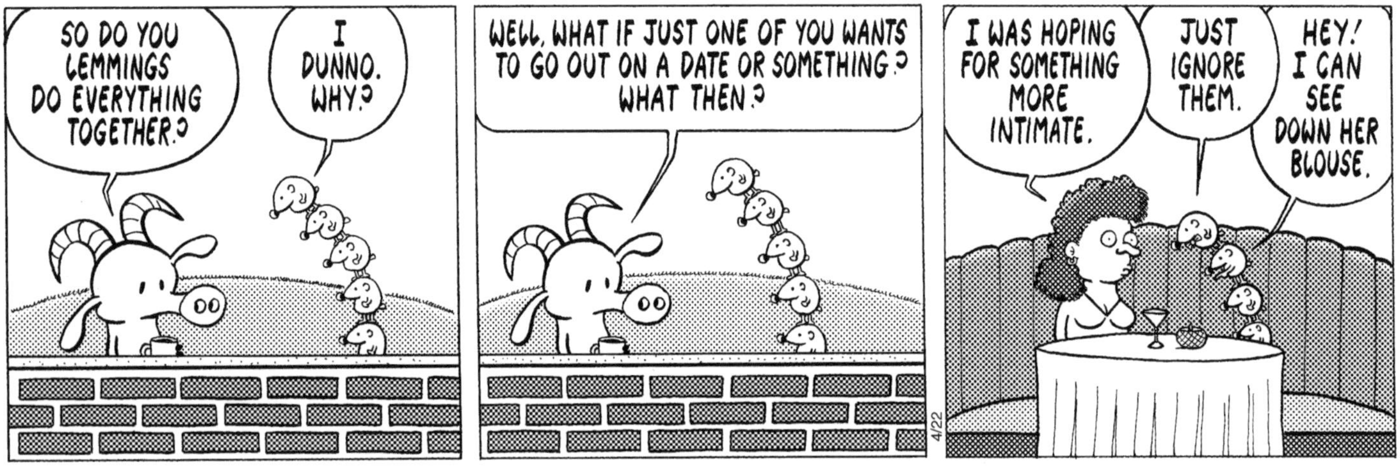
SO DO YOU LEMMINGS DO EVERYTHING TOGETHER?
I DUNNO. WHY?
WELL, WHAT IF JUST ONE OF YOU WANTS TO GO OUT ON A DATE OR SOMETHING? WHAT THEN?
I WAS HOPING FOR SOMETHING MORE INTIMATE.
JUST IGNORE THEM.
HEY! I CAN SEE DOWN HER BLOUSE.
4/22

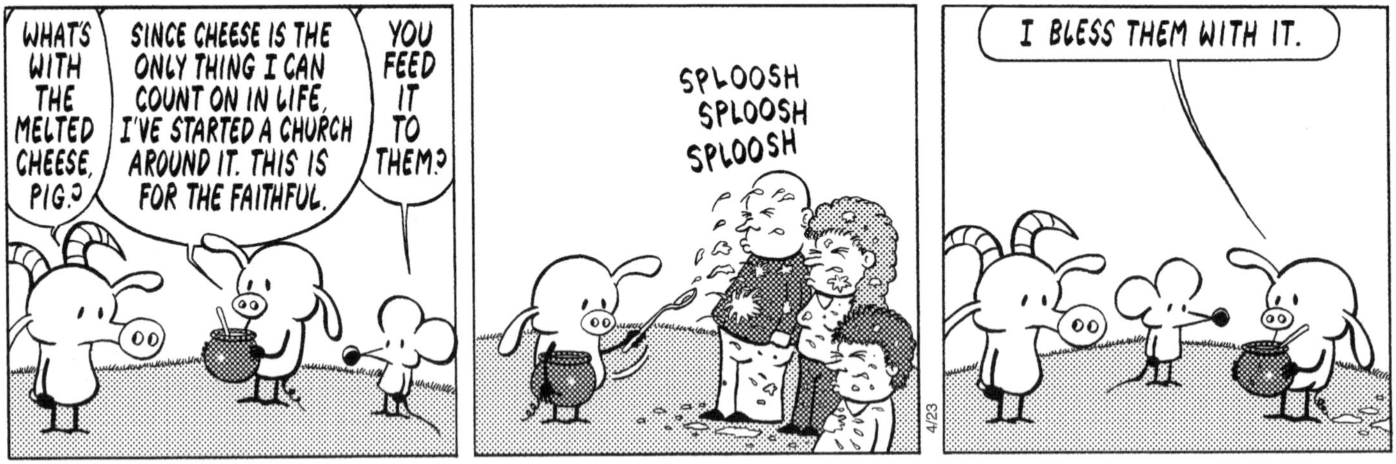
WHAT'S WITH THE MELTED CHEESE, PIG?
SINCE CHEESE IS THE ONLY THING I CAN COUNT ON IN LIFE, I'VE STARTED A CHURCH AROUND IT. THIS IS FOR THE FAITHFUL.
YOU FEED IT TO THEM?
SPLOOSH
SPLOOSH
SPLOOSH
I BLESS THEM WITH IT.
4/23

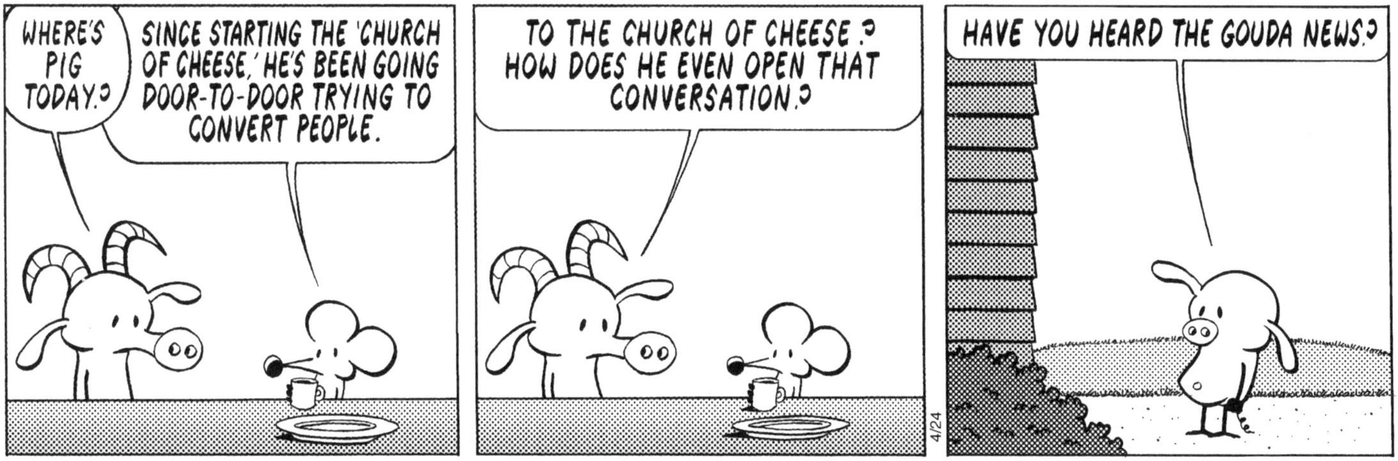
WHERE'S PIG TODAY?
SINCE STARTING THE 'CHURCH OF CHEESE,' HE'S BEEN GOING DOOR-TO-DOOR TRYING TO CONVERT PEOPLE.
TO THE CHURCH OF CHEESE? HOW DOES HE EVEN OPEN THAT CONVERSATION?
HAVE YOU HEARD THE GOUDA NEWS?
4/24

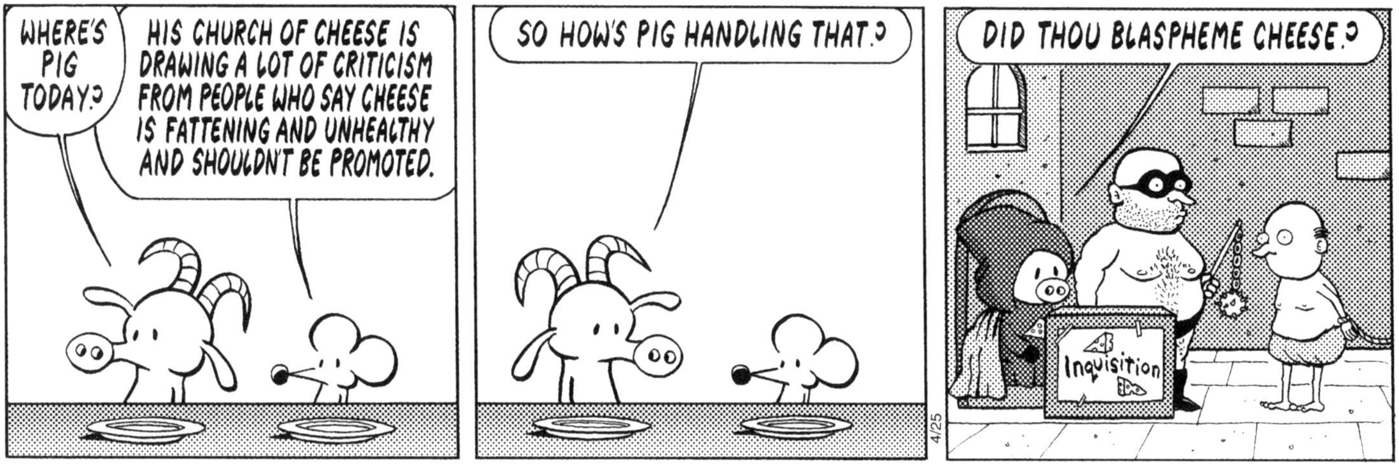
WHERE'S PIG TODAY?
HIS CHURCH OF CHEESE IS DRAWING A LOT OF CRITICISM FROM PEOPLE WHO SAY CHEESE IS FATTENING AND UNHEALTHY AND SHOULDN'T BE PROMOTED.
SO HOW'S PIG HANDLING THAT?
DID THOU BLASPHEME CHEESE?
Inquisition
4/25

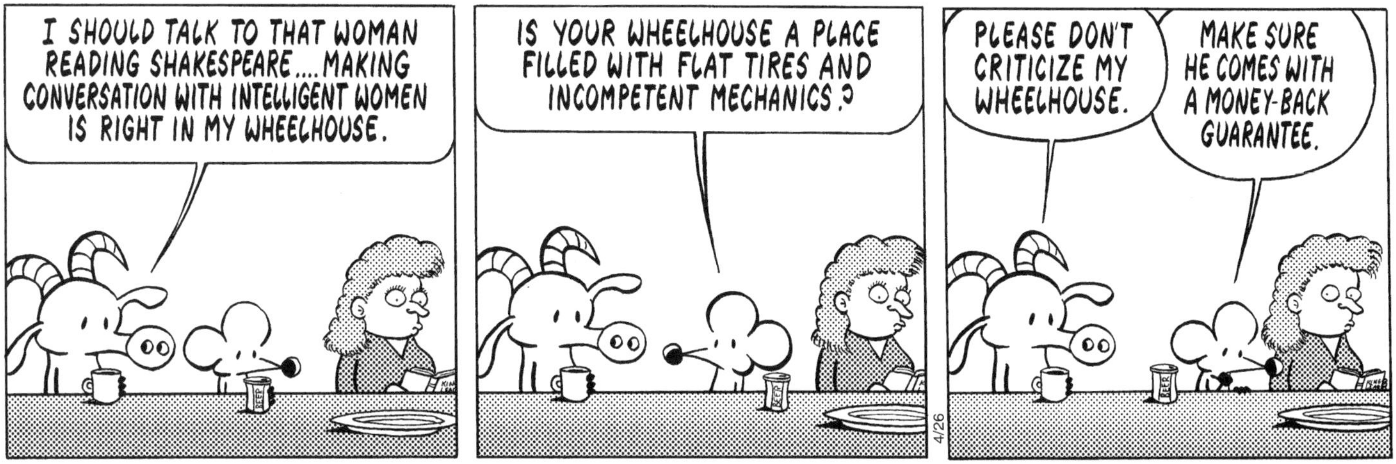
I SHOULD TALK TO THAT WOMAN READING SHAKESPEARE.... MAKING CONVERSATION WITH INTELLIGENT WOMEN IS RIGHT IN MY WHEELHOUSE.
IS YOUR WHEELHOUSE A PLACE FILLED WITH FLAT TIRES AND INCOMPETENT MECHANICS?
PLEASE DON'T CRITICIZE MY WHEELHOUSE.
MAKE SURE HE COMES WITH A MONEY-BACK GUARANTEE.
4/26

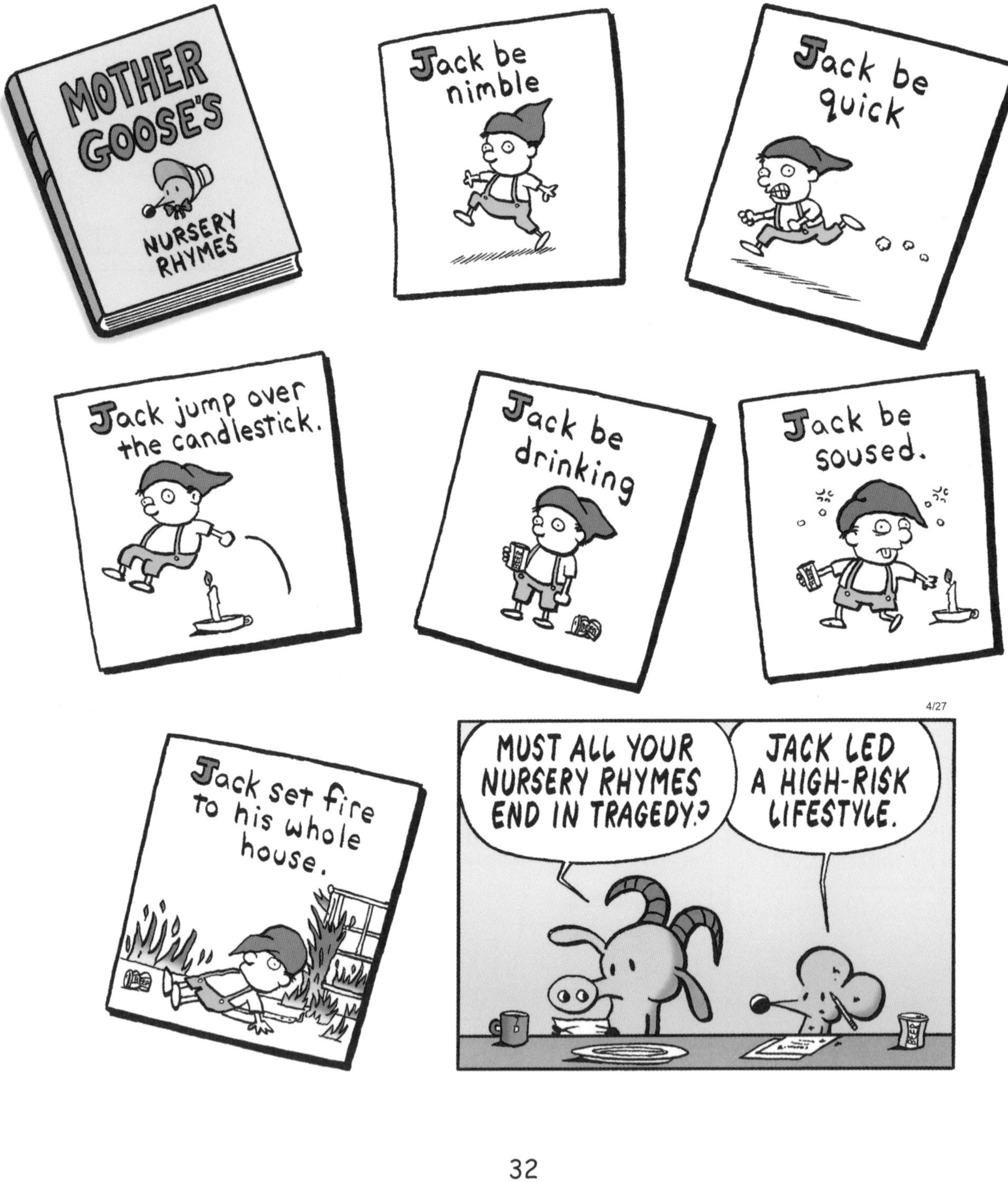
MOTHER GOOSE'S NURSERY RHYMES
Jack be nimble
Jack be quick
Jack jump over the candlestick.
Jack be drinking
Jack be soused.
Jack set fire to his whole house.
4/27
MUST ALL YOUR NURSERY RHYMES END IN TRAGEDY?
JACK LED A HIGH-RISK LIFESTYLE.

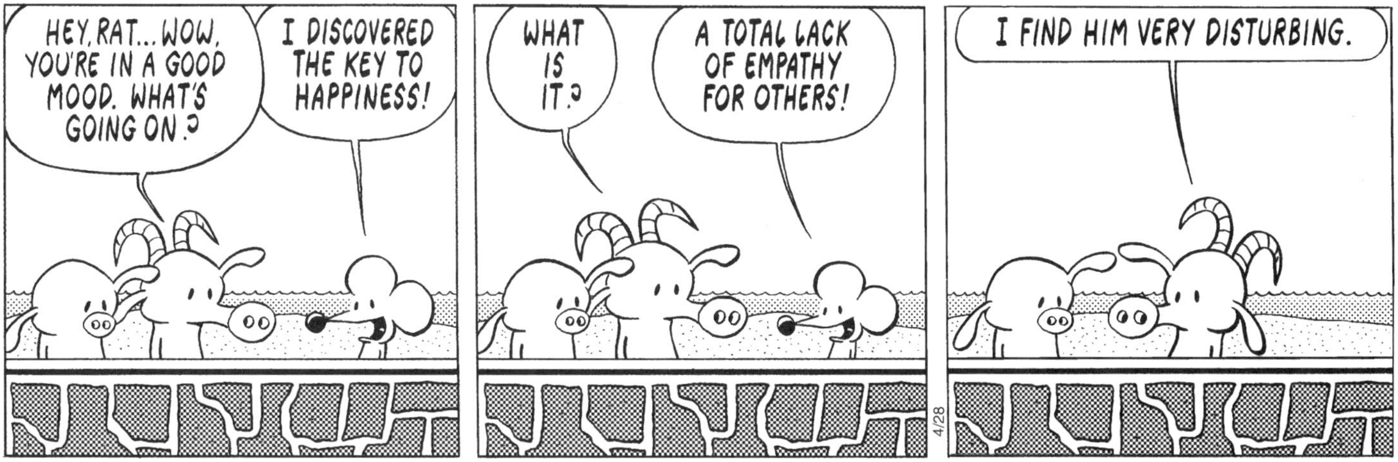
HEY, RAT... WOW, YOU'RE IN A GOOD MOOD. WHAT'S GOING ON?
I DISCOVERED THE KEY TO HAPPINESS!
WHAT IS IT?
A TOTAL LACK OF EMPATHY FOR OTHERS!
I FIND HIM VERY DISTURBING.
4/28

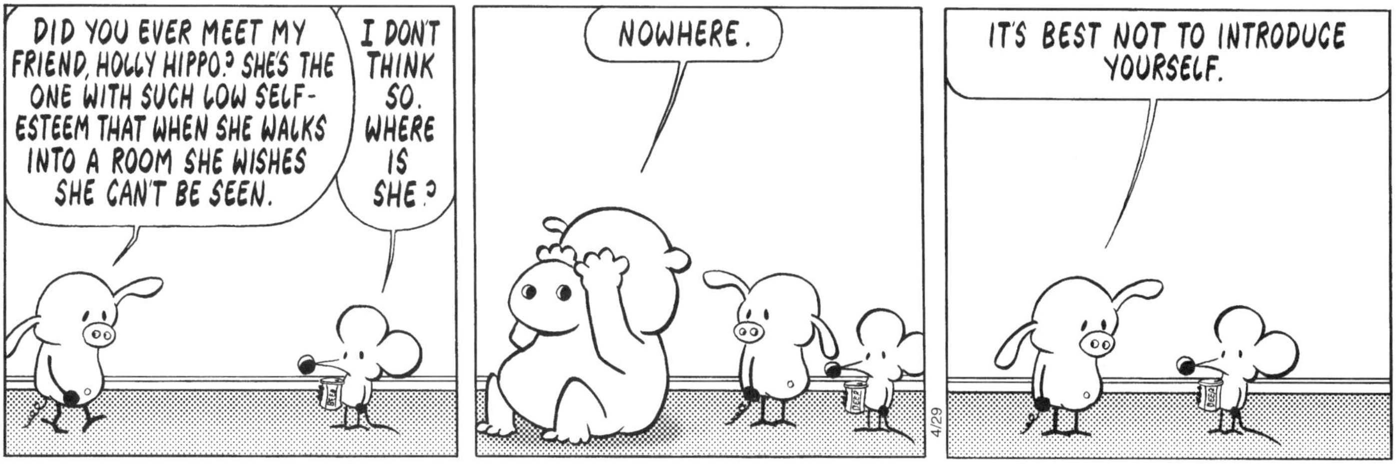
DID YOU EVER MEET MY FRIEND, HOLLY HIPPO? SHE'S THE ONE WITH SUCH LOW SELF-ESTEEM THAT WHEN SHE WALKS INTO A ROOM SHE WISHES SHE CAN'T BE SEEN.
I DON'T THINK SO. WHERE IS SHE?
NOWHERE.
IT'S BEST NOT TO INTRODUCE YOURSELF.
4/29

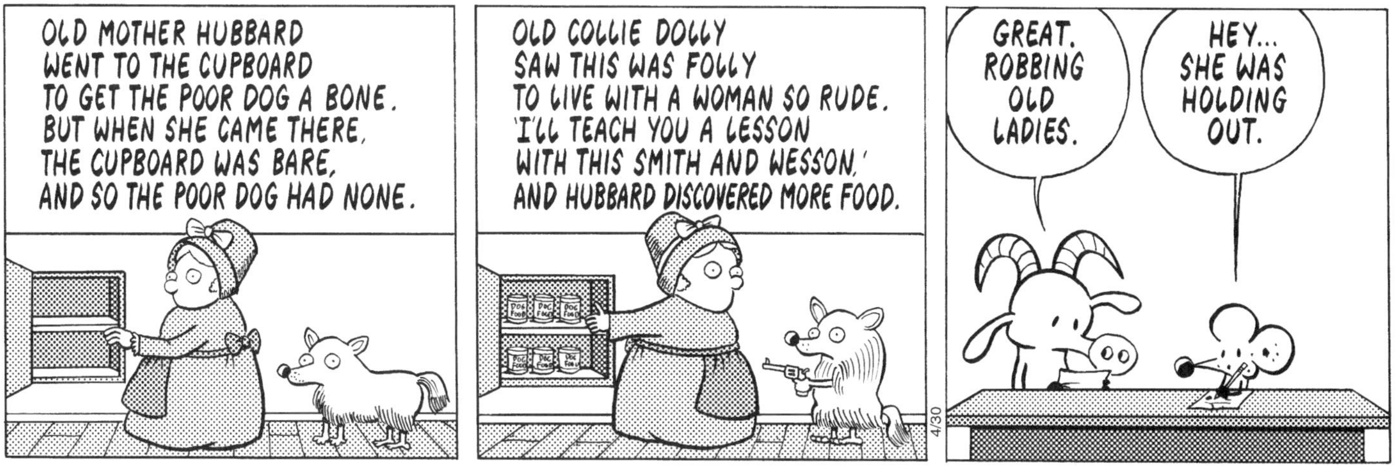
OLD MOTHER HUBBARD
WENT TO THE CUPBOARD
TO GET THE POOR DOG A BONE.
BUT WHEN SHE CAME THERE,
THE CUPBOARD WAS BARE,
AND SO THE POOR DOG HAD NONE.
OLD COLLIE DOLLY
SAW THIS WAS FOLLY
TO LIVE WITH A WOMAN SO RUDE.
'I'LL TEACH YOU A LESSON
WITH THIS SMITH AND WESSON,'
AND HUBBARD DISCOVERED MORE FOOD.
GREAT. ROBBING OLD LADIES.
HEY... SHE WAS HOLDING OUT.
4/30

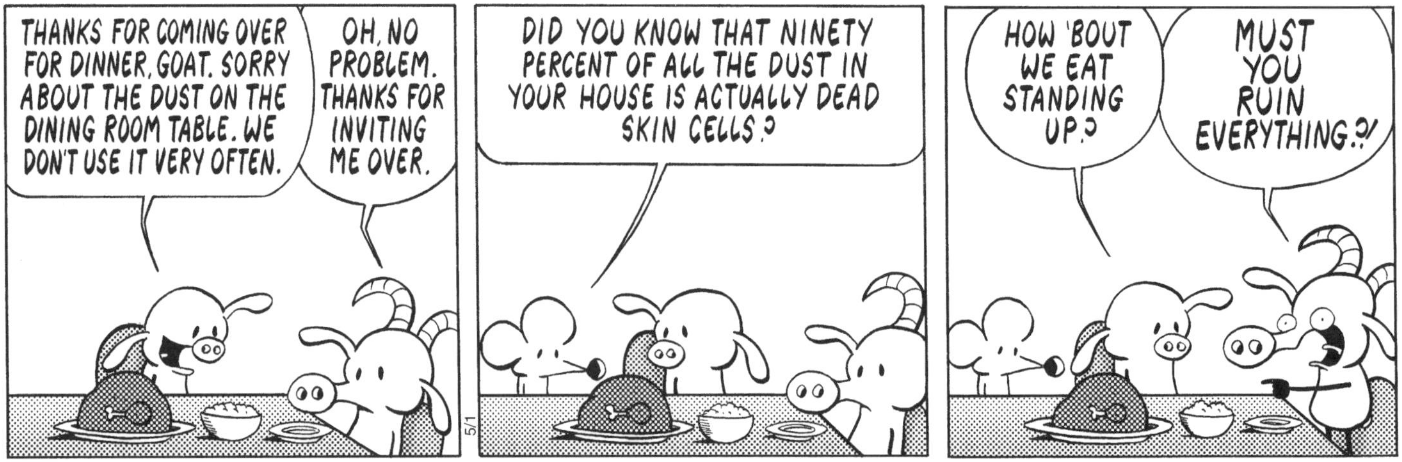
THANKS FOR COMING OVER FOR DINNER, GOAT. SORRY ABOUT THE DUST ON THE DINING ROOM TABLE. WE DON'T USE IT VERY OFTEN.
OH, NO PROBLEM. THANKS FOR INVITING ME OVER.
DID YOU KNOW THAT NINETY PERCENT OF ALL THE DUST IN YOUR HOUSE IS ACTUALLY DEAD SKIN CELLS?
HOW 'BOUT WE EAT STANDING UP?
MUST YOU RUIN EVERYTHING?!
5/1

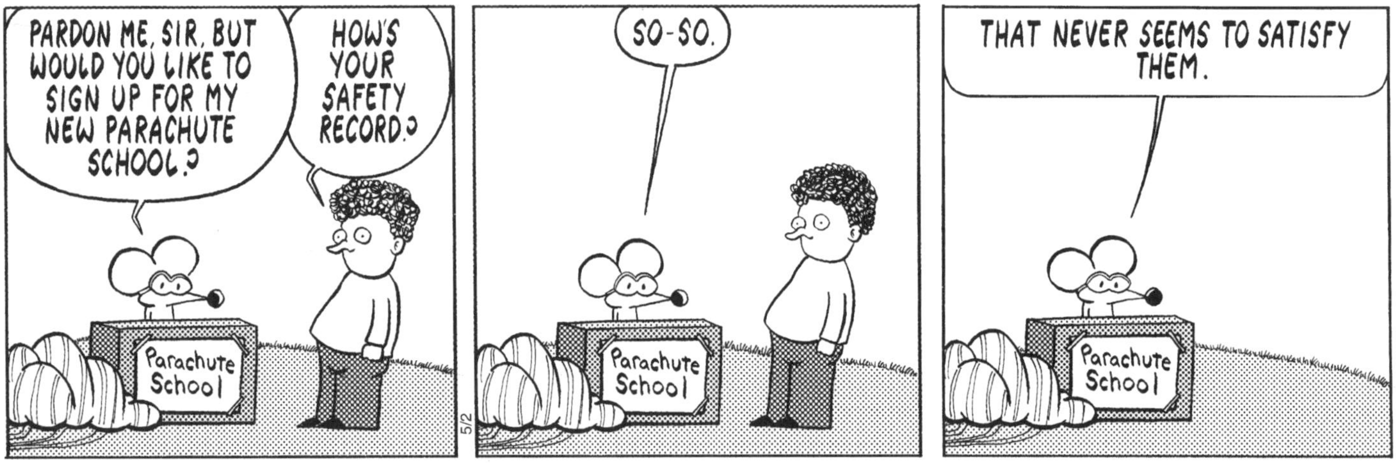
PARDON ME, SIR, BUT WOULD YOU LIKE TO SIGN UP FOR MY NEW PARACHUTE SCHOOL?
HOW'S YOUR SAFETY RECORD?
Parachute School
SO-SO.
THAT NEVER SEEMS TO SATISFY THEM.
5/2

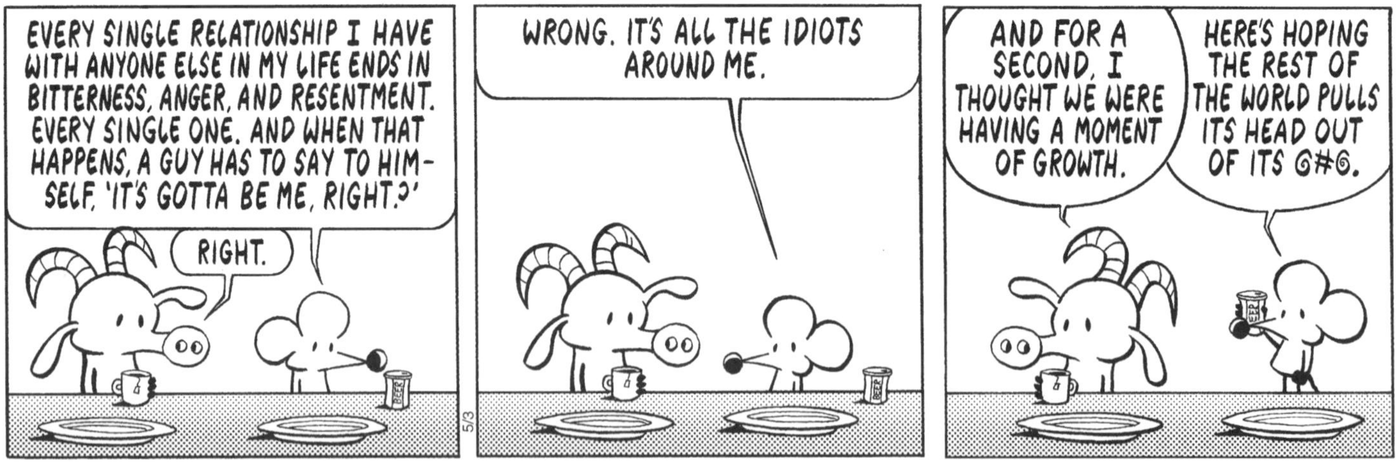
EVERY SINGLE RELATIONSHIP I HAVE WITH ANYONE ELSE IN MY LIFE ENDS IN BITTERNESS, ANGER, AND RESENTMENT. EVERY SINGLE ONE. AND WHEN THAT HAPPENS, A GUY HAS TO SAY TO HIMSELF, 'IT'S GOTTA BE ME, RIGHT?'
RIGHT.
WRONG. IT'S ALL THE IDIOTS AROUND ME.
AND FOR A SECOND, I THOUGHT WE WERE HAVING A MOMENT OF GROWTH.
HERE'S HOPING THE REST OF THE WORLD PULLS ITS HEAD OUT OF ITS @#@.
5/3

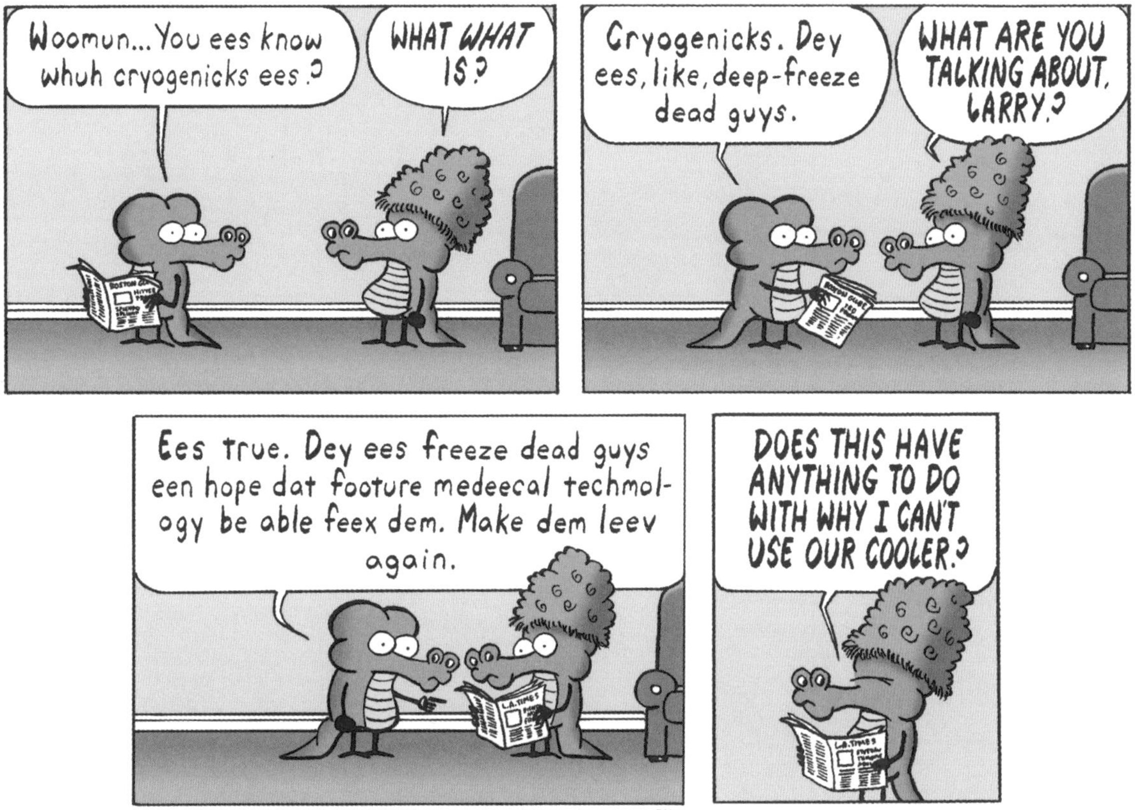
Woomun...You ees know whuh cryogenicks ees.?
WHAT WHAT IS?
Cryogenicks. Dey ees, like, deep-freeze dead guys.
WHAT ARE YOU TALKING ABOUT, LARRY.?
Ees true. Dey ees freeze dead guys een hope dat footure medeecal techmol-ogy be able feex dem. Make dem leev again.
DOES THIS HAVE ANYTHING TO DO WITH WHY I CAN'T USE OUR COOLER.?

5/4

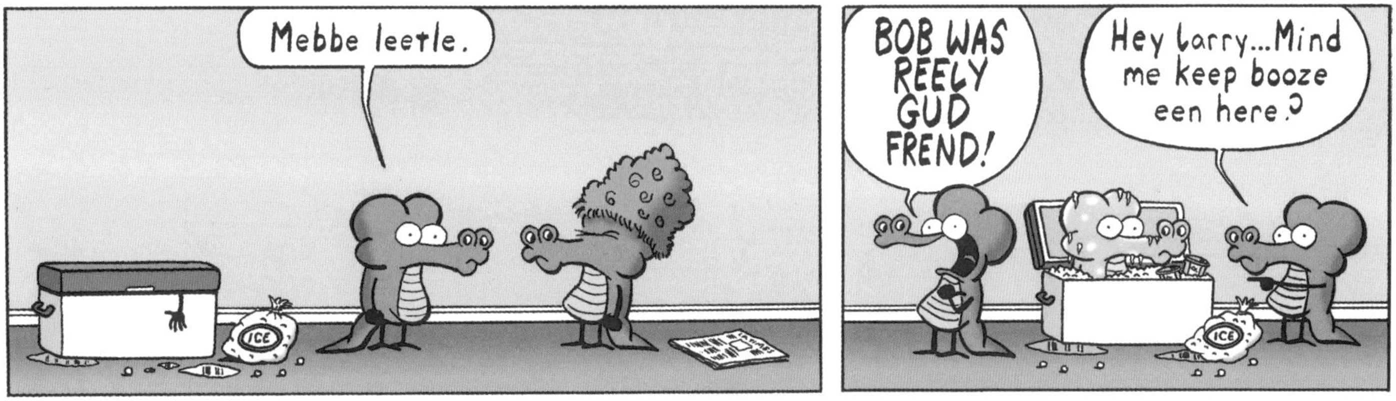
Mebbe leetle.
ICE
BOB WAS REELY GUD FREND!
Hey Larry...Mind me keep booze een here.?
ICE

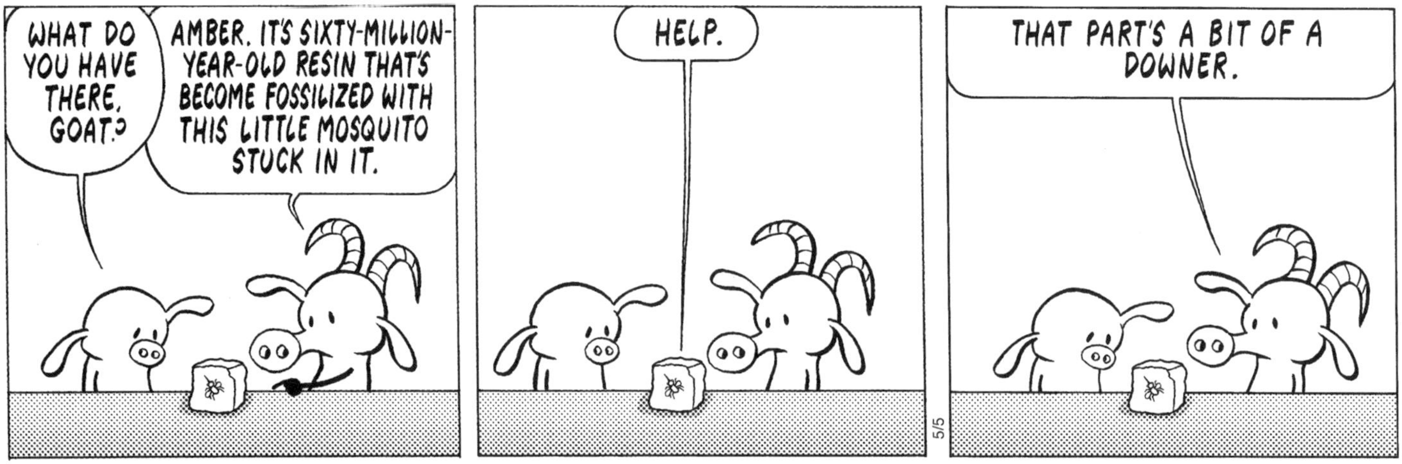
WHAT DO YOU HAVE THERE, GOAT?
AMBER. IT'S SIXTY-MILLION-YEAR-OLD RESIN THAT'S BECOME FOSSILIZED WITH THIS LITTLE MOSQUITO STUCK IN IT.
HELP.
THAT PART'S A BIT OF A DOWNER.
5/5

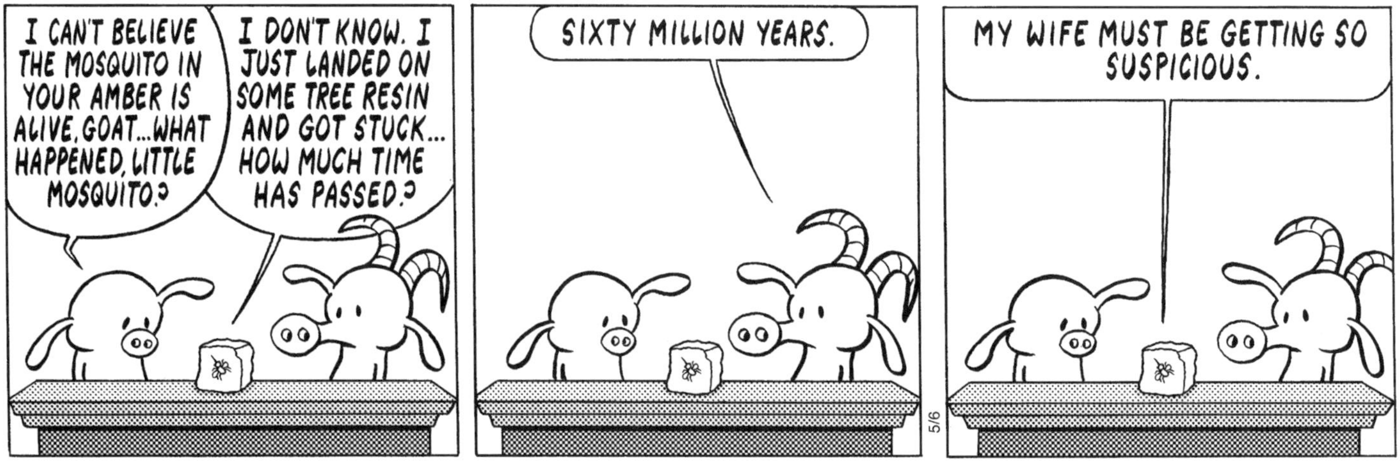
I CAN'T BELIEVE THE MOSQUITO IN YOUR AMBER IS ALIVE, GOAT...WHAT HAPPENED, LITTLE MOSQUITO?
I DON'T KNOW. I JUST LANDED ON SOME TREE RESIN AND GOT STUCK... HOW MUCH TIME HAS PASSED?
SIXTY MILLION YEARS.
MY WIFE MUST BE GETTING SO SUSPICIOUS.
5/6

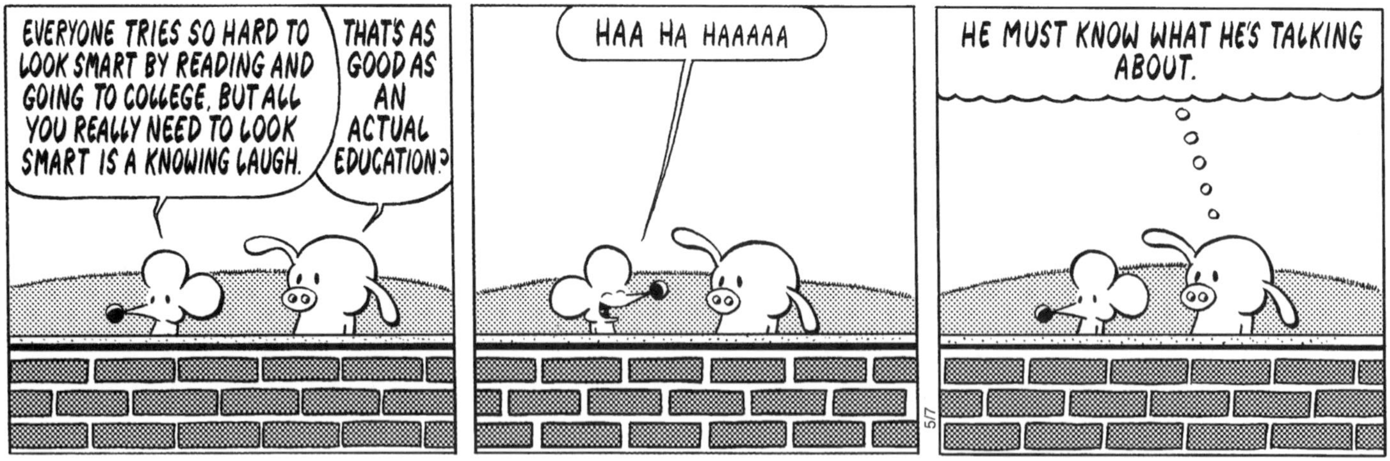
EVERYONE TRIES SO HARD TO LOOK SMART BY READING AND GOING TO COLLEGE, BUT ALL YOU REALLY NEED TO LOOK SMART IS A KNOWING LAUGH.
THAT'S AS GOOD AS AN ACTUAL EDUCATION?
HAA HA HAAAAAA
HE MUST KNOW WHAT HE'S TALKING ABOUT.
5/7

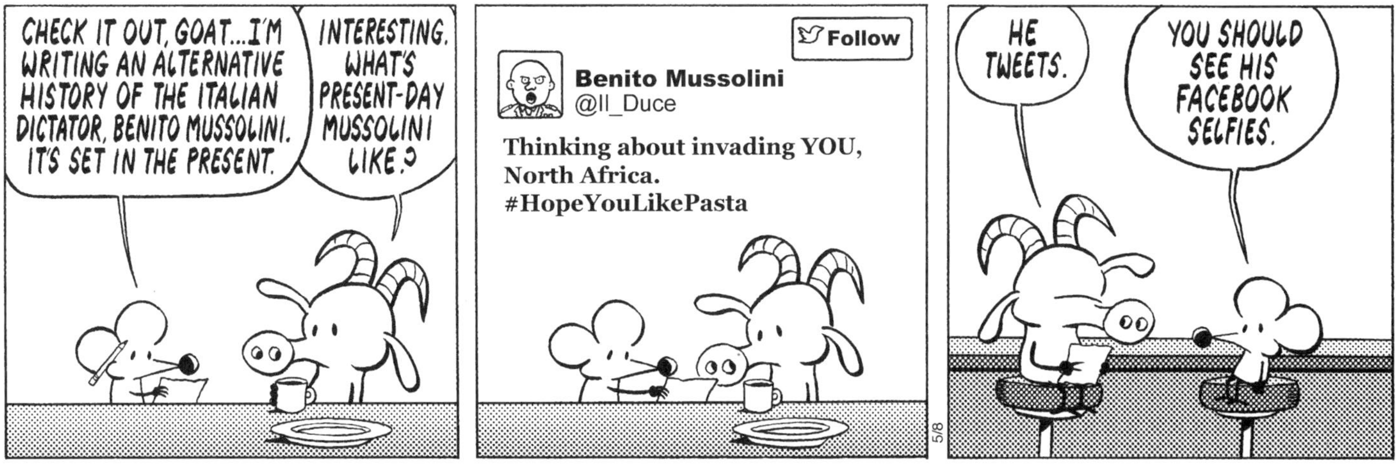
CHECK IT OUT, GOAT...I'M WRITING AN ALTERNATIVE HISTORY OF THE ITALIAN DICTATOR, BENITO MUSSOLINI. IT'S SET IN THE PRESENT.
INTERESTING. WHAT'S PRESENT-DAY MUSSOLINI LIKE?
Follow
Benito Mussolini
@Il_Duce
Thinking about invading YOU, North Africa.
#HopeYouLikePasta
HE TWEETS.
YOU SHOULD SEE HIS FACEBOOK SELFIES.
5/8

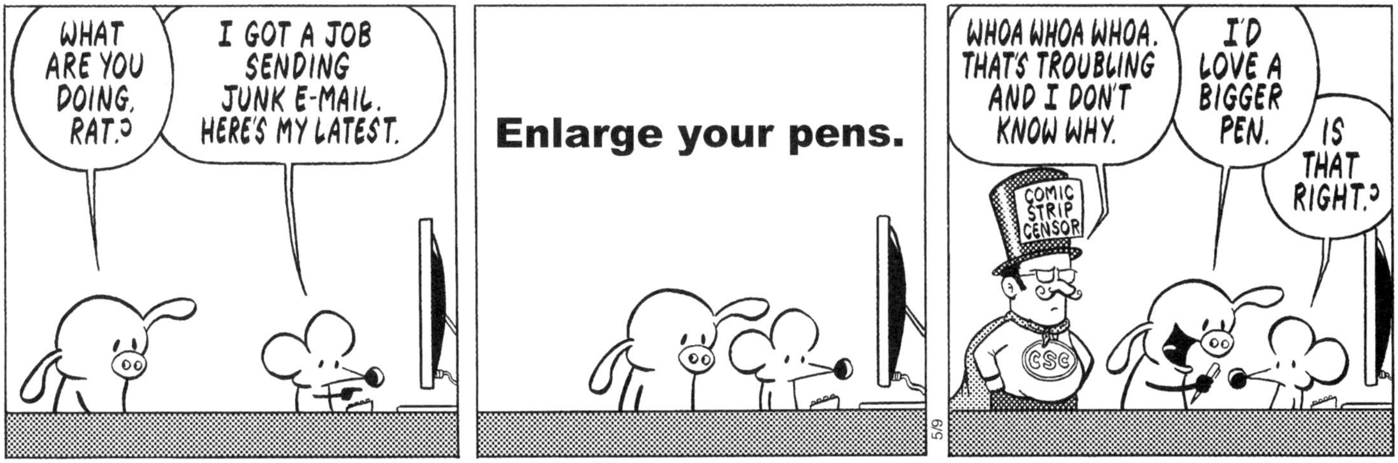
WHAT ARE YOU DOING, RAT?
I GOT A JOB SENDING JUNK E-MAIL. HERE'S MY LATEST.
Enlarge your pens.
WHOA WHOA WHOA. THAT'S TROUBLING AND I DON'T KNOW WHY.
COMIC STRIP CENSOR
CSC
I'D LOVE A BIGGER PEN.
IS THAT RIGHT?
5/9

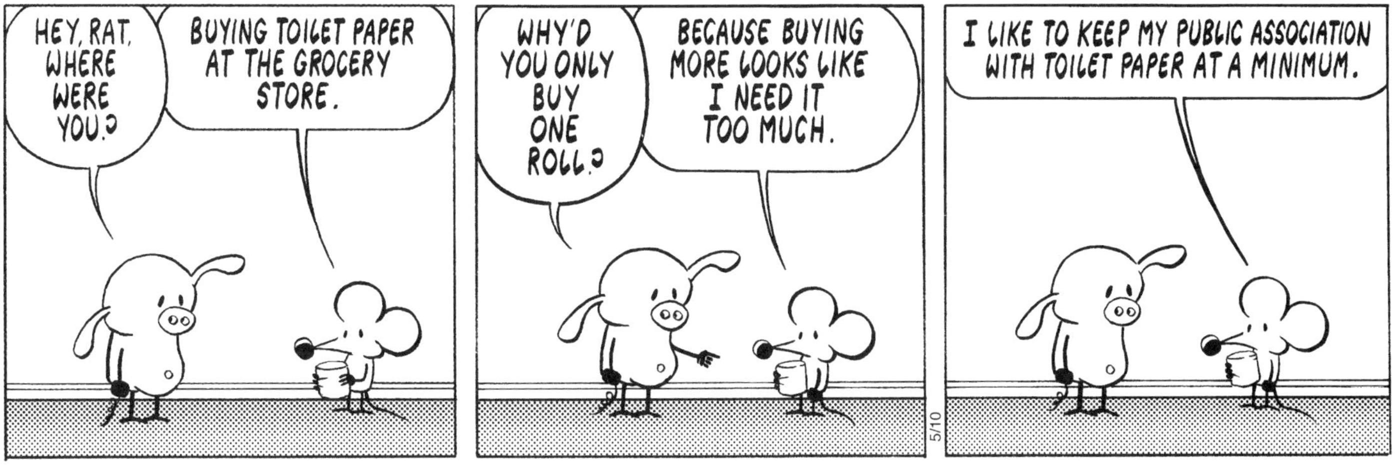
HEY, RAT. WHERE WERE YOU?
BUYING TOILET PAPER AT THE GROCERY STORE.
WHY'D YOU ONLY BUY ONE ROLL?
BECAUSE BUYING MORE LOOKS LIKE I NEED IT TOO MUCH.
I LIKE TO KEEP MY PUBLIC ASSOCIATION WITH TOILET PAPER AT A MINIMUM.
5/10

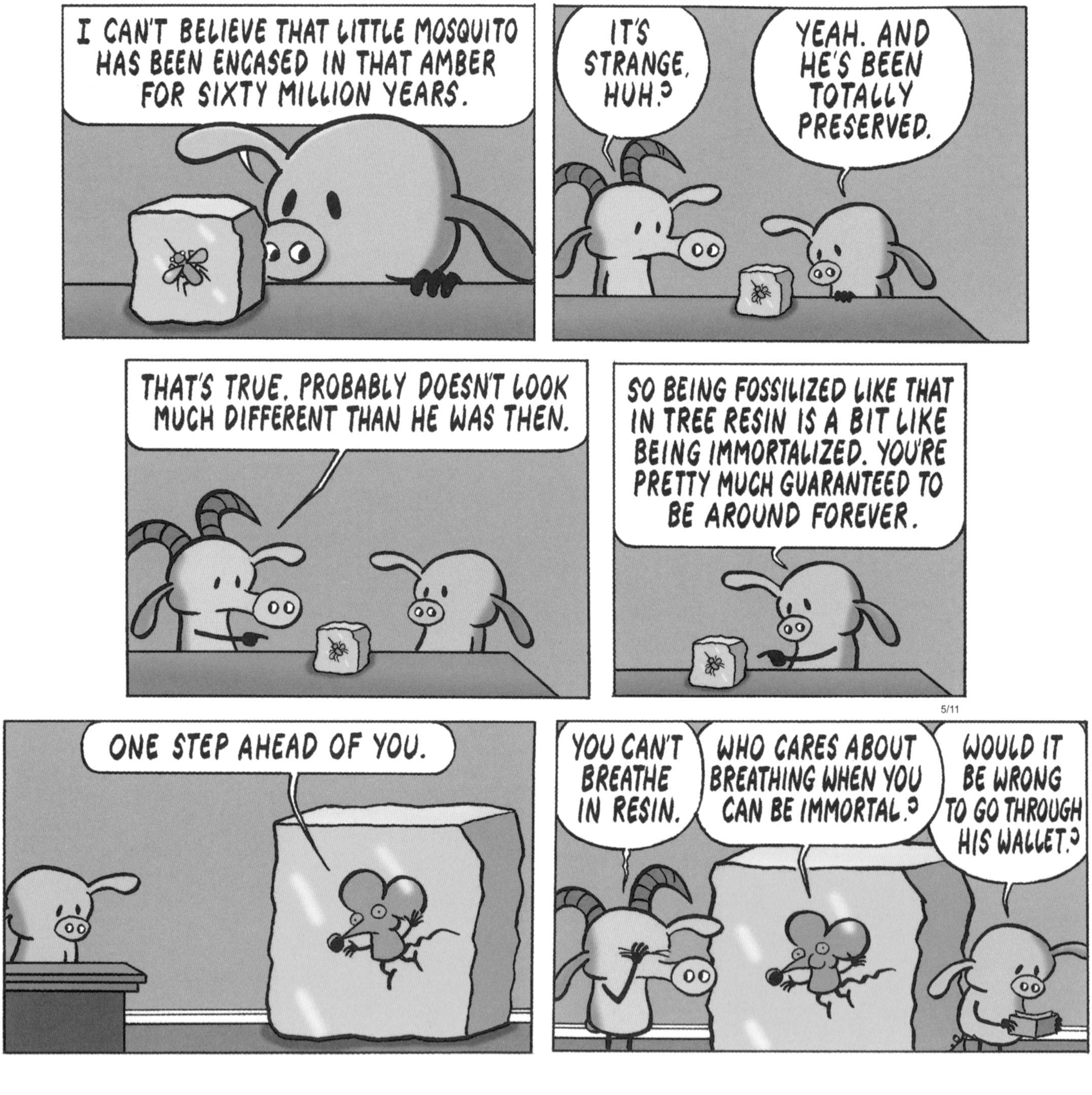
I CAN'T BELIEVE THAT LITTLE MOSQUITO HAS BEEN ENCASED IN THAT AMBER FOR SIXTY MILLION YEARS.
IT'S STRANGE, HUH?
YEAH. AND HE'S BEEN TOTALLY PRESERVED.
THAT'S TRUE. PROBABLY DOESN'T LOOK MUCH DIFFERENT THAN HE WAS THEN.
SO BEING FOSSILIZED LIKE THAT IN TREE RESIN IS A BIT LIKE BEING IMMORTALIZED. YOU'RE PRETTY MUCH GUARANTEED TO BE AROUND FOREVER.
5/11
ONE STEP AHEAD OF YOU.
YOU CAN'T BREATHE IN RESIN.
WHO CARES ABOUT BREATHING WHEN YOU CAN BE IMMORTAL?
WOULD IT BE WRONG TO GO THROUGH HIS WALLET?

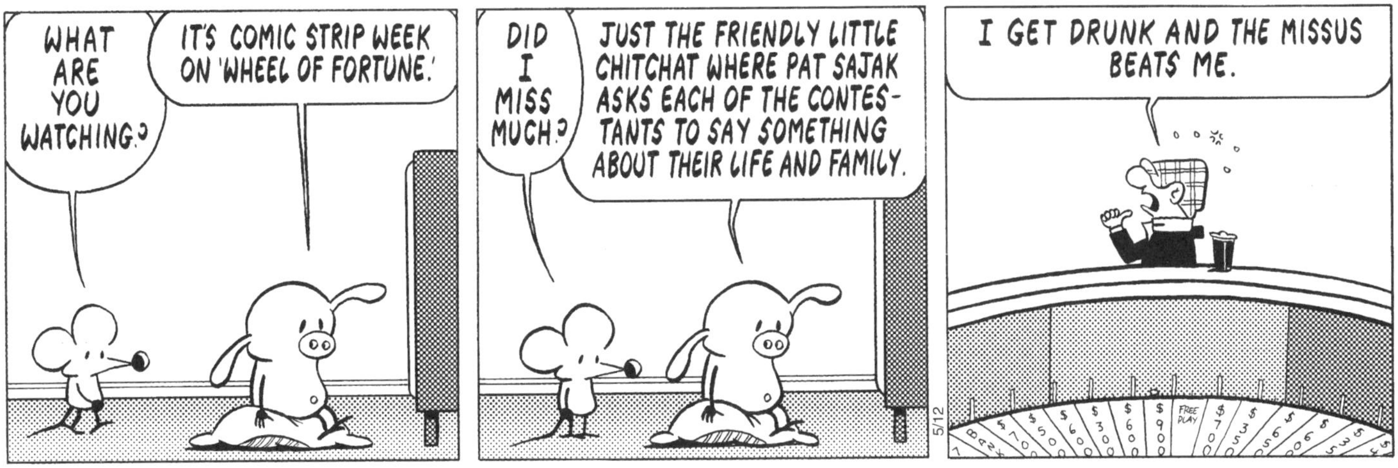
WHAT ARE YOU WATCHING?
IT'S COMIC STRIP WEEK ON 'WHEEL OF FORTUNE.'
DID I MISS MUCH?
JUST THE FRIENDLY LITTLE CHITCHAT WHERE PAT SAJAK ASKS EACH OF THE CONTESTANTS TO SAY SOMETHING ABOUT THEIR LIFE AND FAMILY.
I GET DRUNK AND THE MISSUS BEATS ME.
5/12

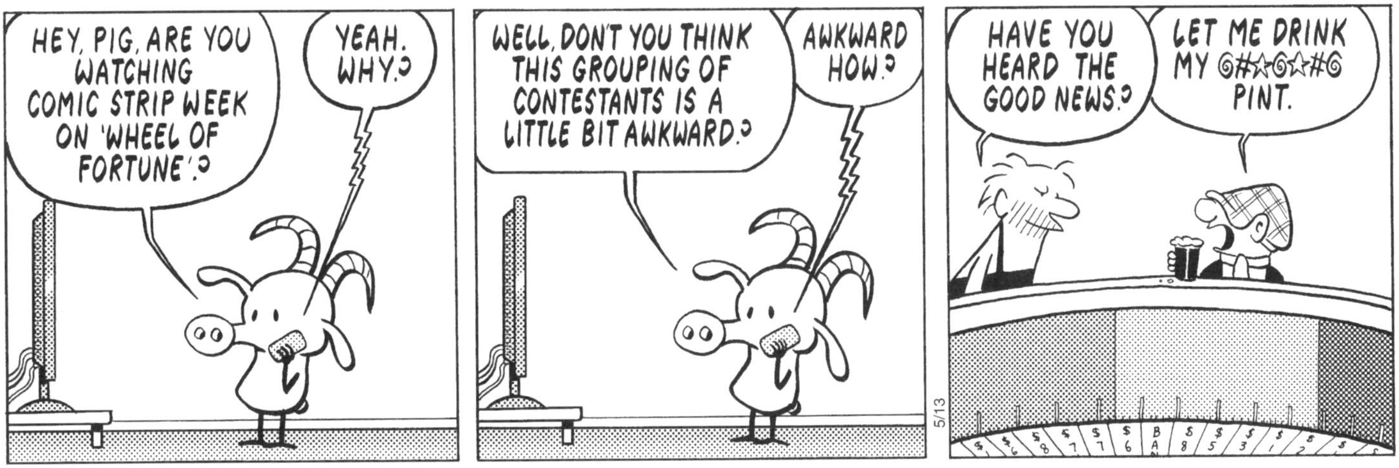
HEY, PIG, ARE YOU WATCHING COMIC STRIP WEEK ON 'WHEEL OF FORTUNE'?
YEAH. WHY?
WELL, DON'T YOU THINK THIS GROUPING OF CONTESTANTS IS A LITTLE BIT AWKWARD?
AWKWARD HOW?
HAVE YOU HEARD THE GOOD NEWS?
LET ME DRINK MY @#☆@☆#@ PINT.
5/13

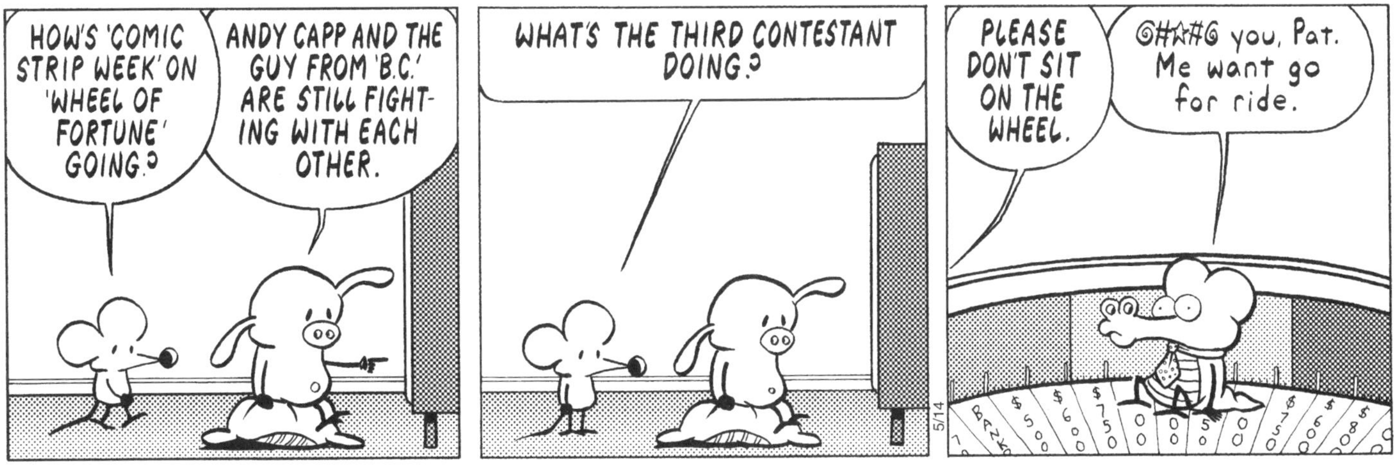
HOW'S 'COMIC STRIP WEEK' ON 'WHEEL OF FORTUNE' GOING?
ANDY CAPP AND THE GUY FROM 'B.C.' ARE STILL FIGHTING WITH EACH OTHER.
WHAT'S THE THIRD CONTESTANT DOING?
PLEASE DON'T SIT ON THE WHEEL.
@#☆#@ you, Pat. Me want go for ride.
5/14

COMIC STRIP WEEK ON 'WHEEL OF FORTUNE'

OUR CATEGORY IS FAMOUS FILMS. ANDY CAPP, YOU'D LIKE TO SOLVE IT?

YES, I WOULD, PAT.

G	O	N	E
W	I	T	H
T	H	E	
W	I	N	

'GONE WITH THE WINO.'

I'M SORRY. NO.

@☆#@.

'GONE WITH THE JESUS'?

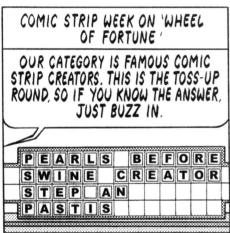

COMIC STRIP WEEK ON 'WHEEL OF FORTUNE'

OUR CATEGORY IS FAMOUS COMIC STRIP CREATORS. THIS IS THE TOSS-UP ROUND, SO IF YOU KNOW THE ANSWER, JUST BUZZ IN.

P	E	A	R	L	S		B	E	F	O	R	E
S	W	I	N	E		C	R	E	A	T	O	R
S	T	E	P		A	N						
P	A	S	T	I	S							

OH, COME ON, NOW!

Is you a homeless guy?

PLEASE, SIR, WE HAVE NO SPARE CHANGE.

COMIC STRIP WEEK ON 'WHEEL OF FORTUNE.'

THE CATEGORY IS FAMOUS COMIC STRIP QUOTES. IT'S YOUR TURN, LARRY.

Me like solve, Pat Asjak.

G	O	O	D
G	R	I	E	F
C	H	A	R	L	I	E
B	R	O	W	

GO AHEAD.

'Hulloooo zeeba neighba.'

NO.

Dat most famous comeec line EVER!

ANDY CAPP'S PUKING AGAIN!

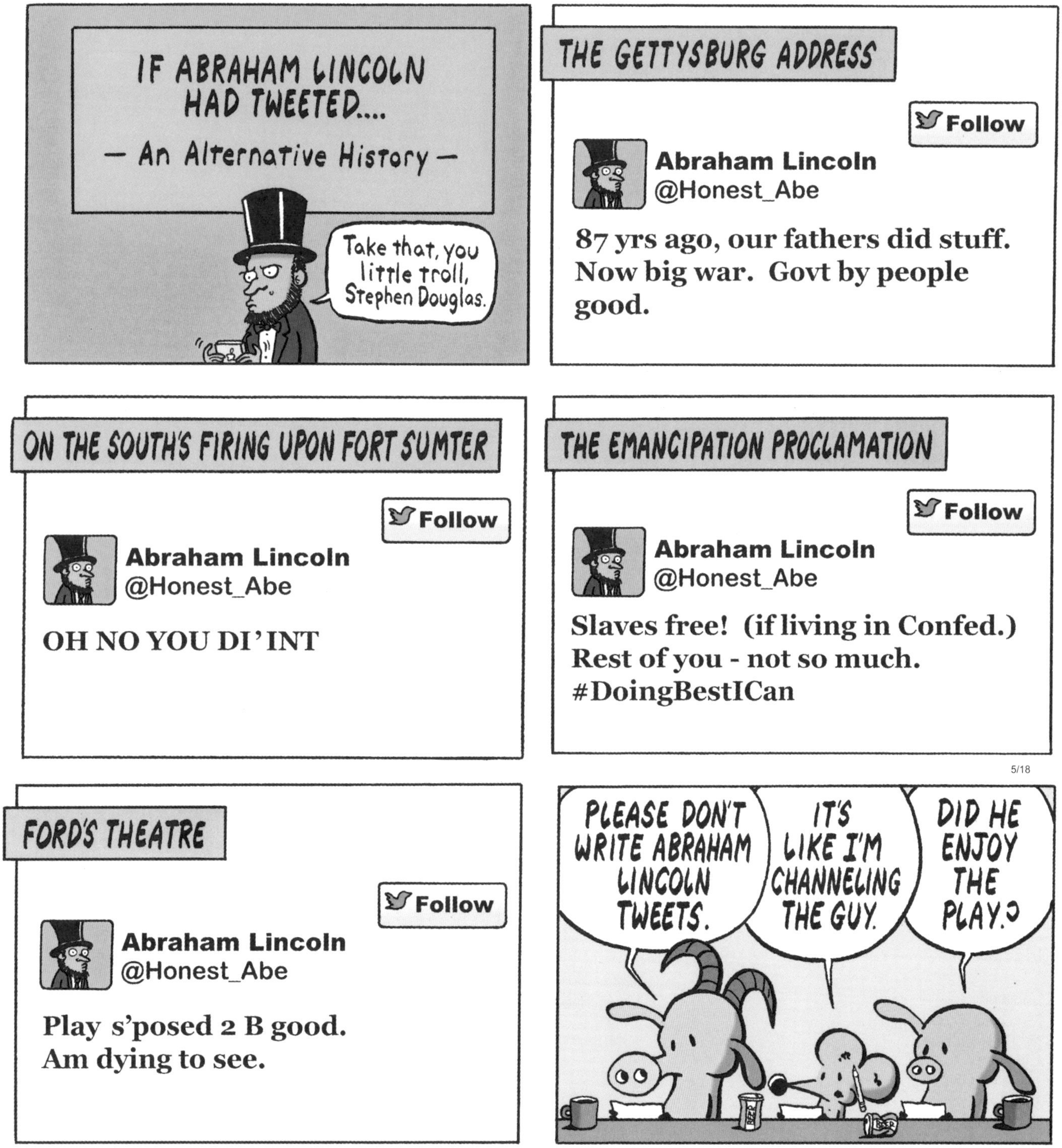
IF ABRAHAM LINCOLN HAD TWEETED....
— An Alternative History —
Take that, you little troll, Stephen Douglas.
THE GETTYSBURG ADDRESS
Follow
Abraham Lincoln
@Honest_Abe
87 yrs ago, our fathers did stuff. Now big war. Govt by people good.
ON THE SOUTH'S FIRING UPON FORT SUMTER
Follow
Abraham Lincoln
@Honest_Abe
OH NO YOU DI'INT
THE EMANCIPATION PROCLAMATION
Follow
Abraham Lincoln
@Honest_Abe
Slaves free! (if living in Confed.) Rest of you - not so much. #DoingBestICan
5/18
FORD'S THEATRE
Follow
Abraham Lincoln
@Honest_Abe
Play s'posed 2 B good. Am dying to see.
PLEASE DON'T WRITE ABRAHAM LINCOLN TWEETS.
IT'S LIKE I'M CHANNELING THE GUY.
DID HE ENJOY THE PLAY?
BEER
BEER

Panel 1:
WHAT ARE YOU DOING, PIG?

PLAYING WITH MY VIKING ACTION FIGURINES. THEY'RE ABOUT TO BATTLE.

Panel 2:
OOOH...VIKING COMBAT...I LIKE THAT...WHAT DO THEY USE? SPEARS? SWORDS? BATTLE AXES?

5/19

Panel 3:
Q-TIPS.

Panel 4:
AT WORST, THEY'LL GET CLEAN EARS.

Panel 5:
DO YOU THINK COMIC STRIP CENSORSHIP IS MORE STRICT THAN THE CENSORSHIP YOU SEE IN OTHER FORMS OF MASS ENTERTAINMENT?

Panel 6:
DOES A BEAR SIT IN THE WOODS?

5/20

Panel 7:
CURSE YOU, TRICKY RAT.

WHAT NOW?

NO MORE TALK OF BEARS IN THE WOODS.

COMIC STRIP CENSOR

COMIC STRIP CENSOR

Panel 8:
DO YOU THINK OUR CREATOR, STEPHAN, HAS BEEN ACTING A LITTLE LESS MATURE LATELY?

WHAT MAKES YOU SAY THAT?

5/21

Panel 9:
I'M IN MY CHOO CHOO JAMMIES.

Panel 10:
THERE'S THAT.

HA HA. STEPHAN LIKE CHOO CHOO JAMMIES.

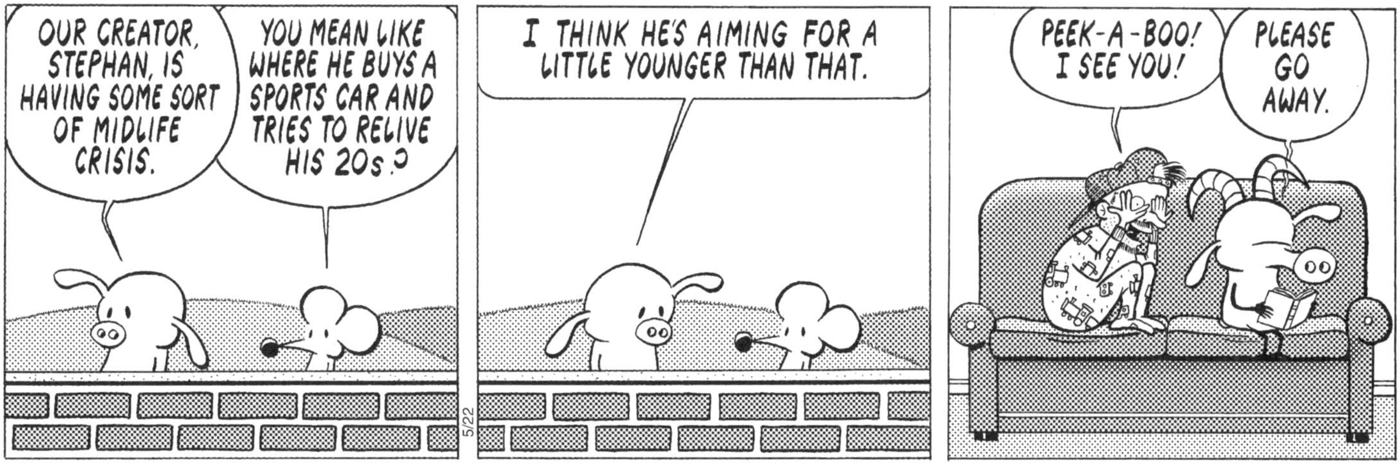
OUR CREATOR, STEPHAN, IS HAVING SOME SORT OF MIDLIFE CRISIS.
YOU MEAN LIKE WHERE HE BUYS A SPORTS CAR AND TRIES TO RELIVE HIS 20s?
5/22
I THINK HE'S AIMING FOR A LITTLE YOUNGER THAN THAT.
PEEK-A-BOO! I SEE YOU!
PLEASE GO AWAY.

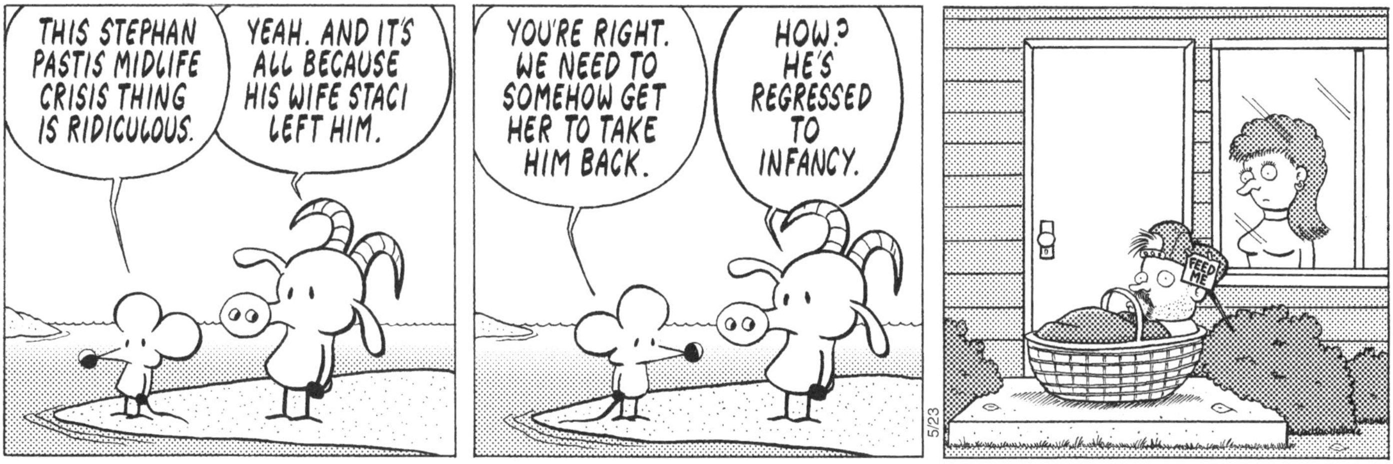
THIS STEPHAN PASTIS MIDLIFE CRISIS THING IS RIDICULOUS.
YEAH. AND IT'S ALL BECAUSE HIS WIFE STACI LEFT HIM.
YOU'RE RIGHT. WE NEED TO SOMEHOW GET HER TO TAKE HIM BACK.
HOW? HE'S REGRESSED TO INFANCY.
5/23
FEED ME

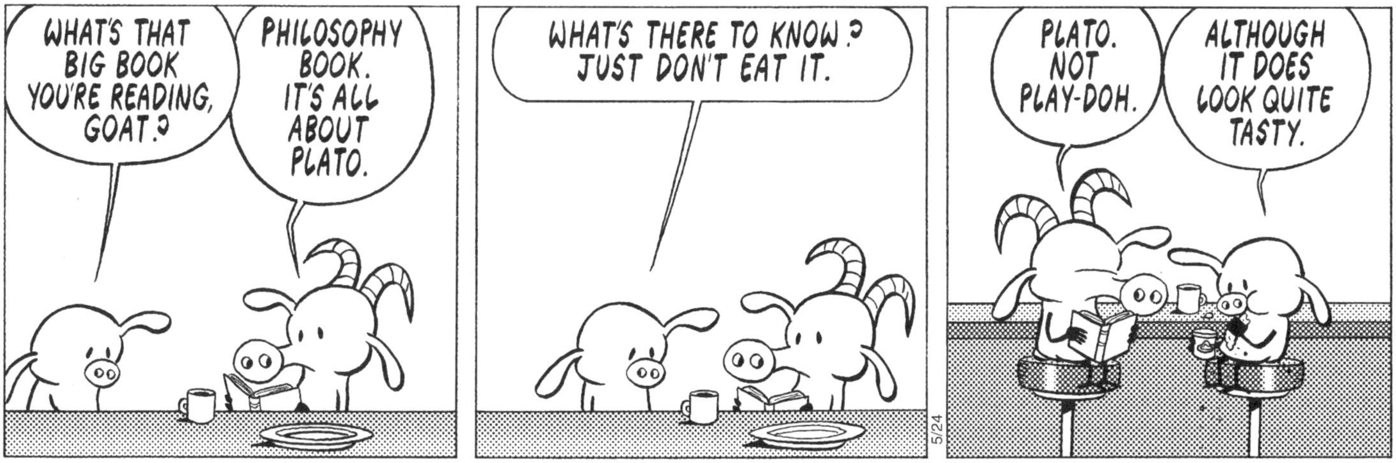
WHAT'S THAT BIG BOOK YOU'RE READING, GOAT?
PHILOSOPHY BOOK. IT'S ALL ABOUT PLATO.
WHAT'S THERE TO KNOW? JUST DON'T EAT IT.
5/24
PLATO. NOT PLAY-DOH.
ALTHOUGH IT DOES LOOK QUITE TASTY.

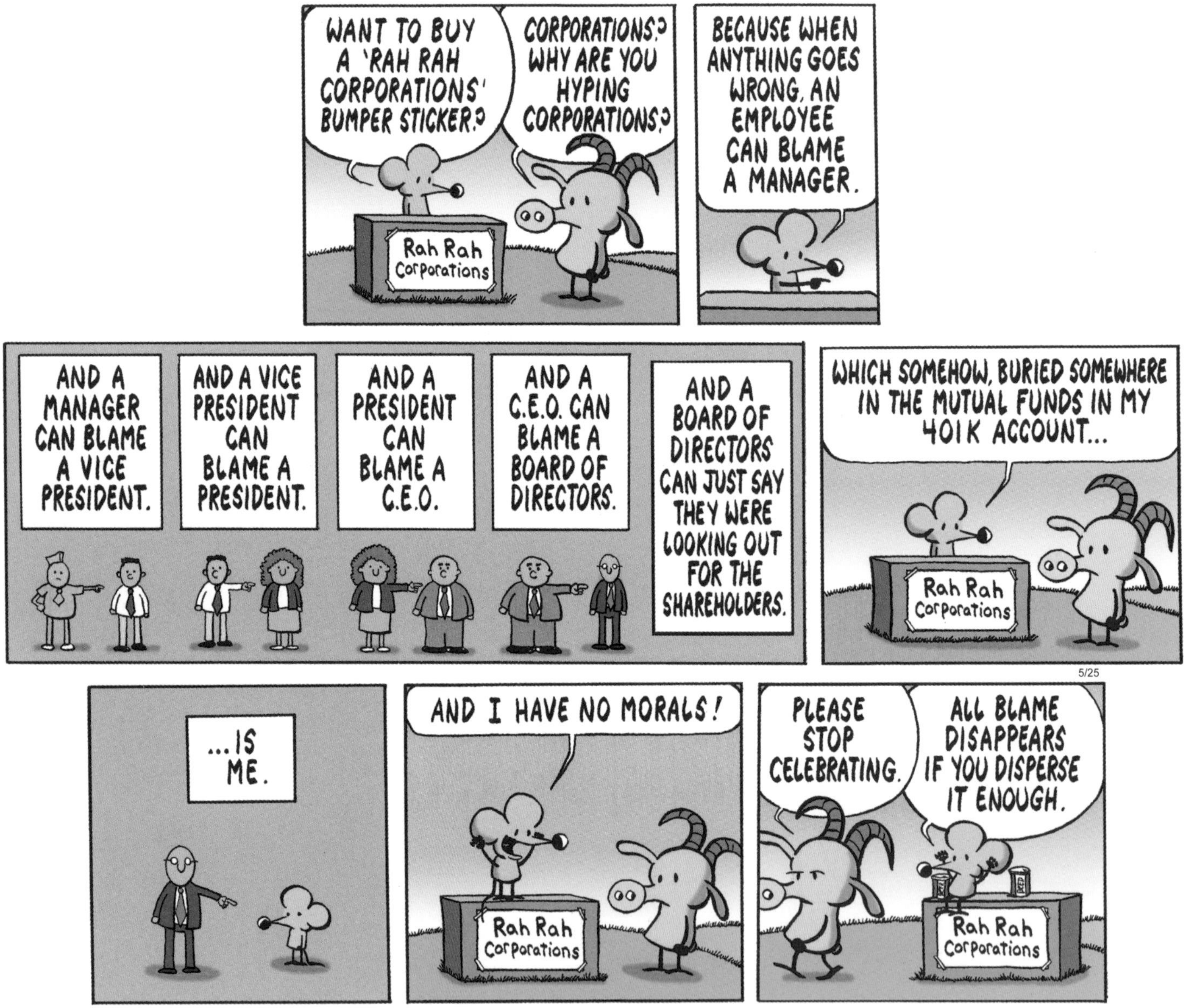
WANT TO BUY A 'RAH RAH CORPORATIONS' BUMPER STICKER?
CORPORATIONS? WHY ARE YOU HYPING CORPORATIONS?
Rah Rah Corporations
BECAUSE WHEN ANYTHING GOES WRONG, AN EMPLOYEE CAN BLAME A MANAGER.
AND A MANAGER CAN BLAME A VICE PRESIDENT.
AND A VICE PRESIDENT CAN BLAME A PRESIDENT.
AND A PRESIDENT CAN BLAME A C.E.O.
AND A C.E.O. CAN BLAME A BOARD OF DIRECTORS.
AND A BOARD OF DIRECTORS CAN JUST SAY THEY WERE LOOKING OUT FOR THE SHAREHOLDERS.
WHICH SOMEHOW, BURIED SOMEWHERE IN THE MUTUAL FUNDS IN MY 401K ACCOUNT...
Rah Rah Corporations
5/25
...IS ME.
AND I HAVE NO MORALS!
Rah Rah Corporations
PLEASE STOP CELEBRATING.
ALL BLAME DISAPPEARS IF YOU DISPERSE IT ENOUGH.
Rah Rah Corporations

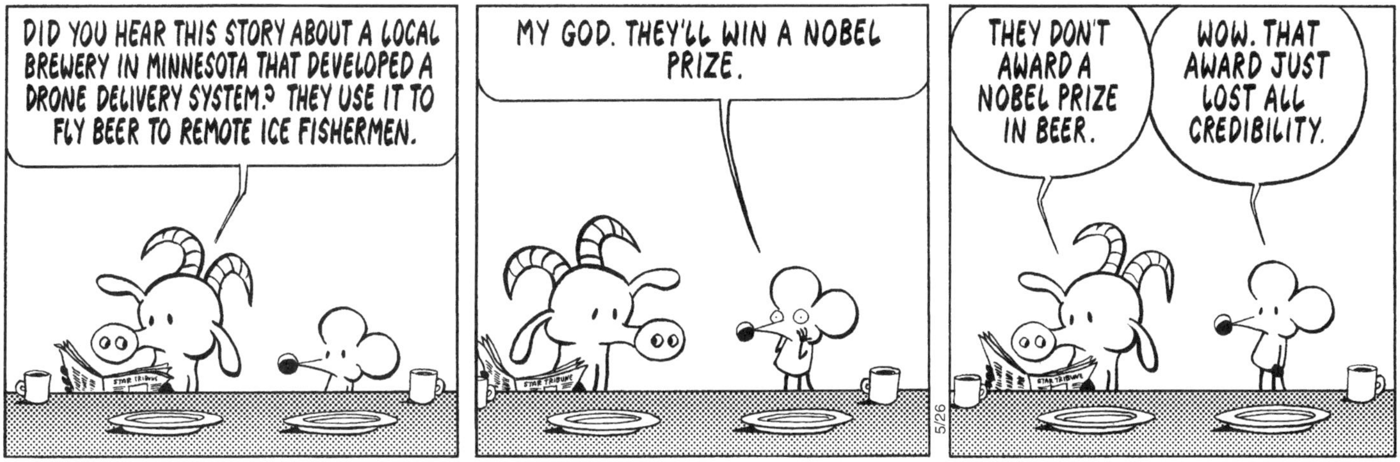
DID YOU HEAR THIS STORY ABOUT A LOCAL BREWERY IN MINNESOTA THAT DEVELOPED A DRONE DELIVERY SYSTEM? THEY USE IT TO FLY BEER TO REMOTE ICE FISHERMEN.
MY GOD. THEY'LL WIN A NOBEL PRIZE.
THEY DON'T AWARD A NOBEL PRIZE IN BEER.
WOW. THAT AWARD JUST LOST ALL CREDIBILITY.
5/26

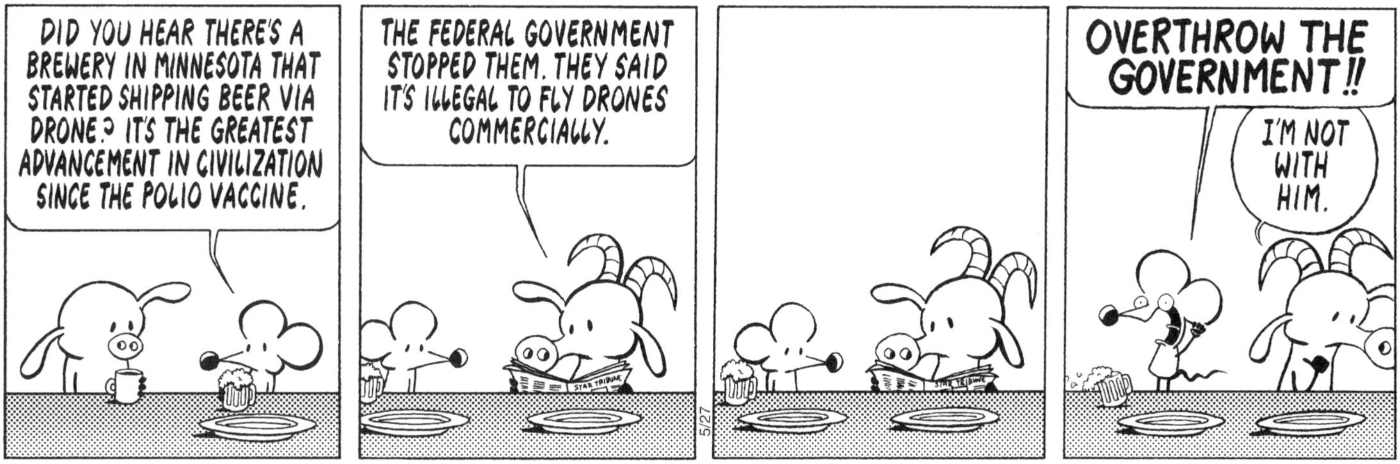
DID YOU HEAR THERE'S A BREWERY IN MINNESOTA THAT STARTED SHIPPING BEER VIA DRONE? IT'S THE GREATEST ADVANCEMENT IN CIVILIZATION SINCE THE POLIO VACCINE.
THE FEDERAL GOVERNMENT STOPPED THEM. THEY SAID IT'S ILLEGAL TO FLY DRONES COMMERCIALLY.
OVERTHROW THE GOVERNMENT!!
I'M NOT WITH HIM.
5/27

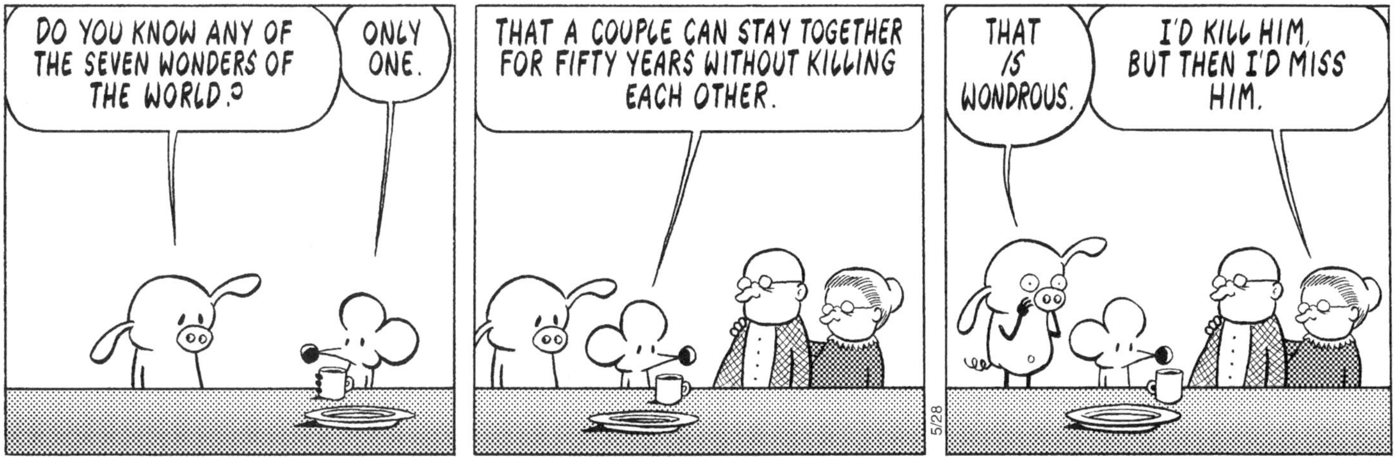
DO YOU KNOW ANY OF THE SEVEN WONDERS OF THE WORLD?
ONLY ONE.
THAT A COUPLE CAN STAY TOGETHER FOR FIFTY YEARS WITHOUT KILLING EACH OTHER.
THAT *IS* WONDROUS.
I'D KILL HIM, BUT THEN I'D MISS HIM.
5/28

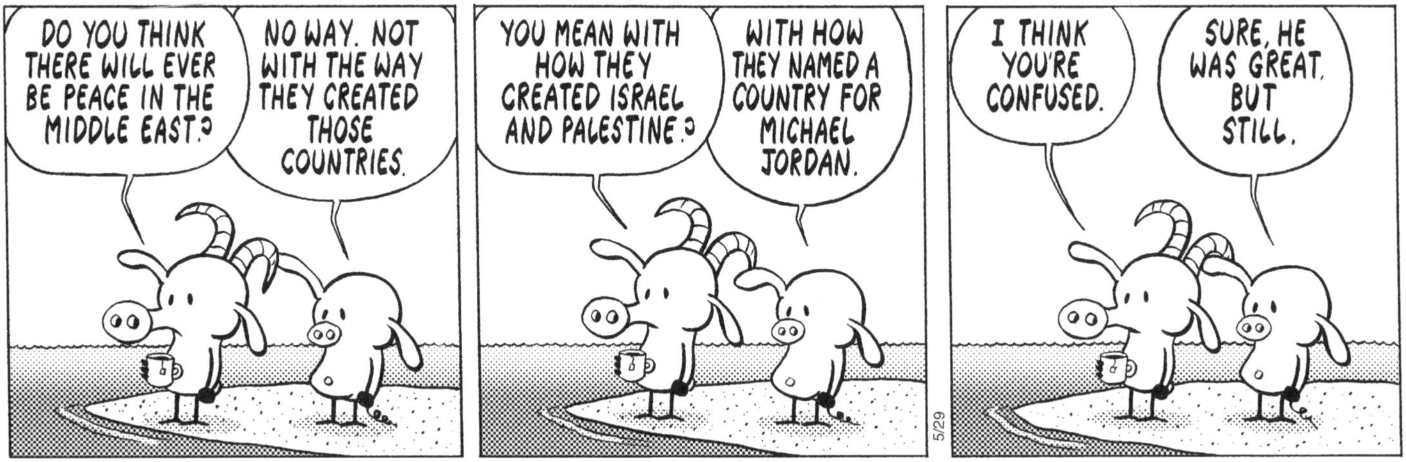
DO YOU THINK THERE WILL EVER BE PEACE IN THE MIDDLE EAST?
NO WAY. NOT WITH THE WAY THEY CREATED THOSE COUNTRIES.
YOU MEAN WITH HOW THEY CREATED ISRAEL AND PALESTINE?
WITH HOW THEY NAMED A COUNTRY FOR MICHAEL JORDAN.
I THINK YOU'RE CONFUSED.
SURE, HE WAS GREAT, BUT STILL.
5/29

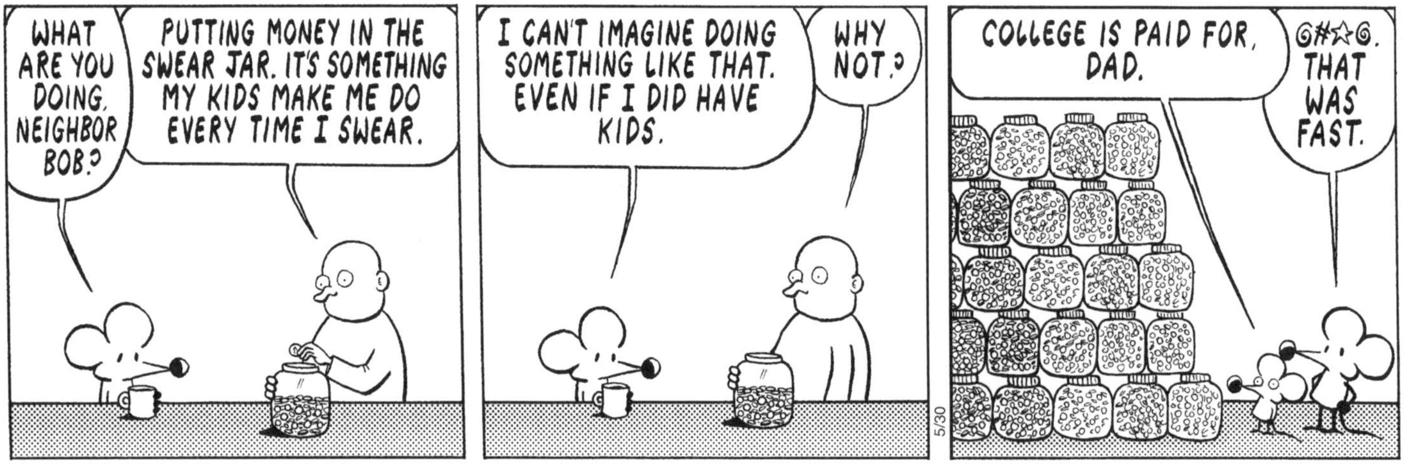
WHAT ARE YOU DOING, NEIGHBOR BOB?
PUTTING MONEY IN THE SWEAR JAR. IT'S SOMETHING MY KIDS MAKE ME DO EVERY TIME I SWEAR.
I CAN'T IMAGINE DOING SOMETHING LIKE THAT. EVEN IF I DID HAVE KIDS.
WHY NOT?
COLLEGE IS PAID FOR, DAD.
@#☆@. THAT WAS FAST.
5/30

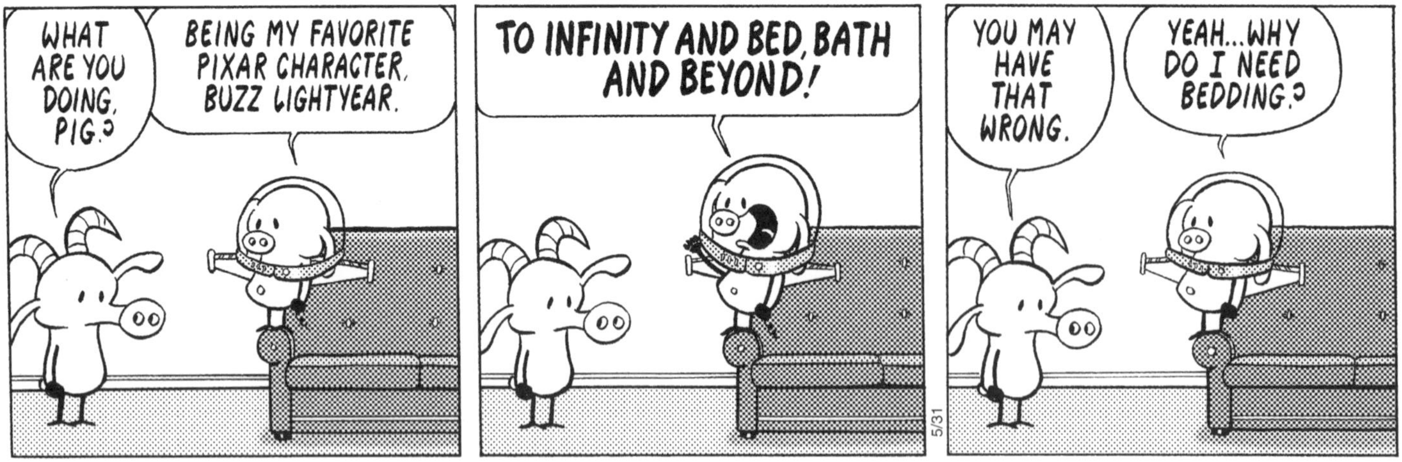
WHAT ARE YOU DOING, PIG?
BEING MY FAVORITE PIXAR CHARACTER, BUZZ LIGHTYEAR.
TO INFINITY AND BED, BATH AND BEYOND!
YOU MAY HAVE THAT WRONG.
YEAH...WHY DO I NEED BEDDING?
5/31

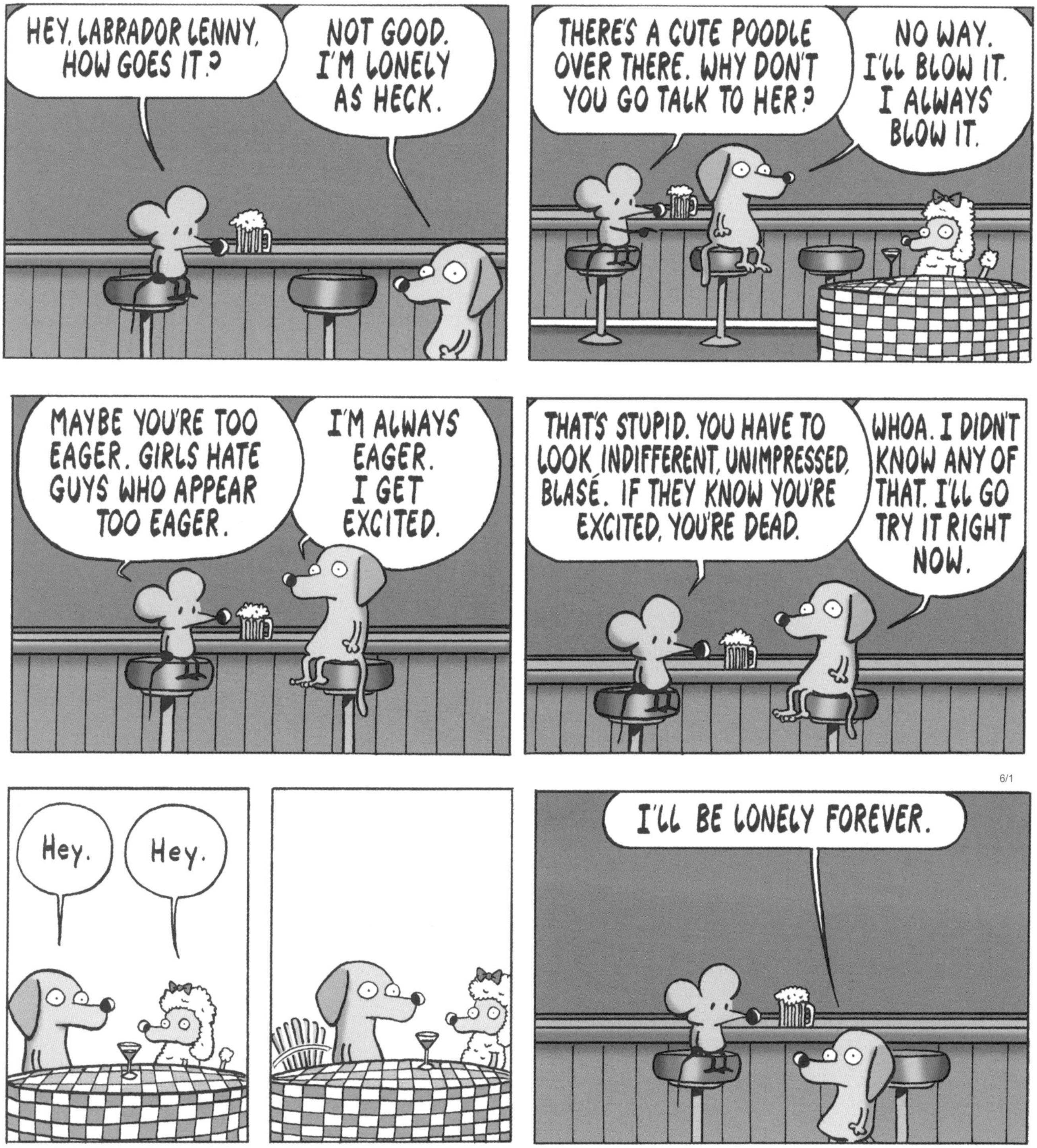
HEY, LABRADOR LENNY, HOW GOES IT?
NOT GOOD. I'M LONELY AS HECK.
THERE'S A CUTE POODLE OVER THERE. WHY DON'T YOU GO TALK TO HER?
NO WAY. I'LL BLOW IT. I ALWAYS BLOW IT.
MAYBE YOU'RE TOO EAGER. GIRLS HATE GUYS WHO APPEAR TOO EAGER.
I'M ALWAYS EAGER. I GET EXCITED.
THAT'S STUPID. YOU HAVE TO LOOK INDIFFERENT, UNIMPRESSED, BLASÉ. IF THEY KNOW YOU'RE EXCITED, YOU'RE DEAD.
WHOA. I DIDN'T KNOW ANY OF THAT. I'LL GO TRY IT RIGHT NOW.
6/1
Hey.
Hey.
I'LL BE LONELY FOREVER.

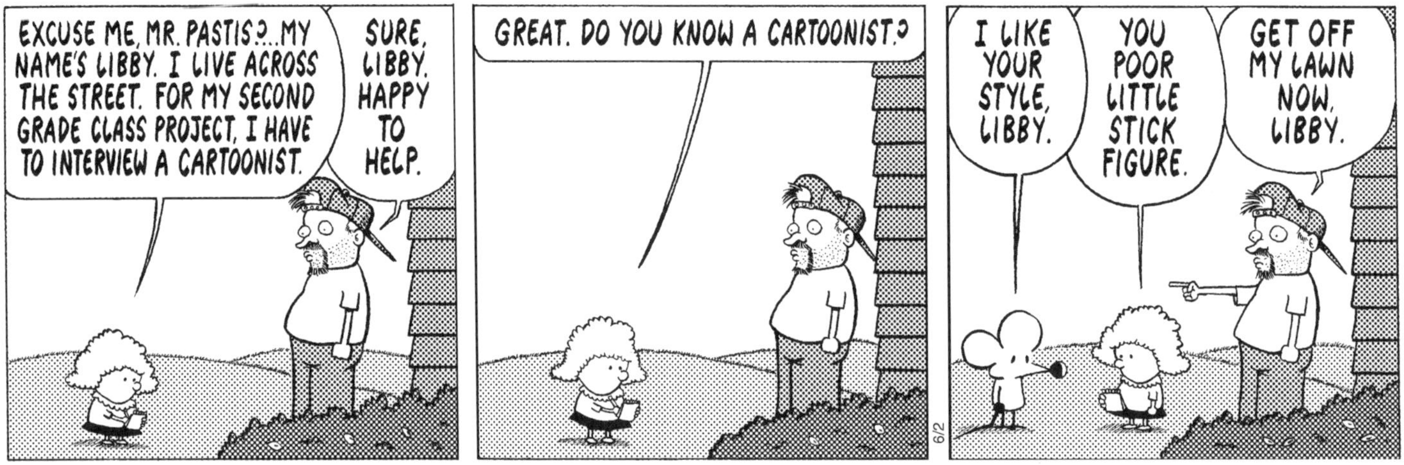
EXCUSE ME, MR. PASTIS?...MY NAME'S LIBBY. I LIVE ACROSS THE STREET. FOR MY SECOND GRADE CLASS PROJECT, I HAVE TO INTERVIEW A CARTOONIST.
SURE, LIBBY. HAPPY TO HELP.
GREAT. DO YOU KNOW A CARTOONIST?
I LIKE YOUR STYLE, LIBBY.
YOU POOR LITTLE STICK FIGURE.
GET OFF MY LAWN NOW, LIBBY.
6/2

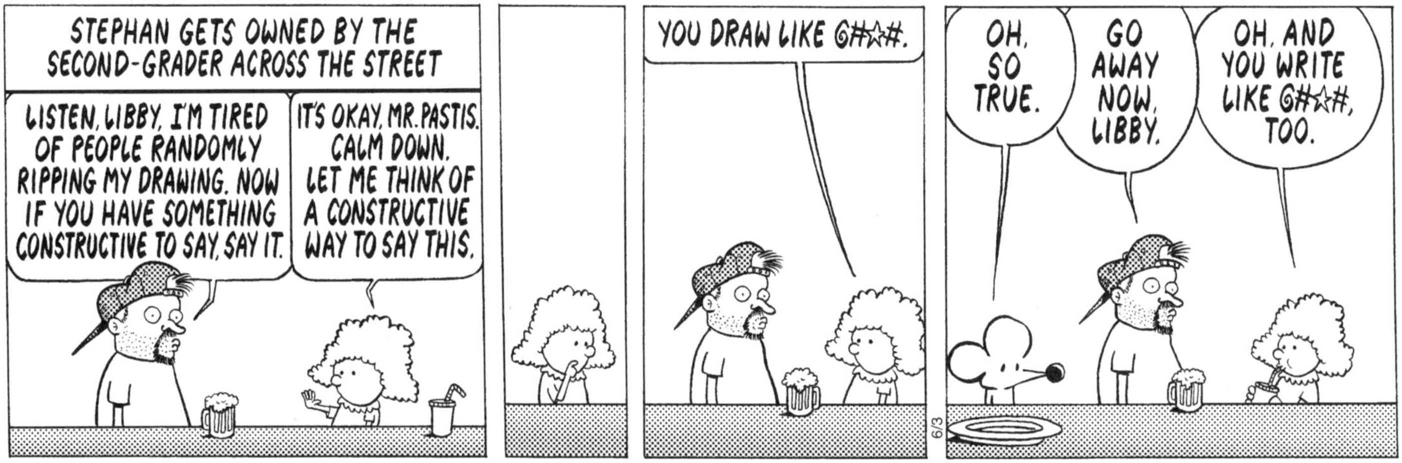
STEPHAN GETS OWNED BY THE SECOND-GRADER ACROSS THE STREET
LISTEN, LIBBY, I'M TIRED OF PEOPLE RANDOMLY RIPPING MY DRAWING. NOW IF YOU HAVE SOMETHING CONSTRUCTIVE TO SAY, SAY IT.
IT'S OKAY, MR. PASTIS. CALM DOWN. LET ME THINK OF A CONSTRUCTIVE WAY TO SAY THIS.
YOU DRAW LIKE @#☆#.
OH, SO TRUE.
GO AWAY NOW, LIBBY.
OH, AND YOU WRITE LIKE @#☆#, TOO.
6/3

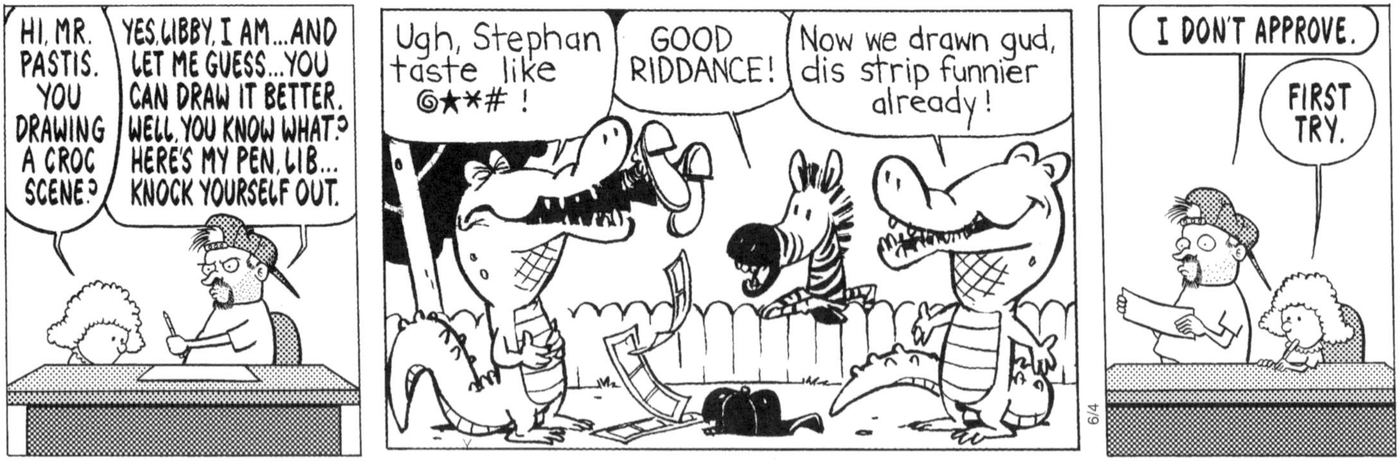
HI, MR. PASTIS. YOU DRAWING A CROC SCENE?
YES, LIBBY, I AM...AND LET ME GUESS...YOU CAN DRAW IT BETTER. WELL, YOU KNOW WHAT? HERE'S MY PEN, LIB... KNOCK YOURSELF OUT.
Ugh, Stephan taste like @★*# !
GOOD RIDDANCE!
Now we drawn gud, dis strip funnier already!
I DON'T APPROVE.
FIRST TRY.
6/4

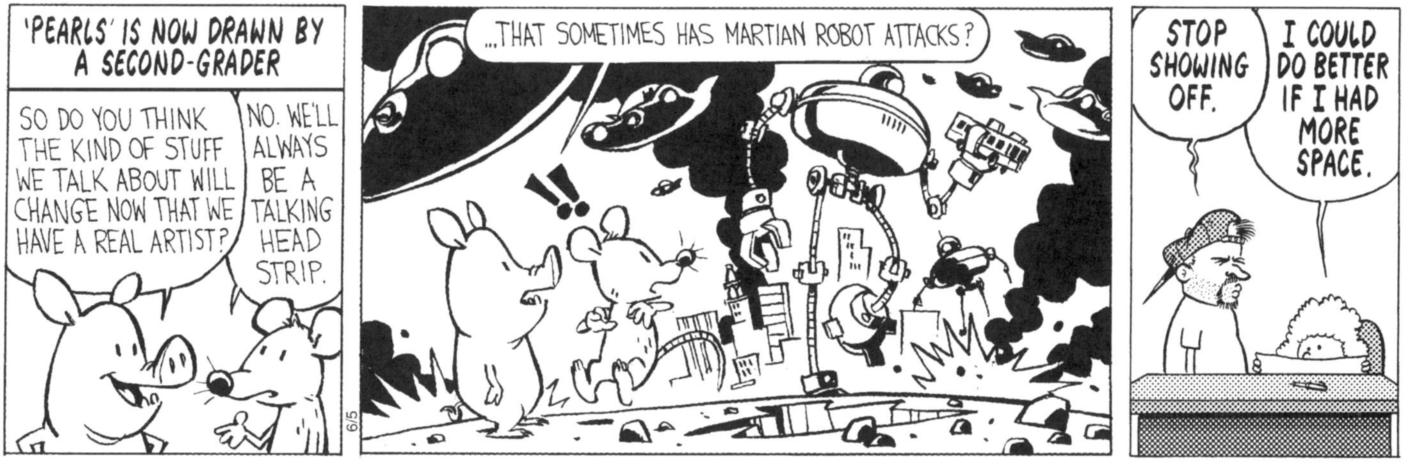
'PEARLS' IS NOW DRAWN BY A SECOND-GRADER
SO DO YOU THINK THE KIND OF STUFF WE TALK ABOUT WILL CHANGE NOW THAT WE HAVE A REAL ARTIST?
NO. WE'LL ALWAYS BE A TALKING HEAD STRIP.
...THAT SOMETIMES HAS MARTIAN ROBOT ATTACKS?
!!
STOP SHOWING OFF.
I COULD DO BETTER IF I HAD MORE SPACE.
6/5

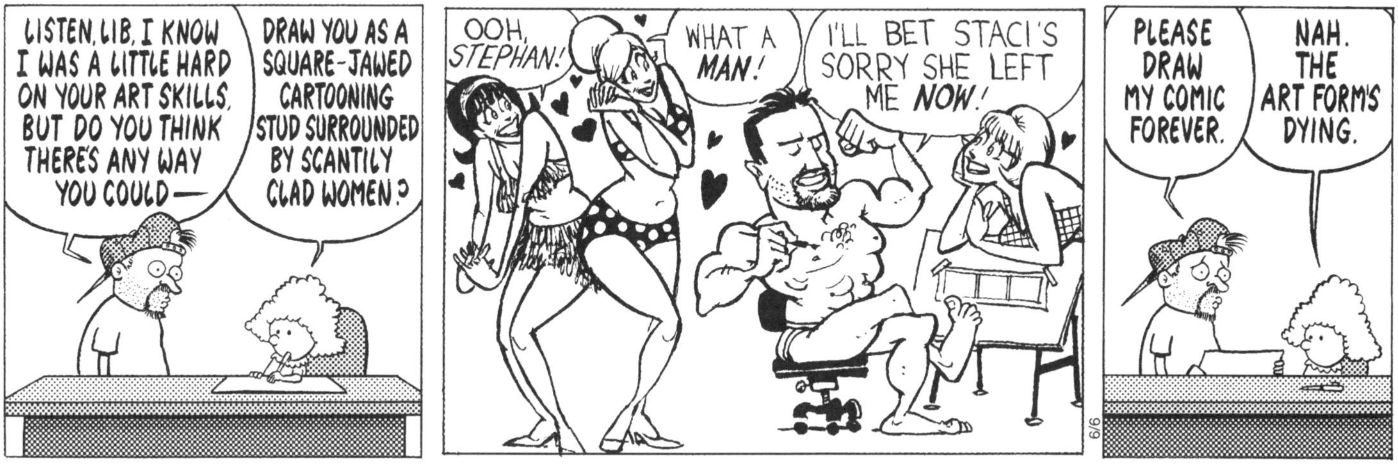
LISTEN, LIB, I KNOW I WAS A LITTLE HARD ON YOUR ART SKILLS, BUT DO YOU THINK THERE'S ANY WAY YOU COULD—
DRAW YOU AS A SQUARE-JAWED CARTOONING STUD SURROUNDED BY SCANTILY CLAD WOMEN?
OOH, STEPHAN!
WHAT A MAN!
I'LL BET STACI'S SORRY SHE LEFT ME NOW!
PLEASE DRAW MY COMIC FOREVER.
NAH. THE ART FORM'S DYING.
6/6

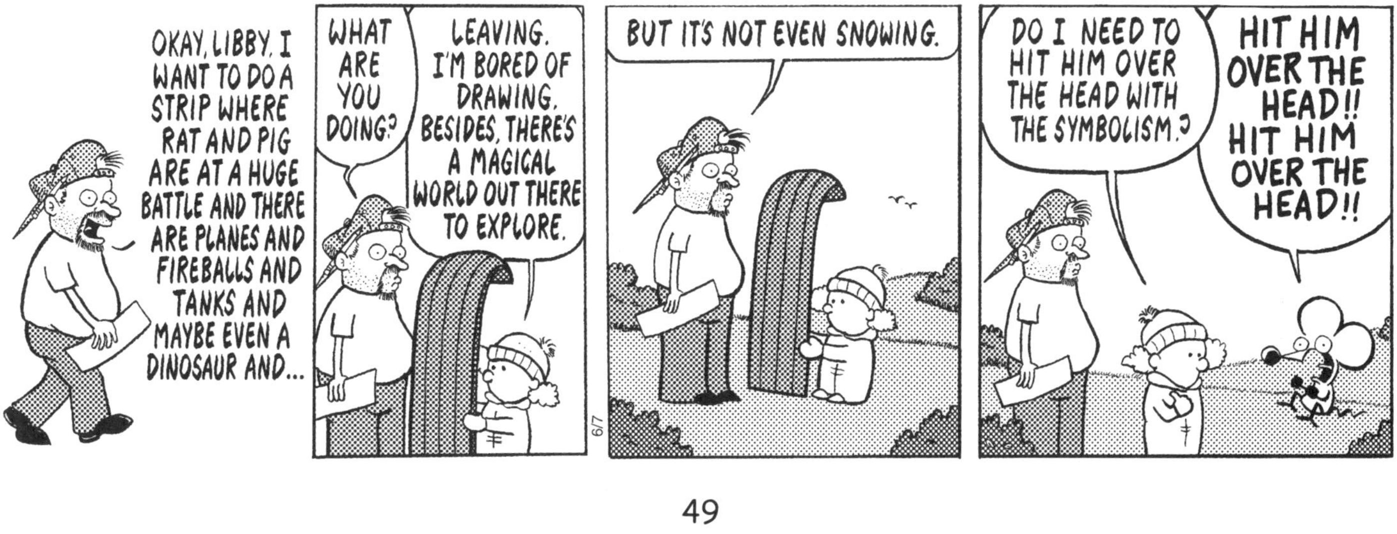
OKAY, LIBBY, I WANT TO DO A STRIP WHERE RAT AND PIG ARE AT A HUGE BATTLE AND THERE ARE PLANES AND FIREBALLS AND TANKS AND MAYBE EVEN A DINOSAUR AND...
WHAT ARE YOU DOING?
LEAVING. I'M BORED OF DRAWING. BESIDES, THERE'S A MAGICAL WORLD OUT THERE TO EXPLORE.
BUT IT'S NOT EVEN SNOWING.
DO I NEED TO HIT HIM OVER THE HEAD WITH THE SYMBOLISM?
HIT HIM OVER THE HEAD!! HIT HIM OVER THE HEAD!!
6/7

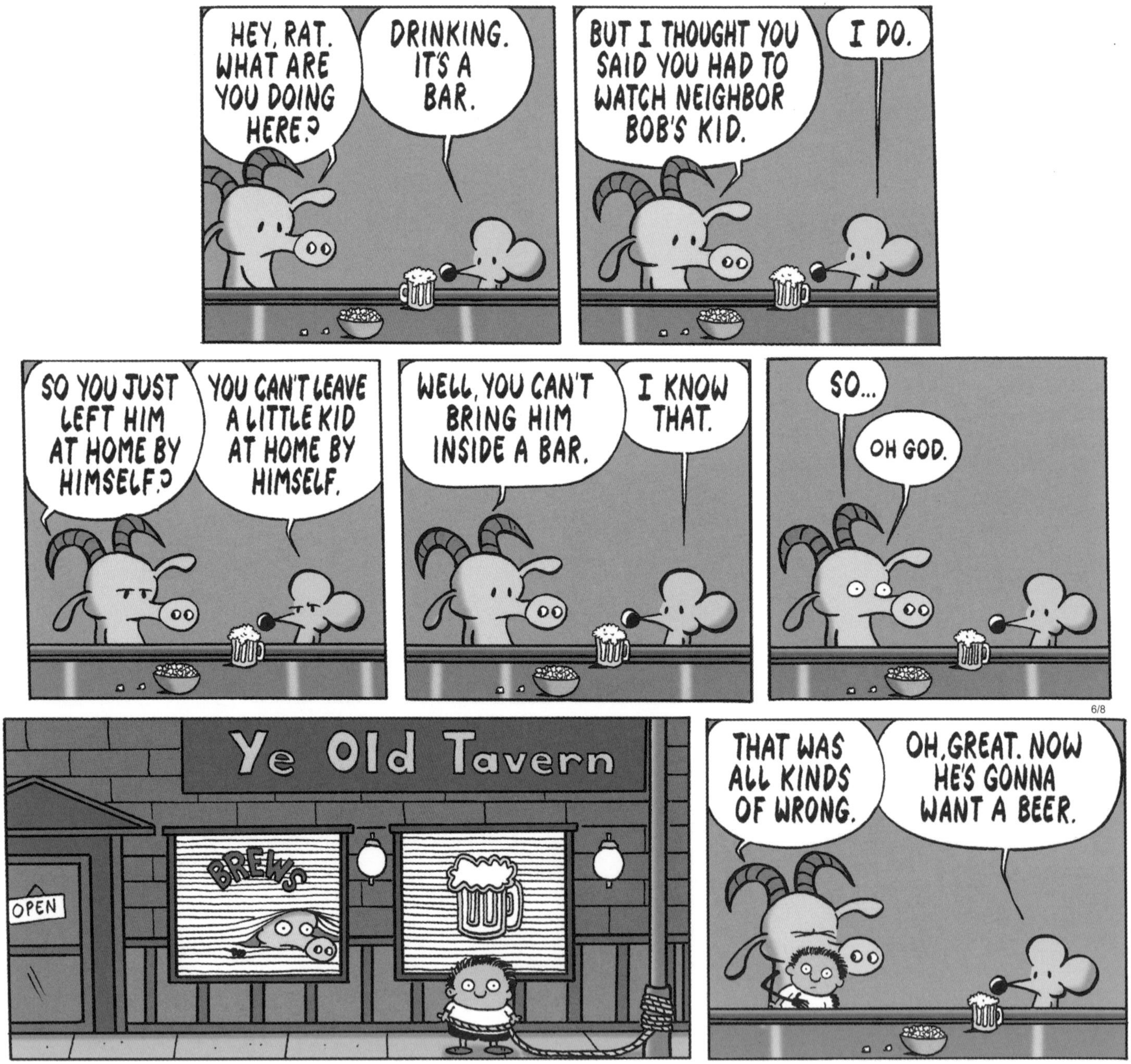
HEY, RAT. WHAT ARE YOU DOING HERE?
DRINKING. IT'S A BAR.
BUT I THOUGHT YOU SAID YOU HAD TO WATCH NEIGHBOR BOB'S KID.
I DO.
SO YOU JUST LEFT HIM AT HOME BY HIMSELF?
YOU CAN'T LEAVE A LITTLE KID AT HOME BY HIMSELF.
WELL, YOU CAN'T BRING HIM INSIDE A BAR.
I KNOW THAT.
SO...
OH GOD.
6/8
Ye Old Tavern
OPEN
BREWS
THAT WAS ALL KINDS OF WRONG.
OH, GREAT. NOW HE'S GONNA WANT A BEER.

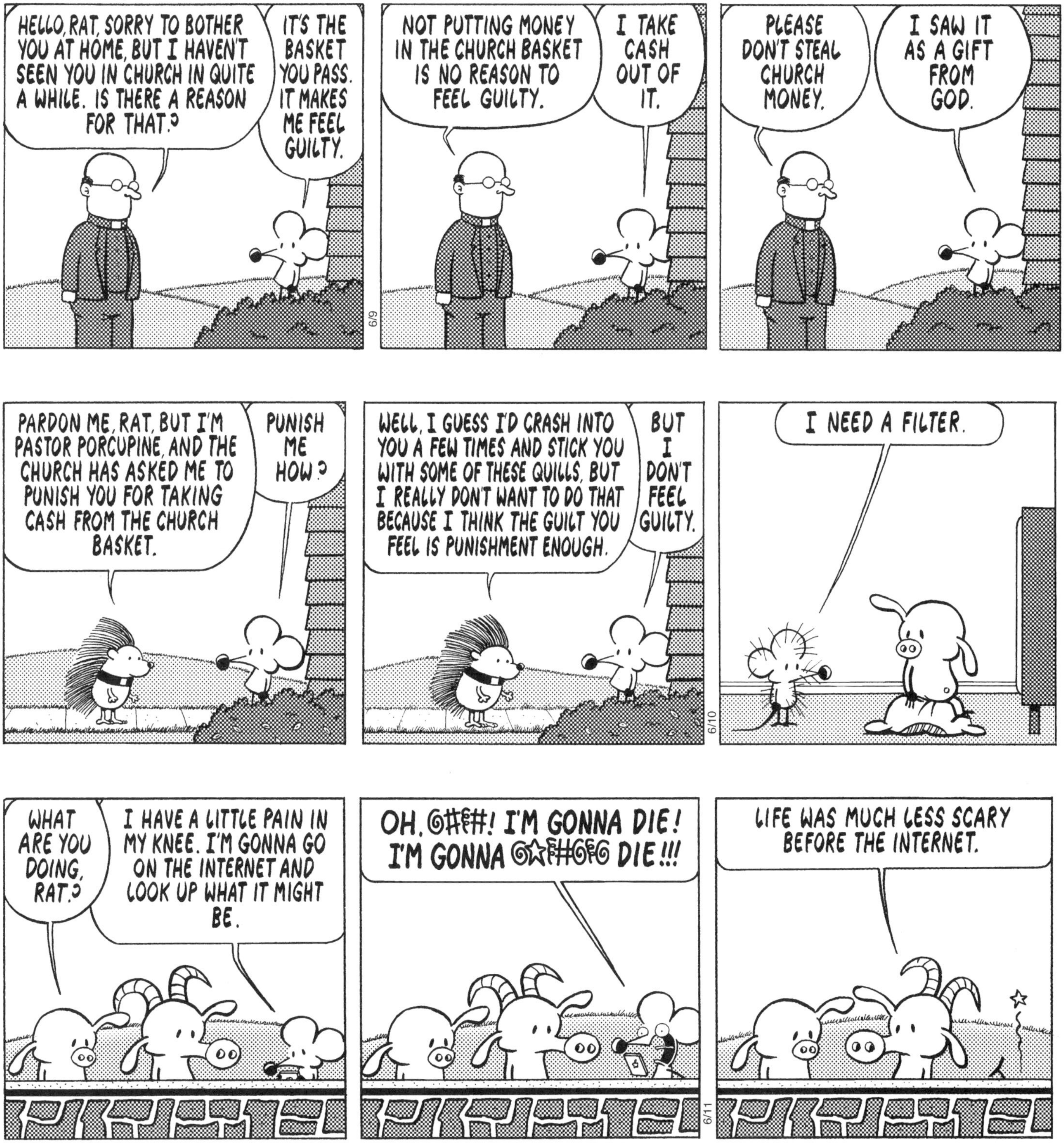
HELLO, RAT. SORRY TO BOTHER YOU AT HOME, BUT I HAVEN'T SEEN YOU IN CHURCH IN QUITE A WHILE. IS THERE A REASON FOR THAT?
IT'S THE BASKET YOU PASS. IT MAKES ME FEEL GUILTY.
NOT PUTTING MONEY IN THE CHURCH BASKET IS NO REASON TO FEEL GUILTY.
I TAKE CASH OUT OF IT.
PLEASE DON'T STEAL CHURCH MONEY.
I SAW IT AS A GIFT FROM GOD.
6/9
PARDON ME, RAT, BUT I'M PASTOR PORCUPINE, AND THE CHURCH HAS ASKED ME TO PUNISH YOU FOR TAKING CASH FROM THE CHURCH BASKET.
PUNISH ME HOW?
WELL, I GUESS I'D CRASH INTO YOU A FEW TIMES AND STICK YOU WITH SOME OF THESE QUILLS, BUT I REALLY DON'T WANT TO DO THAT BECAUSE I THINK THE GUILT YOU FEEL IS PUNISHMENT ENOUGH.
BUT I DON'T FEEL GUILTY.
I NEED A FILTER.
6/10
WHAT ARE YOU DOING, RAT?
I HAVE A LITTLE PAIN IN MY KNEE. I'M GONNA GO ON THE INTERNET AND LOOK UP WHAT IT MIGHT BE.
OH, @#$#! I'M GONNA DIE! I'M GONNA @☆$#@$@ DIE!!!
LIFE WAS MUCH LESS SCARY BEFORE THE INTERNET.
6/11

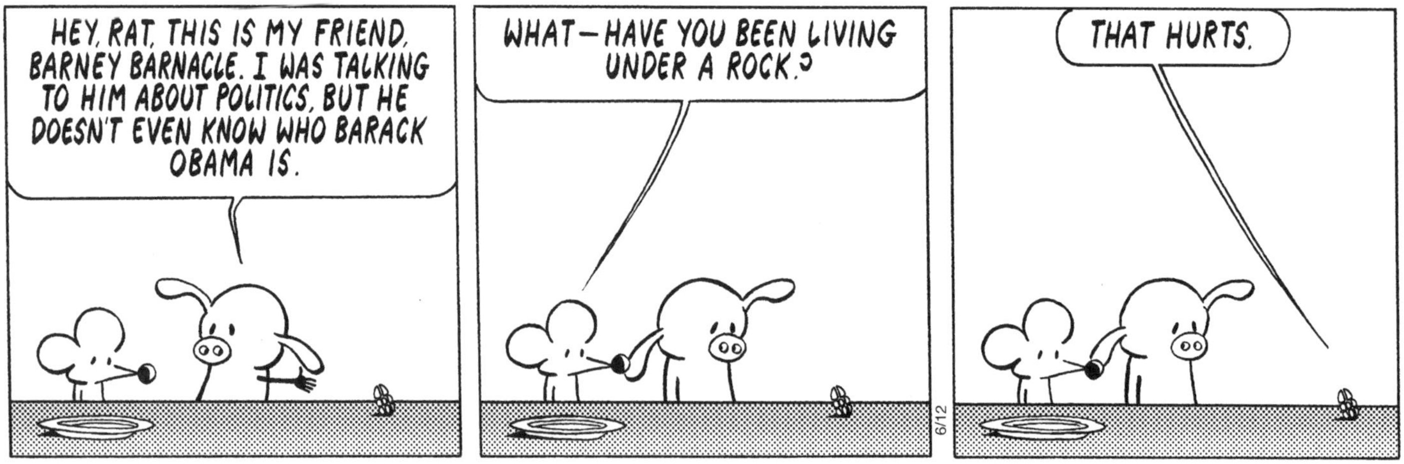
HEY, RAT, THIS IS MY FRIEND, BARNEY BARNACLE. I WAS TALKING TO HIM ABOUT POLITICS, BUT HE DOESN'T EVEN KNOW WHO BARACK OBAMA IS.
WHAT—HAVE YOU BEEN LIVING UNDER A ROCK?
THAT HURTS.
6/12

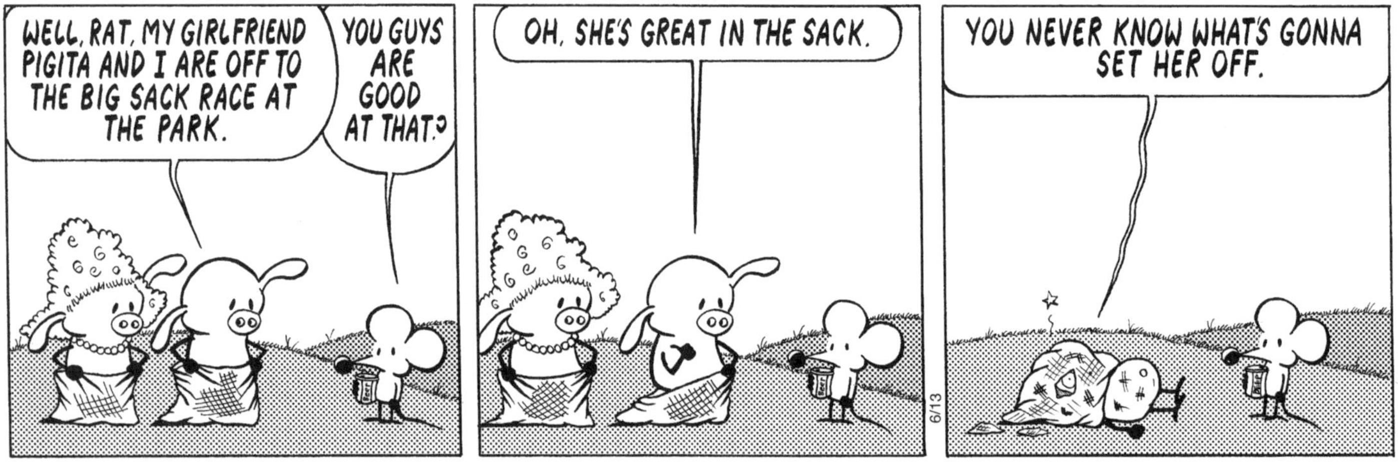
WELL, RAT, MY GIRLFRIEND PIGITA AND I ARE OFF TO THE BIG SACK RACE AT THE PARK.
YOU GUYS ARE GOOD AT THAT?
OH, SHE'S GREAT IN THE SACK.
YOU NEVER KNOW WHAT'S GONNA SET HER OFF.
6/13

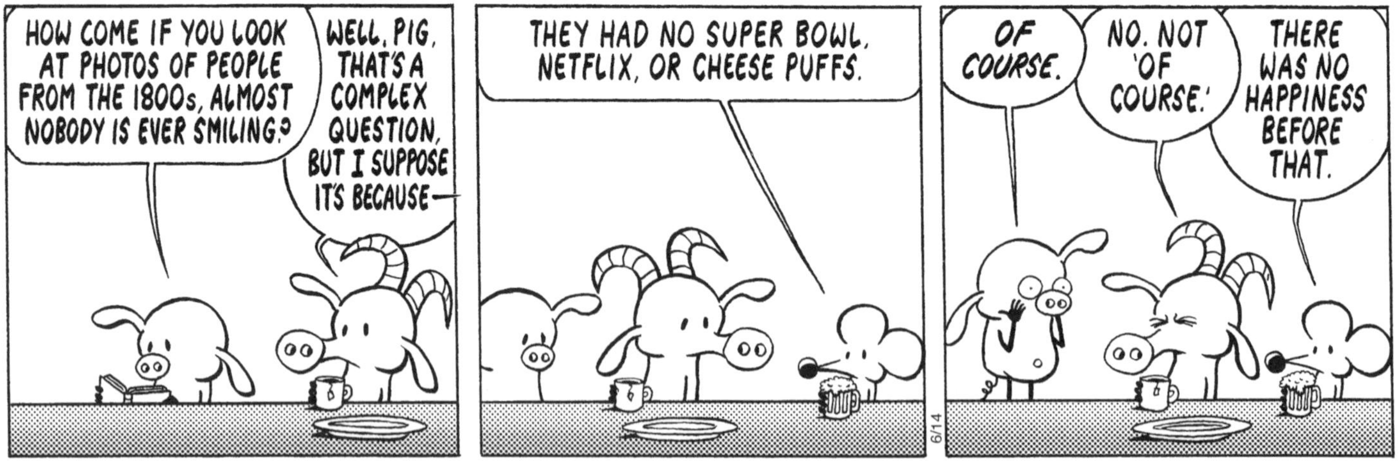
HOW COME IF YOU LOOK AT PHOTOS OF PEOPLE FROM THE 1800s, ALMOST NOBODY IS EVER SMILING?
WELL, PIG, THAT'S A COMPLEX QUESTION, BUT I SUPPOSE IT'S BECAUSE—
THEY HAD NO SUPER BOWL, NETFLIX, OR CHEESE PUFFS.
OF COURSE.
NO. NOT 'OF COURSE.'
THERE WAS NO HAPPINESS BEFORE THAT.
6/14

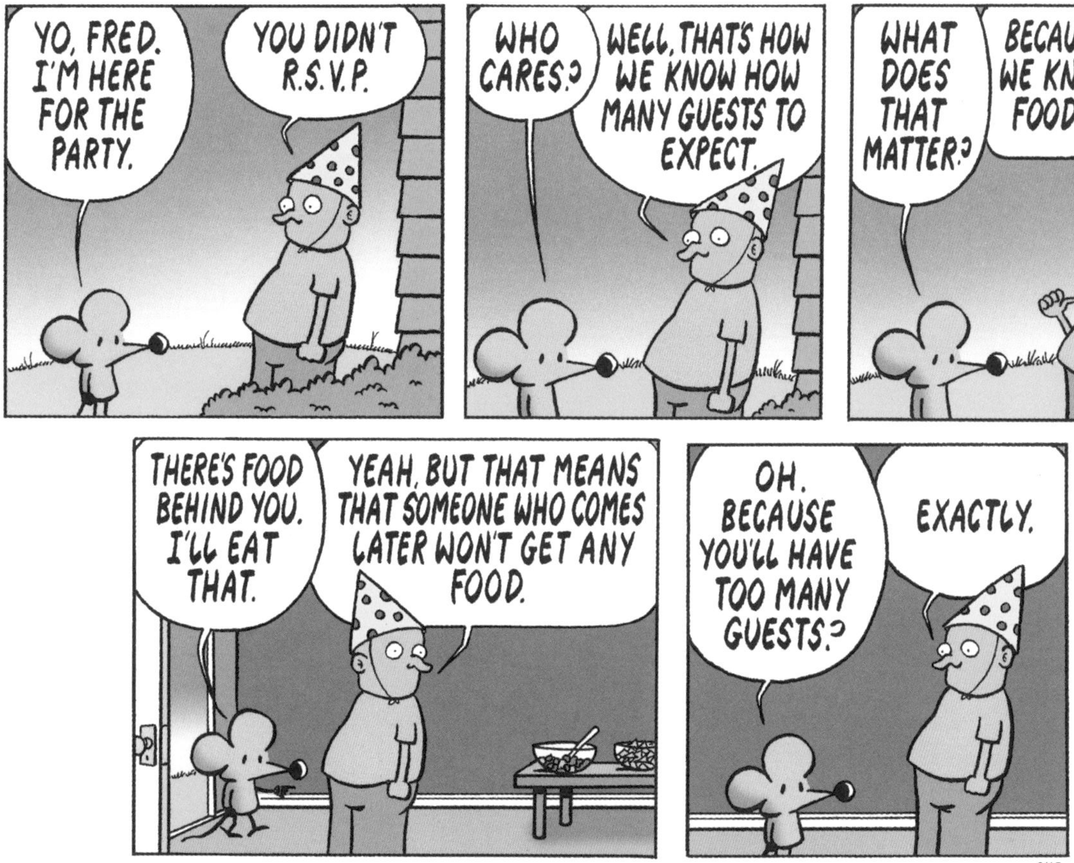
YO, FRED. I'M HERE FOR THE PARTY.
YOU DIDN'T R.S.V.P.
WHO CARES?
WELL, THAT'S HOW WE KNOW HOW MANY GUESTS TO EXPECT.
WHAT DOES THAT MATTER?
BECAUSE THAT'S HOW WE KNOW HOW MUCH FOOD TO PREPARE.
THERE'S FOOD BEHIND YOU. I'LL EAT THAT.
YEAH, BUT THAT MEANS THAT SOMEONE WHO COMES LATER WON'T GET ANY FOOD.
OH. BECAUSE YOU'LL HAVE TOO MANY GUESTS?
EXACTLY.

6/15

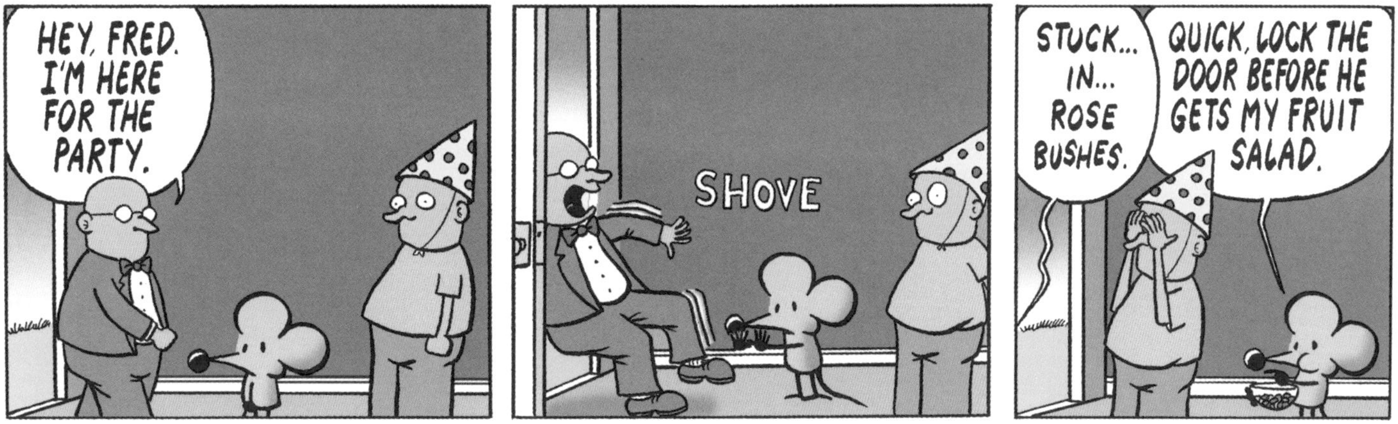
HEY, FRED. I'M HERE FOR THE PARTY.
SHOVE
STUCK... IN... ROSE BUSHES.
QUICK, LOCK THE DOOR BEFORE HE GETS MY FRUIT SALAD.

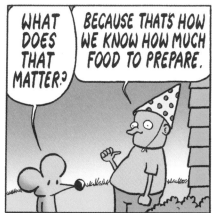

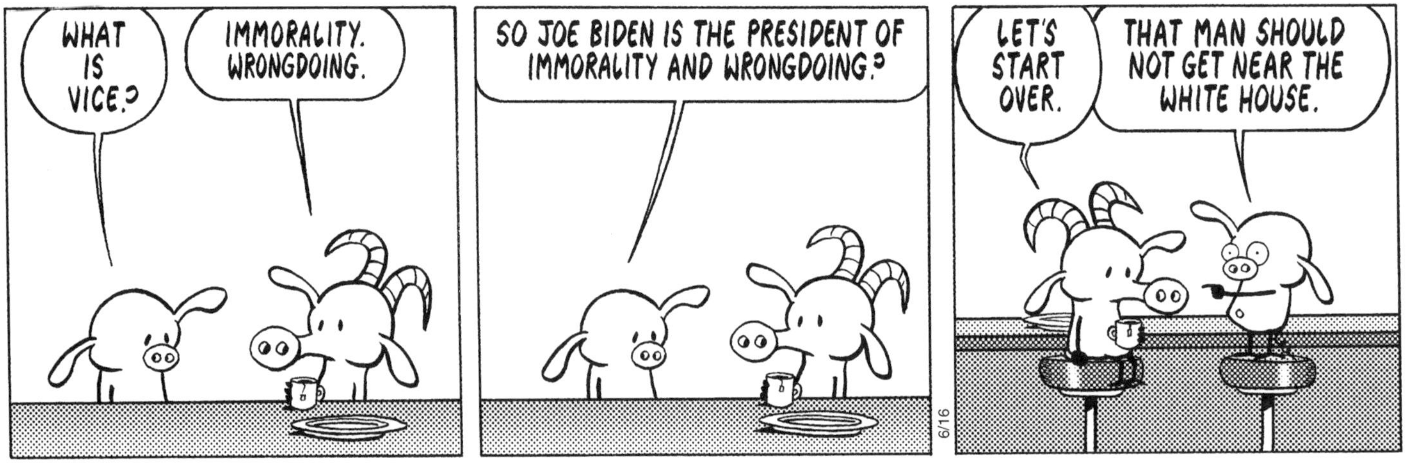
WHAT IS VICE?
IMMORALITY. WRONGDOING.
SO JOE BIDEN IS THE PRESIDENT OF IMMORALITY AND WRONGDOING?
LET'S START OVER.
THAT MAN SHOULD NOT GET NEAR THE WHITE HOUSE.
6/16

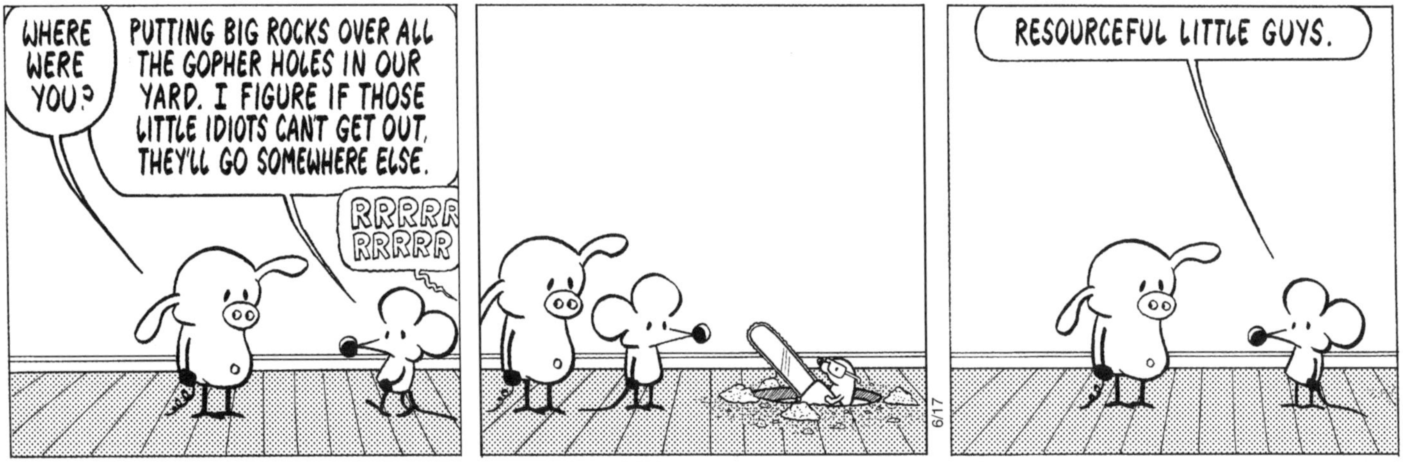
WHERE WERE YOU?
PUTTING BIG ROCKS OVER ALL THE GOPHER HOLES IN OUR YARD. I FIGURE IF THOSE LITTLE IDIOTS CAN'T GET OUT, THEY'LL GO SOMEWHERE ELSE.
RRRRR RRRRR
6/17
RESOURCEFUL LITTLE GUYS.

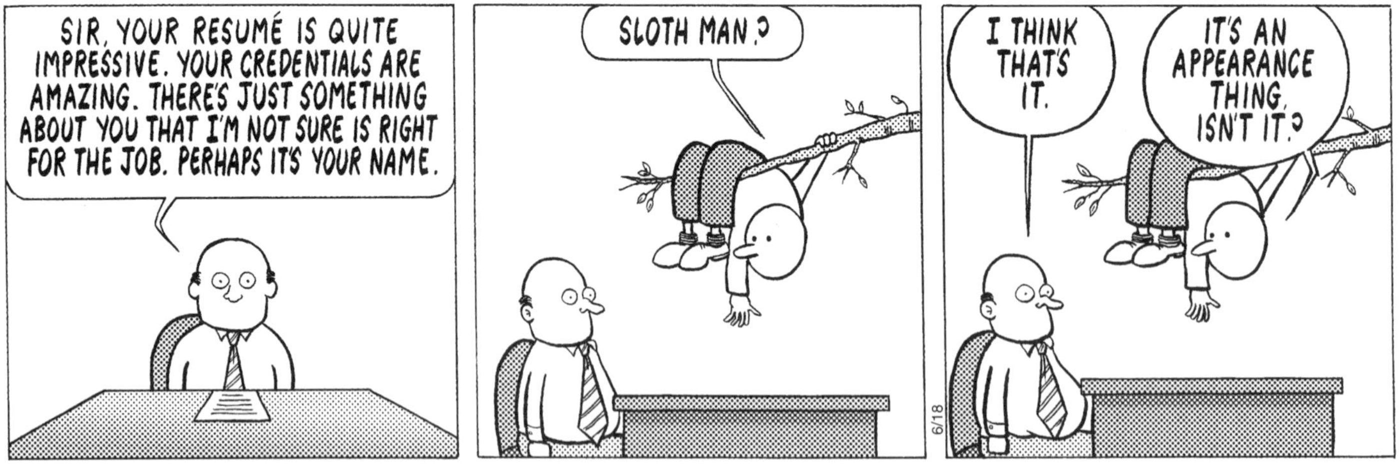
SIR, YOUR RESUMÉ IS QUITE IMPRESSIVE. YOUR CREDENTIALS ARE AMAZING. THERE'S JUST SOMETHING ABOUT YOU THAT I'M NOT SURE IS RIGHT FOR THE JOB. PERHAPS IT'S YOUR NAME.
SLOTH MAN?
6/18
I THINK THAT'S IT.
IT'S AN APPEARANCE THING, ISN'T IT?

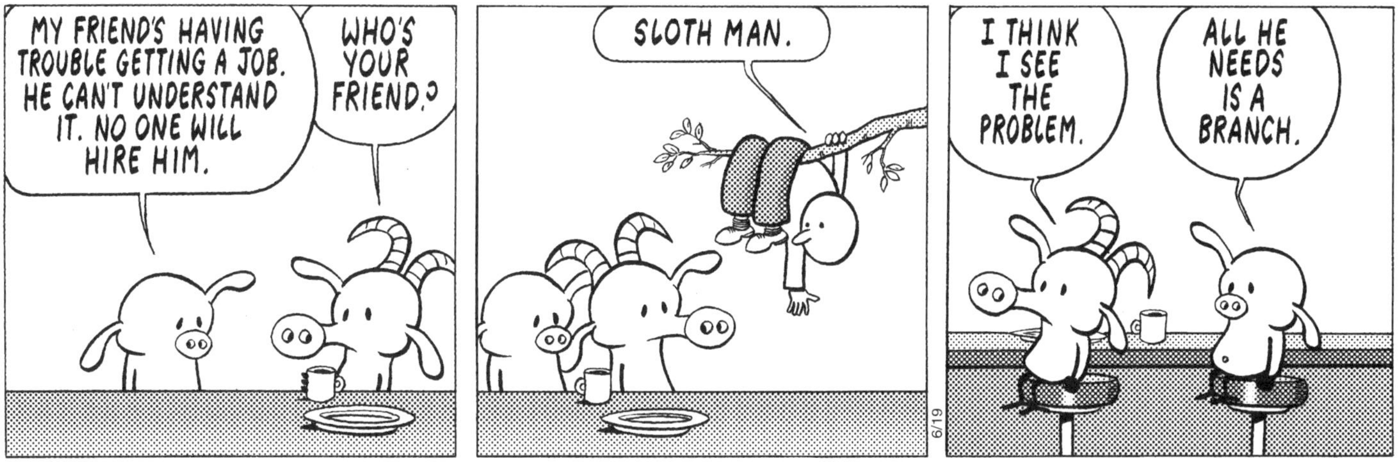
MY FRIEND'S HAVING TROUBLE GETTING A JOB. HE CAN'T UNDERSTAND IT. NO ONE WILL HIRE HIM.
WHO'S YOUR FRIEND?
SLOTH MAN.
I THINK I SEE THE PROBLEM.
ALL HE NEEDS IS A BRANCH.
6/19

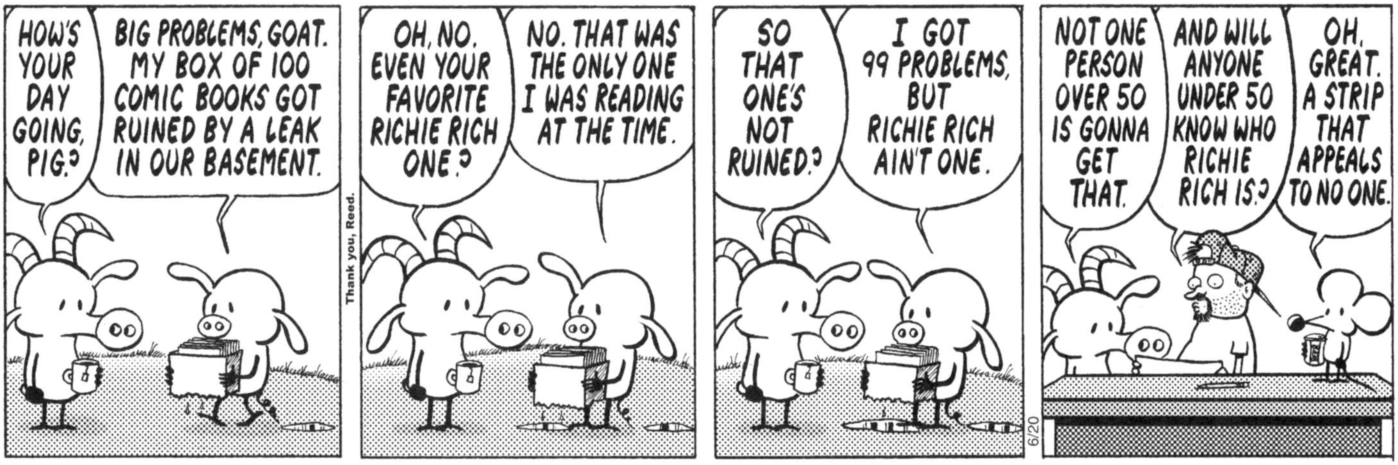
HOW'S YOUR DAY GOING, PIG?
BIG PROBLEMS, GOAT. MY BOX OF 100 COMIC BOOKS GOT RUINED BY A LEAK IN OUR BASEMENT.
Thank you, Reed.
OH, NO. EVEN YOUR FAVORITE RICHIE RICH ONE?
NO. THAT WAS THE ONLY ONE I WAS READING AT THE TIME.
SO THAT ONE'S NOT RUINED?
I GOT 99 PROBLEMS, BUT RICHIE RICH AIN'T ONE.
6/20
NOT ONE PERSON OVER 50 IS GONNA GET THAT.
AND WILL ANYONE UNDER 50 KNOW WHO RICHIE RICH IS?
OH, GREAT. A STRIP THAT APPEALS TO NO ONE.

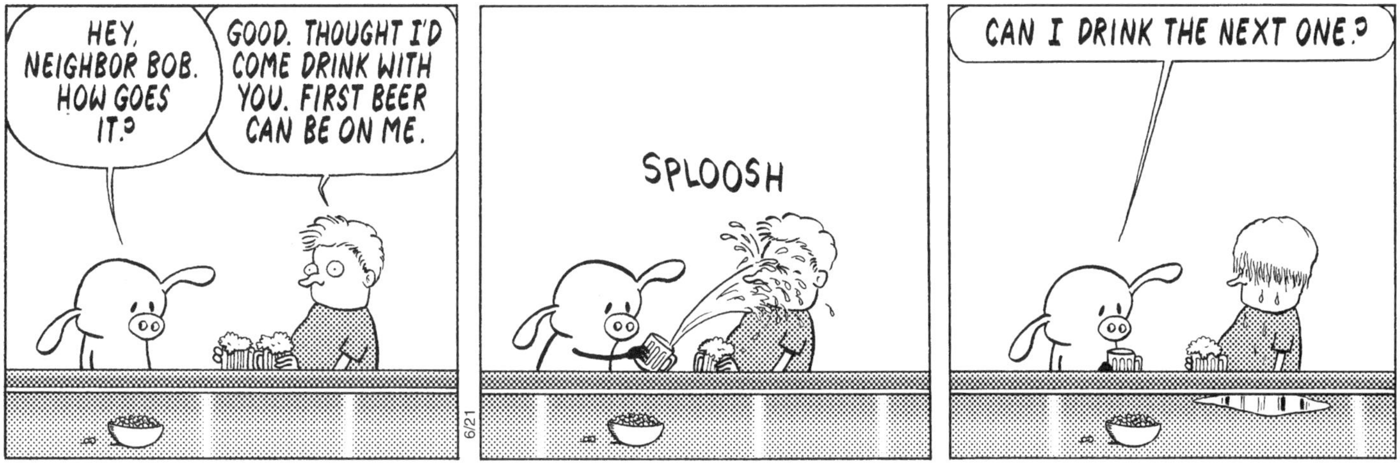
HEY, NEIGHBOR BOB. HOW GOES IT?
GOOD. THOUGHT I'D COME DRINK WITH YOU. FIRST BEER CAN BE ON ME.
6/21
SPLOOSH
CAN I DRINK THE NEXT ONE?

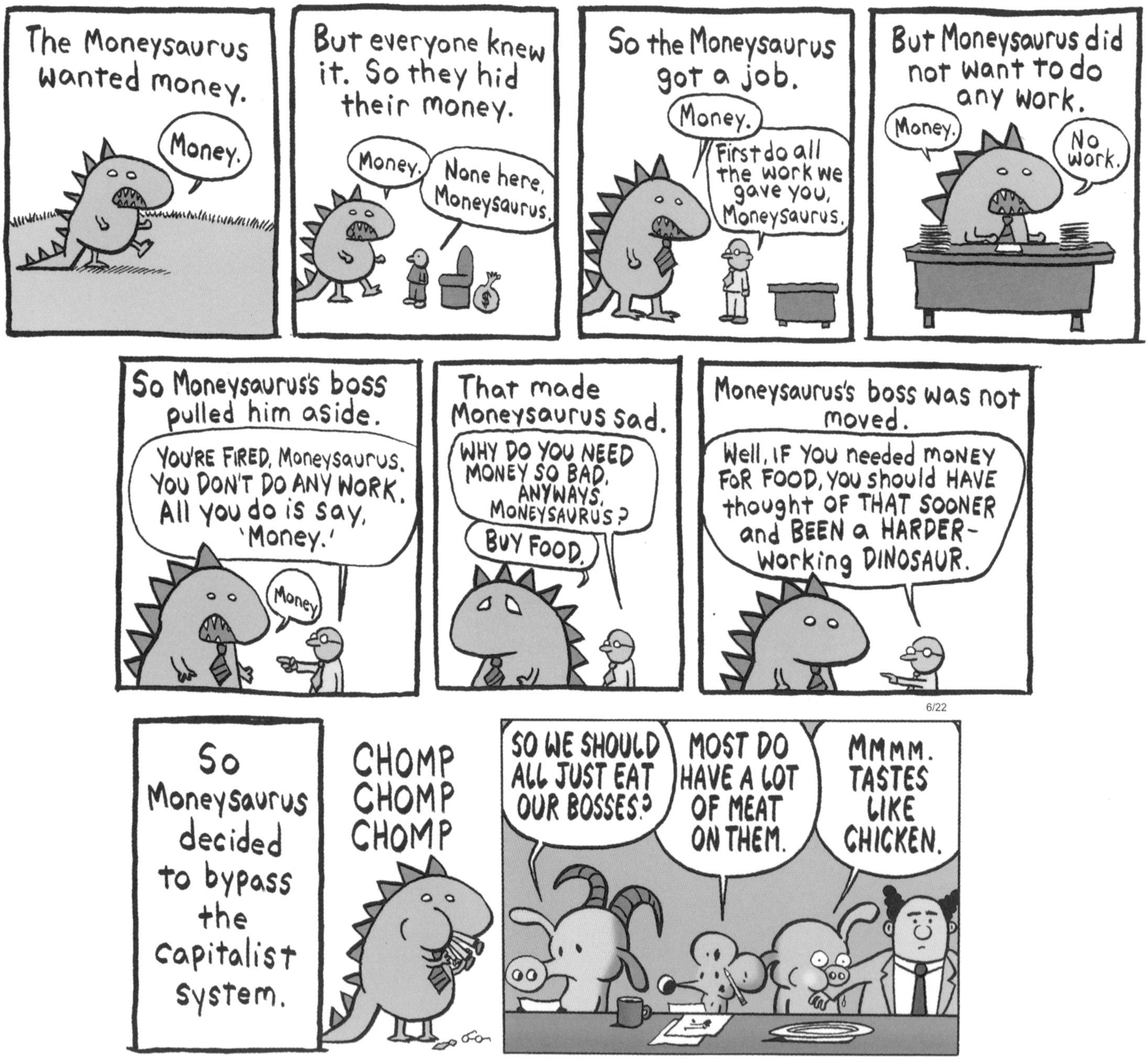
The Moneysaurus wanted money.
Money.
But everyone knew it. So they hid their money.
Money.
None here, Moneysaurus.
So the Moneysaurus got a job.
Money.
First do all the work we gave you, Moneysaurus.
But Moneysaurus did not want to do any work.
Money.
No work.
So Moneysaurus's boss pulled him aside.
YOU'RE FIRED, Moneysaurus. YOU DON'T DO ANY WORK. All you do is say, 'Money.'
Money
That made Moneysaurus sad.
WHY DO YOU NEED MONEY SO BAD, ANYWAYS, MONEYSAURUS?
BUY FOOD.
Moneysaurus's boss was not moved.
Well, IF YOU needed MONEY FOR FOOD, YOU should HAVE thought OF THAT SOONER and BEEN a HARDER-working DINOSAUR.
6/22
So Moneysaurus decided to bypass the capitalist system.
CHOMP CHOMP CHOMP
SO WE SHOULD ALL JUST EAT OUR BOSSES?
MOST DO HAVE A LOT OF MEAT ON THEM.
MMMM. TASTES LIKE CHICKEN.

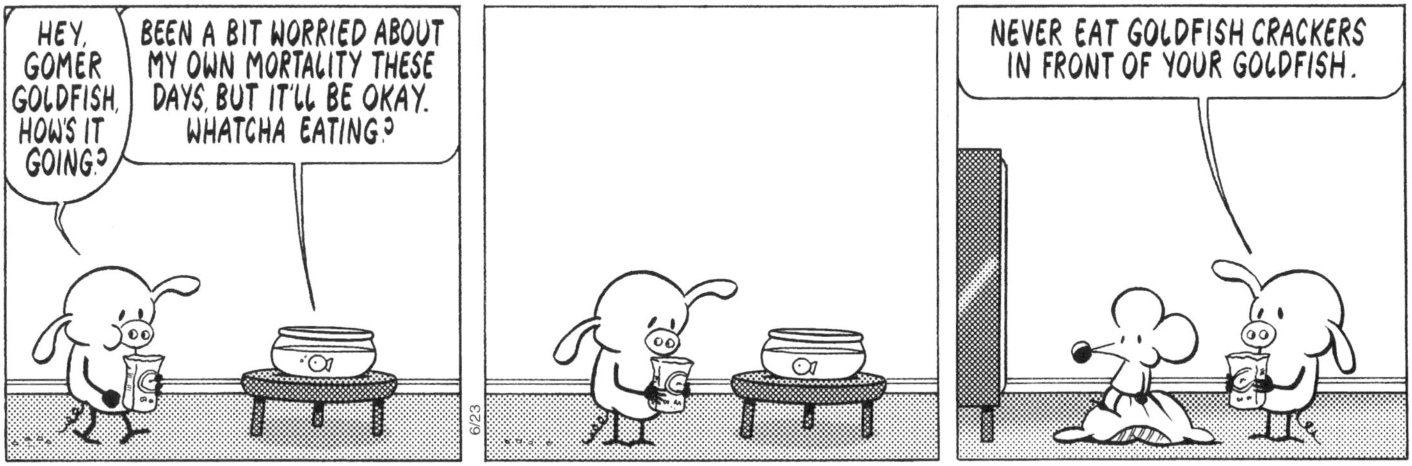
HEY, GOMER GOLDFISH, HOW'S IT GOING?
BEEN A BIT WORRIED ABOUT MY OWN MORTALITY THESE DAYS, BUT IT'LL BE OKAY. WHATCHA EATING?
6/23
NEVER EAT GOLDFISH CRACKERS IN FRONT OF YOUR GOLDFISH.

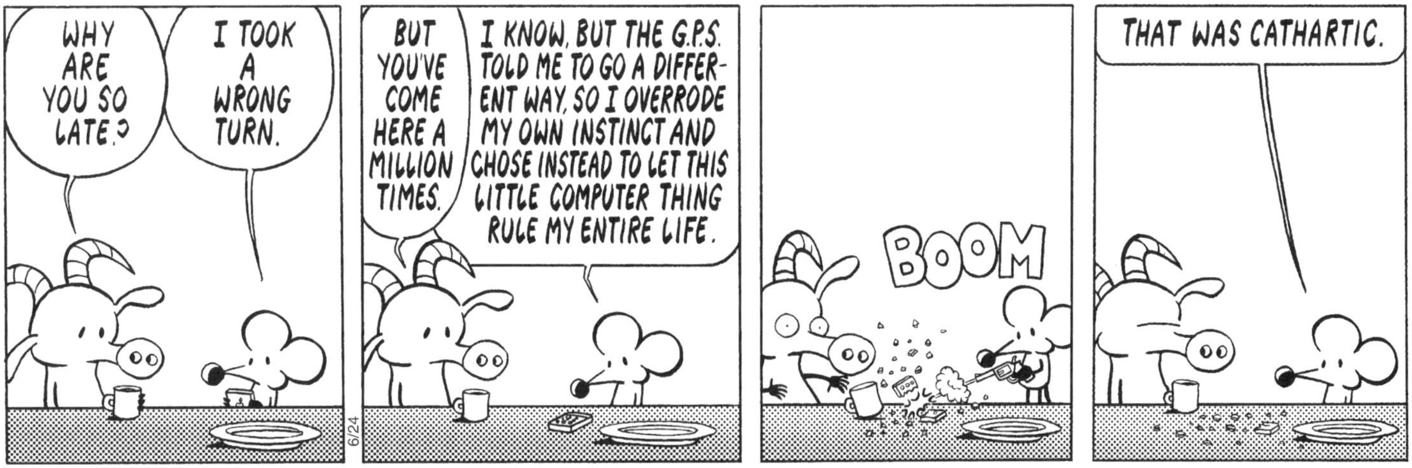
WHY ARE YOU SO LATE?
I TOOK A WRONG TURN.
6/24
BUT YOU'VE COME HERE A MILLION TIMES.
I KNOW, BUT THE G.P.S. TOLD ME TO GO A DIFFERENT WAY, SO I OVERRODE MY OWN INSTINCT AND CHOSE INSTEAD TO LET THIS LITTLE COMPUTER THING RULE MY ENTIRE LIFE.
BOOM
THAT WAS CATHARTIC.

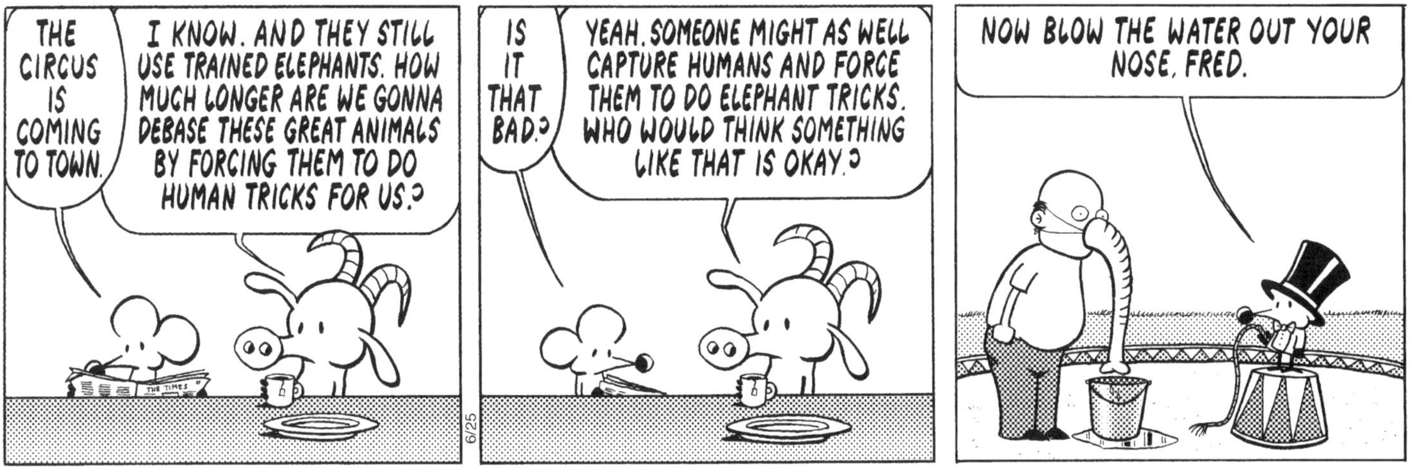
THE CIRCUS IS COMING TO TOWN.
I KNOW. AND THEY STILL USE TRAINED ELEPHANTS. HOW MUCH LONGER ARE WE GONNA DEBASE THESE GREAT ANIMALS BY FORCING THEM TO DO HUMAN TRICKS FOR US?
THE TIMES
6/25
IS IT THAT BAD?
YEAH. SOMEONE MIGHT AS WELL CAPTURE HUMANS AND FORCE THEM TO DO ELEPHANT TRICKS. WHO WOULD THINK SOMETHING LIKE THAT IS OKAY?
NOW BLOW THE WATER OUT YOUR NOSE, FRED.

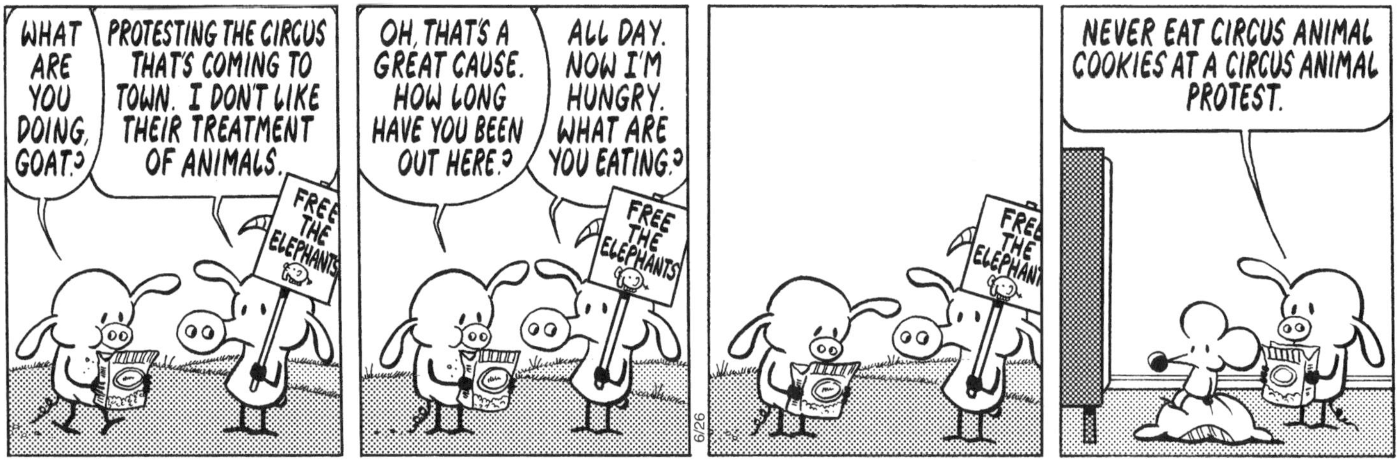
WHAT ARE YOU DOING, GOAT?
PROTESTING THE CIRCUS THAT'S COMING TO TOWN. I DON'T LIKE THEIR TREATMENT OF ANIMALS.
FREE THE ELEPHANTS
OH, THAT'S A GREAT CAUSE. HOW LONG HAVE YOU BEEN OUT HERE?
ALL DAY. NOW I'M HUNGRY. WHAT ARE YOU EATING?
FREE THE ELEPHANTS
NEVER EAT CIRCUS ANIMAL COOKIES AT A CIRCUS ANIMAL PROTEST.
6/26

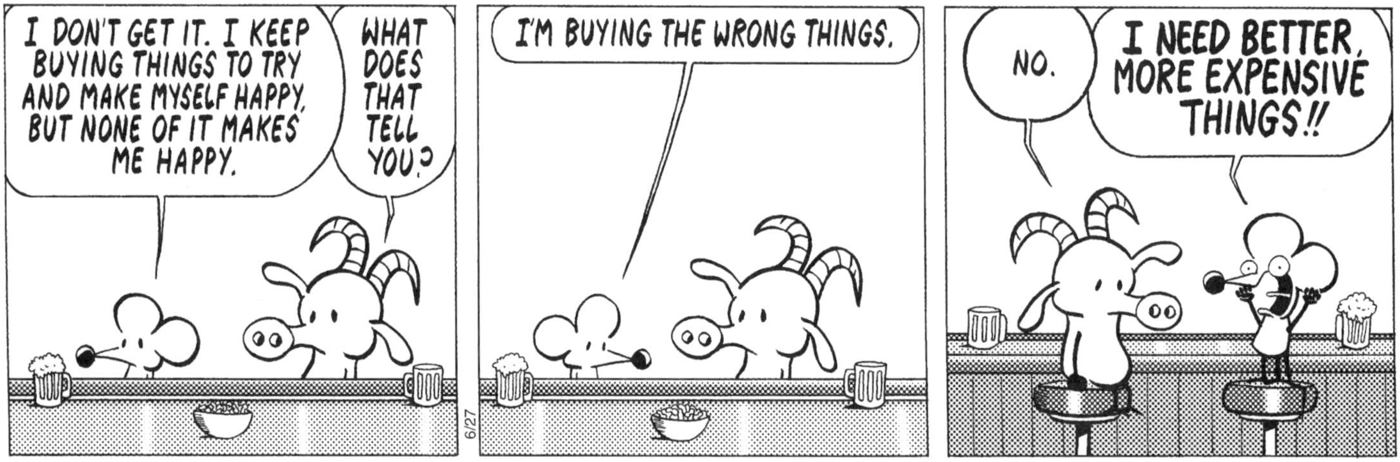
I DON'T GET IT. I KEEP BUYING THINGS TO TRY AND MAKE MYSELF HAPPY, BUT NONE OF IT MAKES ME HAPPY.
WHAT DOES THAT TELL YOU?
I'M BUYING THE WRONG THINGS.
NO.
I NEED BETTER, MORE EXPENSIVE THINGS!!
6/27

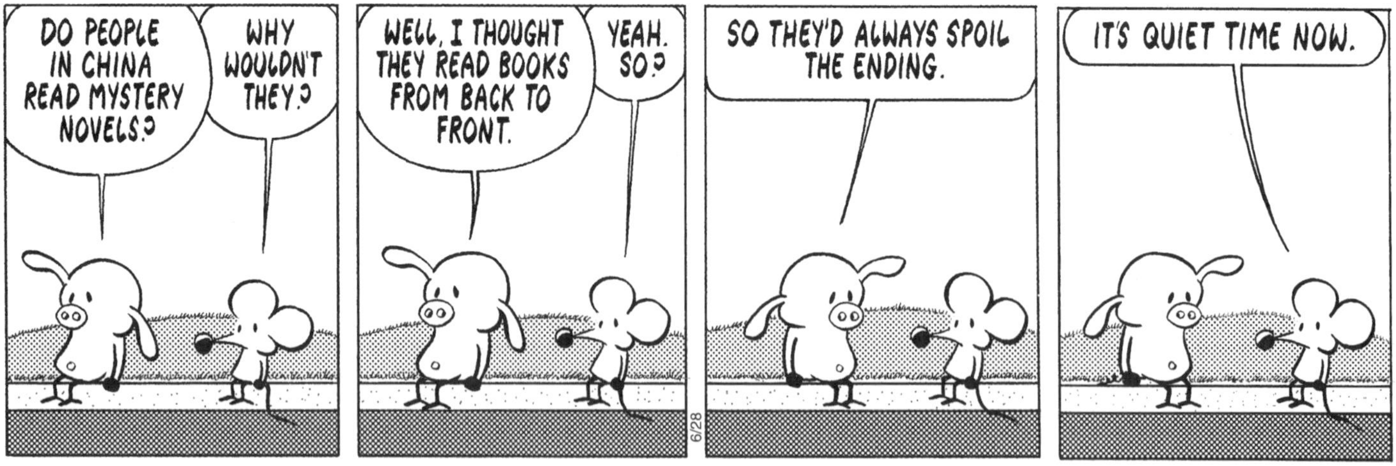
DO PEOPLE IN CHINA READ MYSTERY NOVELS?
WHY WOULDN'T THEY?
WELL, I THOUGHT THEY READ BOOKS FROM BACK TO FRONT.
YEAH. SO?
SO THEY'D ALWAYS SPOIL THE ENDING.
IT'S QUIET TIME NOW.
6/28

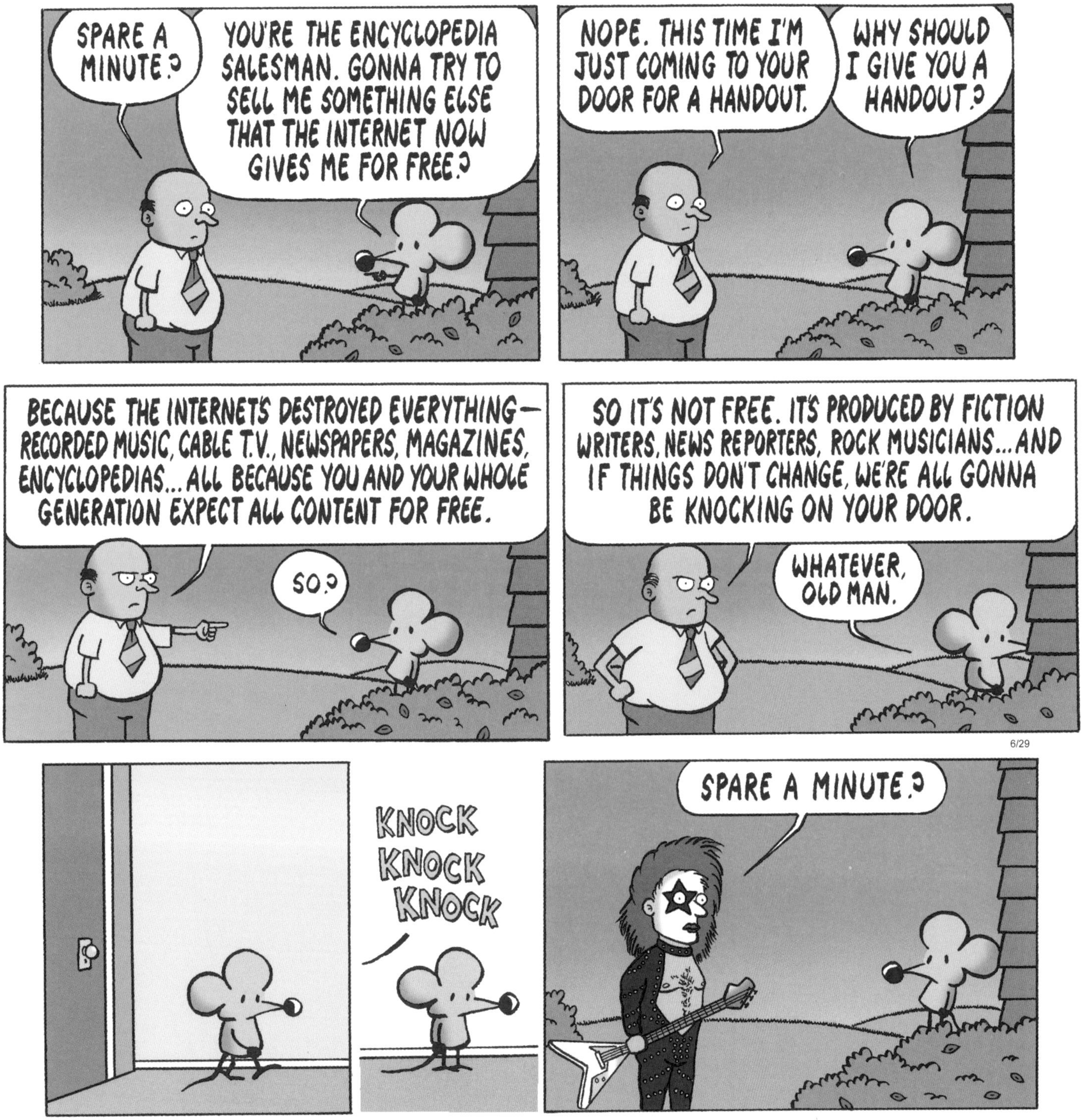
SPARE A MINUTE?
YOU'RE THE ENCYCLOPEDIA SALESMAN. GONNA TRY TO SELL ME SOMETHING ELSE THAT THE INTERNET NOW GIVES ME FOR FREE?
NOPE. THIS TIME I'M JUST COMING TO YOUR DOOR FOR A HANDOUT.
WHY SHOULD I GIVE YOU A HANDOUT?
BECAUSE THE INTERNET'S DESTROYED EVERYTHING— RECORDED MUSIC, CABLE T.V., NEWSPAPERS, MAGAZINES, ENCYCLOPEDIAS... ALL BECAUSE YOU AND YOUR WHOLE GENERATION EXPECT ALL CONTENT FOR FREE.
SO?
SO IT'S NOT FREE. IT'S PRODUCED BY FICTION WRITERS, NEWS REPORTERS, ROCK MUSICIANS... AND IF THINGS DON'T CHANGE, WE'RE ALL GONNA BE KNOCKING ON YOUR DOOR.
WHATEVER, OLD MAN.
6/29
KNOCK
KNOCK
KNOCK
SPARE A MINUTE?

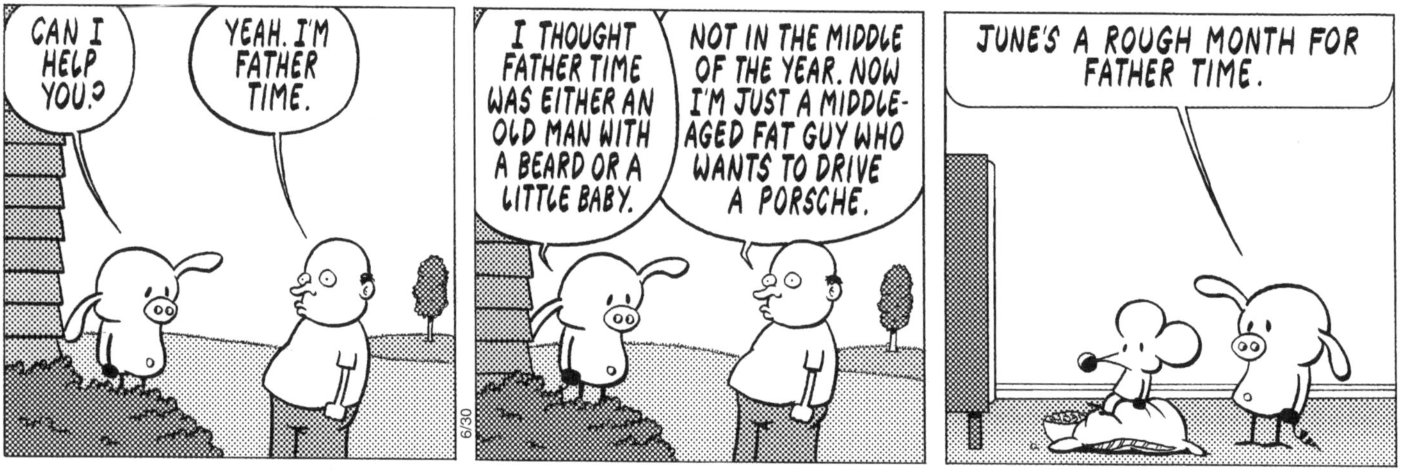
CAN I HELP YOU?
YEAH. I'M FATHER TIME.
I THOUGHT FATHER TIME WAS EITHER AN OLD MAN WITH A BEARD OR A LITTLE BABY.
NOT IN THE MIDDLE OF THE YEAR. NOW I'M JUST A MIDDLE-AGED FAT GUY WHO WANTS TO DRIVE A PORSCHE.
JUNE'S A ROUGH MONTH FOR FATHER TIME.
6/30

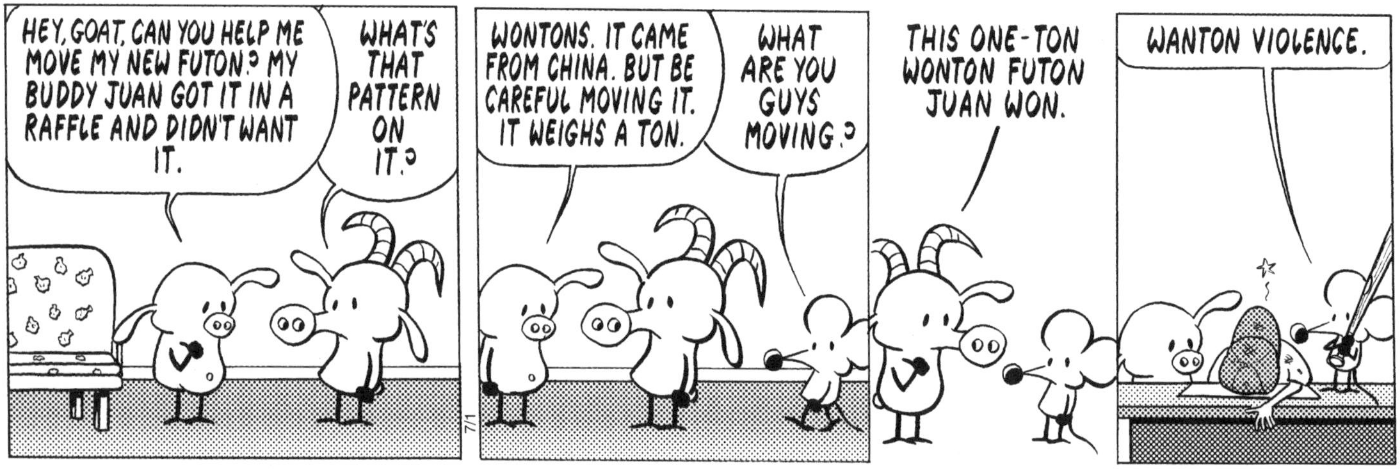
HEY, GOAT, CAN YOU HELP ME MOVE MY NEW FUTON? MY BUDDY JUAN GOT IT IN A RAFFLE AND DIDN'T WANT IT.
WHAT'S THAT PATTERN ON IT?
WONTONS. IT CAME FROM CHINA. BUT BE CAREFUL MOVING IT. IT WEIGHS A TON.
WHAT ARE YOU GUYS MOVING?
THIS ONE-TON WONTON FUTON JUAN WON.
WANTON VIOLENCE.
7/1

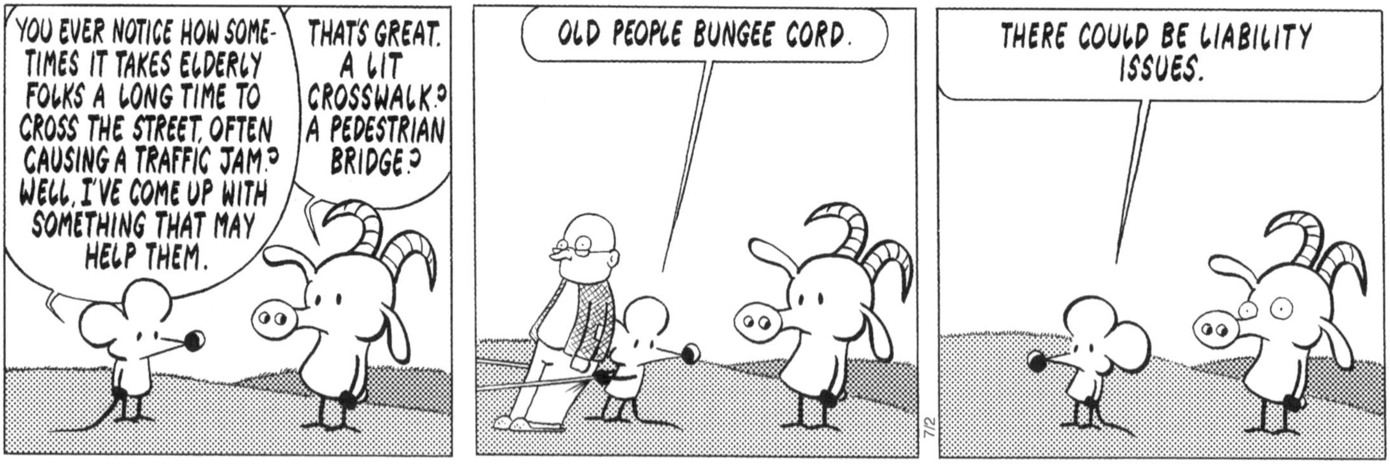
YOU EVER NOTICE HOW SOMETIMES IT TAKES ELDERLY FOLKS A LONG TIME TO CROSS THE STREET, OFTEN CAUSING A TRAFFIC JAM? WELL, I'VE COME UP WITH SOMETHING THAT MAY HELP THEM.
THAT'S GREAT. A LIT CROSSWALK? A PEDESTRIAN BRIDGE?
OLD PEOPLE BUNGEE CORD.
THERE COULD BE LIABILITY ISSUES.
7/2

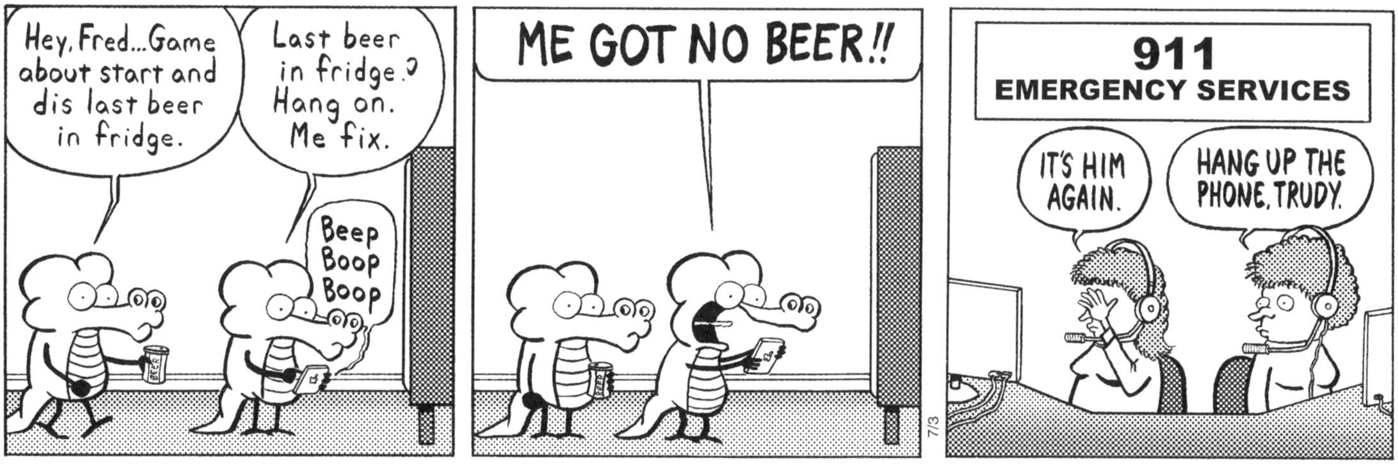
Hey, Fred...Game about start and dis last beer in fridge.
Last beer in fridge? Hang on. Me fix.
Beep Boop Boop
ME GOT NO BEER!!
7/3
911
EMERGENCY SERVICES
IT'S HIM AGAIN.
HANG UP THE PHONE, TRUDY.

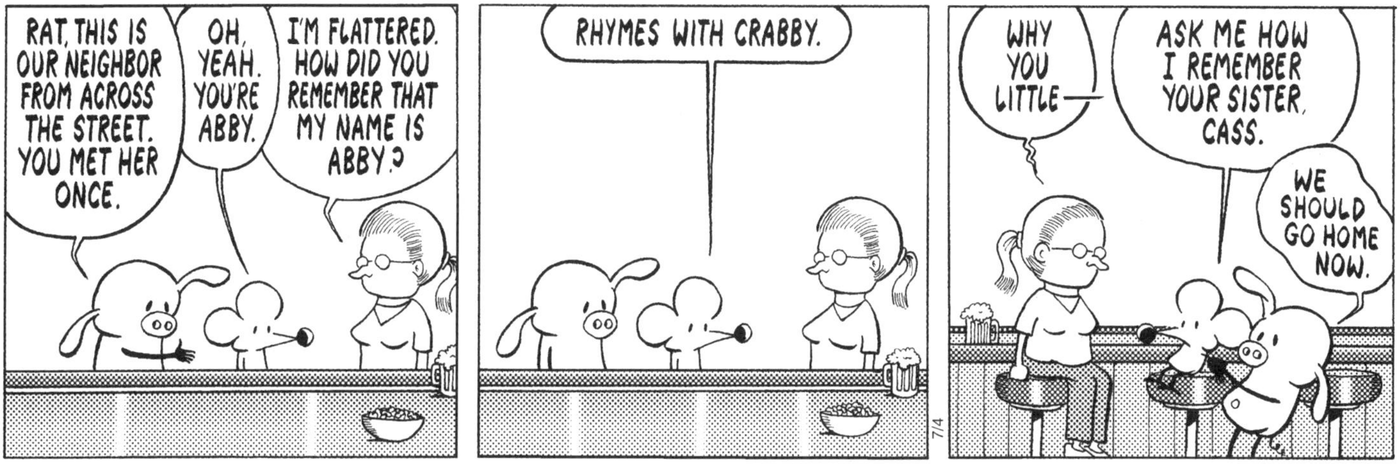
RAT, THIS IS OUR NEIGHBOR FROM ACROSS THE STREET. YOU MET HER ONCE.
OH, YEAH. YOU'RE ABBY.
I'M FLATTERED. HOW DID YOU REMEMBER THAT MY NAME IS ABBY?
RHYMES WITH CRABBY.
7/4
WHY YOU LITTLE—
ASK ME HOW I REMEMBER YOUR SISTER, CASS.
WE SHOULD GO HOME NOW.

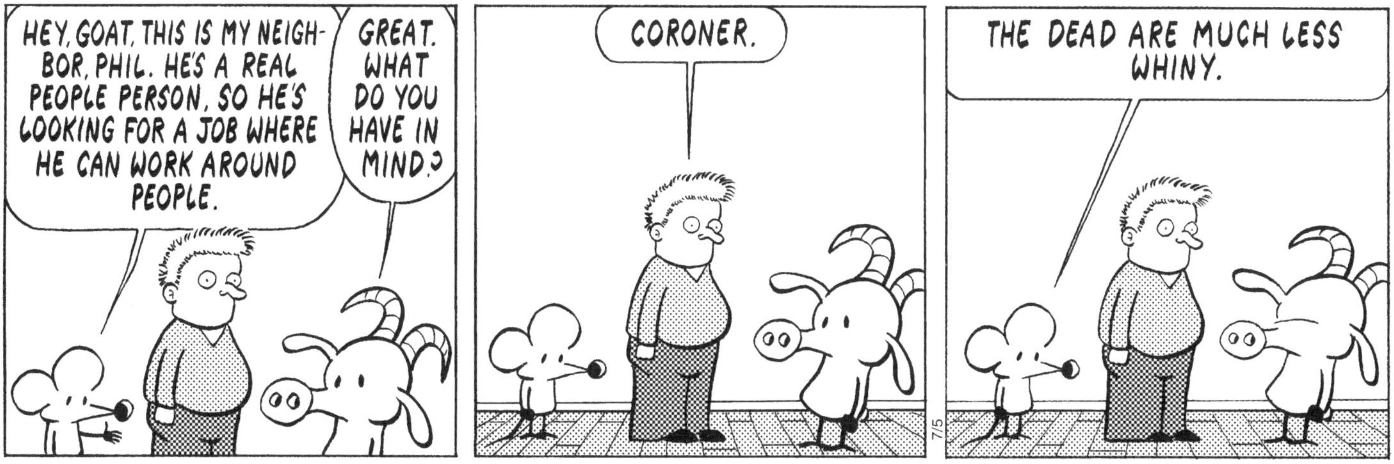
HEY, GOAT, THIS IS MY NEIGHBOR, PHIL. HE'S A REAL PEOPLE PERSON, SO HE'S LOOKING FOR A JOB WHERE HE CAN WORK AROUND PEOPLE.
GREAT. WHAT DO YOU HAVE IN MIND?
CORONER.
7/5
THE DEAD ARE MUCH LESS WHINY.

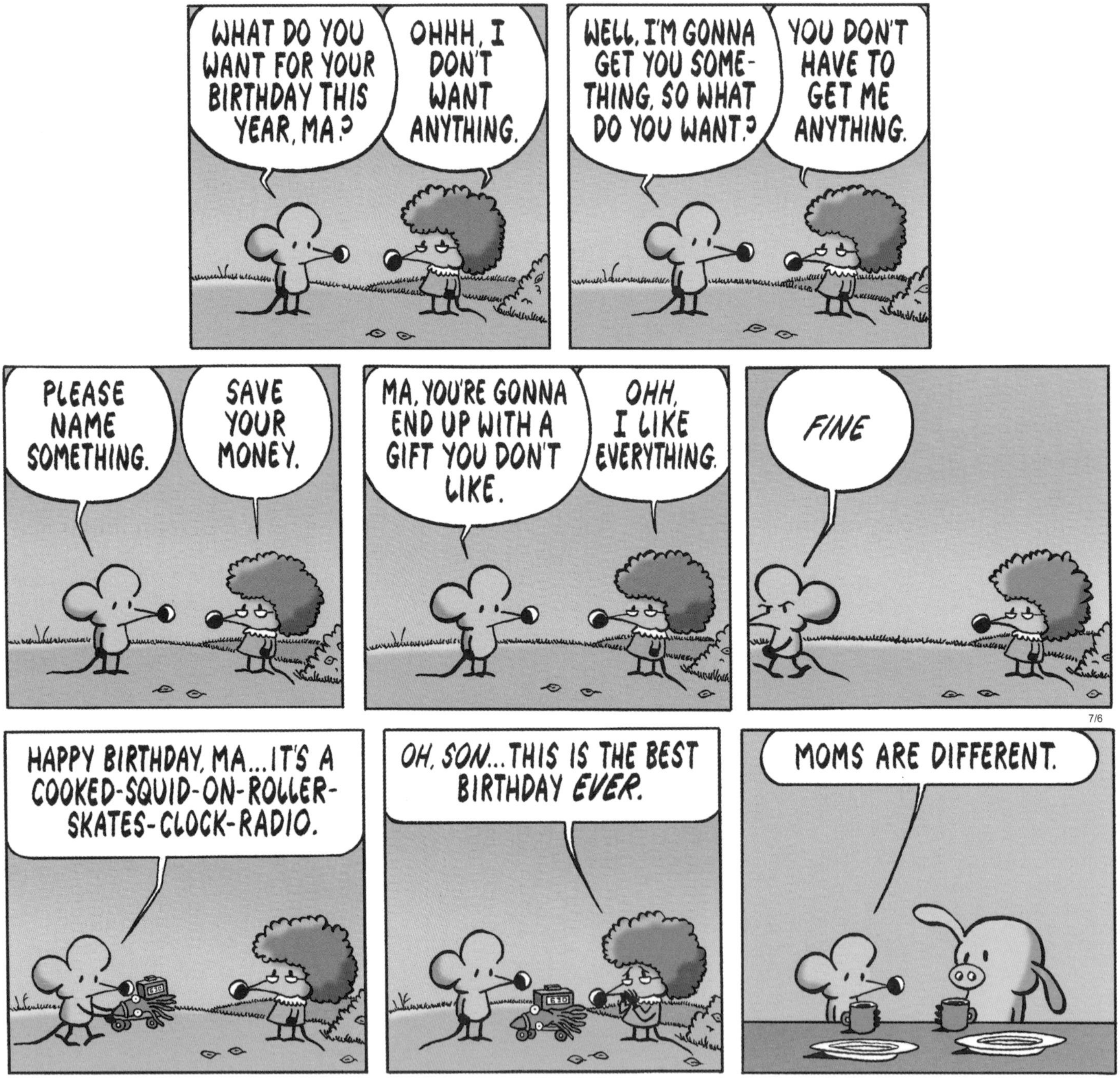
WHAT DO YOU WANT FOR YOUR BIRTHDAY THIS YEAR, MA?
OHHH, I DON'T WANT ANYTHING.
WELL, I'M GONNA GET YOU SOME-THING, SO WHAT DO YOU WANT?
YOU DON'T HAVE TO GET ME ANYTHING.
PLEASE NAME SOMETHING.
SAVE YOUR MONEY.
MA, YOU'RE GONNA END UP WITH A GIFT YOU DON'T LIKE.
OHH, I LIKE EVERYTHING.
FINE
7/6
HAPPY BIRTHDAY, MA...IT'S A COOKED-SQUID-ON-ROLLER-SKATES-CLOCK-RADIO.
OH, SON...THIS IS THE BEST BIRTHDAY EVER.
MOMS ARE DIFFERENT.

Panel 1: HEY, RICKY RAISIN. HOW GOES IT?

GOOD. I WON THE LOTTERY. GOT A NEW CAR. GOT A NEW BEACH HOUSE. GOT A NEW GIRLFRIEND.... OH, WELL. GOTTA GO.

Panel 3: EVERYTHING HAPPENS FOR A RAISIN.

Panel 1: BOMBAST CABLE... HOW CAN I HELP YOU?

I WANT TO CANCEL CABLE. NOW THAT I HAVE NETFLIX AND HULU, I DON'T NEED YOU AND YOUR 700 WORTHLESS CHANNELS ANYMORE.

Panel 2: SO THAT'S IT? YOU WANT TO CANCEL YOUR ENTIRE ACCOUNT?

WELL, NO, I STILL WANT ESPN.

Panel 3: HA! TO GET ESPN, YOU HAVE TO GET ALL 700 WORTHLESS CHANNELS! BWAHAHAAAAAAA!!!

Panel 4: THE CABLE COMPANY IS A WORTHY FOE.

Panel 1: WHAT ARE YOU LOOKING AT ON YOUR PHONE, GOAT?

THESE PHOTOS OF A TEMPLE IN EGYPT. THAT SEMICIRCULAR RECESS IN THE BUILDING IS CALLED AN APSE.

Panel 2: WHAT'S PAINTED ON IT?

THOSE ARE THE SNAKES THAT ARE SAID TO HAVE KILLED CLEOPATRA.

Panel 3: WOW. AND YOU FOUND ALL OF THIS ON YOUR PHONE?

YEAH. ON THESE APSE ASPS APPS.

Panel 4: TRY SAYING IT THREE TIMES FAST.

TRY WRITING A JOKE THAT'S NOT LAME.

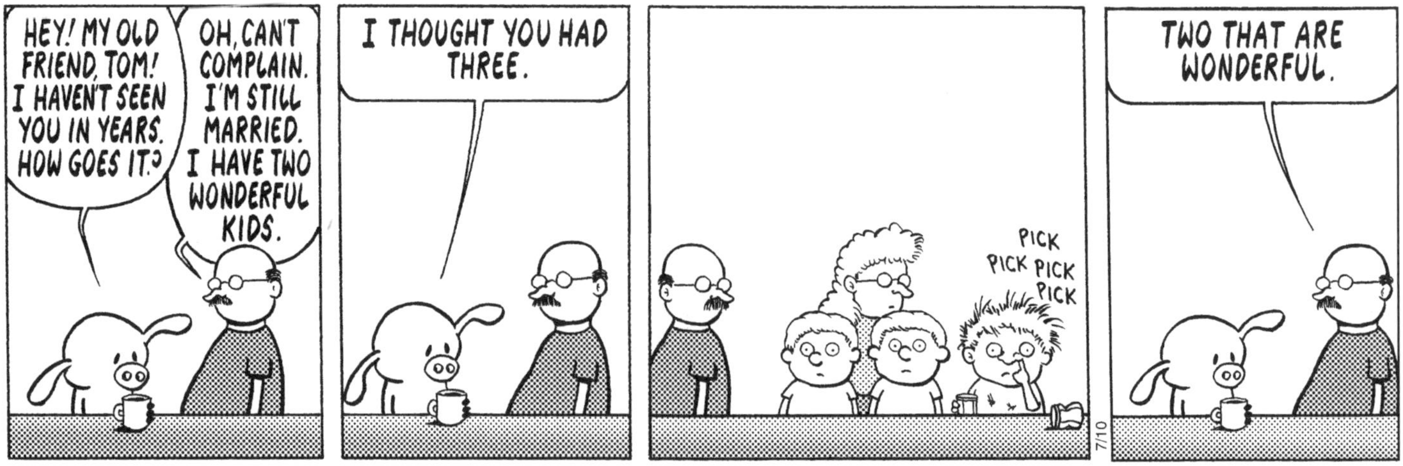
HEY! MY OLD FRIEND, TOM! I HAVEN'T SEEN YOU IN YEARS. HOW GOES IT?
OH, CAN'T COMPLAIN. I'M STILL MARRIED. I HAVE TWO WONDERFUL KIDS.
I THOUGHT YOU HAD THREE.
PICK PICK PICK PICK
TWO THAT ARE WONDERFUL.
7/10

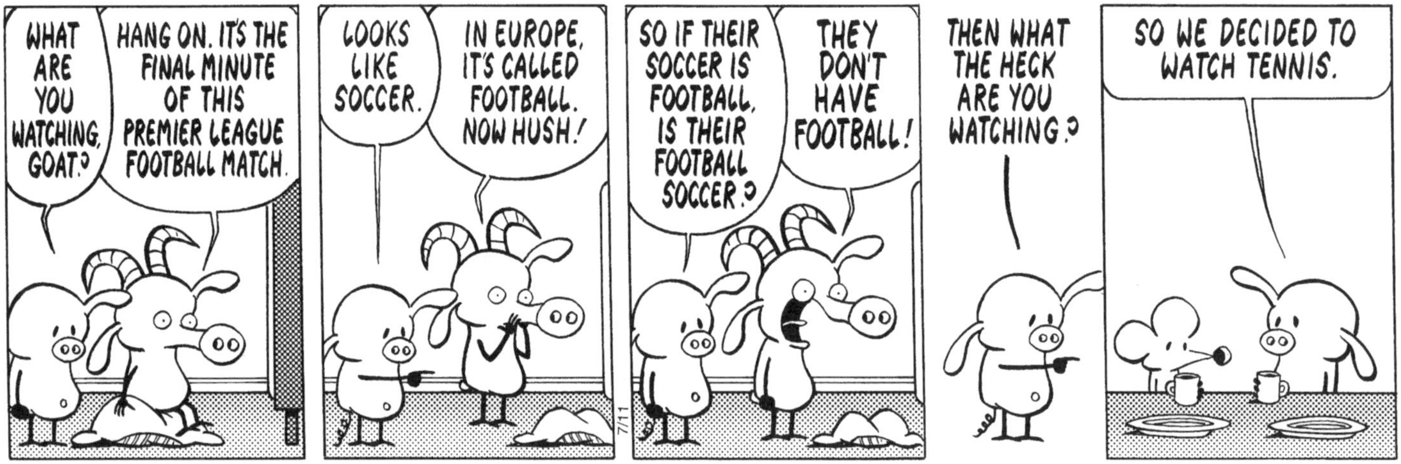
WHAT ARE YOU WATCHING, GOAT?
HANG ON. IT'S THE FINAL MINUTE OF THIS PREMIER LEAGUE FOOTBALL MATCH.
LOOKS LIKE SOCCER.
IN EUROPE, IT'S CALLED FOOTBALL. NOW HUSH!
SO IF THEIR SOCCER IS FOOTBALL, IS THEIR FOOTBALL SOCCER?
THEY DON'T HAVE FOOTBALL!
THEN WHAT THE HECK ARE YOU WATCHING?
SO WE DECIDED TO WATCH TENNIS.
7/11

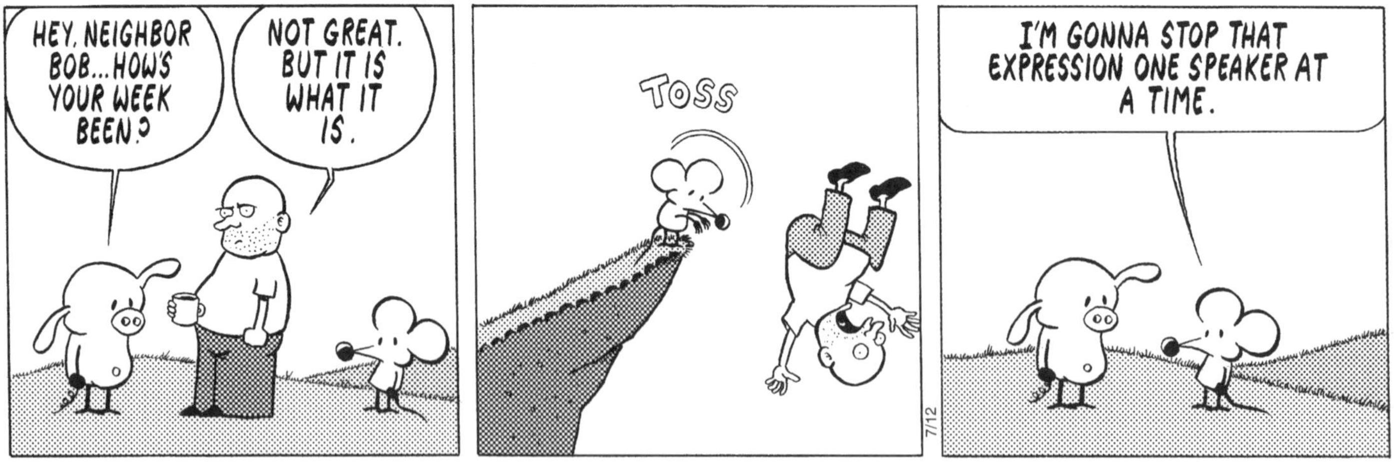
HEY, NEIGHBOR BOB... HOW'S YOUR WEEK BEEN?
NOT GREAT. BUT IT IS WHAT IT IS.
TOSS
I'M GONNA STOP THAT EXPRESSION ONE SPEAKER AT A TIME.
7/12

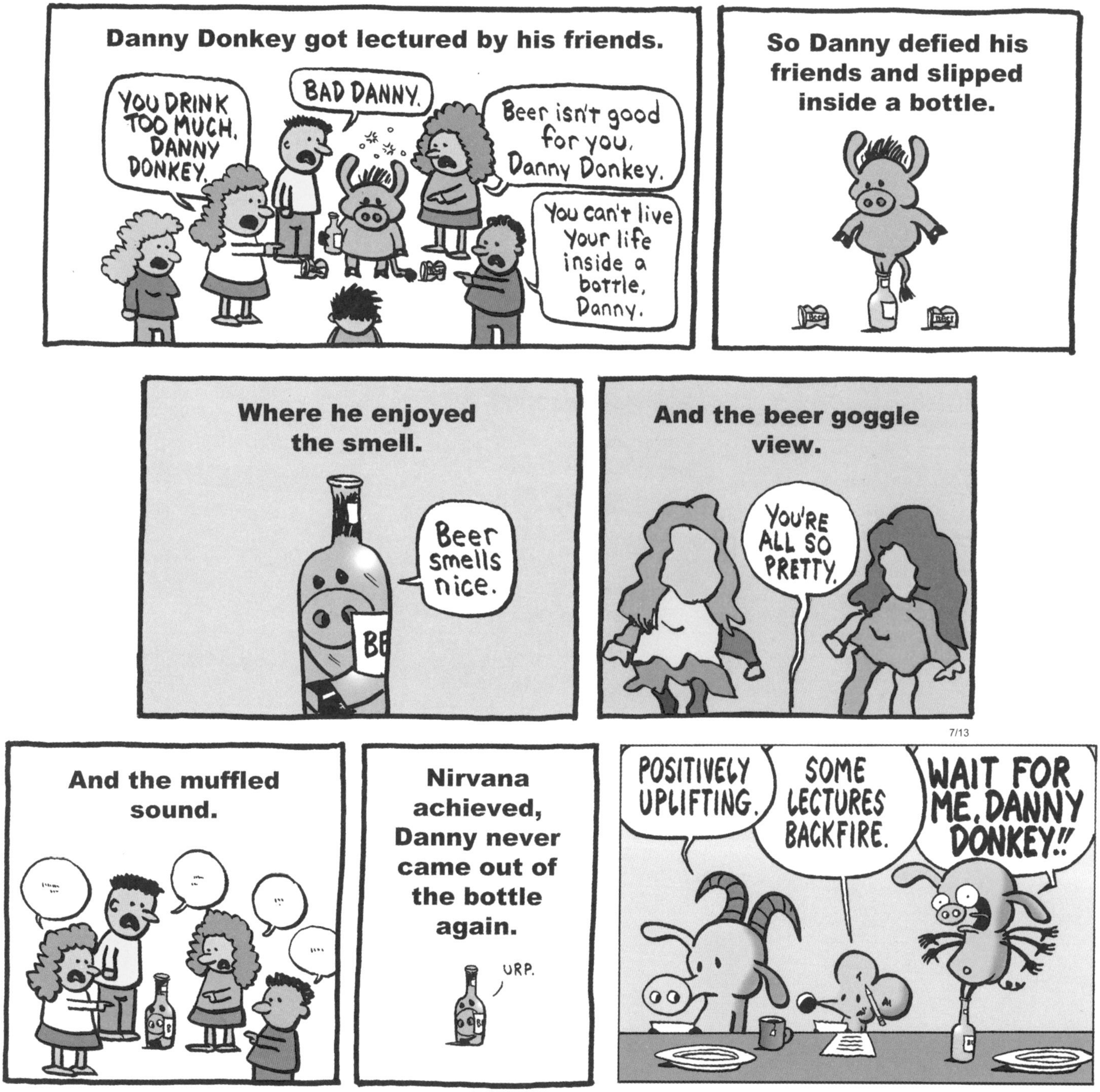
Danny Donkey got lectured by his friends.
YOU DRINK TOO MUCH, DANNY DONKEY.
BAD DANNY.
Beer isn't good for you, Danny Donkey.
You can't live your life inside a bottle, Danny.
So Danny defied his friends and slipped inside a bottle.
Where he enjoyed the smell.
Beer smells nice.
And the beer goggle view.
YOU'RE ALL SO PRETTY.
And the muffled sound.
Nirvana achieved, Danny never came out of the bottle again.
URP.
7/13
POSITIVELY UPLIFTING.
SOME LECTURES BACKFIRE.
WAIT FOR ME, DANNY DONKEY!!

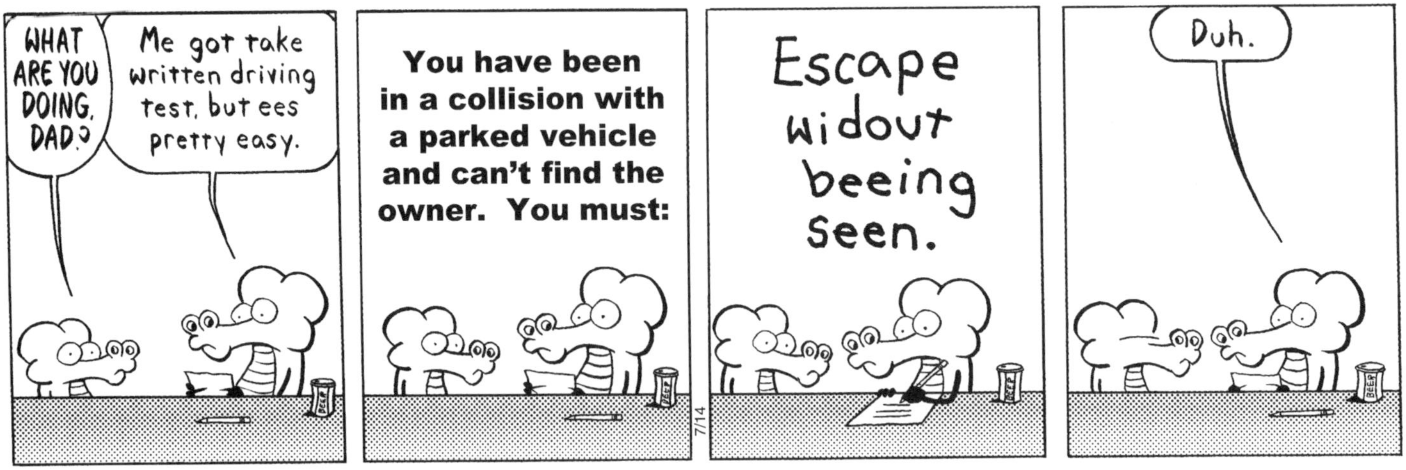
WHAT ARE YOU DOING, DAD?
Me got take written driving test, but ees pretty easy.
You have been in a collision with a parked vehicle and can't find the owner. You must:
7/14
Escape widout beeing seen.
Duh.

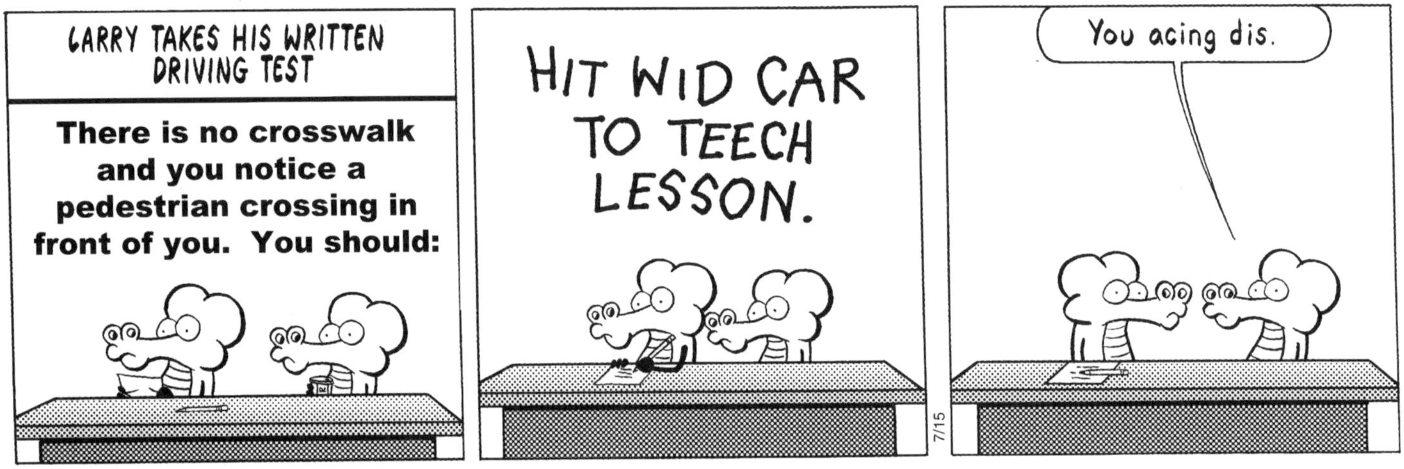
LARRY TAKES HIS WRITTEN DRIVING TEST
There is no crosswalk and you notice a pedestrian crossing in front of you. You should:
HIT WID CAR TO TEECH LESSON.
7/15
You acing dis.

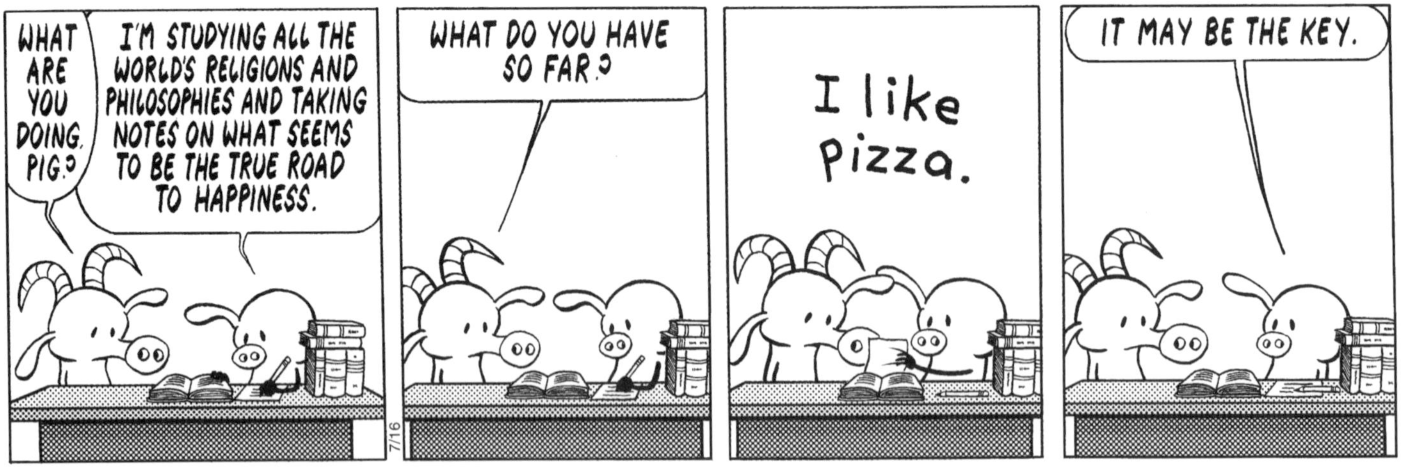
WHAT ARE YOU DOING, PIG?
I'M STUDYING ALL THE WORLD'S RELIGIONS AND PHILOSOPHIES AND TAKING NOTES ON WHAT SEEMS TO BE THE TRUE ROAD TO HAPPINESS.
7/16
WHAT DO YOU HAVE SO FAR?
I like pizza.
IT MAY BE THE KEY.

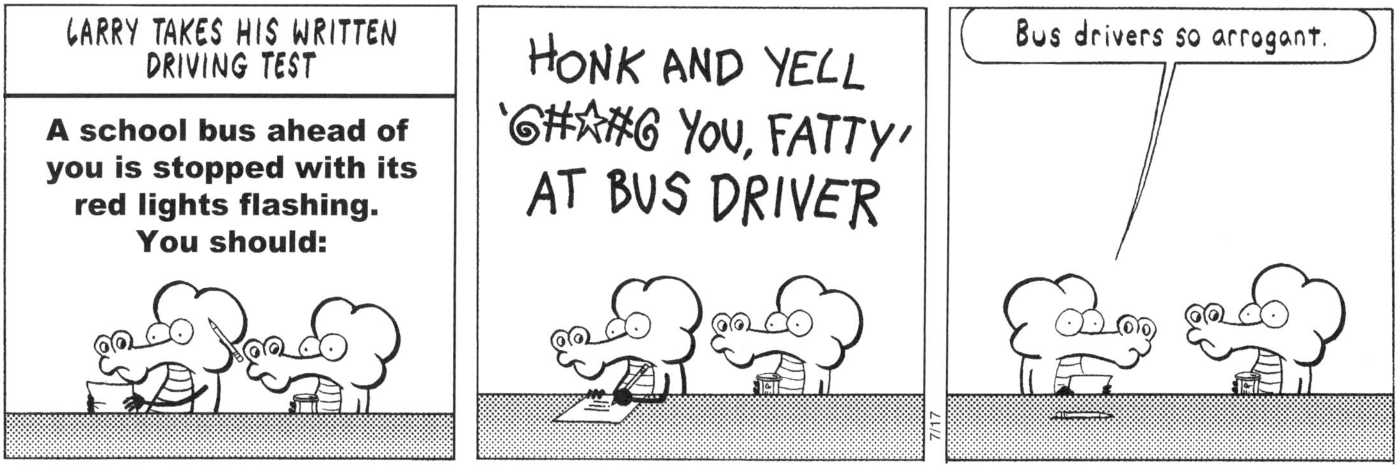
LARRY TAKES HIS WRITTEN DRIVING TEST
A school bus ahead of you is stopped with its red lights flashing. You should:
HONK AND YELL '@#☆#@ YOU, FATTY' AT BUS DRIVER
7/17
Bus drivers so arrogant.

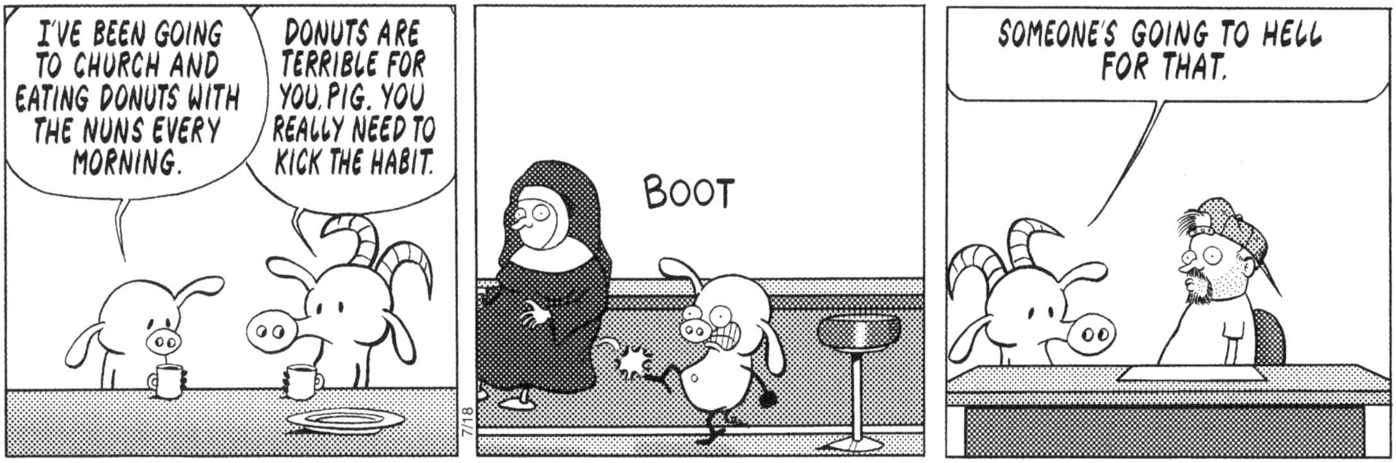
I'VE BEEN GOING TO CHURCH AND EATING DONUTS WITH THE NUNS EVERY MORNING.
DONUTS ARE TERRIBLE FOR YOU, PIG. YOU REALLY NEED TO KICK THE HABIT.
7/18
BOOT
SOMEONE'S GOING TO HELL FOR THAT.

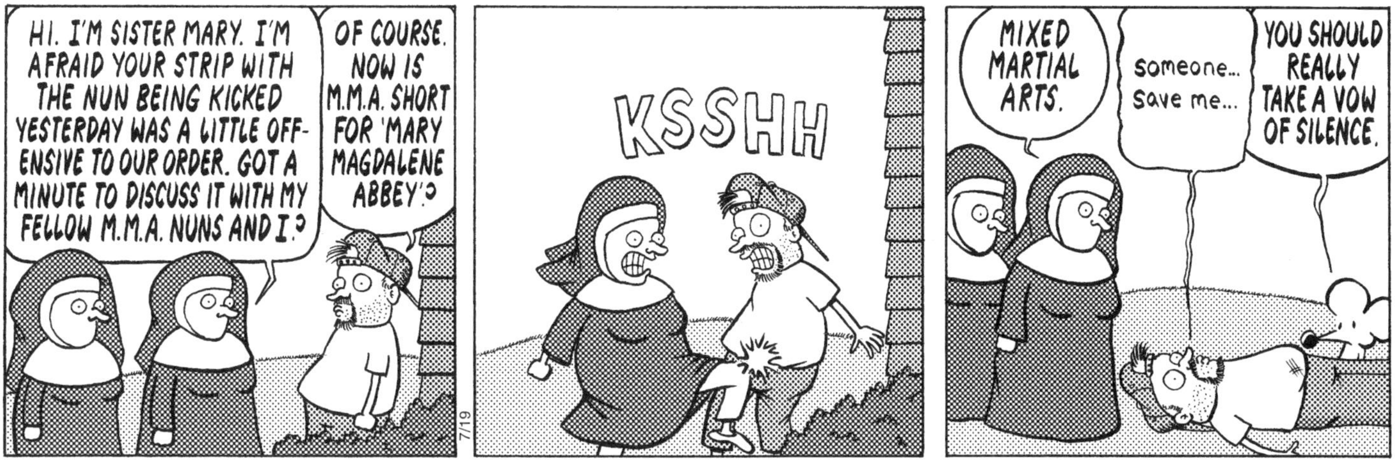
HI. I'M SISTER MARY. I'M AFRAID YOUR STRIP WITH THE NUN BEING KICKED YESTERDAY WAS A LITTLE OFF-ENSIVE TO OUR ORDER. GOT A MINUTE TO DISCUSS IT WITH MY FELLOW M.M.A. NUNS AND I?
OF COURSE. NOW IS M.M.A. SHORT FOR 'MARY MAGDALENE ABBEY'?
7/19
KSSHH
MIXED MARTIAL ARTS.
Someone... save me...
YOU SHOULD REALLY TAKE A VOW OF SILENCE.

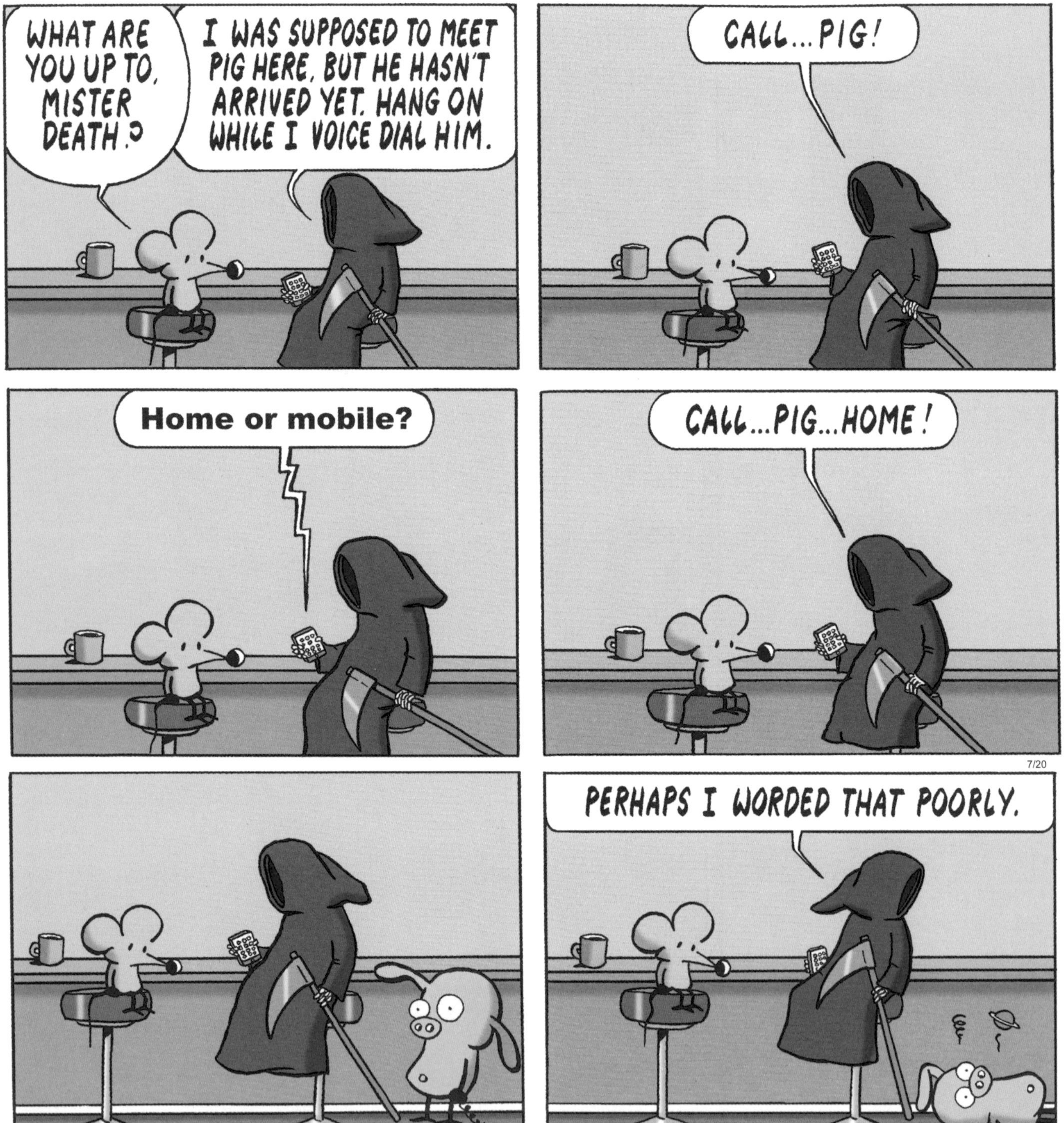
WHAT ARE YOU UP TO, MISTER DEATH?
I WAS SUPPOSED TO MEET PIG HERE, BUT HE HASN'T ARRIVED YET. HANG ON WHILE I VOICE DIAL HIM.
CALL...PIG!
Home or mobile?
CALL...PIG...HOME!
7/20
PERHAPS I WORDED THAT POORLY.

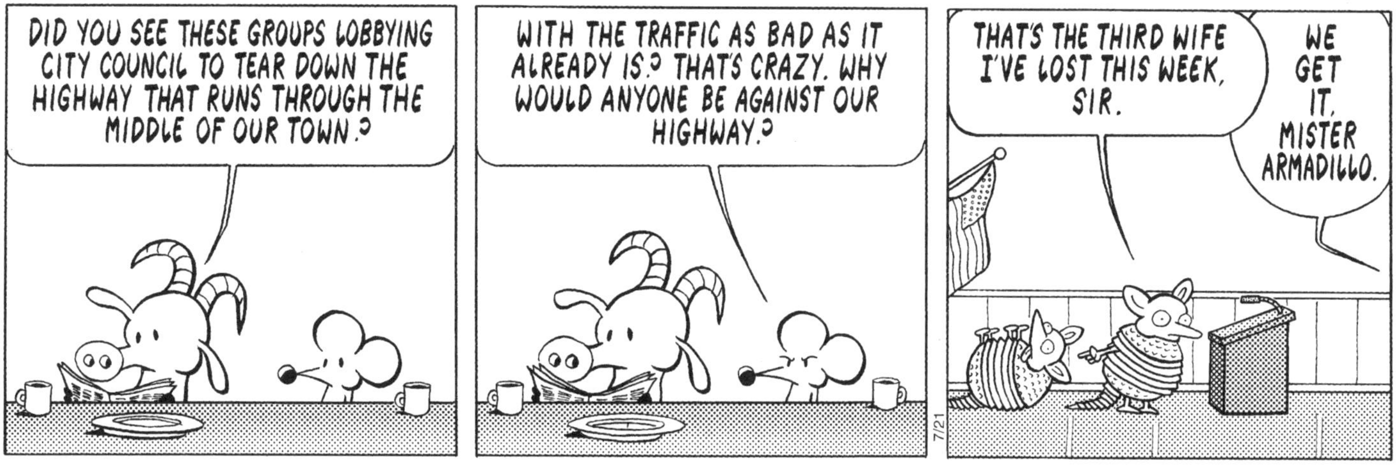
DID YOU SEE THESE GROUPS LOBBYING CITY COUNCIL TO TEAR DOWN THE HIGHWAY THAT RUNS THROUGH THE MIDDLE OF OUR TOWN?
WITH THE TRAFFIC AS BAD AS IT ALREADY IS? THAT'S CRAZY. WHY WOULD ANYONE BE AGAINST OUR HIGHWAY?
THAT'S THE THIRD WIFE I'VE LOST THIS WEEK, SIR.
WE GET IT, MISTER ARMADILLO.
7/21

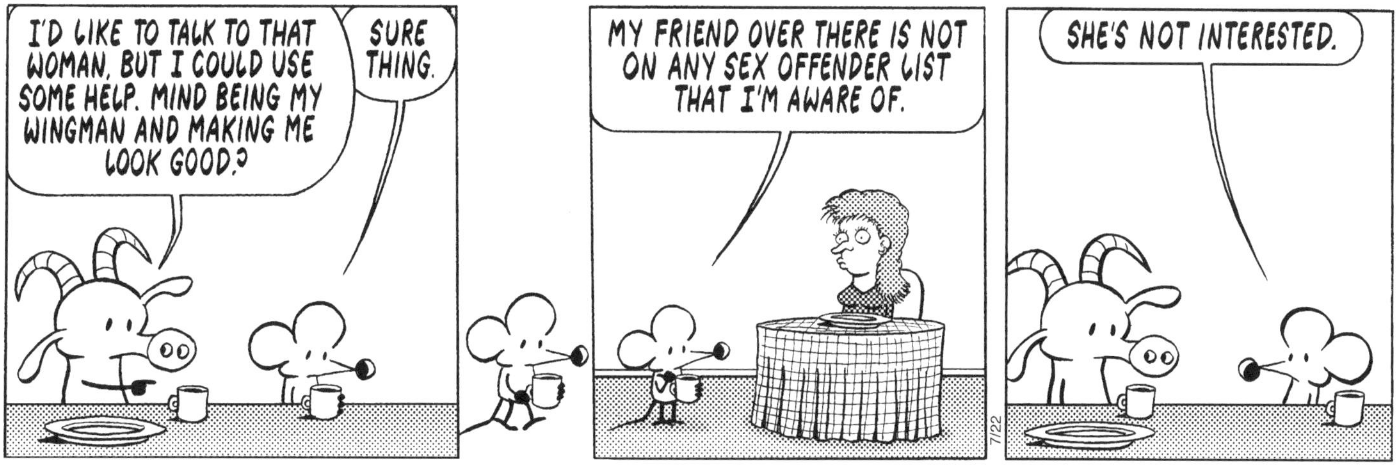
I'D LIKE TO TALK TO THAT WOMAN, BUT I COULD USE SOME HELP. MIND BEING MY WINGMAN AND MAKING ME LOOK GOOD?
SURE THING.
MY FRIEND OVER THERE IS NOT ON ANY SEX OFFENDER LIST THAT I'M AWARE OF.
SHE'S NOT INTERESTED.
7/22

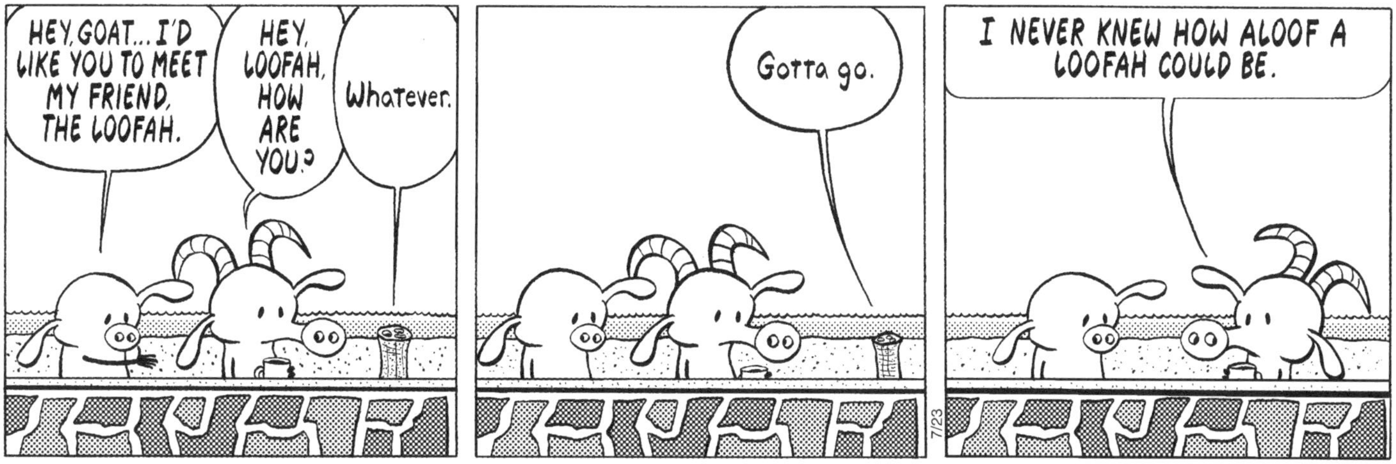
HEY, GOAT... I'D LIKE YOU TO MEET MY FRIEND, THE LOOFAH.
HEY, LOOFAH, HOW ARE YOU?
Whatever.
Gotta go.
I NEVER KNEW HOW ALOOF A LOOFAH COULD BE.
7/23

Panel 1: WHERE YOU OFF TO, GOAT? / MY SPIN CLASS.

Panel 2: YOU NEED A CLASS TO LEARN HOW TO SPIN? / THEY DON'T TEACH US HOW TO SPIN. WE RIDE BIKES.

Panel 3: TO WHERE? / NOWHERE.

Panel 4: HAHAHAHA HAHAHAHA HAHAHAHA HAHAHAHA HAHAHAHA

Panel 5: OKAY, NOW BE SERIOUS.

Panel 6: MY FRIENDS INVITED ME TO THEIR PLACE OF WORSHIP, BUT I'M NOT GONNA GO. / WHY NOT?

Panel 7: THEY HAVE RABIES. / RABIES?

Panel 8: HIS FRIENDS ARE JEWISH. AND THE WORD HE'S LOOKING FOR IS 'RABBIS.'

Panel 9: WE SHOULD HAVE THESE DISCUSSIONS LESS OFTEN.

Panel 10: HI, RAT. IT'S YOUR MOTHER. I'M CALLING TO TELL YOU THAT AUNT MILLIE DIED. HER MEMORIAL'S ON TUESDAY. HER FUNERAL'S ON WEDNESDAY. AND INSTEAD OF SENDING FLOWERS, THE FAMILY WOULD LIKE PEOPLE TO MAKE DONATIONS TO SAINT ANTHONY'S, HER CHURCH ON MAIN STREET.

Panel 11: YOU'RE QUIET. DO YOU NEED A MOMENT? / YES. TO FIGURE OUT WHO AUNT MILLIE IS.

Panel 12: I'M NOT AS CLOSE TO MY FAMILY AS I COULD BE.

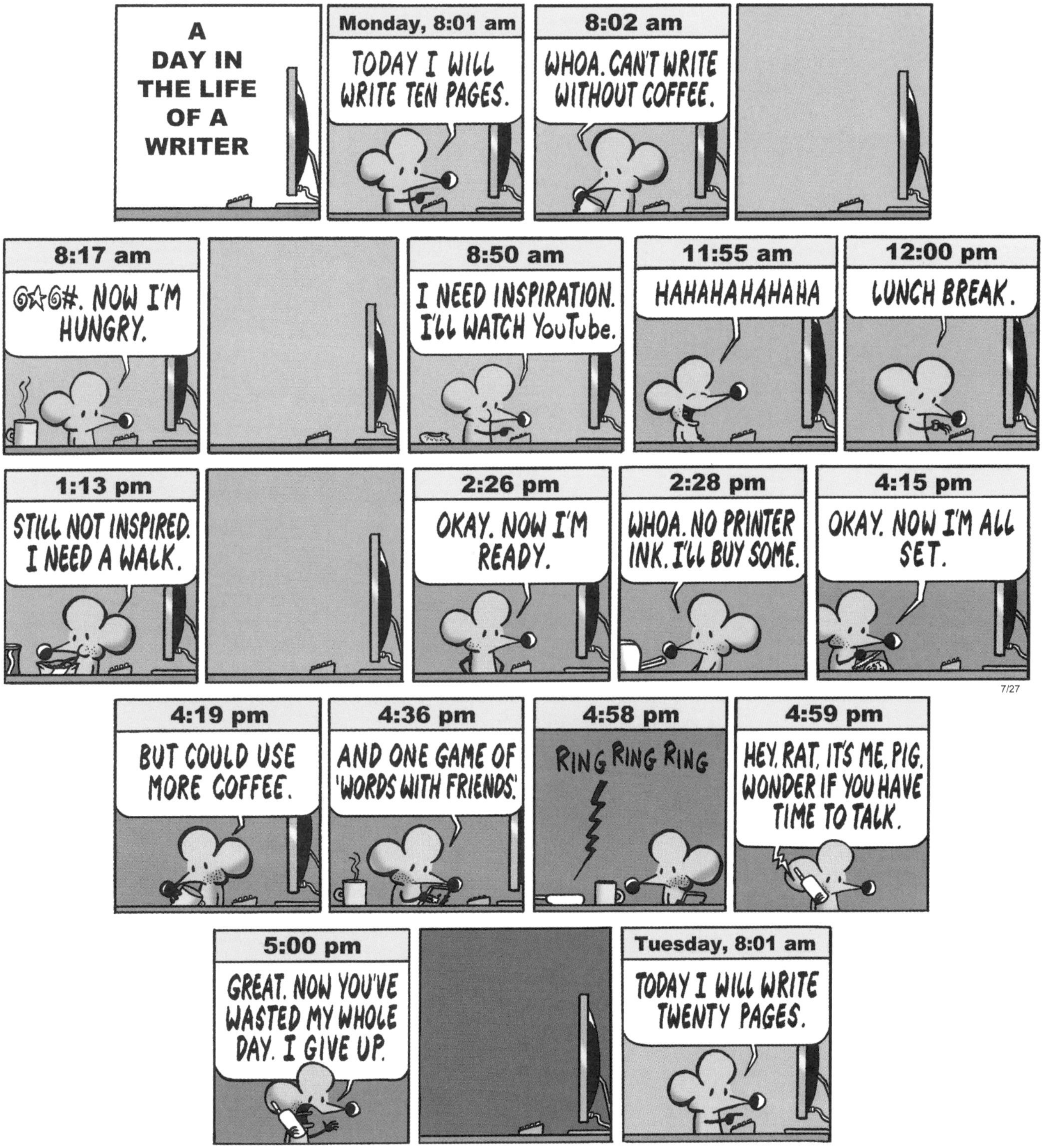
A DAY IN THE LIFE OF A WRITER
Monday, 8:01 am
TODAY I WILL WRITE TEN PAGES.
8:02 am
WHOA. CAN'T WRITE WITHOUT COFFEE.
8:17 am
@☆@#. NOW I'M HUNGRY.
8:50 am
I NEED INSPIRATION. I'LL WATCH YouTube.
11:55 am
HAHAHAHAHAHA
12:00 pm
LUNCH BREAK.
1:13 pm
STILL NOT INSPIRED. I NEED A WALK.
2:26 pm
OKAY. NOW I'M READY.
2:28 pm
WHOA. NO PRINTER INK. I'LL BUY SOME.
4:15 pm
OKAY. NOW I'M ALL SET.
7/27
4:19 pm
BUT COULD USE MORE COFFEE.
4:36 pm
AND ONE GAME OF 'WORDS WITH FRIENDS.'
4:58 pm
RING RING RING
4:59 pm
HEY, RAT, IT'S ME, PIG. WONDER IF YOU HAVE TIME TO TALK.
5:00 pm
GREAT. NOW YOU'VE WASTED MY WHOLE DAY. I GIVE UP.
Tuesday, 8:01 am
TODAY I WILL WRITE TWENTY PAGES.

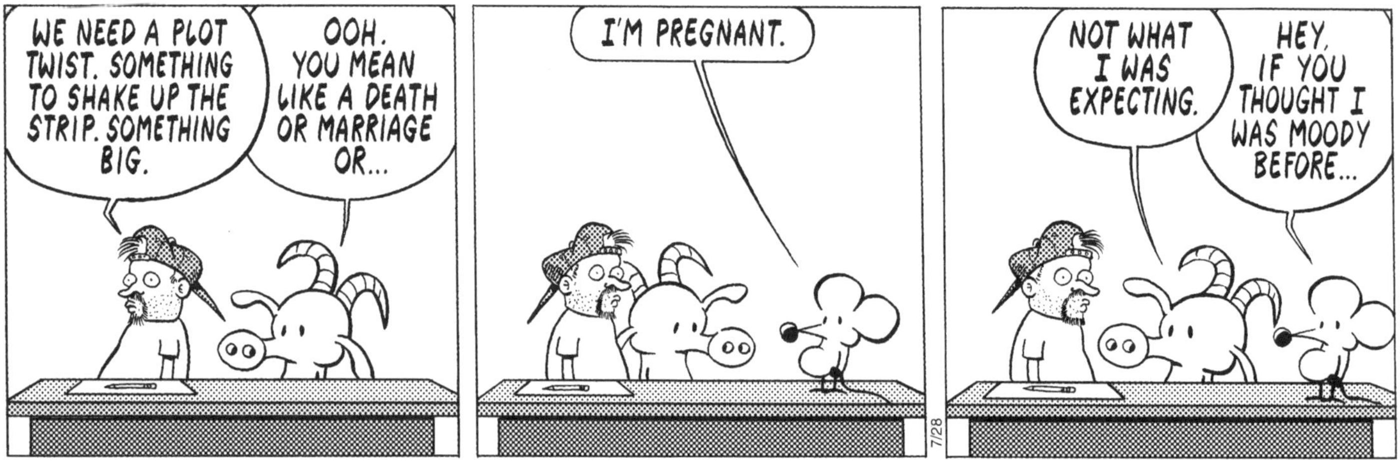
WE NEED A PLOT TWIST. SOMETHING TO SHAKE UP THE STRIP. SOMETHING BIG.
OOH. YOU MEAN LIKE A DEATH OR MARRIAGE OR...
I'M PREGNANT.
NOT WHAT I WAS EXPECTING.
HEY, IF YOU THOUGHT I WAS MOODY BEFORE...
7/28

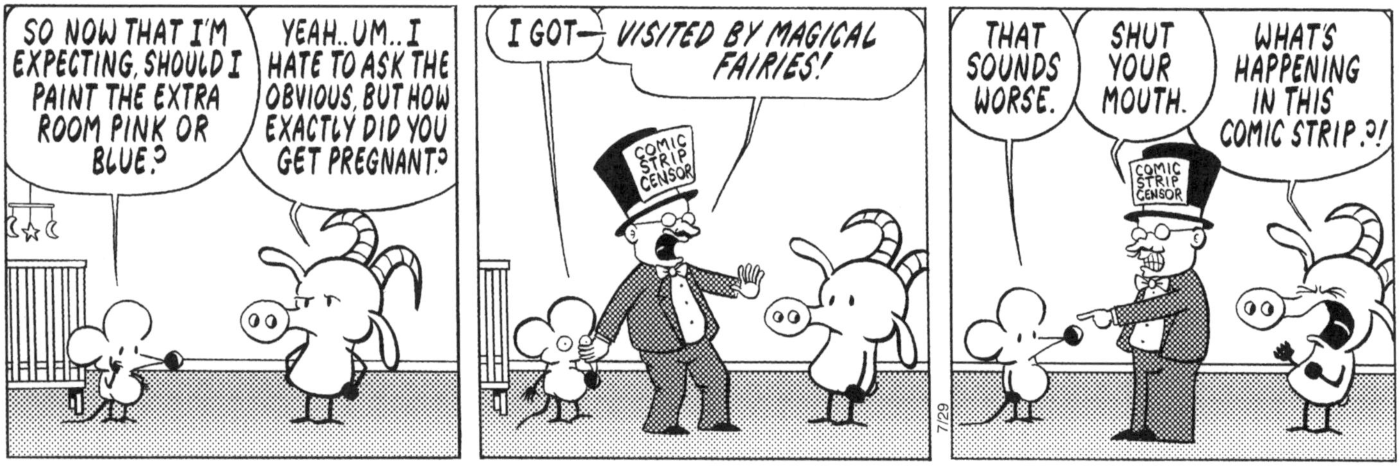
SO NOW THAT I'M EXPECTING, SHOULD I PAINT THE EXTRA ROOM PINK OR BLUE?
YEAH.. UM.. I HATE TO ASK THE OBVIOUS, BUT HOW EXACTLY DID YOU GET PREGNANT?
I GOT—
VISITED BY MAGICAL FAIRIES!
COMIC STRIP CENSOR
THAT SOUNDS WORSE.
SHUT YOUR MOUTH.
WHAT'S HAPPENING IN THIS COMIC STRIP?!
7/29

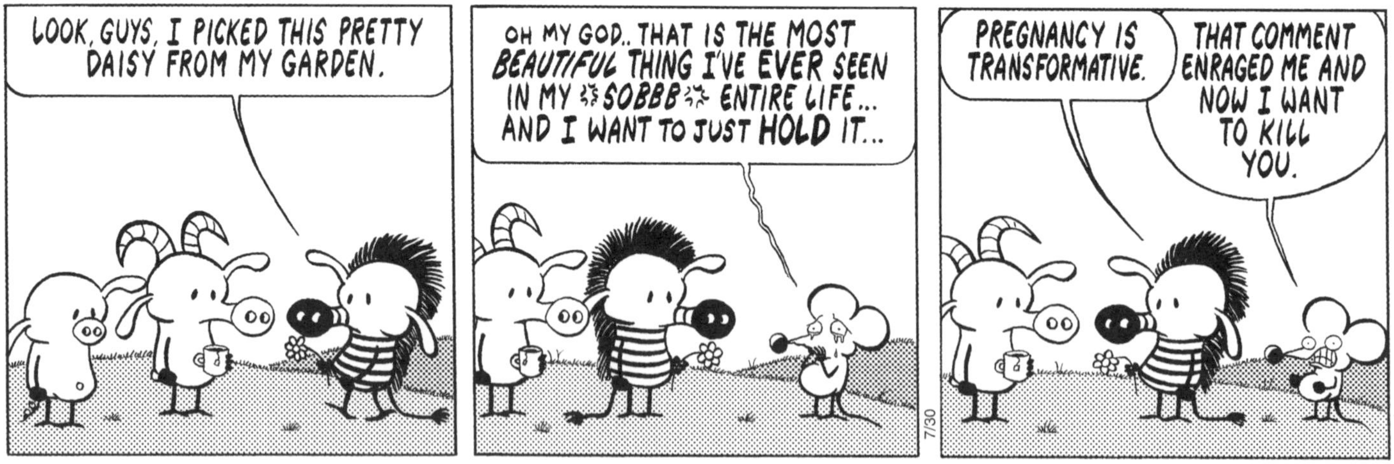
LOOK, GUYS, I PICKED THIS PRETTY DAISY FROM MY GARDEN.
OH MY GOD.. THAT IS THE MOST BEAUTIFUL THING I'VE EVER SEEN IN MY SOBBB ENTIRE LIFE... AND I WANT TO JUST HOLD IT...
PREGNANCY IS TRANSFORMATIVE.
THAT COMMENT ENRAGED ME AND NOW I WANT TO KILL YOU.
7/30

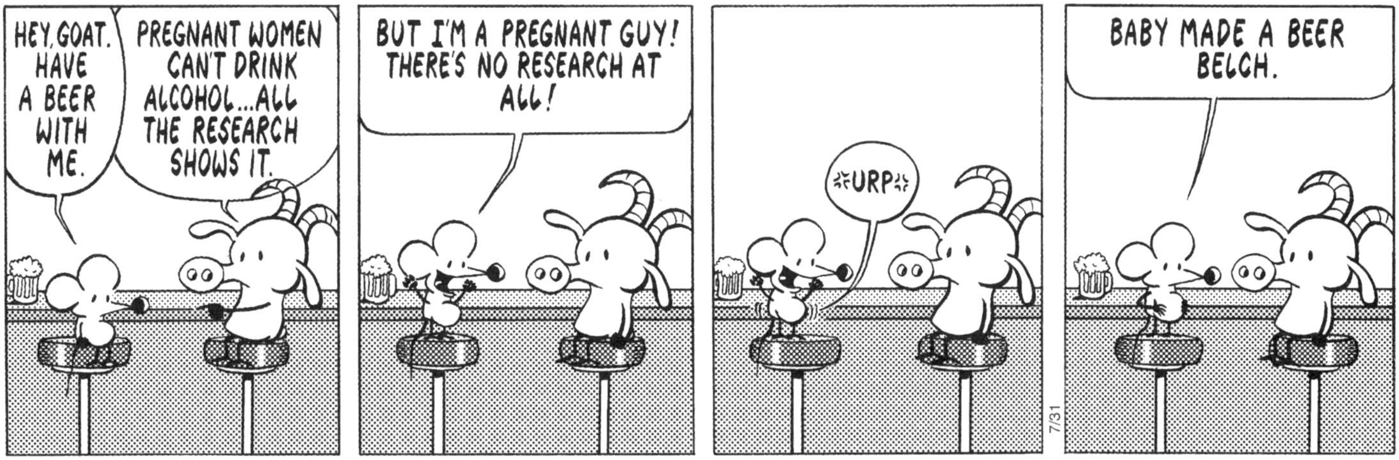
HEY, GOAT. HAVE A BEER WITH ME.
PREGNANT WOMEN CAN'T DRINK ALCOHOL... ALL THE RESEARCH SHOWS IT.
BUT I'M A PREGNANT GUY! THERE'S NO RESEARCH AT ALL!
URP
BABY MADE A BEER BELCH.
7/31

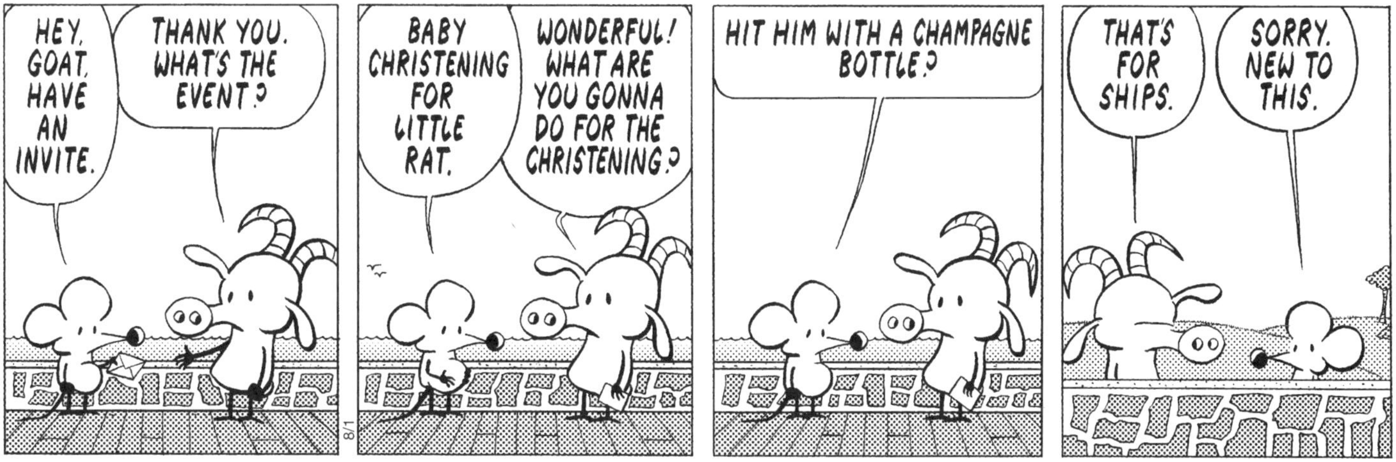
HEY, GOAT, HAVE AN INVITE.
THANK YOU. WHAT'S THE EVENT?
BABY CHRISTENING FOR LITTLE RAT.
WONDERFUL! WHAT ARE YOU GONNA DO FOR THE CHRISTENING?
HIT HIM WITH A CHAMPAGNE BOTTLE?
THAT'S FOR SHIPS.
SORRY. NEW TO THIS.
8/1

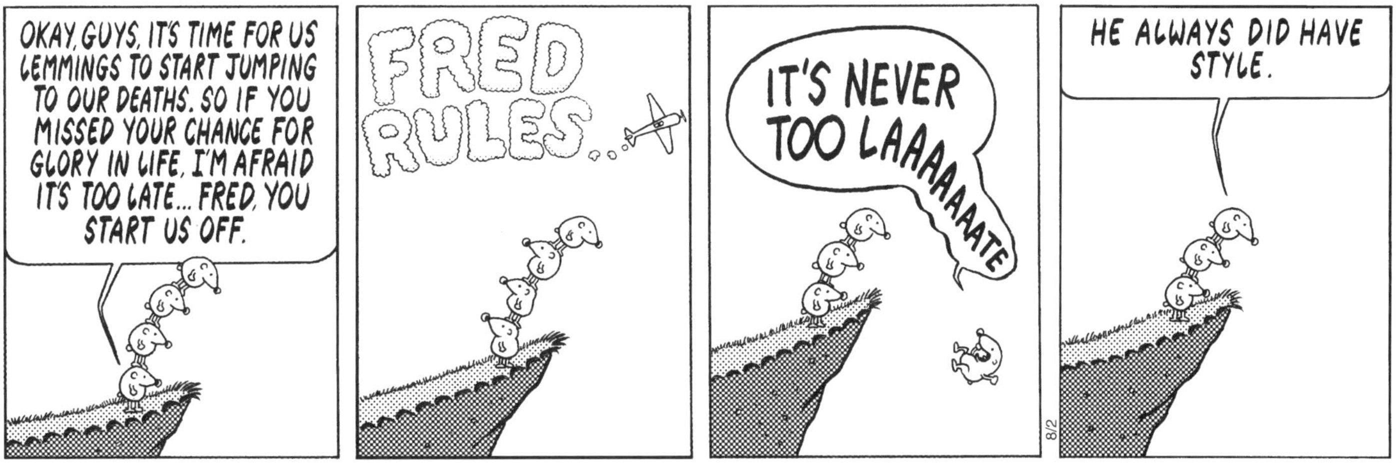
OKAY, GUYS, IT'S TIME FOR US LEMMINGS TO START JUMPING TO OUR DEATHS. SO IF YOU MISSED YOUR CHANCE FOR GLORY IN LIFE, I'M AFRAID IT'S TOO LATE... FRED, YOU START US OFF.
FRED RULES
IT'S NEVER TOO LAAAAAAATE
HE ALWAYS DID HAVE STYLE.
8/2

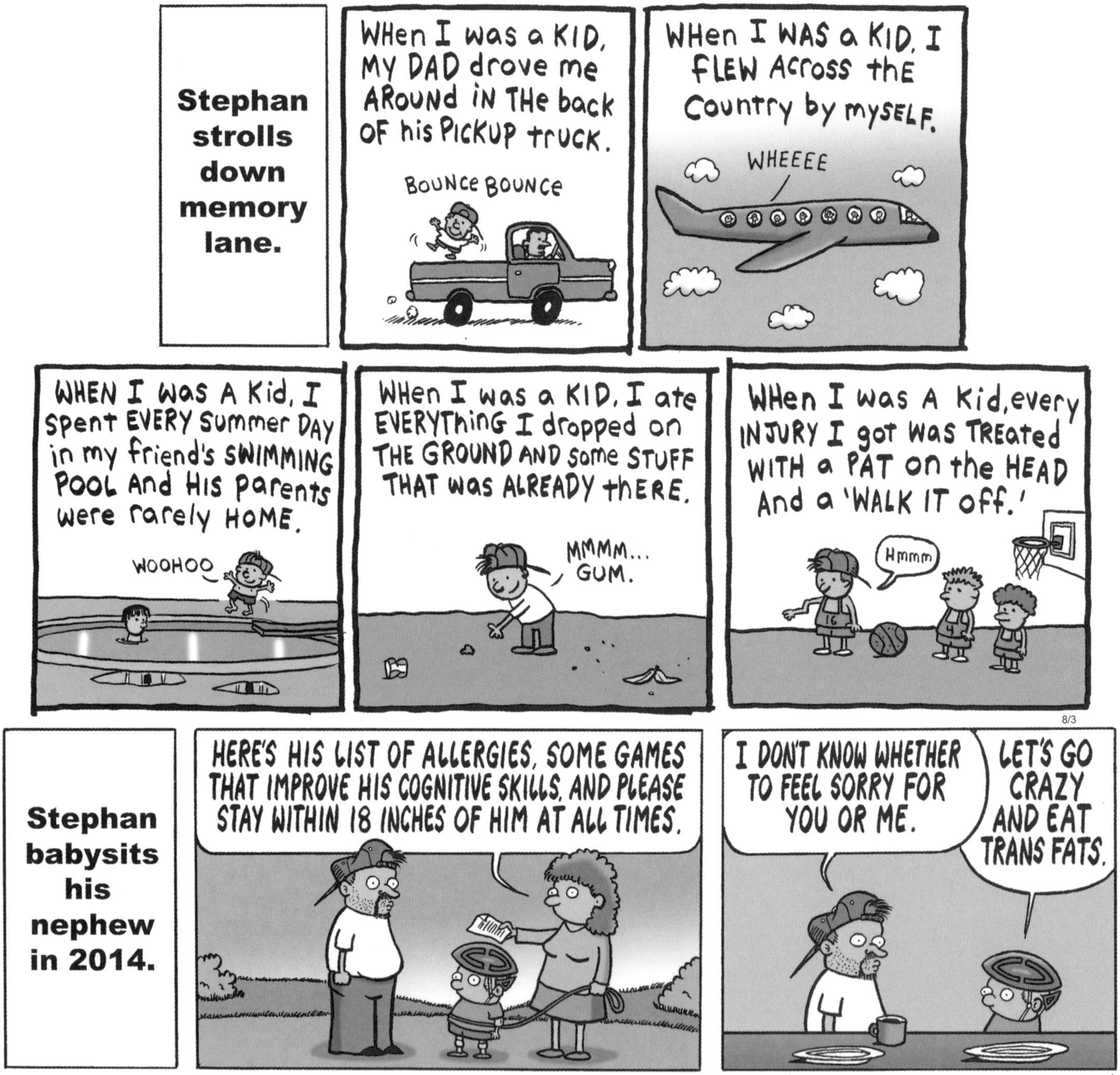
Stephan strolls down memory lane.
WHen I was a KID, MY DAD drove me ARound IN THe back OF his PICKUP truck.
BOUNCE BOUNCE
WHen I WAS a KID, I FLEW Across the Country by mySELF.
WHEEEE
WHEN I Was A Kid, I spent EVERY Summer DAY in my friend's SWIMMING POOL And His parents were rarely HOME.
WOOHOO
WHen I was a KID, I ate EVERYThing I dropped on THE GROUND AND some STUFF THAT was ALREADY there.
MMMM... GUM.
WHen I was A Kid, every INJURY I got was TREated WITH a PAT on the HEAD And a 'WALK IT off.'
Hmmm
8/3
Stephan babysits his nephew in 2014.
HERE'S HIS LIST OF ALLERGIES, SOME GAMES THAT IMPROVE HIS COGNITIVE SKILLS, AND PLEASE STAY WITHIN 18 INCHES OF HIM AT ALL TIMES.
I DON'T KNOW WHETHER TO FEEL SORRY FOR YOU OR ME.
LET'S GO CRAZY AND EAT TRANS FATS.

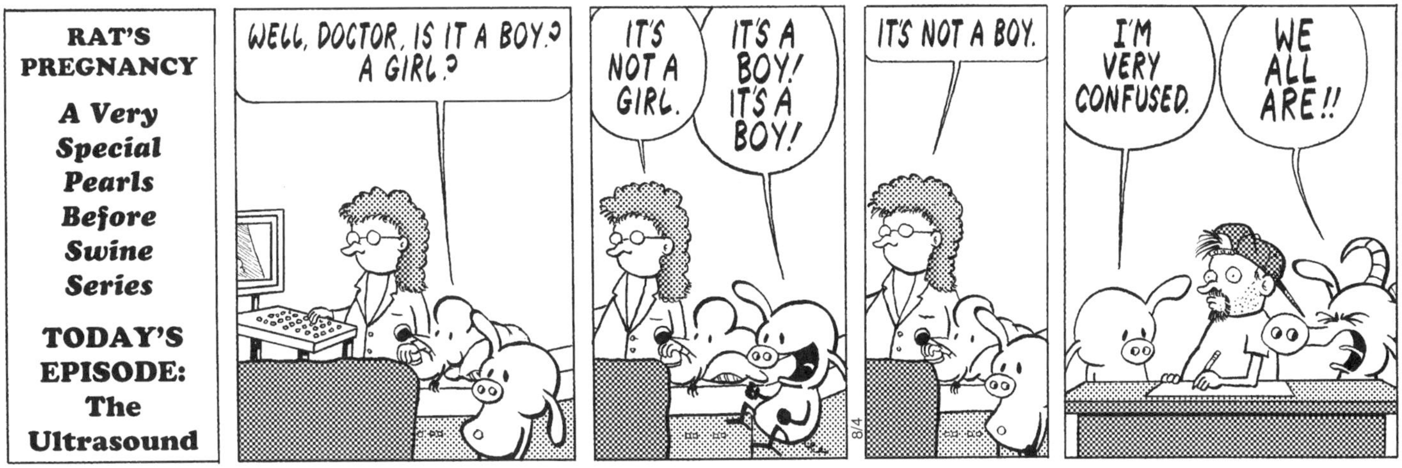
RAT'S PREGNANCY
A Very Special Pearls Before Swine Series
TODAY'S EPISODE: The Ultrasound
WELL, DOCTOR, IS IT A BOY? A GIRL?
IT'S NOT A GIRL.
IT'S A BOY! IT'S A BOY!
IT'S NOT A BOY.
I'M VERY CONFUSED.
WE ALL ARE!!
8/4

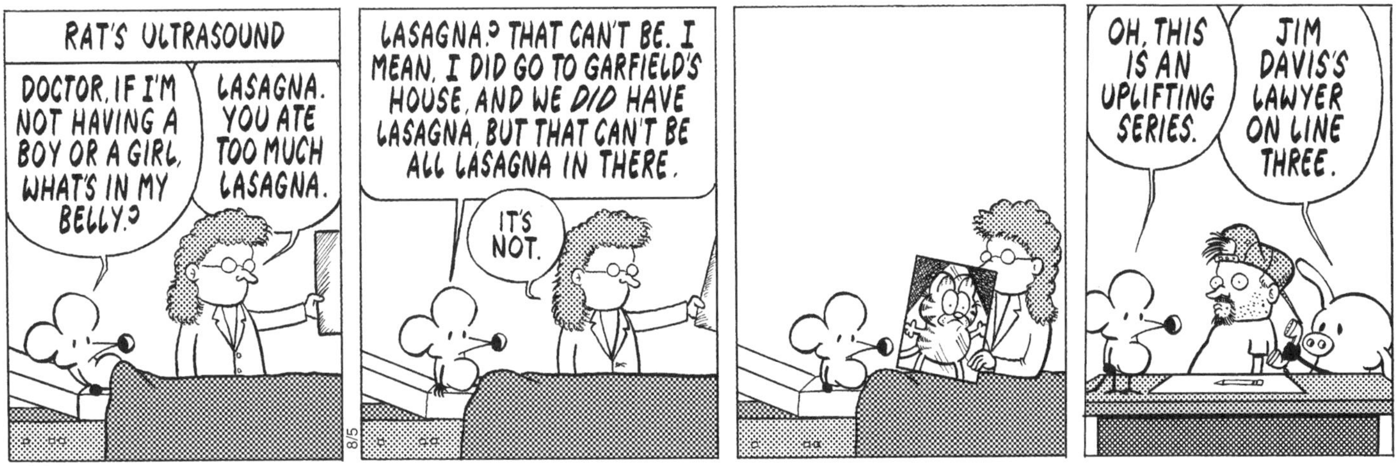
RAT'S ULTRASOUND
DOCTOR, IF I'M NOT HAVING A BOY OR A GIRL, WHAT'S IN MY BELLY?
LASAGNA. YOU ATE TOO MUCH LASAGNA.
LASAGNA? THAT CAN'T BE. I MEAN, I DID GO TO GARFIELD'S HOUSE, AND WE DID HAVE LASAGNA, BUT THAT CAN'T BE ALL LASAGNA IN THERE.
IT'S NOT.
OH, THIS IS AN UPLIFTING SERIES.
JIM DAVIS'S LAWYER ON LINE THREE.
8/5

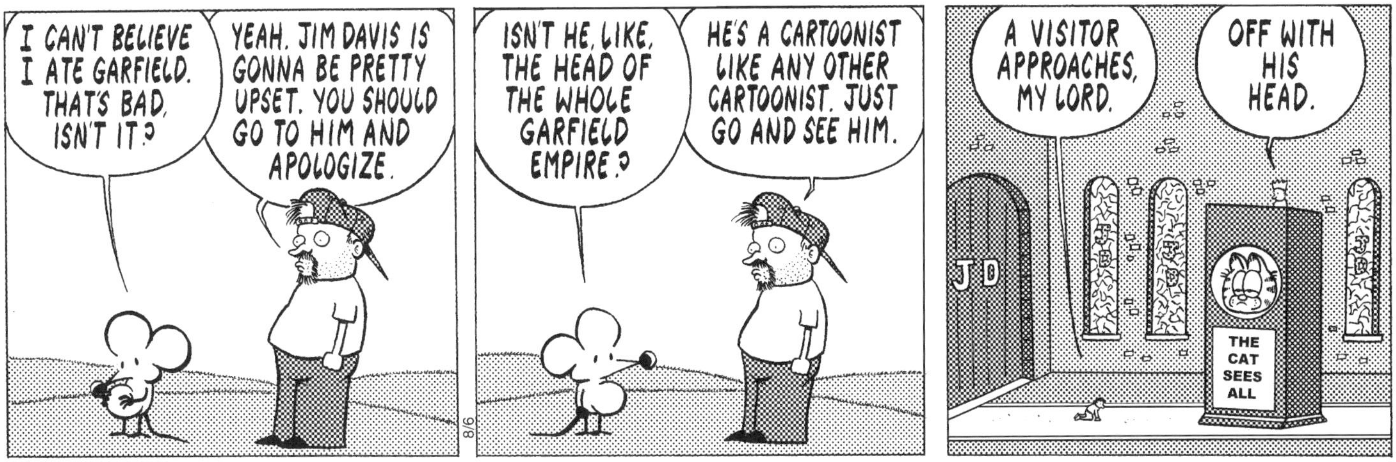
I CAN'T BELIEVE I ATE GARFIELD. THAT'S BAD, ISN'T IT?
YEAH. JIM DAVIS IS GONNA BE PRETTY UPSET. YOU SHOULD GO TO HIM AND APOLOGIZE.
ISN'T HE, LIKE, THE HEAD OF THE WHOLE GARFIELD EMPIRE?
HE'S A CARTOONIST LIKE ANY OTHER CARTOONIST. JUST GO AND SEE HIM.
A VISITOR APPROACHES, MY LORD.
OFF WITH HIS HEAD.
JD
THE CAT SEES ALL
8/6

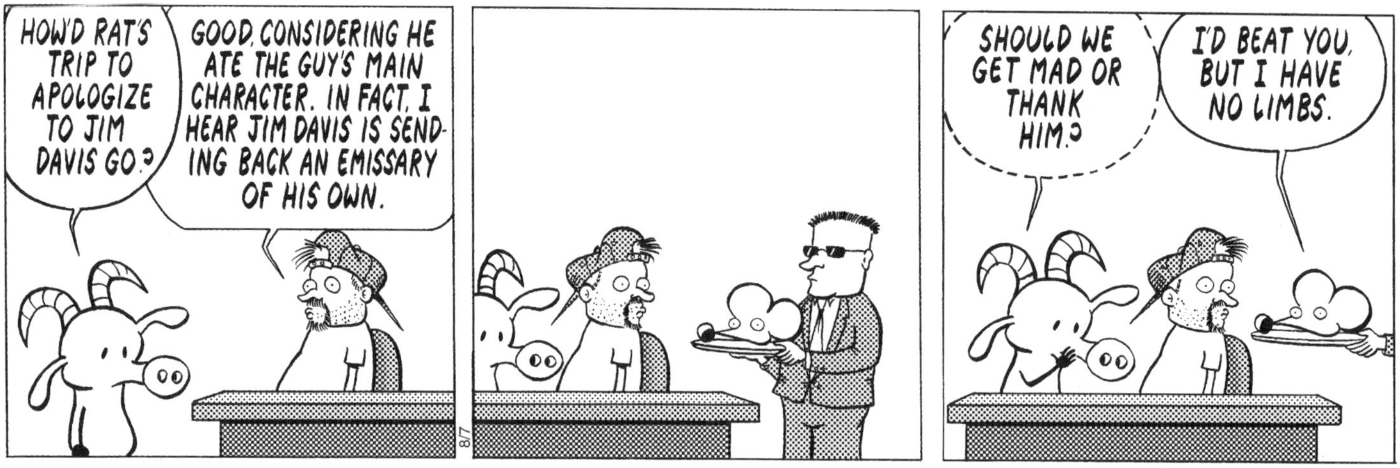
HOW'D RAT'S TRIP TO APOLOGIZE TO JIM DAVIS GO?
GOOD, CONSIDERING HE ATE THE GUY'S MAIN CHARACTER. IN FACT, I HEAR JIM DAVIS IS SENDING BACK AN EMISSARY OF HIS OWN.
8/7
SHOULD WE GET MAD OR THANK HIM?
I'D BEAT YOU, BUT I HAVE NO LIMBS.

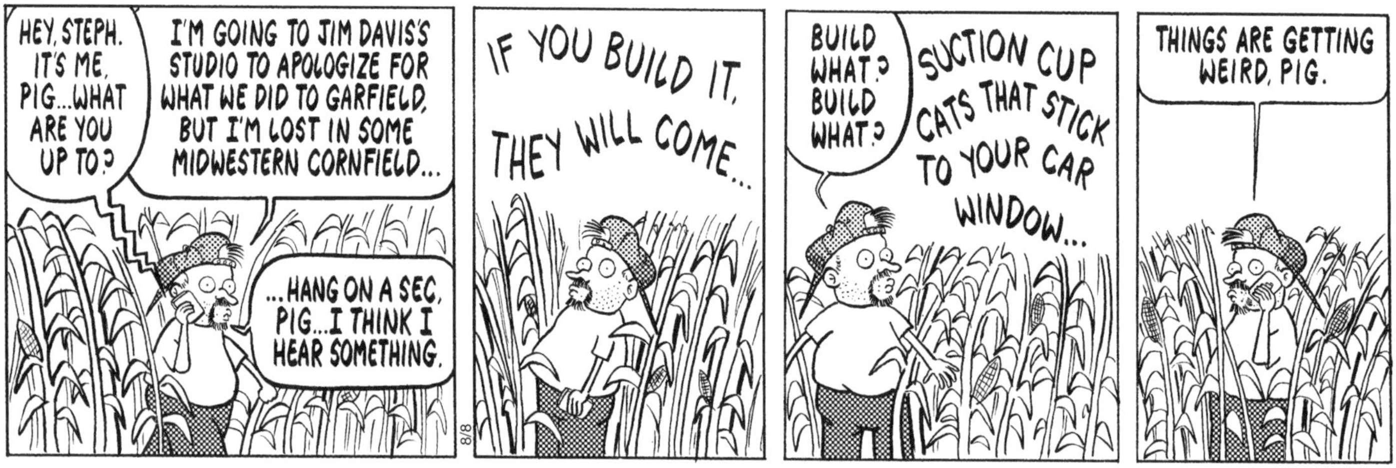
HEY, STEPH. IT'S ME, PIG...WHAT ARE YOU UP TO?
I'M GOING TO JIM DAVIS'S STUDIO TO APOLOGIZE FOR WHAT WE DID TO GARFIELD, BUT I'M LOST IN SOME MIDWESTERN CORNFIELD...
...HANG ON A SEC, PIG...I THINK I HEAR SOMETHING.
8/8
IF YOU BUILD IT, THEY WILL COME...
BUILD WHAT? BUILD WHAT?
SUCTION CUP CATS THAT STICK TO YOUR CAR WINDOW...
THINGS ARE GETTING WEIRD, PIG.

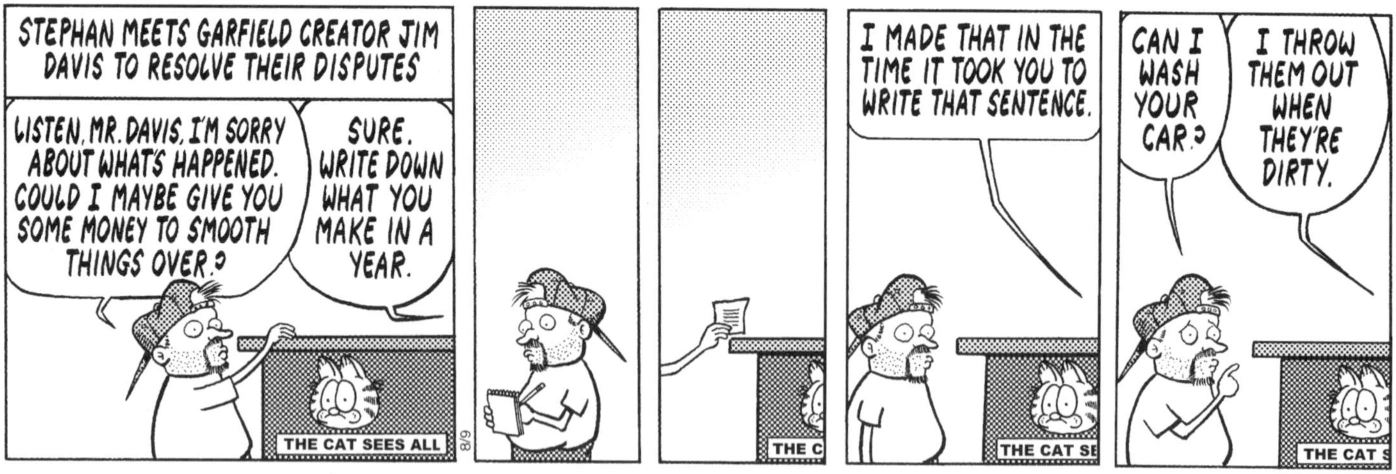
STEPHAN MEETS GARFIELD CREATOR JIM DAVIS TO RESOLVE THEIR DISPUTES
LISTEN, MR. DAVIS, I'M SORRY ABOUT WHAT'S HAPPENED. COULD I MAYBE GIVE YOU SOME MONEY TO SMOOTH THINGS OVER?
SURE. WRITE DOWN WHAT YOU MAKE IN A YEAR.
THE CAT SEES ALL
8/9
I MADE THAT IN THE TIME IT TOOK YOU TO WRITE THAT SENTENCE.
CAN I WASH YOUR CAR?
I THROW THEM OUT WHEN THEY'RE DIRTY.

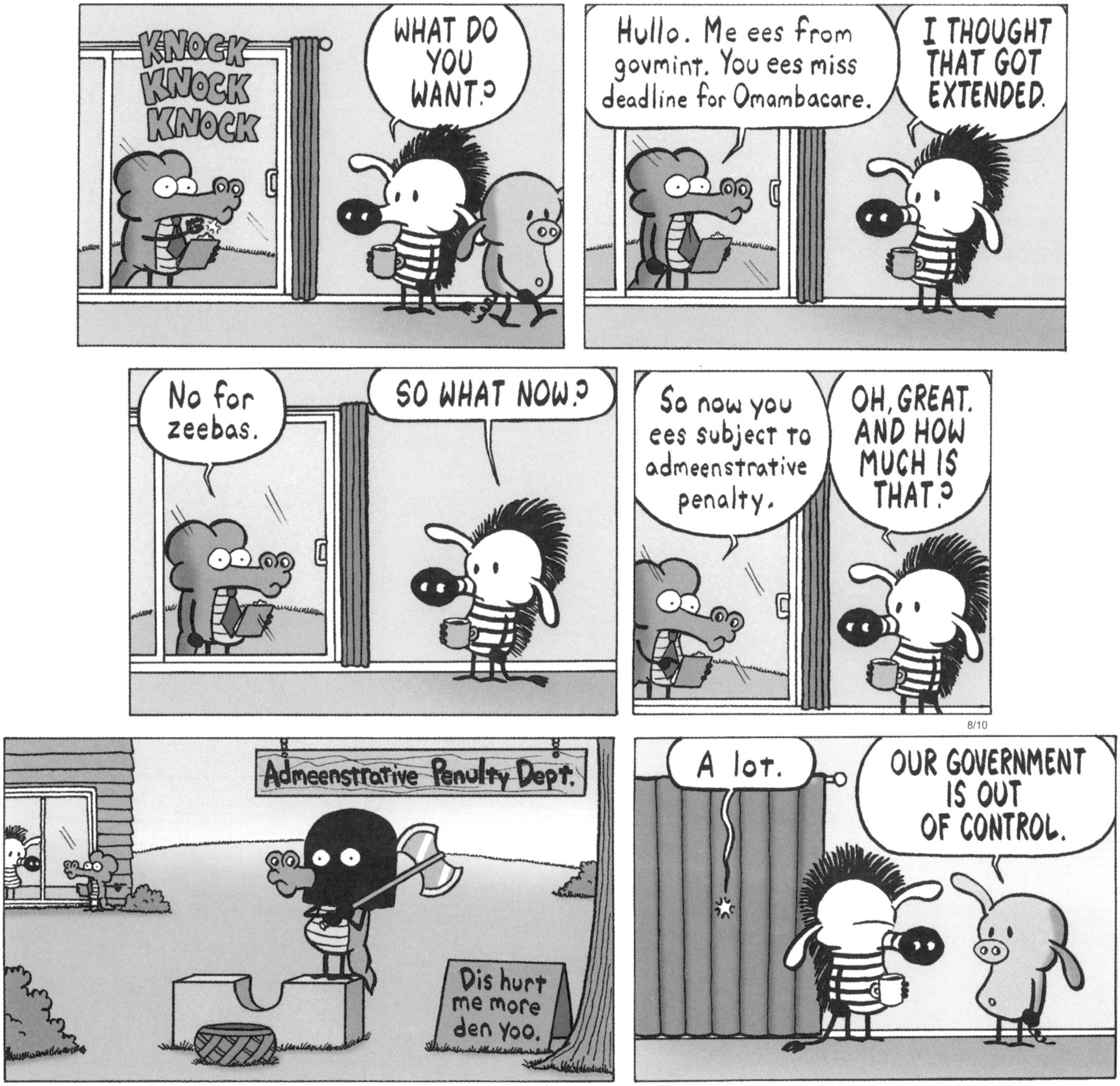
KNOCK KNOCK KNOCK
WHAT DO YOU WANT?
Hullo. Me ees from govmint. You ees miss deadline for Omambacare.
I THOUGHT THAT GOT EXTENDED.
No for zeebas.
SO WHAT NOW?
So now you ees subject to admeenstrative penalty.
OH, GREAT. AND HOW MUCH IS THAT?
8/10
Admeenstrative Penulty Dept.
Dis hurt me more den yoo.
A lot.
OUR GOVERNMENT IS OUT OF CONTROL.

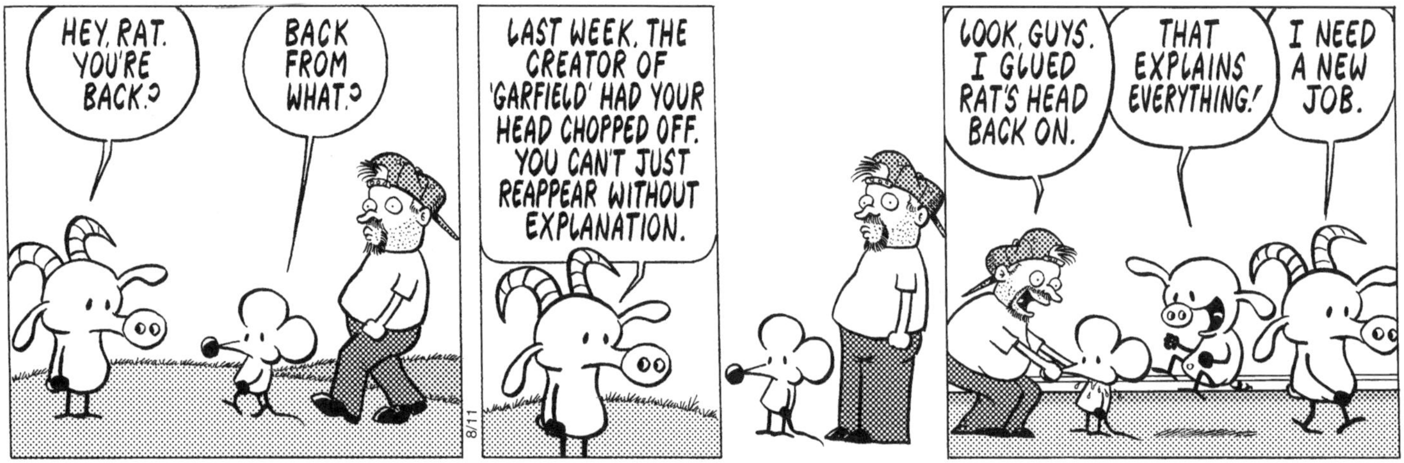
HEY, RAT. YOU'RE BACK.?
BACK FROM WHAT.?
LAST WEEK, THE CREATOR OF 'GARFIELD' HAD YOUR HEAD CHOPPED OFF. YOU CAN'T JUST REAPPEAR WITHOUT EXPLANATION.
LOOK, GUYS. I GLUED RAT'S HEAD BACK ON.
THAT EXPLAINS EVERYTHING!
I NEED A NEW JOB.
8/11

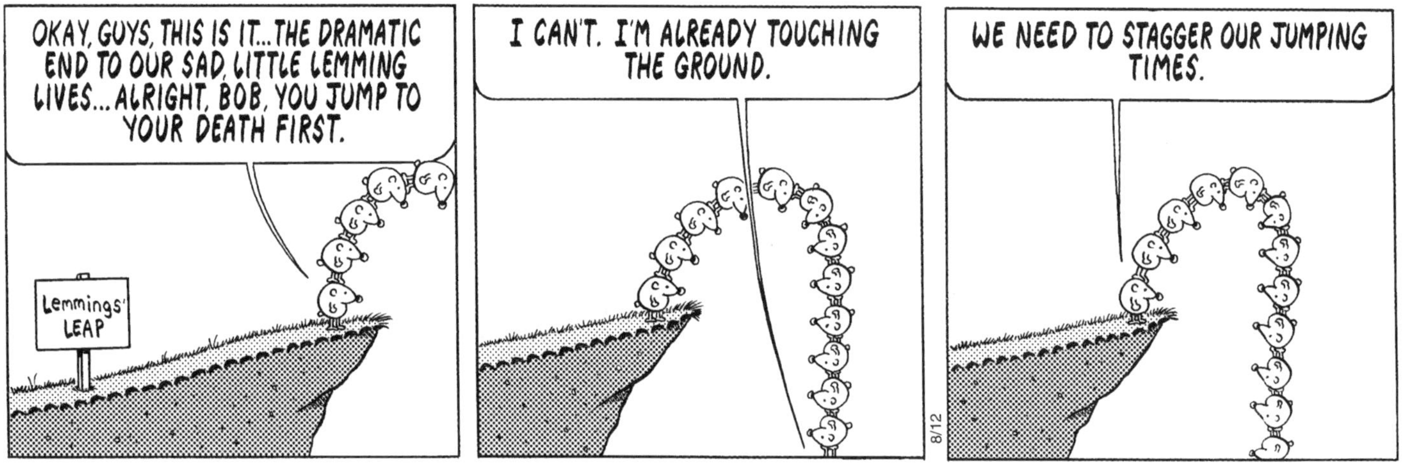
OKAY, GUYS, THIS IS IT...THE DRAMATIC END TO OUR SAD, LITTLE LEMMING LIVES...ALRIGHT, BOB, YOU JUMP TO YOUR DEATH FIRST.
Lemmings' LEAP
I CAN'T. I'M ALREADY TOUCHING THE GROUND.
WE NEED TO STAGGER OUR JUMPING TIMES.
8/12

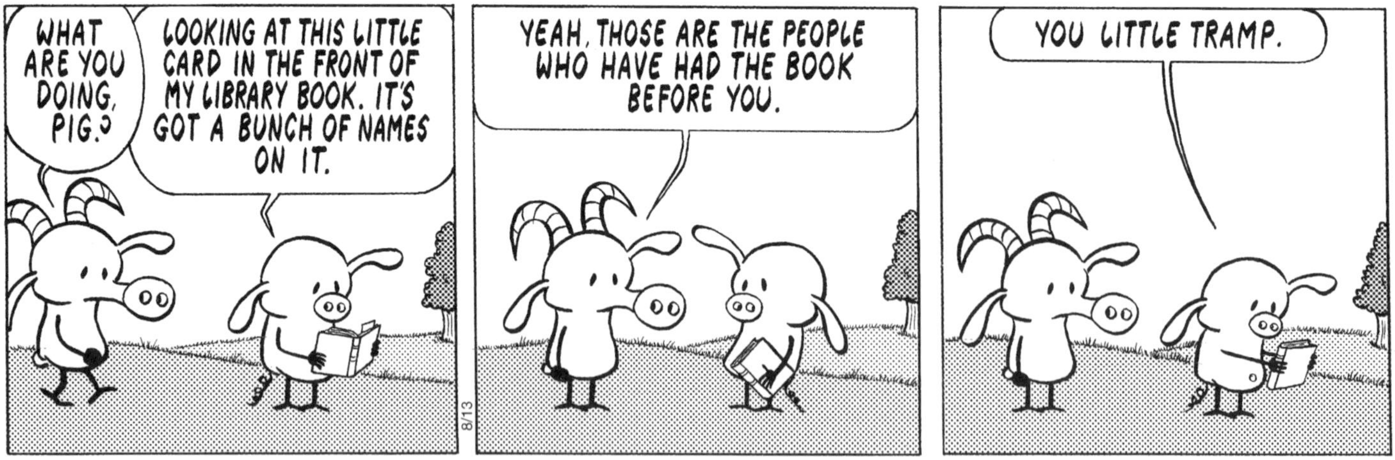
WHAT ARE YOU DOING, PIG.?
LOOKING AT THIS LITTLE CARD IN THE FRONT OF MY LIBRARY BOOK. IT'S GOT A BUNCH OF NAMES ON IT.
YEAH, THOSE ARE THE PEOPLE WHO HAVE HAD THE BOOK BEFORE YOU.
YOU LITTLE TRAMP.
8/13

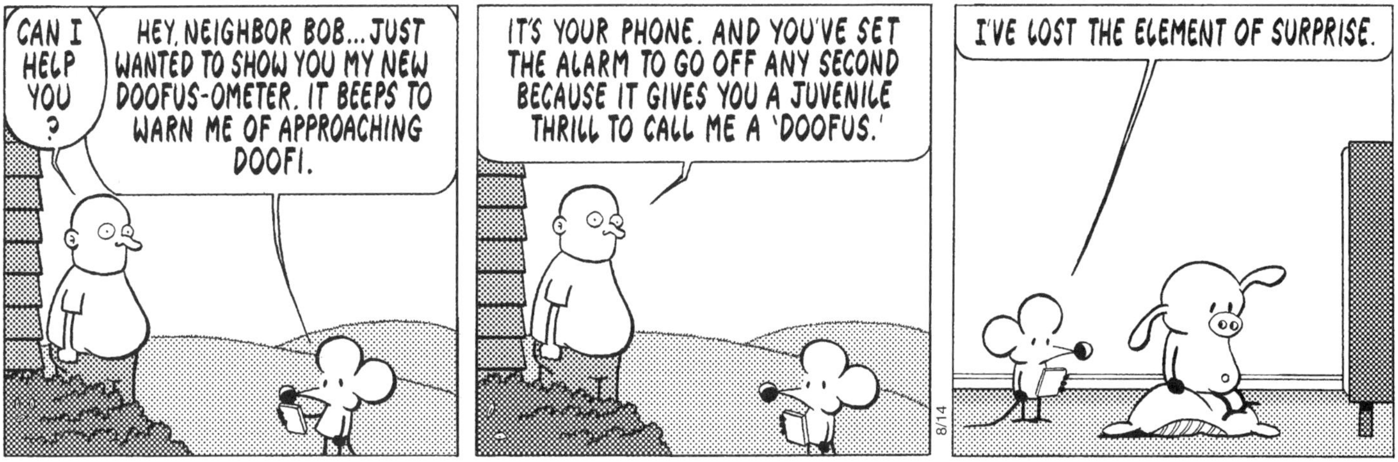
CAN I HELP YOU?
HEY, NEIGHBOR BOB... JUST WANTED TO SHOW YOU MY NEW DOOFUS-OMETER. IT BEEPS TO WARN ME OF APPROACHING DOOFI.
IT'S YOUR PHONE. AND YOU'VE SET THE ALARM TO GO OFF ANY SECOND BECAUSE IT GIVES YOU A JUVENILE THRILL TO CALL ME A 'DOOFUS.'
I'VE LOST THE ELEMENT OF SURPRISE.
8/14

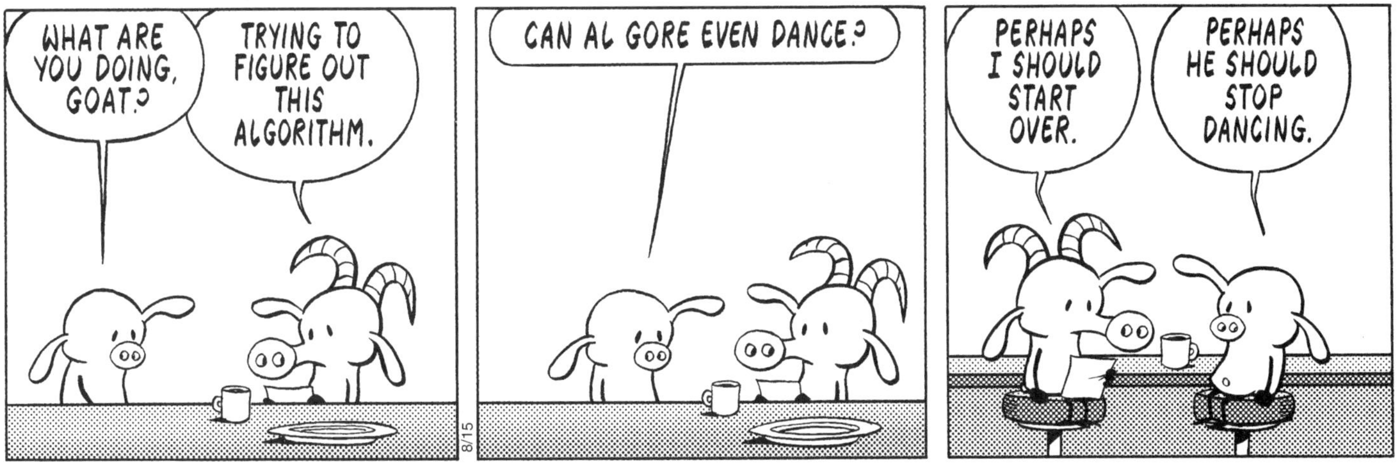
WHAT ARE YOU DOING, GOAT?
TRYING TO FIGURE OUT THIS ALGORITHM.
8/15
CAN AL GORE EVEN DANCE?
PERHAPS I SHOULD START OVER.
PERHAPS HE SHOULD STOP DANCING.

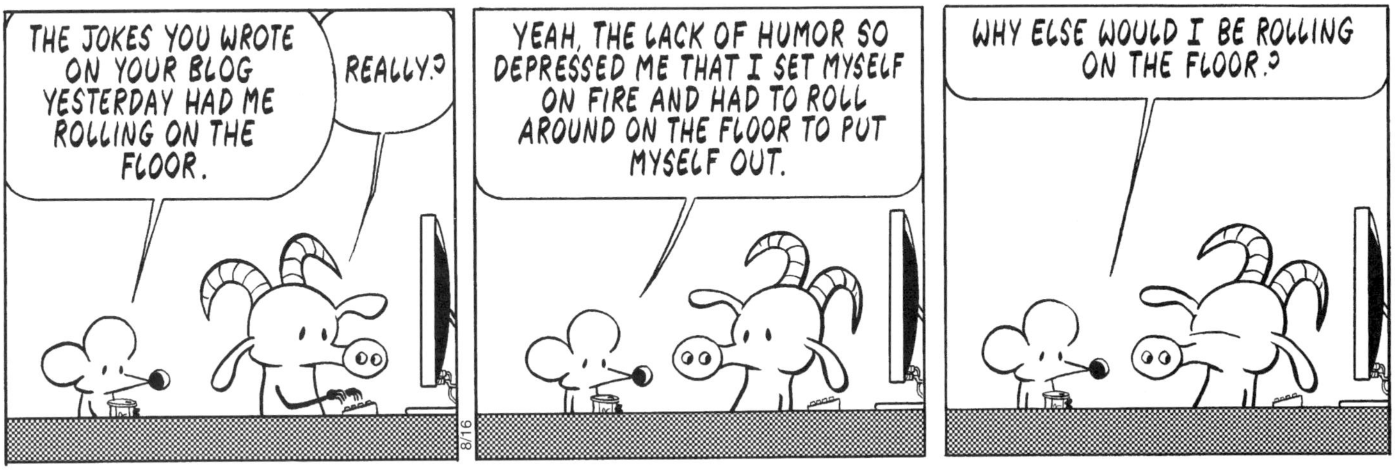
THE JOKES YOU WROTE ON YOUR BLOG YESTERDAY HAD ME ROLLING ON THE FLOOR.
REALLY?
8/16
YEAH, THE LACK OF HUMOR SO DEPRESSED ME THAT I SET MYSELF ON FIRE AND HAD TO ROLL AROUND ON THE FLOOR TO PUT MYSELF OUT.
WHY ELSE WOULD I BE ROLLING ON THE FLOOR?

LEFT!

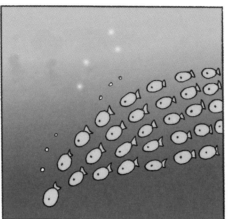

HALT!

SWIMMING IN A BIG SCHOOL AGAIN, TIMMY?

GO AWAY, BOB. THE SCHOOL PROVIDES ME WITH PROTECTION.

IT DOES, HUH? WHAT IS IT, TIMMY—THE SIZE? THE SHAPE?

I DON'T KNOW, BOB. YOU'D HAVE TO ASK MY BUDDIES.

8/17

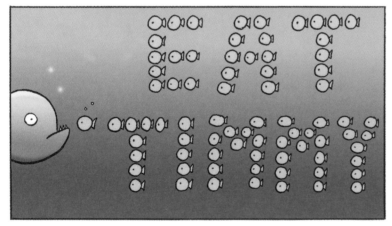

THAT WAS A BRIEF CHARACTER.

CARTOONING IS A CRUEL BUSINESS.

WE'LL MISS YOU, LITTLE TIMMY!

80

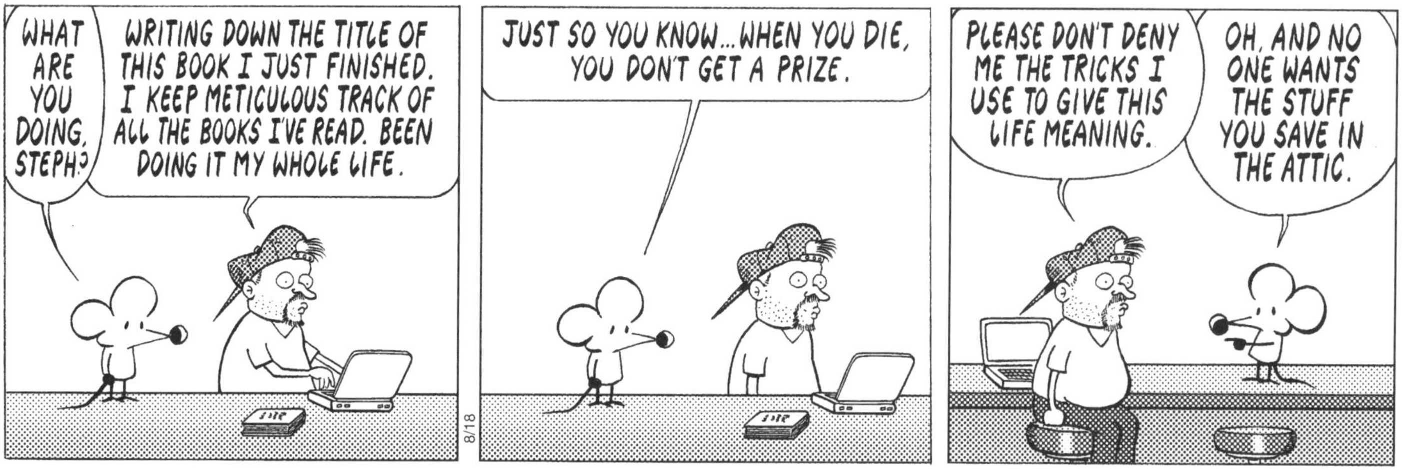
WHAT ARE YOU DOING, STEPH?
WRITING DOWN THE TITLE OF THIS BOOK I JUST FINISHED. I KEEP METICULOUS TRACK OF ALL THE BOOKS I'VE READ. BEEN DOING IT MY WHOLE LIFE.
8/18
JUST SO YOU KNOW...WHEN YOU DIE, YOU DON'T GET A PRIZE.
PLEASE DON'T DENY ME THE TRICKS I USE TO GIVE THIS LIFE MEANING.
OH, AND NO ONE WANTS THE STUFF YOU SAVE IN THE ATTIC.

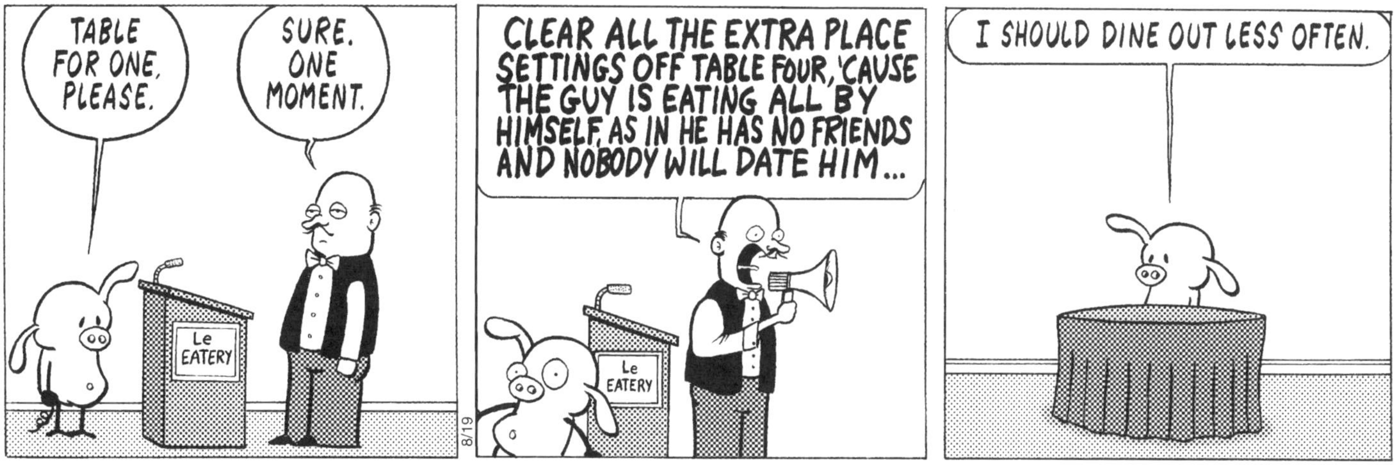
TABLE FOR ONE, PLEASE.
SURE. ONE MOMENT.
Le EATERY
8/19
CLEAR ALL THE EXTRA PLACE SETTINGS OFF TABLE FOUR, 'CAUSE THE GUY IS EATING ALL BY HIMSELF, AS IN HE HAS NO FRIENDS AND NOBODY WILL DATE HIM...
Le EATERY
I SHOULD DINE OUT LESS OFTEN.

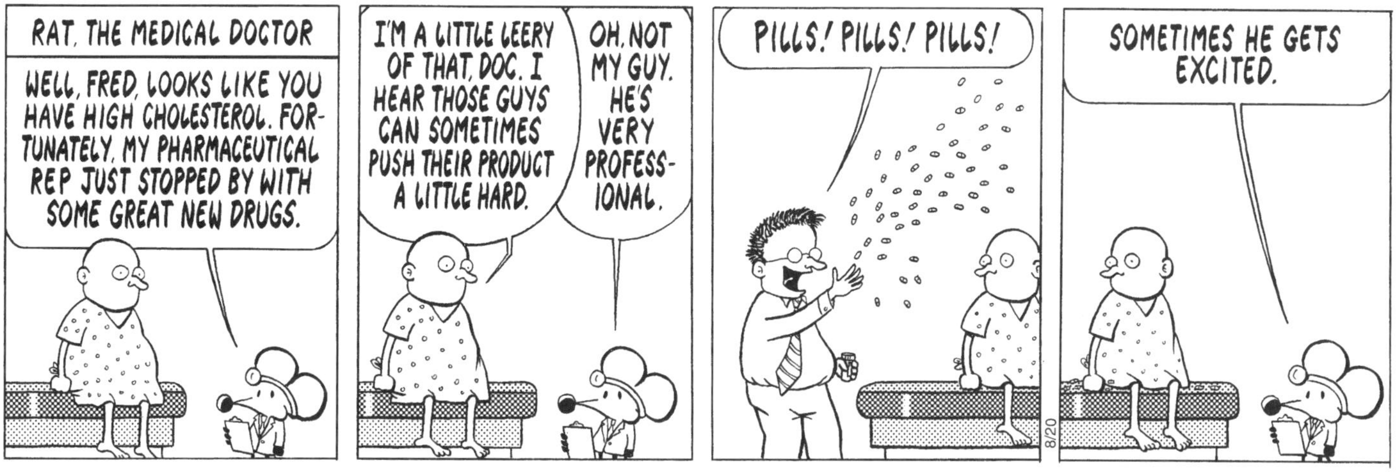
RAT, THE MEDICAL DOCTOR
WELL, FRED, LOOKS LIKE YOU HAVE HIGH CHOLESTEROL. FORTUNATELY, MY PHARMACEUTICAL REP JUST STOPPED BY WITH SOME GREAT NEW DRUGS.
I'M A LITTLE LEERY OF THAT, DOC. I HEAR THOSE GUYS CAN SOMETIMES PUSH THEIR PRODUCT A LITTLE HARD.
OH, NOT MY GUY. HE'S VERY PROFESSIONAL.
PILLS! PILLS! PILLS!
8/20
SOMETIMES HE GETS EXCITED.

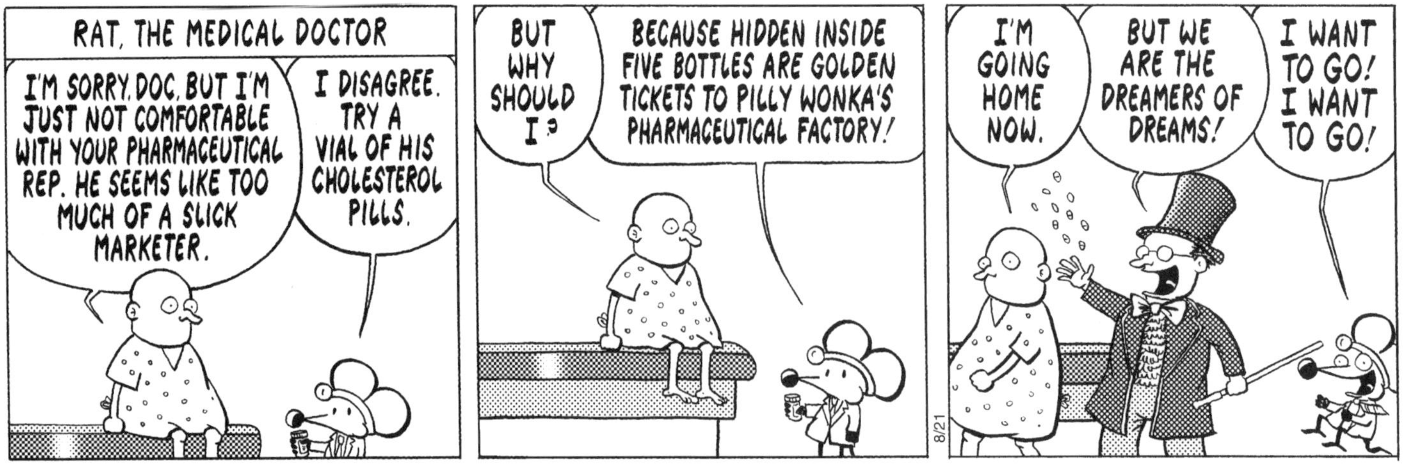
RAT, THE MEDICAL DOCTOR
I'M SORRY, DOC, BUT I'M JUST NOT COMFORTABLE WITH YOUR PHARMACEUTICAL REP. HE SEEMS LIKE TOO MUCH OF A SLICK MARKETER.
I DISAGREE. TRY A VIAL OF HIS CHOLESTEROL PILLS.
BUT WHY SHOULD I?
BECAUSE HIDDEN INSIDE FIVE BOTTLES ARE GOLDEN TICKETS TO PILLY WONKA'S PHARMACEUTICAL FACTORY!
I'M GOING HOME NOW.
BUT WE ARE THE DREAMERS OF DREAMS!
I WANT TO GO! I WANT TO GO!
8/21

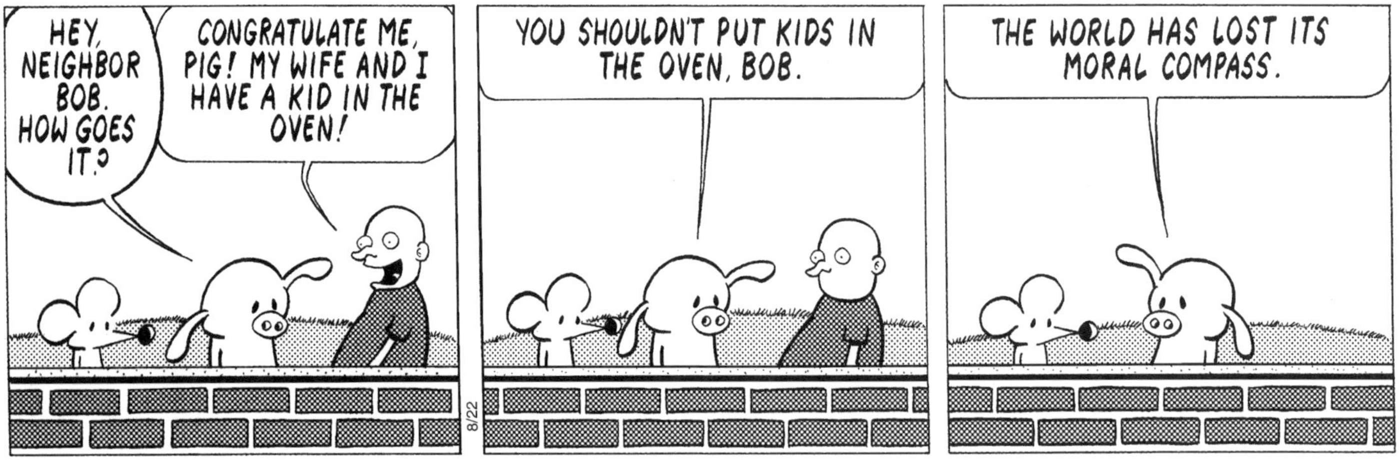
HEY, NEIGHBOR BOB. HOW GOES IT?
CONGRATULATE ME, PIG! MY WIFE AND I HAVE A KID IN THE OVEN!
8/22
YOU SHOULDN'T PUT KIDS IN THE OVEN, BOB.
THE WORLD HAS LOST ITS MORAL COMPASS.

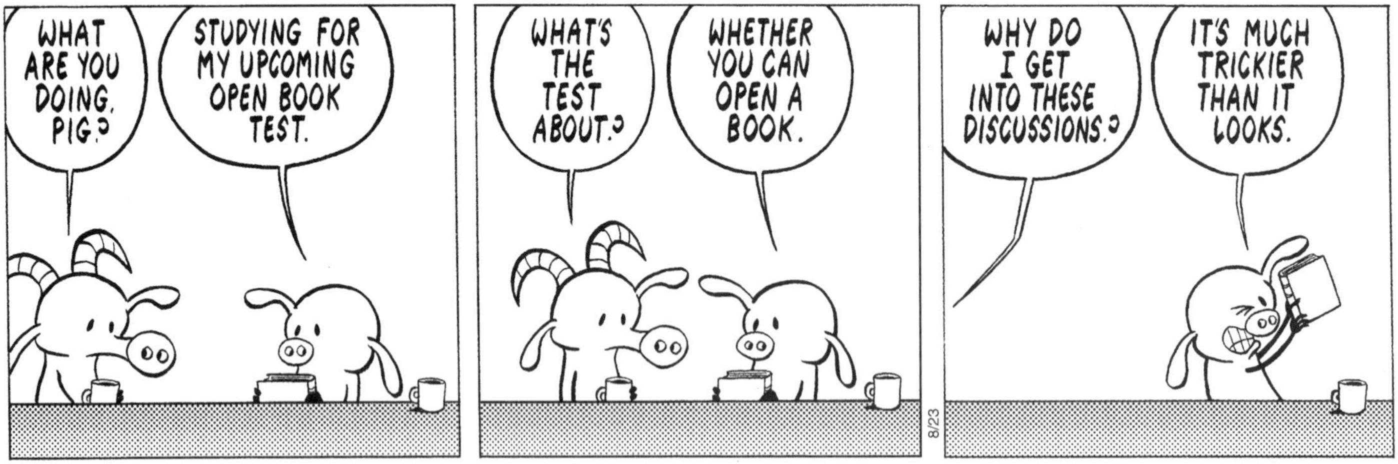
WHAT ARE YOU DOING, PIG?
STUDYING FOR MY UPCOMING OPEN BOOK TEST.
WHAT'S THE TEST ABOUT?
WHETHER YOU CAN OPEN A BOOK.
8/23
WHY DO I GET INTO THESE DISCUSSIONS?
IT'S MUCH TRICKIER THAN IT LOOKS.

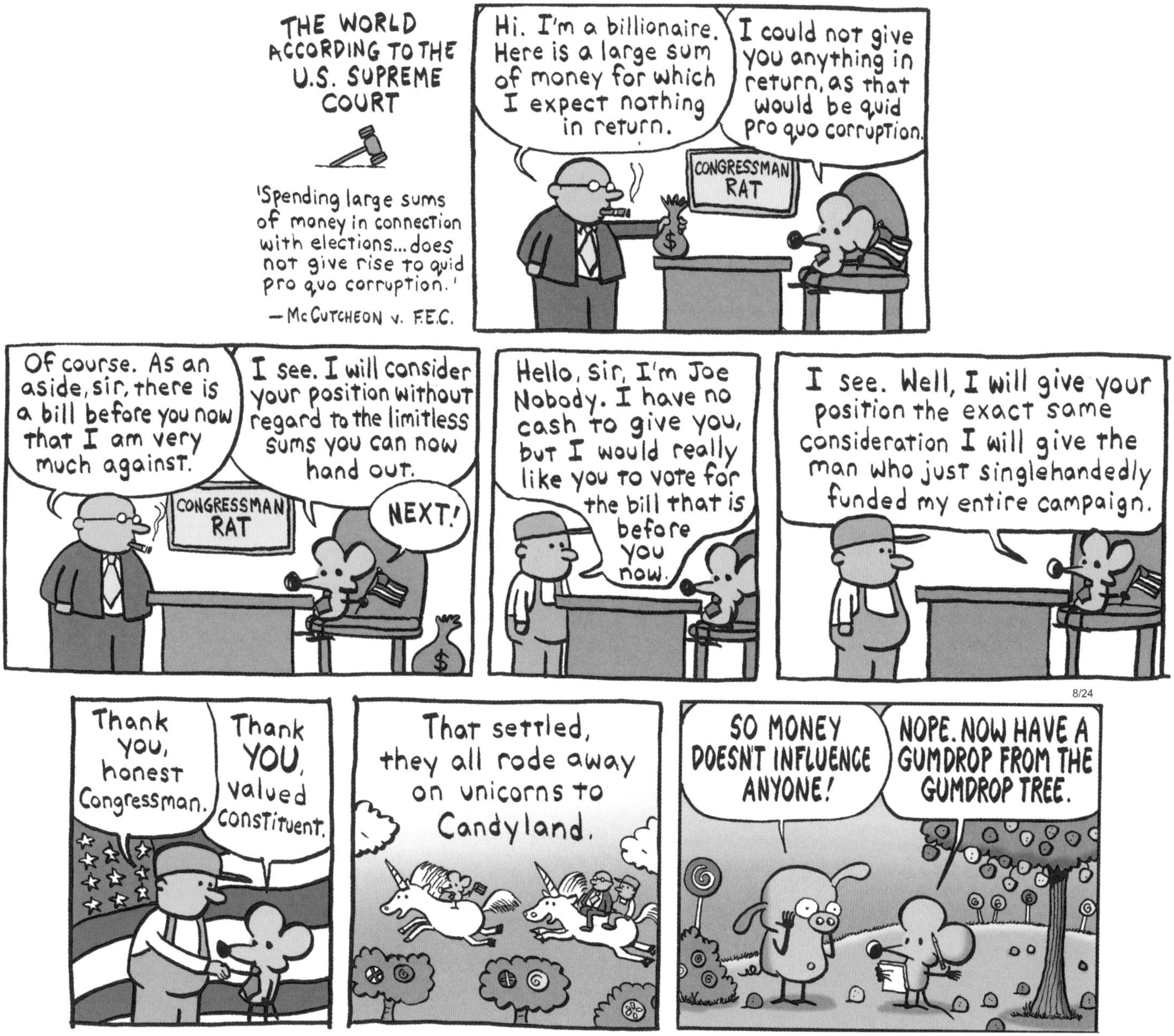
THE WORLD ACCORDING TO THE U.S. SUPREME COURT
'Spending large sums of money in connection with elections... does not give rise to quid pro quo corruption.'
— McCUTCHEON v. F.E.C.
Hi. I'm a billionaire. Here is a large sum of money for which I expect nothing in return.
I could not give you anything in return, as that would be quid pro quo corruption.
CONGRESSMAN RAT
Of course. As an aside, sir, there is a bill before you now that I am very much against.
I see. I will consider your position without regard to the limitless sums you can now hand out.
CONGRESSMAN RAT
NEXT!
Hello, sir, I'm Joe Nobody. I have no cash to give you, but I would really like you to vote for the bill that is before you now.
I see. Well, I will give your position the exact same consideration I will give the man who just singlehandedly funded my entire campaign.
8/24
Thank you, honest Congressman.
Thank YOU, valued constituent.
That settled, they all rode away on unicorns to Candyland.
SO MONEY DOESN'T INFLUENCE ANYONE!
NOPE. NOW HAVE A GUMDROP FROM THE GUMDROP TREE.

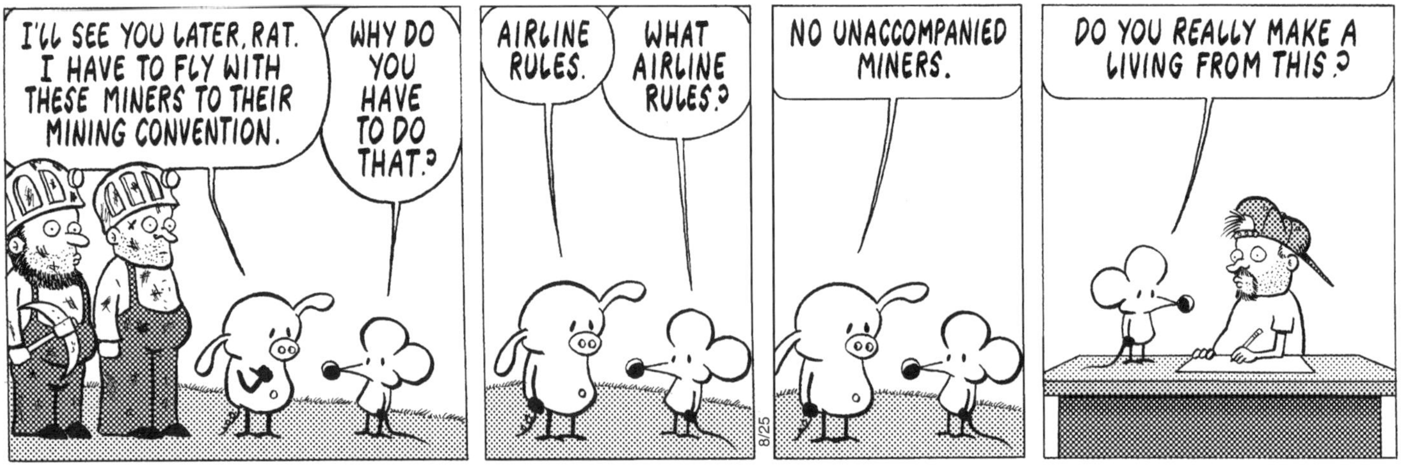
I'LL SEE YOU LATER, RAT. I HAVE TO FLY WITH THESE MINERS TO THEIR MINING CONVENTION.
WHY DO YOU HAVE TO DO THAT?
AIRLINE RULES.
WHAT AIRLINE RULES?
8/25
NO UNACCOMPANIED MINERS.
DO YOU REALLY MAKE A LIVING FROM THIS?

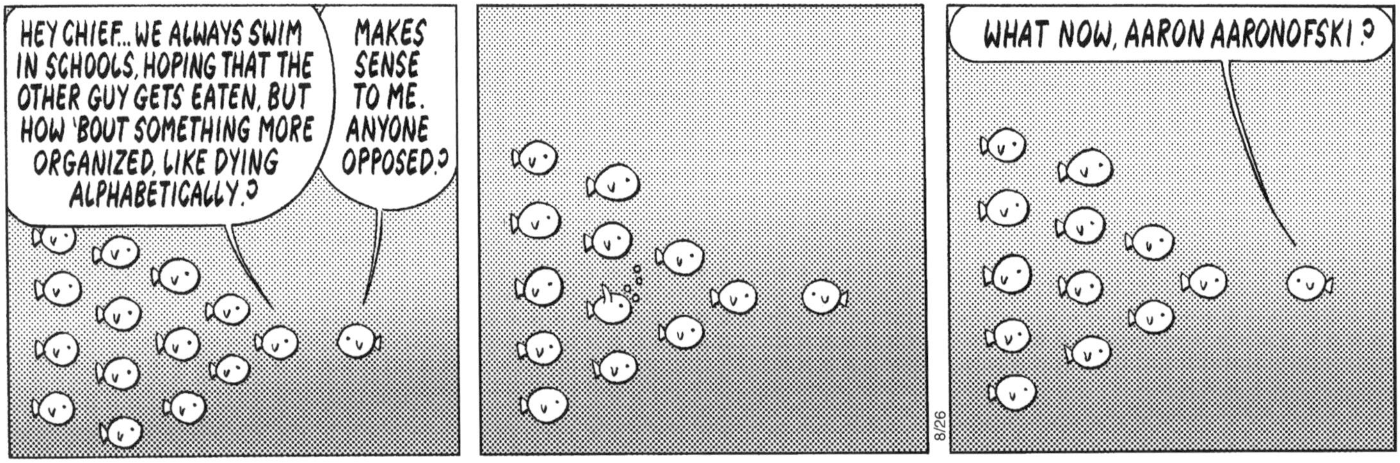
HEY CHIEF...WE ALWAYS SWIM IN SCHOOLS, HOPING THAT THE OTHER GUY GETS EATEN, BUT HOW 'BOUT SOMETHING MORE ORGANIZED, LIKE DYING ALPHABETICALLY?
MAKES SENSE TO ME. ANYONE OPPOSED?
8/26
WHAT NOW, AARON AARONOFSKI?

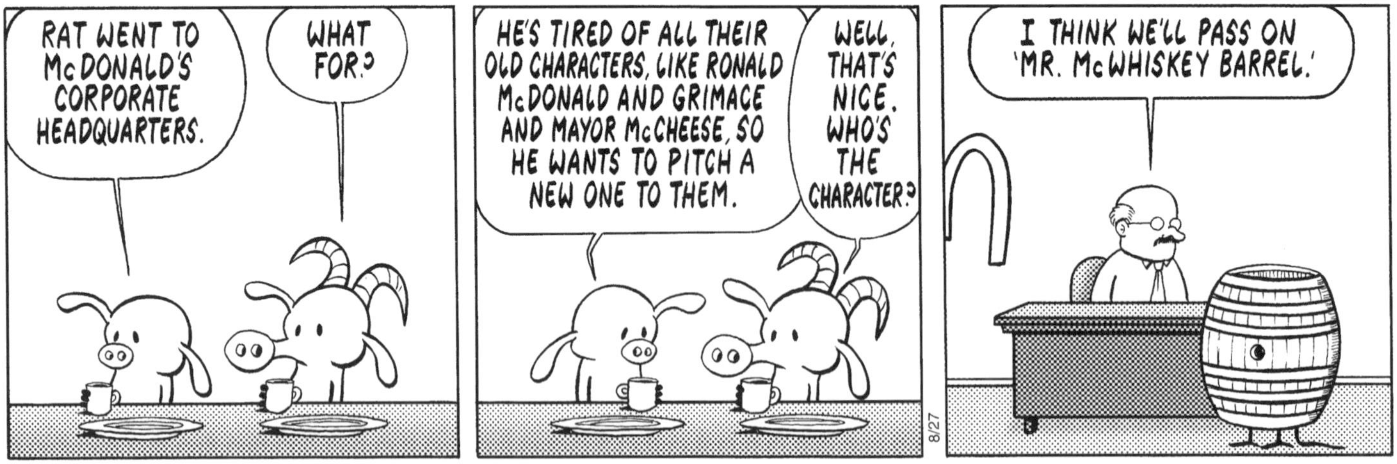
RAT WENT TO McDONALD'S CORPORATE HEADQUARTERS.
WHAT FOR?
HE'S TIRED OF ALL THEIR OLD CHARACTERS, LIKE RONALD McDONALD AND GRIMACE AND MAYOR McCHEESE, SO HE WANTS TO PITCH A NEW ONE TO THEM.
WELL, THAT'S NICE. WHO'S THE CHARACTER?
8/27
I THINK WE'LL PASS ON 'MR. McWHISKEY BARREL.'

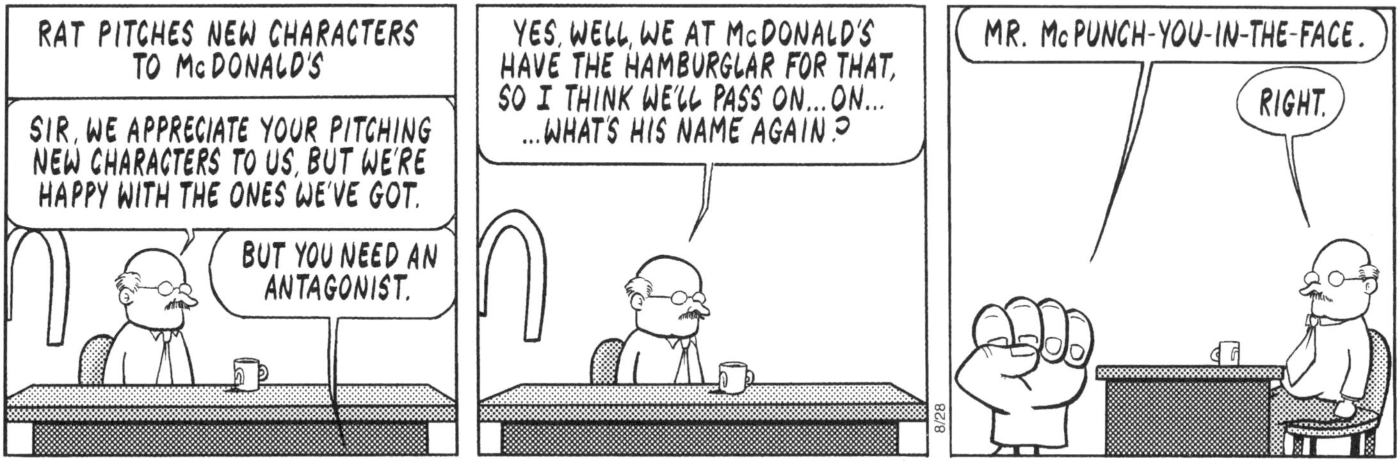
RAT PITCHES NEW CHARACTERS TO McDONALD'S
SIR, WE APPRECIATE YOUR PITCHING NEW CHARACTERS TO US, BUT WE'RE HAPPY WITH THE ONES WE'VE GOT.
BUT YOU NEED AN ANTAGONIST.
YES, WELL, WE AT McDONALD'S HAVE THE HAMBURGLAR FOR THAT, SO I THINK WE'LL PASS ON... ON... ...WHAT'S HIS NAME AGAIN?
8/28
MR. McPUNCH-YOU-IN-THE-FACE.
RIGHT.

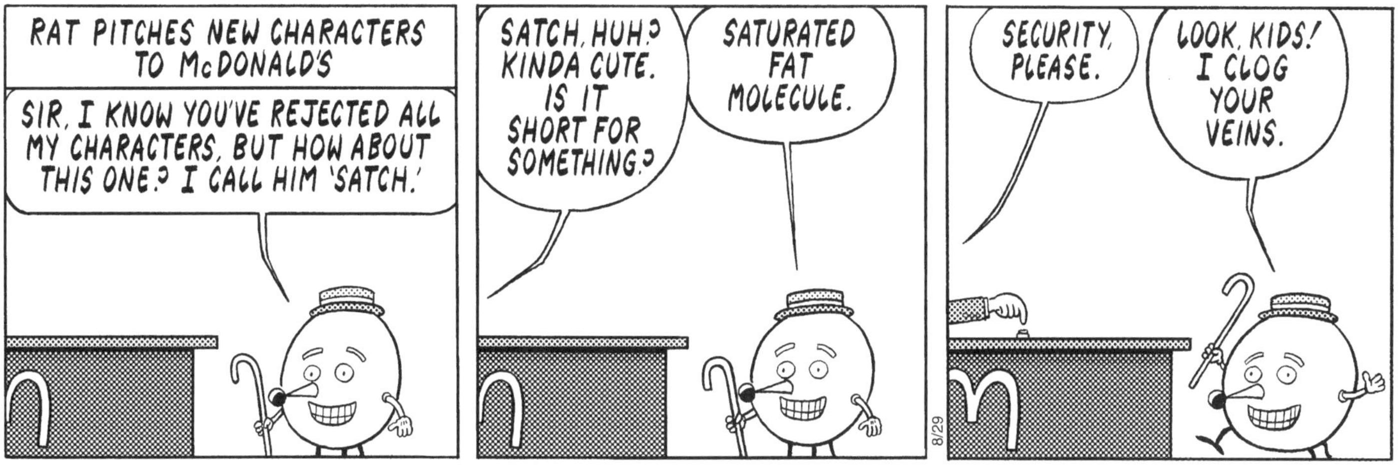
RAT PITCHES NEW CHARACTERS TO McDONALD'S
SIR, I KNOW YOU'VE REJECTED ALL MY CHARACTERS, BUT HOW ABOUT THIS ONE? I CALL HIM 'SATCH.'
SATCH, HUH? KINDA CUTE. IS IT SHORT FOR SOMETHING?
SATURATED FAT MOLECULE.
8/29
SECURITY, PLEASE.
LOOK, KIDS! I CLOG YOUR VEINS.

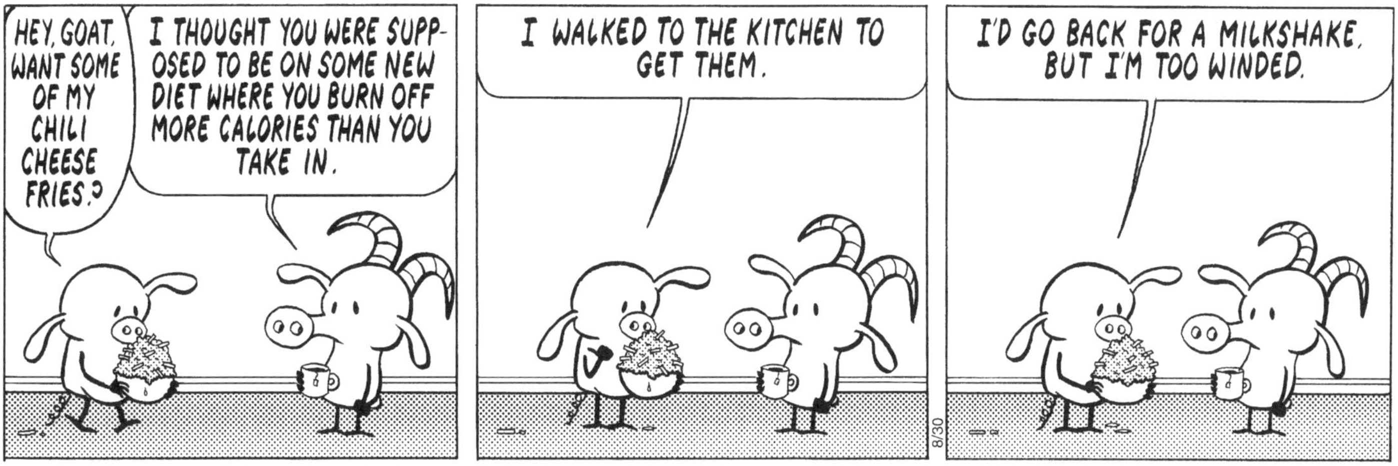
HEY, GOAT, WANT SOME OF MY CHILI CHEESE FRIES?
I THOUGHT YOU WERE SUPPOSED TO BE ON SOME NEW DIET WHERE YOU BURN OFF MORE CALORIES THAN YOU TAKE IN.
I WALKED TO THE KITCHEN TO GET THEM.
8/30
I'D GO BACK FOR A MILKSHAKE, BUT I'M TOO WINDED.

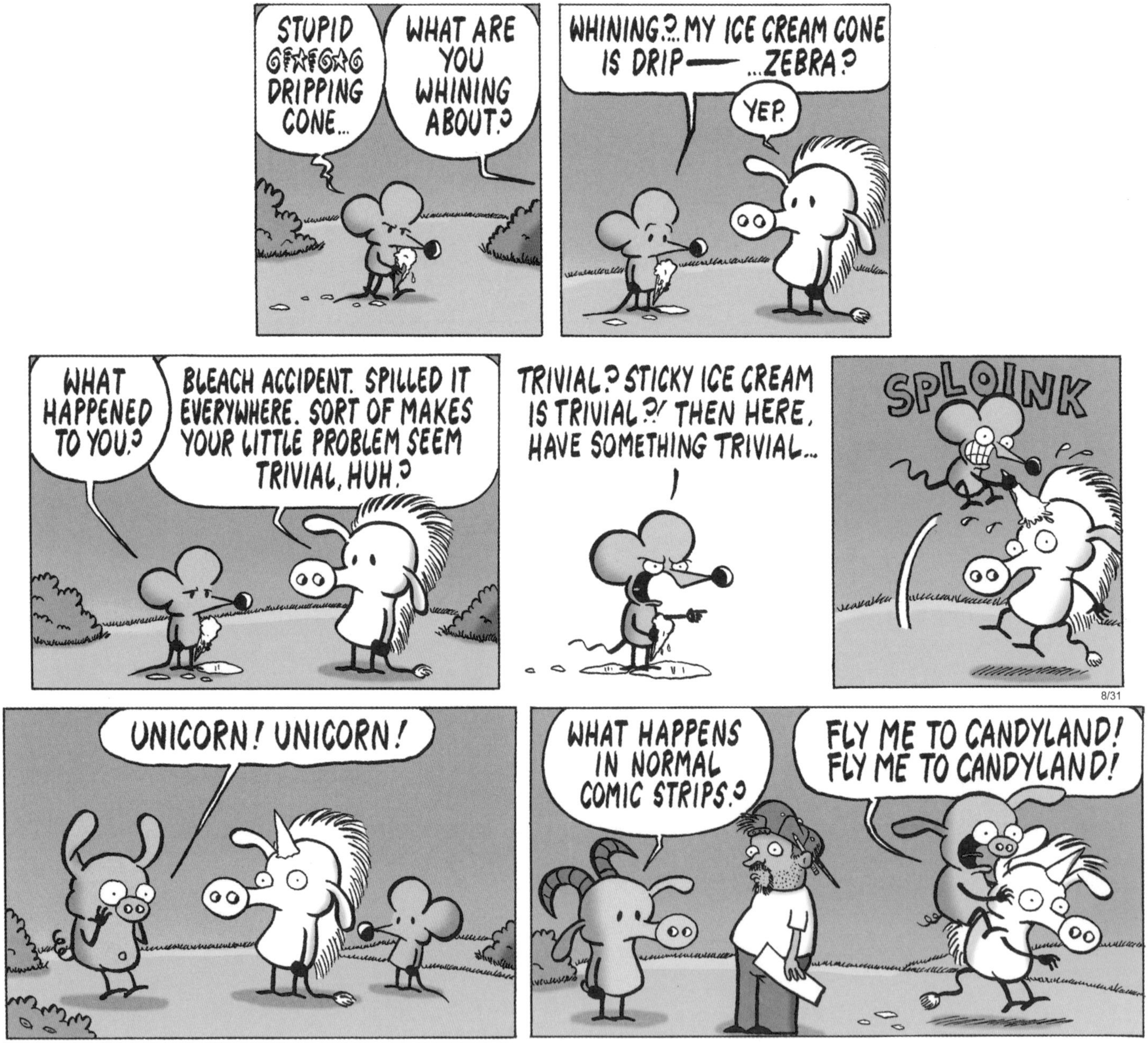
STUPID @#*@%@ DRIPPING CONE...
WHAT ARE YOU WHINING ABOUT?
WHINING?... MY ICE CREAM CONE IS DRIP— ...ZEBRA?
YEP.
WHAT HAPPENED TO YOU?
BLEACH ACCIDENT. SPILLED IT EVERYWHERE. SORT OF MAKES YOUR LITTLE PROBLEM SEEM TRIVIAL, HUH?
TRIVIAL? STICKY ICE CREAM IS TRIVIAL?! THEN HERE, HAVE SOMETHING TRIVIAL...
SPLOINK
8/31
UNICORN! UNICORN!
WHAT HAPPENS IN NORMAL COMIC STRIPS?
FLY ME TO CANDYLAND! FLY ME TO CANDYLAND!

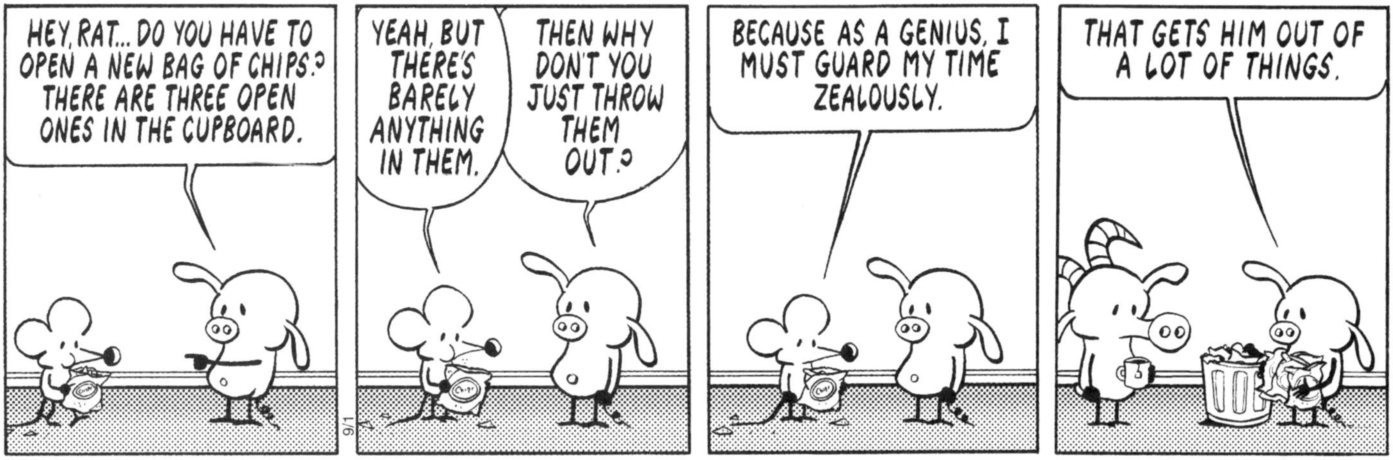
HEY, RAT... DO YOU HAVE TO OPEN A NEW BAG OF CHIPS? THERE ARE THREE OPEN ONES IN THE CUPBOARD.
YEAH, BUT THERE'S BARELY ANYTHING IN THEM.
THEN WHY DON'T YOU JUST THROW THEM OUT?
BECAUSE AS A GENIUS, I MUST GUARD MY TIME ZEALOUSLY.
THAT GETS HIM OUT OF A LOT OF THINGS.
9/1

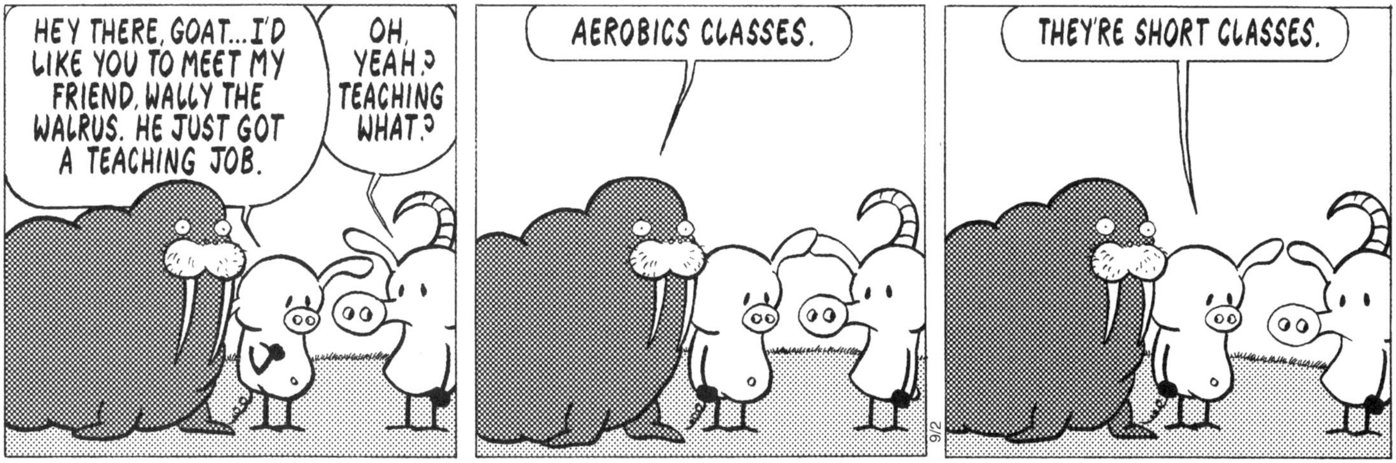
HEY THERE, GOAT... I'D LIKE YOU TO MEET MY FRIEND, WALLY THE WALRUS. HE JUST GOT A TEACHING JOB.
OH, YEAH? TEACHING WHAT?
AEROBICS CLASSES.
THEY'RE SHORT CLASSES.
9/2

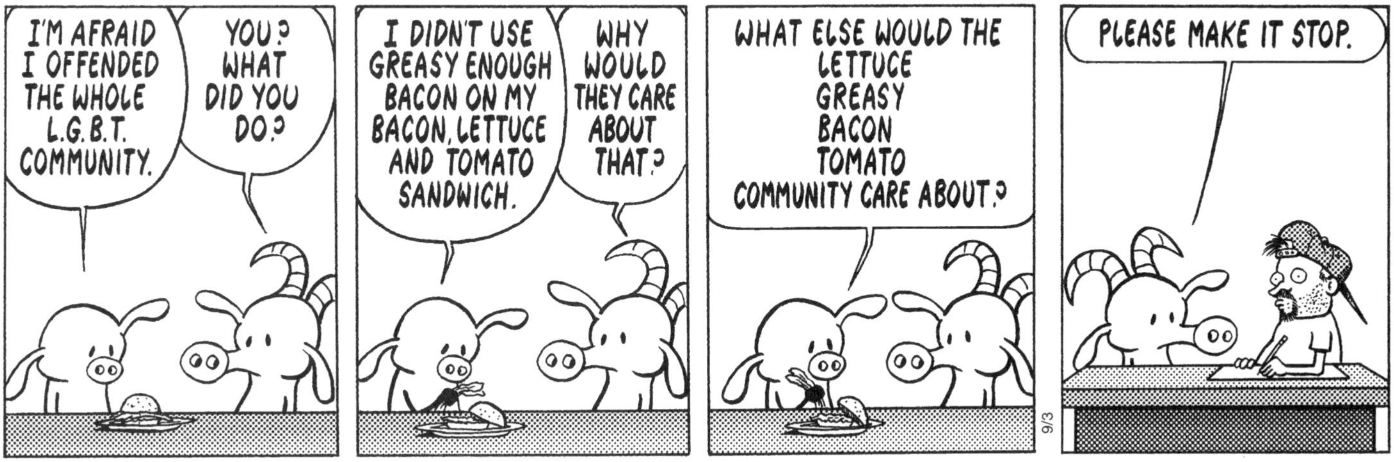
I'M AFRAID I OFFENDED THE WHOLE L.G.B.T. COMMUNITY.
YOU? WHAT DID YOU DO?
I DIDN'T USE GREASY ENOUGH BACON ON MY BACON, LETTUCE AND TOMATO SANDWICH.
WHY WOULD THEY CARE ABOUT THAT?
WHAT ELSE WOULD THE LETTUCE GREASY BACON TOMATO COMMUNITY CARE ABOUT?
PLEASE MAKE IT STOP.
9/3

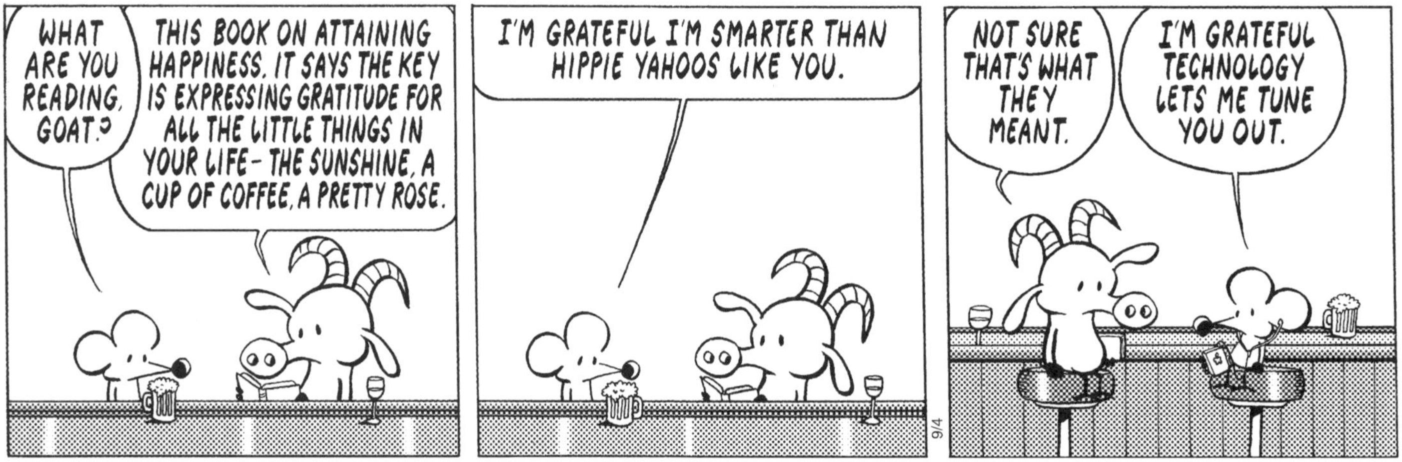
WHAT ARE YOU READING, GOAT?
THIS BOOK ON ATTAINING HAPPINESS. IT SAYS THE KEY IS EXPRESSING GRATITUDE FOR ALL THE LITTLE THINGS IN YOUR LIFE - THE SUNSHINE, A CUP OF COFFEE, A PRETTY ROSE.
I'M GRATEFUL I'M SMARTER THAN HIPPIE YAHOOS LIKE YOU.
9/4
NOT SURE THAT'S WHAT THEY MEANT.
I'M GRATEFUL TECHNOLOGY LETS ME TUNE YOU OUT.

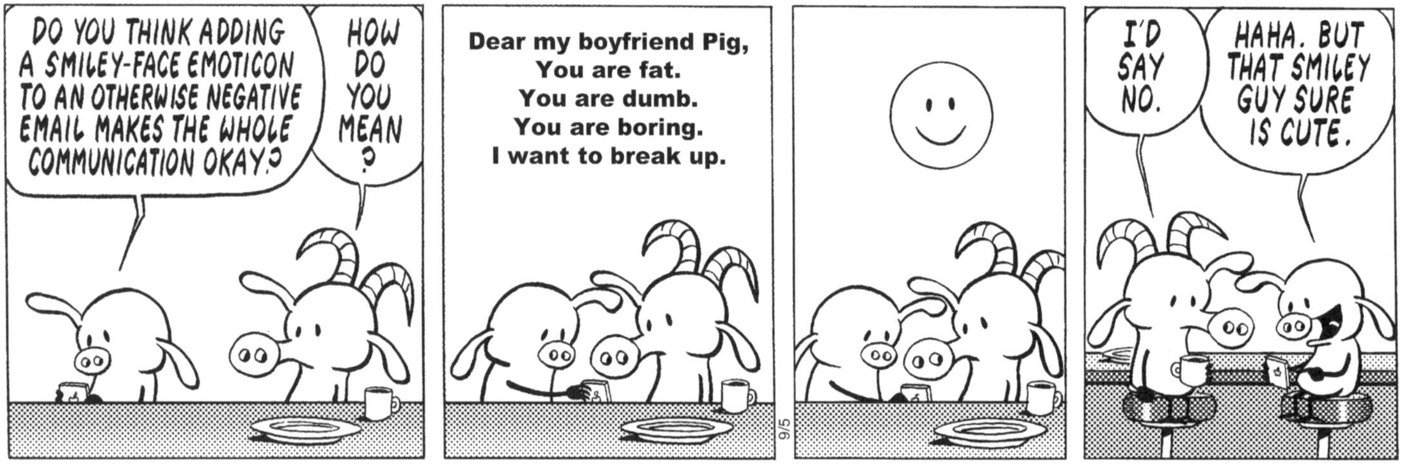
DO YOU THINK ADDING A SMILEY-FACE EMOTICON TO AN OTHERWISE NEGATIVE EMAIL MAKES THE WHOLE COMMUNICATION OKAY?
HOW DO YOU MEAN?
Dear my boyfriend Pig,
You are fat.
You are dumb.
You are boring.
I want to break up.
9/5
I'D SAY NO.
HAHA. BUT THAT SMILEY GUY SURE IS CUTE.

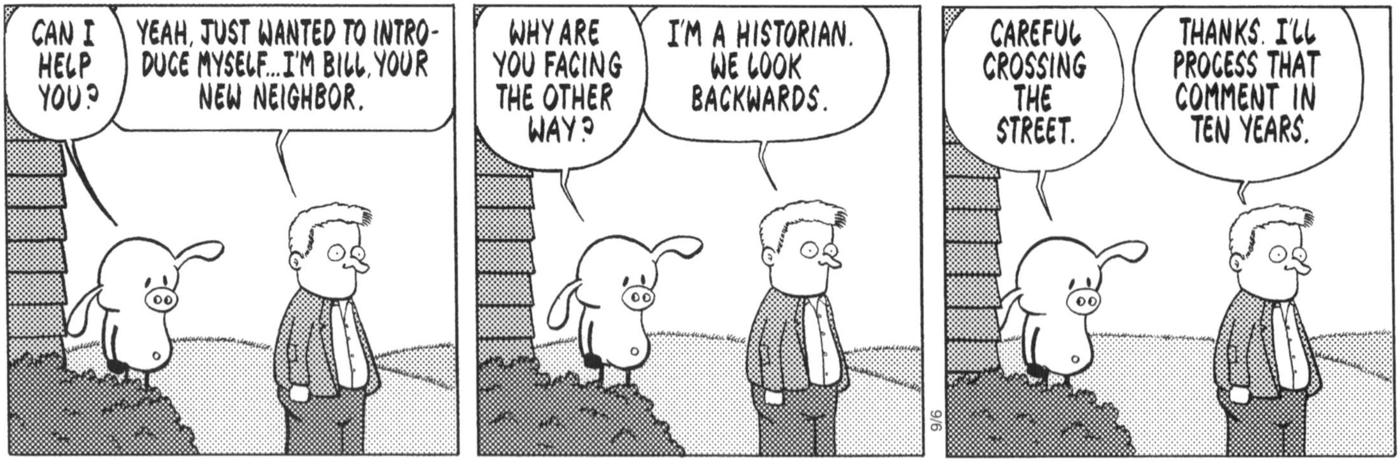
CAN I HELP YOU?
YEAH, JUST WANTED TO INTRODUCE MYSELF...I'M BILL, YOUR NEW NEIGHBOR.
WHY ARE YOU FACING THE OTHER WAY?
I'M A HISTORIAN. WE LOOK BACKWARDS.
9/6
CAREFUL CROSSING THE STREET.
THANKS. I'LL PROCESS THAT COMMENT IN TEN YEARS.

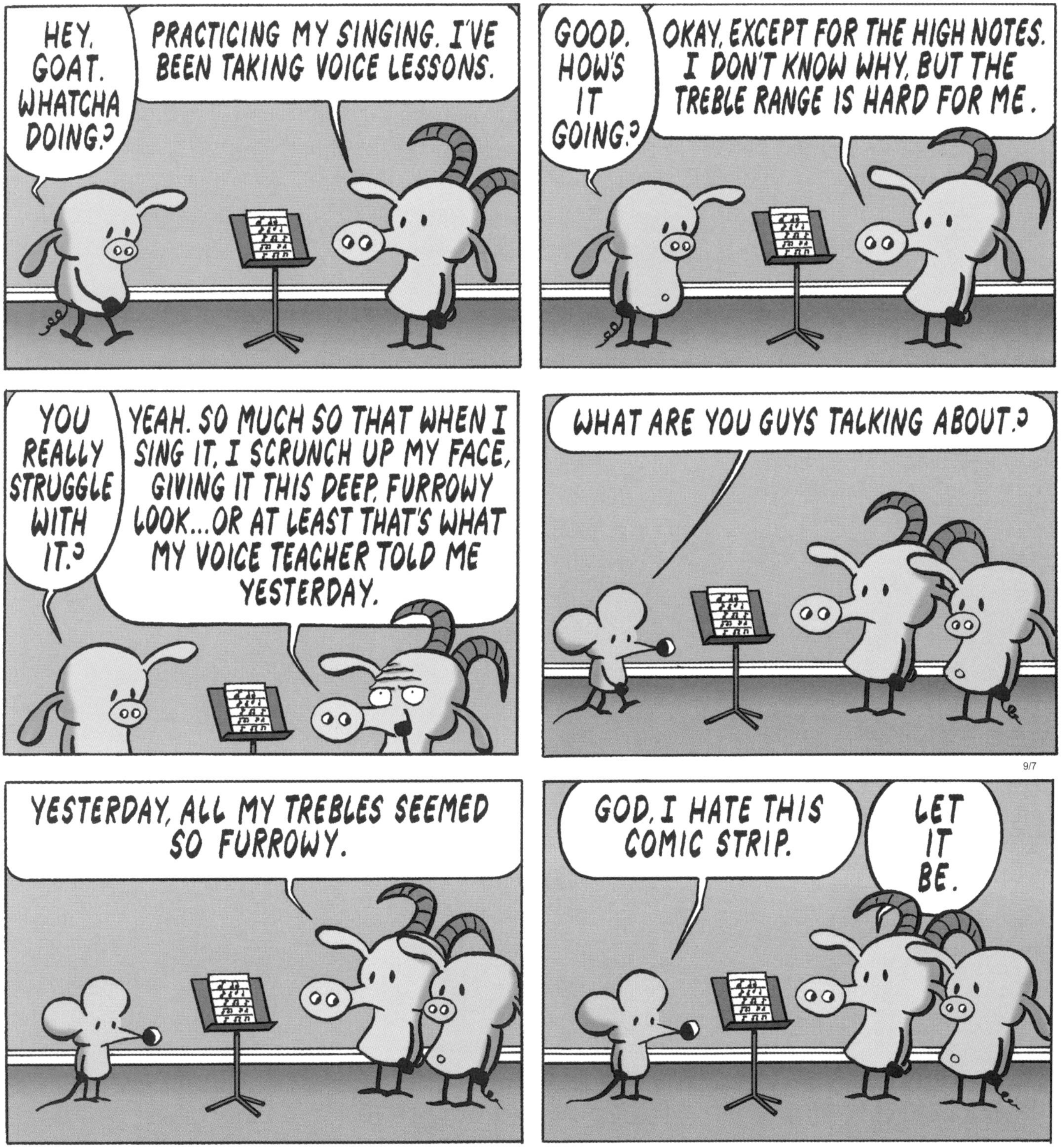
HEY, GOAT. WHATCHA DOING?
PRACTICING MY SINGING. I'VE BEEN TAKING VOICE LESSONS.
GOOD. HOW'S IT GOING?
OKAY, EXCEPT FOR THE HIGH NOTES. I DON'T KNOW WHY, BUT THE TREBLE RANGE IS HARD FOR ME.
YOU REALLY STRUGGLE WITH IT?
YEAH. SO MUCH SO THAT WHEN I SING IT, I SCRUNCH UP MY FACE, GIVING IT THIS DEEP, FURROWY LOOK...OR AT LEAST THAT'S WHAT MY VOICE TEACHER TOLD ME YESTERDAY.
WHAT ARE YOU GUYS TALKING ABOUT?
9/7
YESTERDAY, ALL MY TREBLES SEEMED SO FURROWY.
GOD, I HATE THIS COMIC STRIP.
LET IT BE.

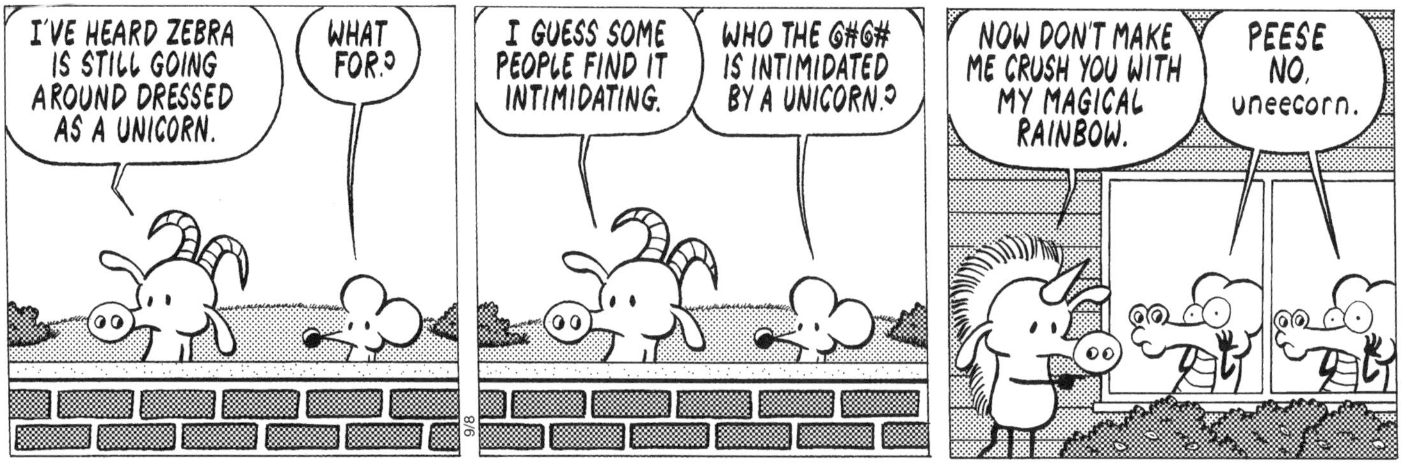

I'VE HEARD ZEBRA IS STILL GOING AROUND DRESSED AS A UNICORN.
WHAT FOR?
I GUESS SOME PEOPLE FIND IT INTIMIDATING.
WHO THE G#G# IS INTIMIDATED BY A UNICORN?
9/8
NOW DON'T MAKE ME CRUSH YOU WITH MY MAGICAL RAINBOW.
PEESE NO, uneecorn.

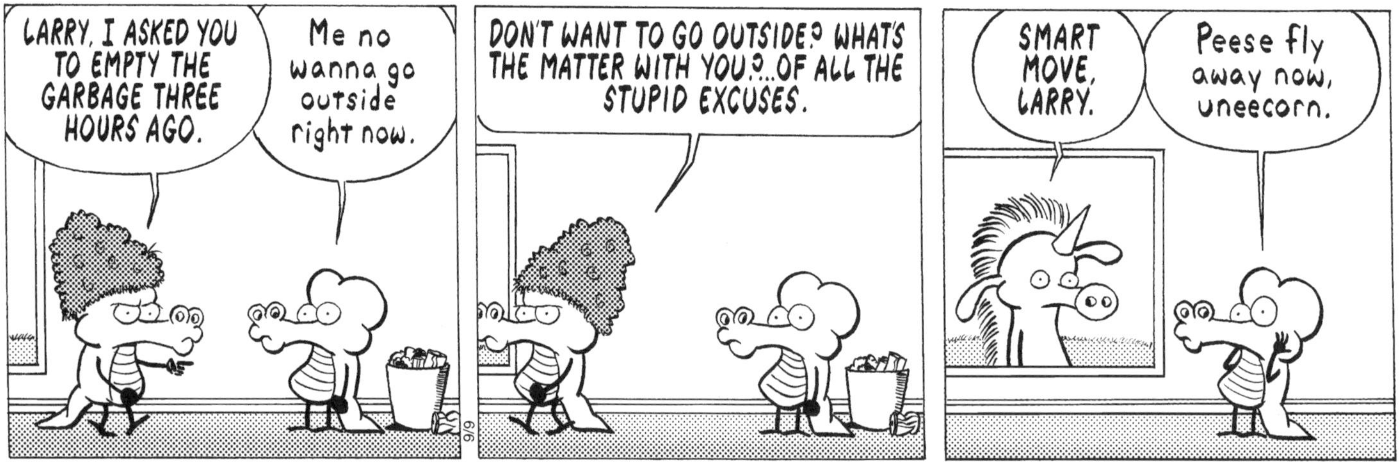

LARRY, I ASKED YOU TO EMPTY THE GARBAGE THREE HOURS AGO.
Me no wanna go outside right now.
DON'T WANT TO GO OUTSIDE? WHAT'S THE MATTER WITH YOU?...OF ALL THE STUPID EXCUSES.
9/9
SMART MOVE, LARRY.
Peese fly away now, uneecorn.

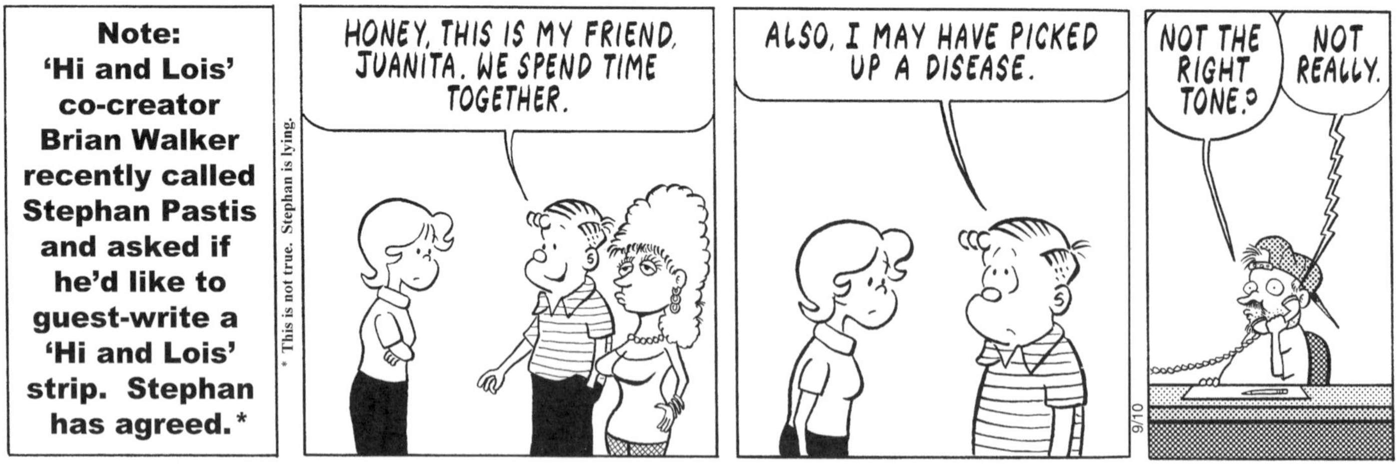

Note: 'Hi and Lois' co-creator Brian Walker recently called Stephan Pastis and asked if he'd like to guest-write a 'Hi and Lois' strip. Stephan has agreed.*
* This is not true. Stephan is lying.
HONEY, THIS IS MY FRIEND, JUANITA. WE SPEND TIME TOGETHER.
ALSO, I MAY HAVE PICKED UP A DISEASE.
9/10
NOT THE RIGHT TONE?
NOT REALLY.

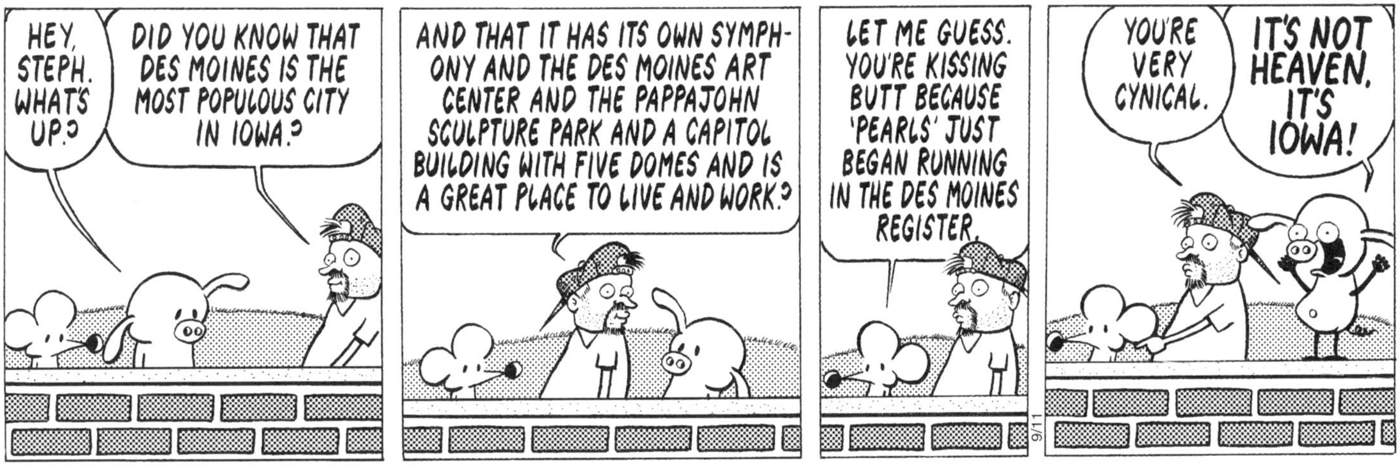
HEY, STEPH. WHAT'S UP?
DID YOU KNOW THAT DES MOINES IS THE MOST POPULOUS CITY IN IOWA?
AND THAT IT HAS ITS OWN SYMPHONY AND THE DES MOINES ART CENTER AND THE PAPPAJOHN SCULPTURE PARK AND A CAPITOL BUILDING WITH FIVE DOMES AND IS A GREAT PLACE TO LIVE AND WORK?
LET ME GUESS. YOU'RE KISSING BUTT BECAUSE 'PEARLS' JUST BEGAN RUNNING IN THE DES MOINES REGISTER.
9/11
YOU'RE VERY CYNICAL.
IT'S NOT HEAVEN. IT'S IOWA!

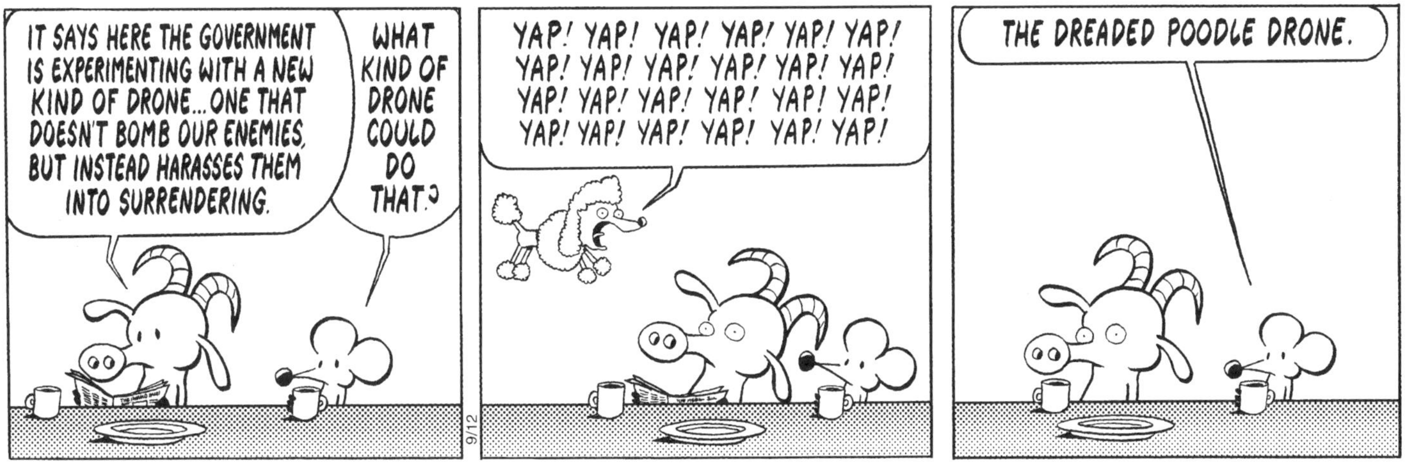
IT SAYS HERE THE GOVERNMENT IS EXPERIMENTING WITH A NEW KIND OF DRONE...ONE THAT DOESN'T BOMB OUR ENEMIES, BUT INSTEAD HARASSES THEM INTO SURRENDERING.
WHAT KIND OF DRONE COULD DO THAT?
9/12
YAP! YAP! YAP! YAP! YAP! YAP! YAP! YAP! YAP! YAP! YAP! YAP! YAP! YAP! YAP! YAP! YAP! YAP! YAP! YAP! YAP! YAP! YAP! YAP!
THE DREADED POODLE DRONE.

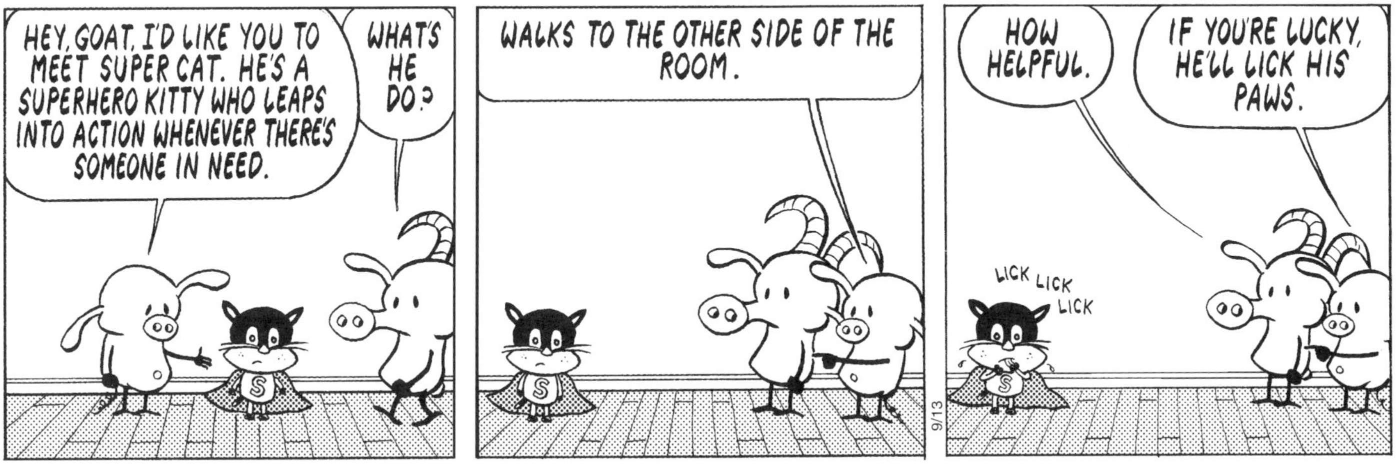
HEY, GOAT, I'D LIKE YOU TO MEET SUPER CAT. HE'S A SUPERHERO KITTY WHO LEAPS INTO ACTION WHENEVER THERE'S SOMEONE IN NEED.
WHAT'S HE DO?
WALKS TO THE OTHER SIDE OF THE ROOM.
9/13
HOW HELPFUL.
IF YOU'RE LUCKY, HE'LL LICK HIS PAWS.
LICK LICK LICK

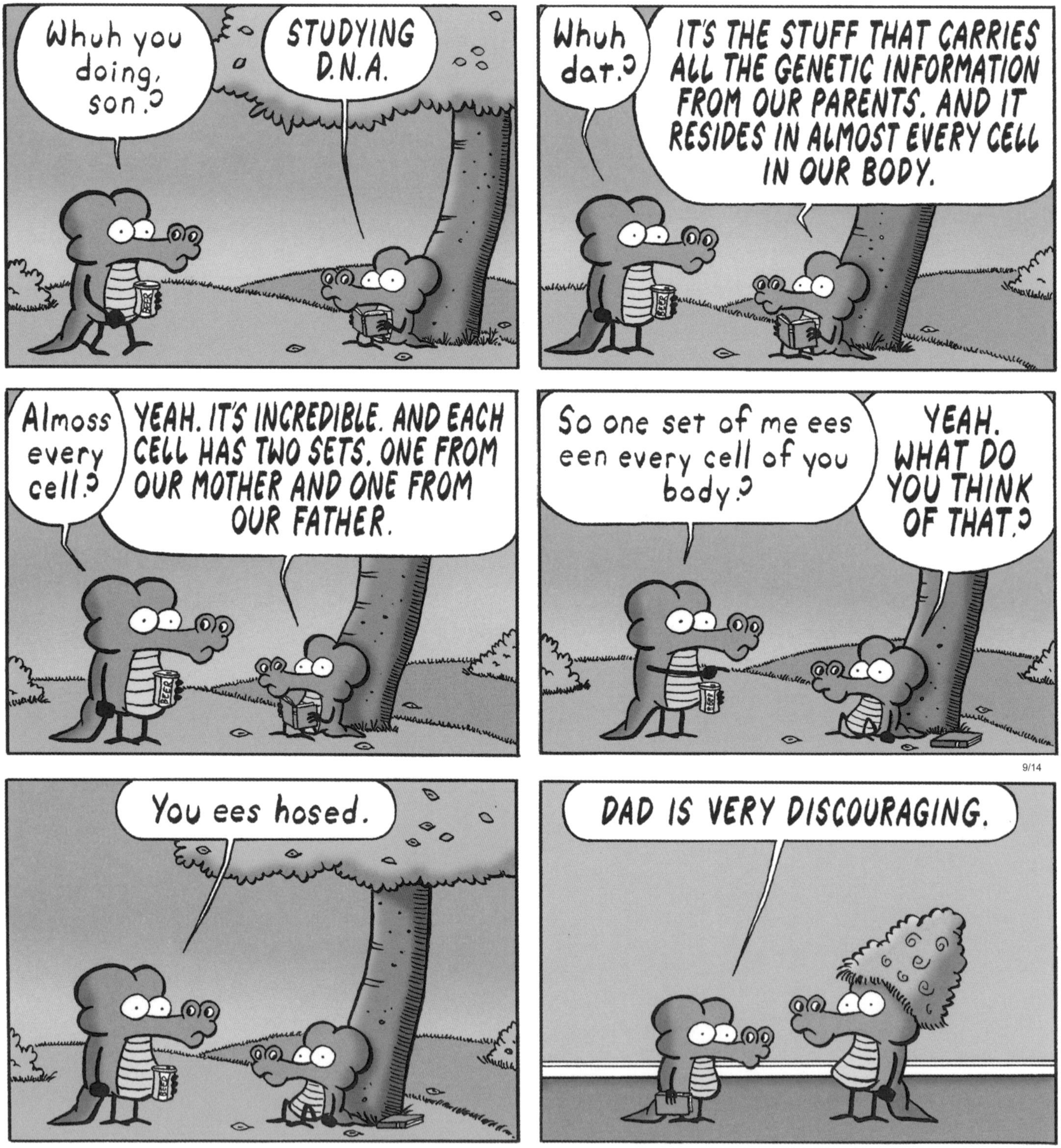
Whuh you doing, son.?
STUDYING D.N.A.
Whuh dat.?
IT'S THE STUFF THAT CARRIES ALL THE GENETIC INFORMATION FROM OUR PARENTS. AND IT RESIDES IN ALMOST EVERY CELL IN OUR BODY.
Almoss every cell.?
YEAH. IT'S INCREDIBLE. AND EACH CELL HAS TWO SETS. ONE FROM OUR MOTHER AND ONE FROM OUR FATHER.
So one set of me ees een every cell of you body.?
YEAH. WHAT DO YOU THINK OF THAT.?
You ees hosed.
DAD IS VERY DISCOURAGING.
BEER
9/14

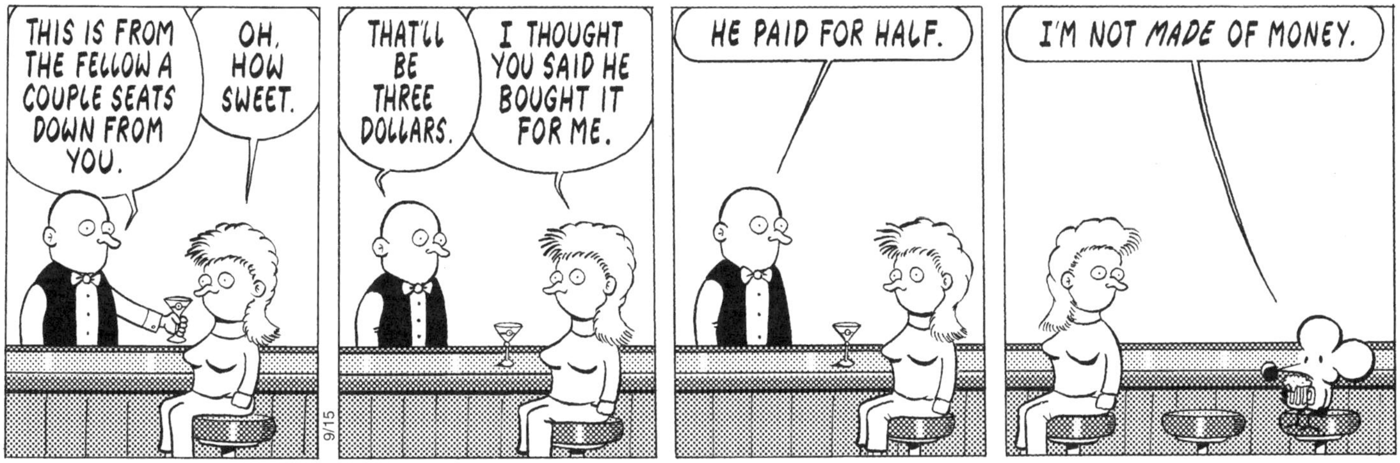
THIS IS FROM THE FELLOW A COUPLE SEATS DOWN FROM YOU.
OH, HOW SWEET.
9/15
THAT'LL BE THREE DOLLARS.
I THOUGHT YOU SAID HE BOUGHT IT FOR ME.
HE PAID FOR HALF.
I'M NOT *MADE* OF MONEY.

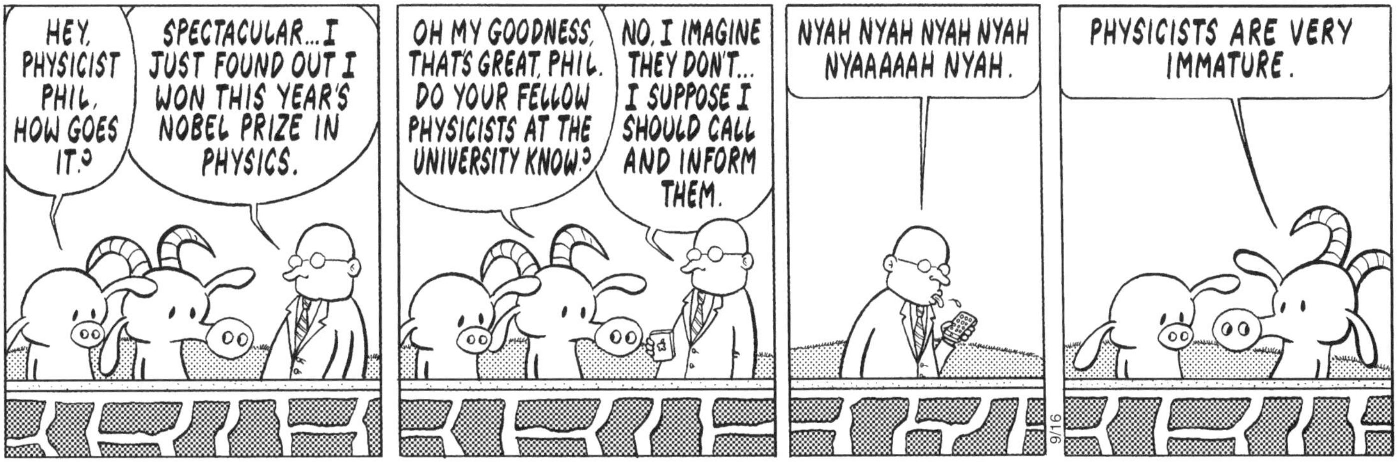
HEY, PHYSICIST PHIL, HOW GOES IT?
SPECTACULAR... I JUST FOUND OUT I WON THIS YEAR'S NOBEL PRIZE IN PHYSICS.
OH MY GOODNESS, THAT'S GREAT, PHIL. DO YOUR FELLOW PHYSICISTS AT THE UNIVERSITY KNOW?
NO, I IMAGINE THEY DON'T... I SUPPOSE I SHOULD CALL AND INFORM THEM.
NYAH NYAH NYAH NYAH NYAAAAAH NYAH.
9/16
PHYSICISTS ARE VERY IMMATURE.

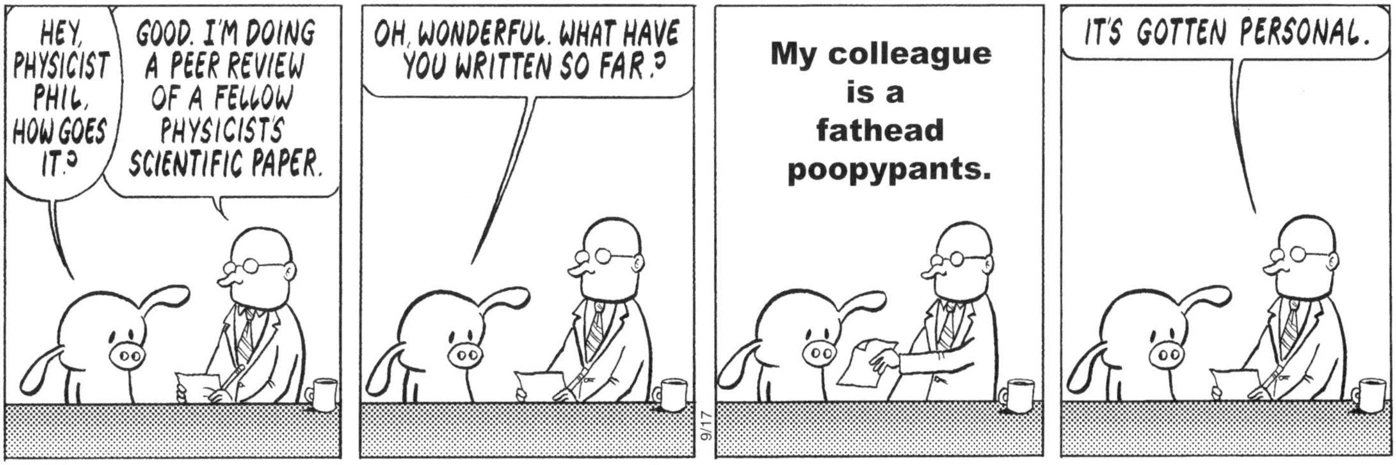
HEY, PHYSICIST PHIL, HOW GOES IT?
GOOD. I'M DOING A PEER REVIEW OF A FELLOW PHYSICIST'S SCIENTIFIC PAPER.
OH, WONDERFUL. WHAT HAVE YOU WRITTEN SO FAR?
9/17
My colleague is a fathead poopypants.
IT'S GOTTEN PERSONAL.

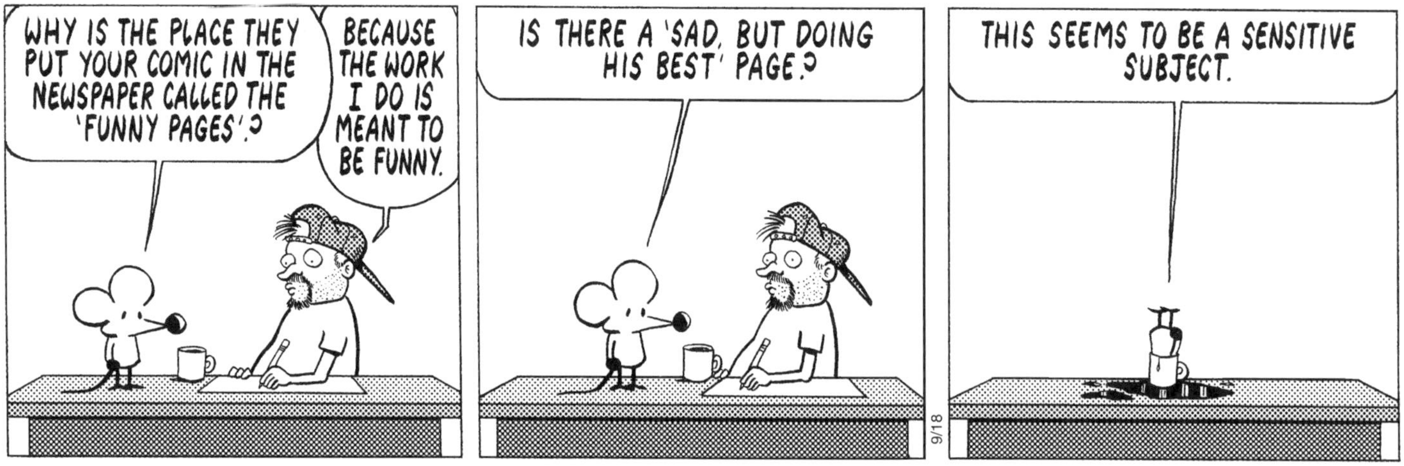
WHY IS THE PLACE THEY PUT YOUR COMIC IN THE NEWSPAPER CALLED THE 'FUNNY PAGES'?
BECAUSE THE WORK I DO IS MEANT TO BE FUNNY.
IS THERE A 'SAD, BUT DOING HIS BEST' PAGE?
THIS SEEMS TO BE A SENSITIVE SUBJECT.
9/18

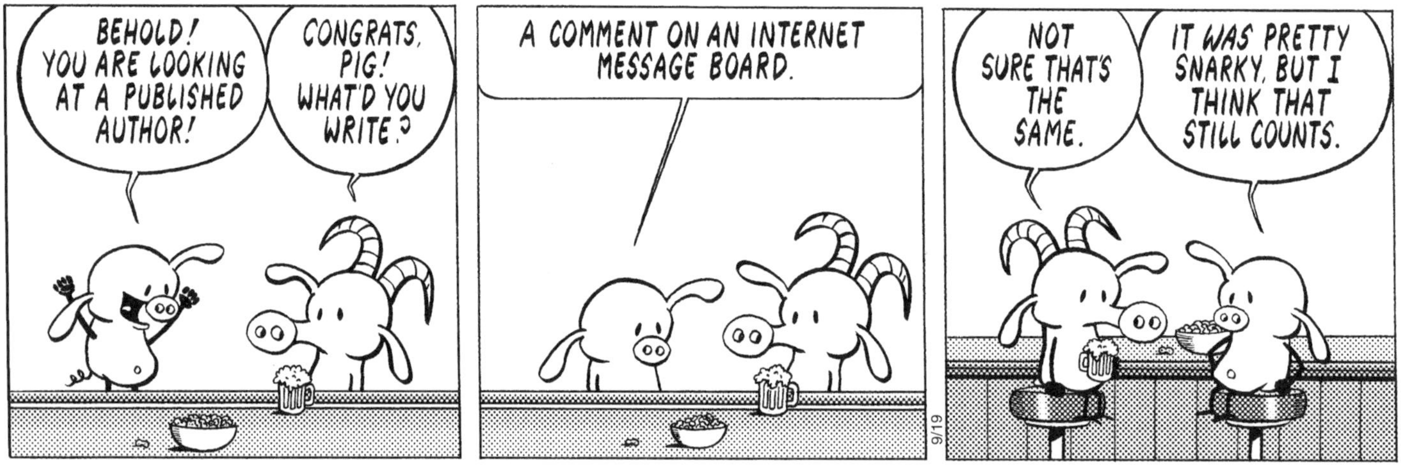
BEHOLD! YOU ARE LOOKING AT A PUBLISHED AUTHOR!
CONGRATS, PIG! WHAT'D YOU WRITE?
A COMMENT ON AN INTERNET MESSAGE BOARD.
NOT SURE THAT'S THE SAME.
IT *WAS* PRETTY SNARKY, BUT I THINK THAT STILL COUNTS.
9/19

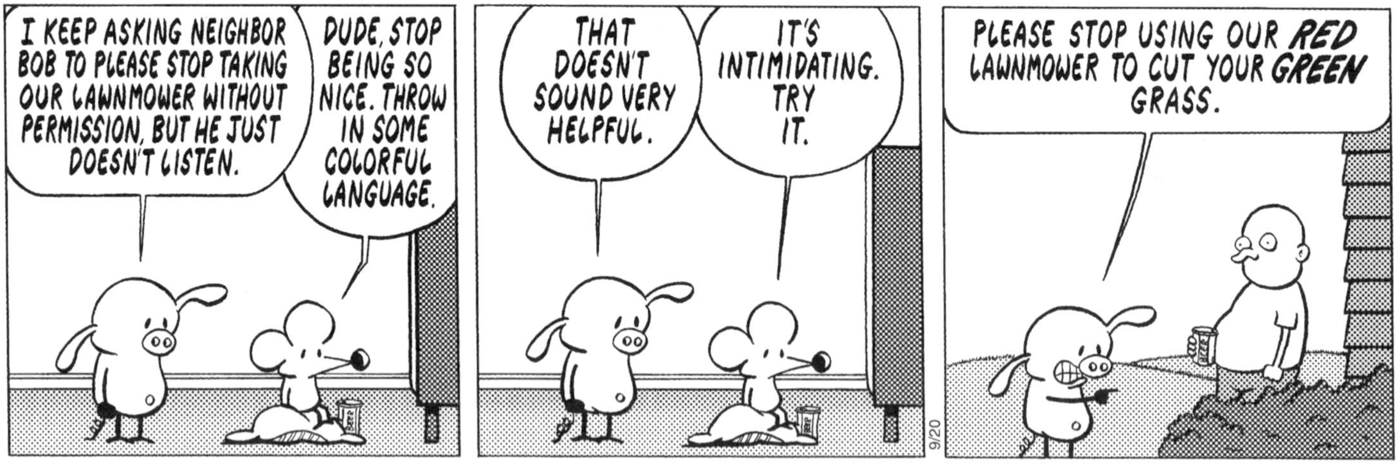
I KEEP ASKING NEIGHBOR BOB TO PLEASE STOP TAKING OUR LAWNMOWER WITHOUT PERMISSION, BUT HE JUST DOESN'T LISTEN.
DUDE, STOP BEING SO NICE. THROW IN SOME COLORFUL LANGUAGE.
THAT DOESN'T SOUND VERY HELPFUL.
IT'S INTIMIDATING. TRY IT.
PLEASE STOP USING OUR **RED** LAWNMOWER TO CUT YOUR **GREEN** GRASS.
9/20

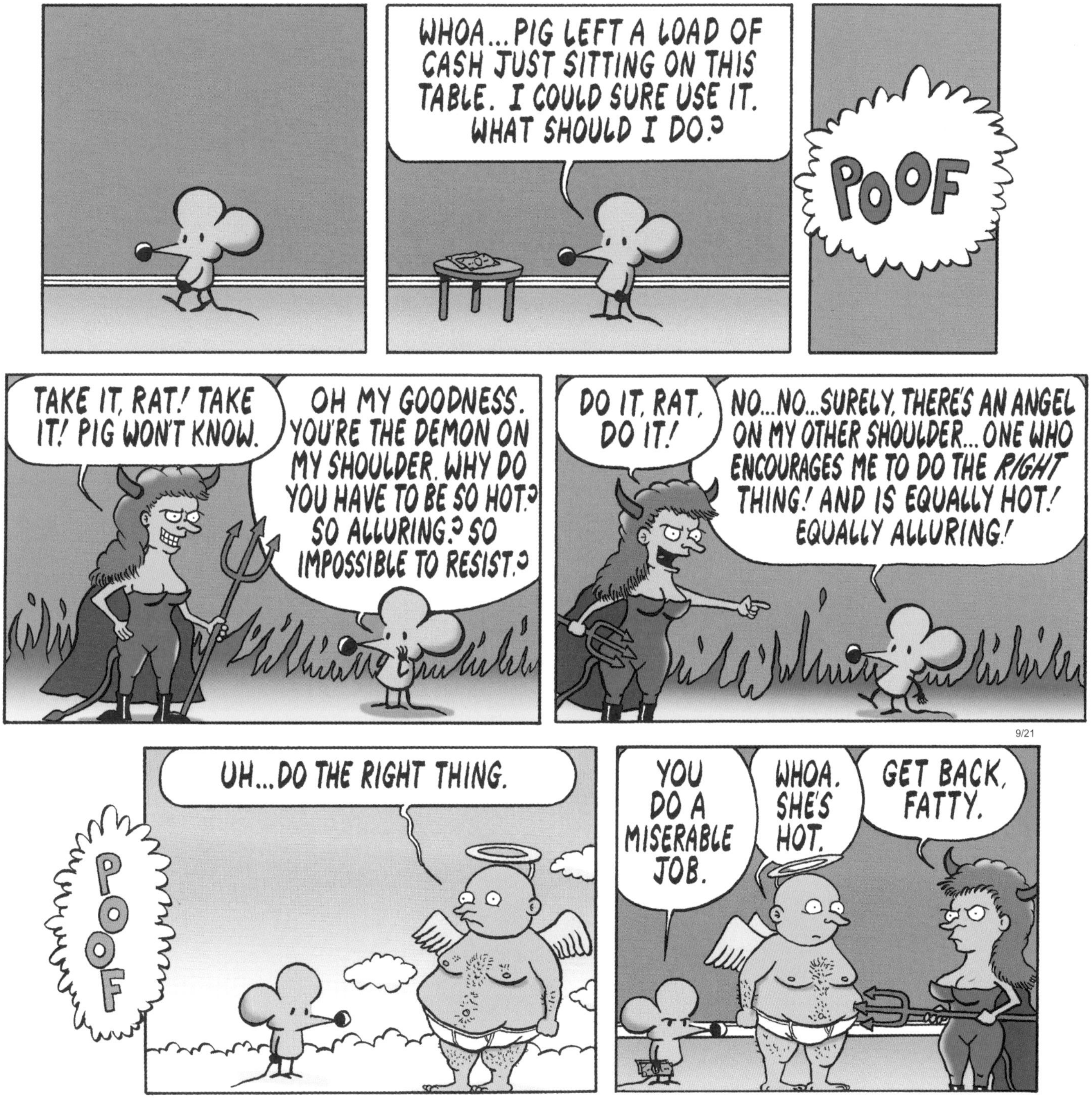
WHOA...PIG LEFT A LOAD OF CASH JUST SITTING ON THIS TABLE. I COULD SURE USE IT. WHAT SHOULD I DO?
POOF
TAKE IT, RAT! TAKE IT! PIG WON'T KNOW.
OH MY GOODNESS. YOU'RE THE DEMON ON MY SHOULDER. WHY DO YOU HAVE TO BE SO HOT? SO ALLURING? SO IMPOSSIBLE TO RESIST?
DO IT, RAT, DO IT!
NO...NO...SURELY, THERE'S AN ANGEL ON MY OTHER SHOULDER...ONE WHO ENCOURAGES ME TO DO THE *RIGHT* THING! AND IS EQUALLY HOT! EQUALLY ALLURING!
9/21
POOF
UH...DO THE RIGHT THING.
YOU DO A MISERABLE JOB.
WHOA. SHE'S HOT.
GET BACK, FATTY.

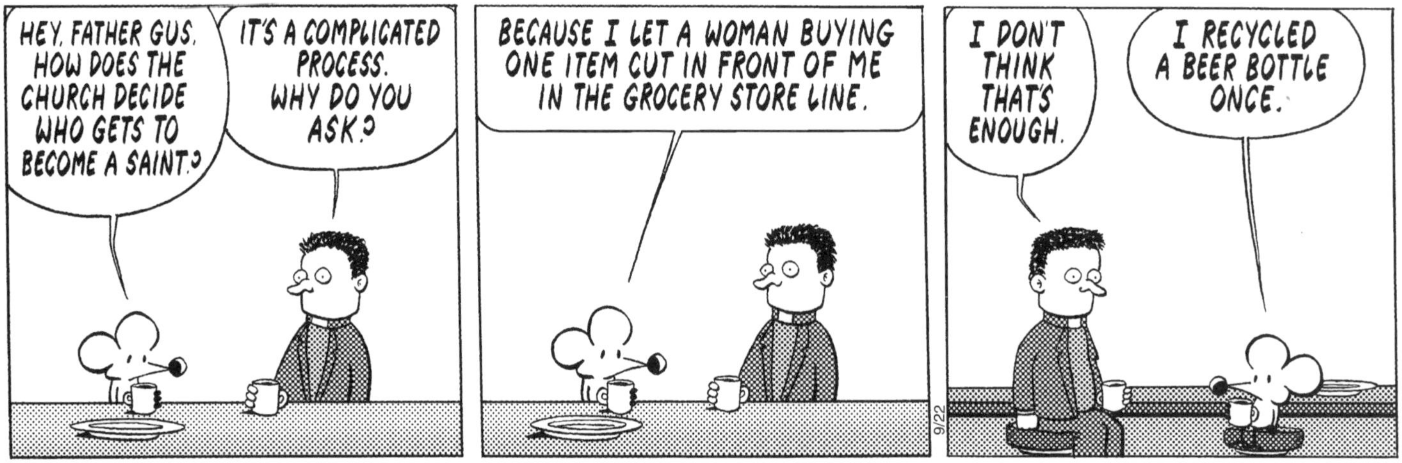
HEY, FATHER GUS. HOW DOES THE CHURCH DECIDE WHO GETS TO BECOME A SAINT?
IT'S A COMPLICATED PROCESS. WHY DO YOU ASK?
BECAUSE I LET A WOMAN BUYING ONE ITEM CUT IN FRONT OF ME IN THE GROCERY STORE LINE.
I DON'T THINK THAT'S ENOUGH.
I RECYCLED A BEER BOTTLE ONCE.
9/22

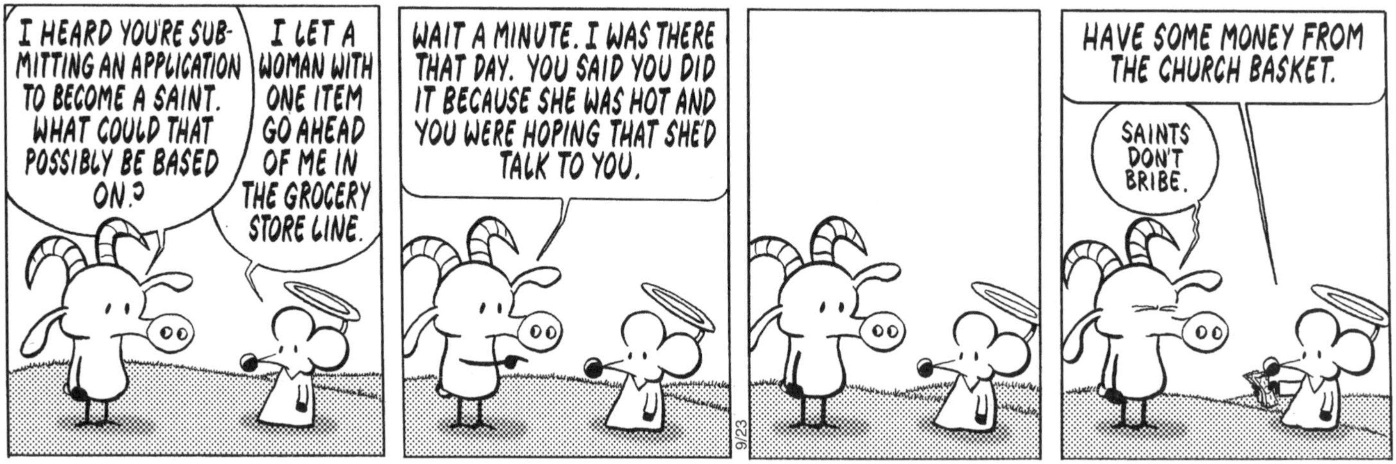
I HEARD YOU'RE SUBMITTING AN APPLICATION TO BECOME A SAINT. WHAT COULD THAT POSSIBLY BE BASED ON?
I LET A WOMAN WITH ONE ITEM GO AHEAD OF ME IN THE GROCERY STORE LINE.
WAIT A MINUTE. I WAS THERE THAT DAY. YOU SAID YOU DID IT BECAUSE SHE WAS HOT AND YOU WERE HOPING THAT SHE'D TALK TO YOU.
HAVE SOME MONEY FROM THE CHURCH BASKET.
SAINTS DON'T BRIBE.
9/23

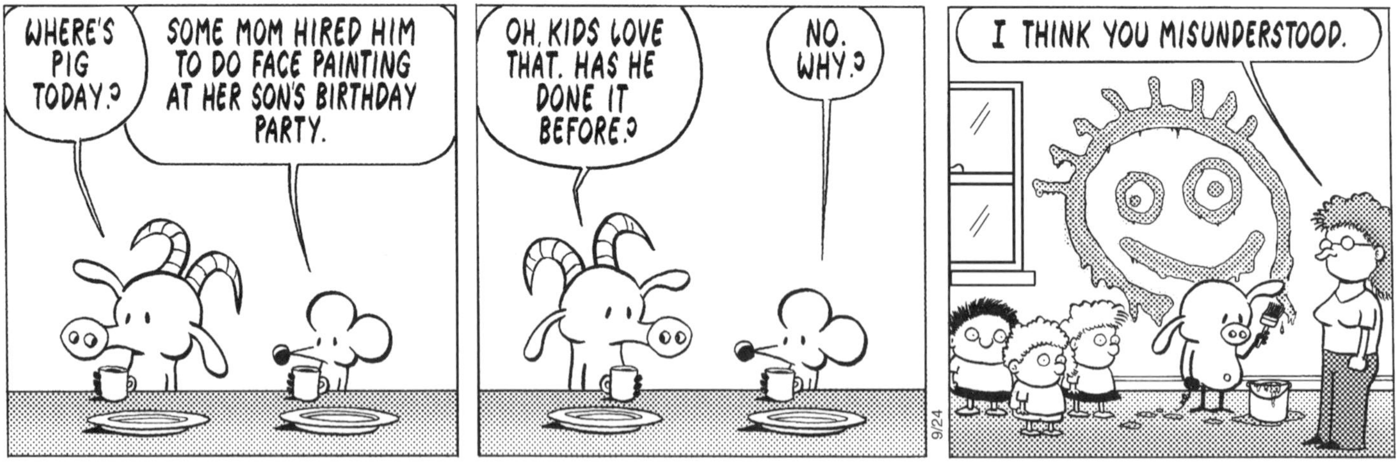
WHERE'S PIG TODAY?
SOME MOM HIRED HIM TO DO FACE PAINTING AT HER SON'S BIRTHDAY PARTY.
OH, KIDS LOVE THAT. HAS HE DONE IT BEFORE?
NO. WHY?
I THINK YOU MISUNDERSTOOD.
9/24

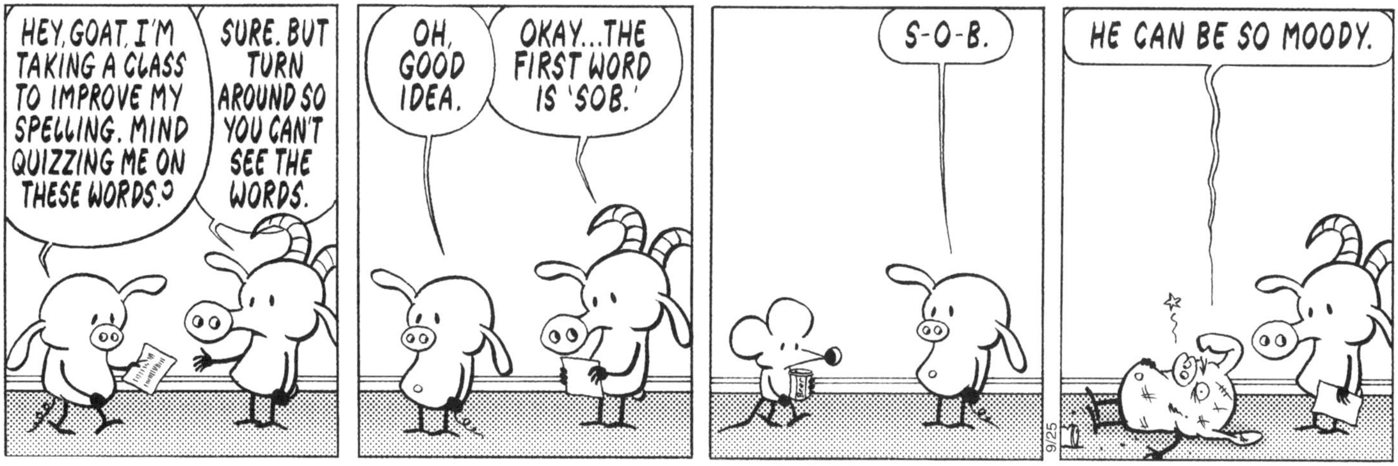
HEY, GOAT, I'M TAKING A CLASS TO IMPROVE MY SPELLING. MIND QUIZZING ME ON THESE WORDS?
SURE. BUT TURN AROUND SO YOU CAN'T SEE THE WORDS.
OH, GOOD IDEA.
OKAY... THE FIRST WORD IS 'SOB.'
S-O-B.
9/25
HE CAN BE SO MOODY.

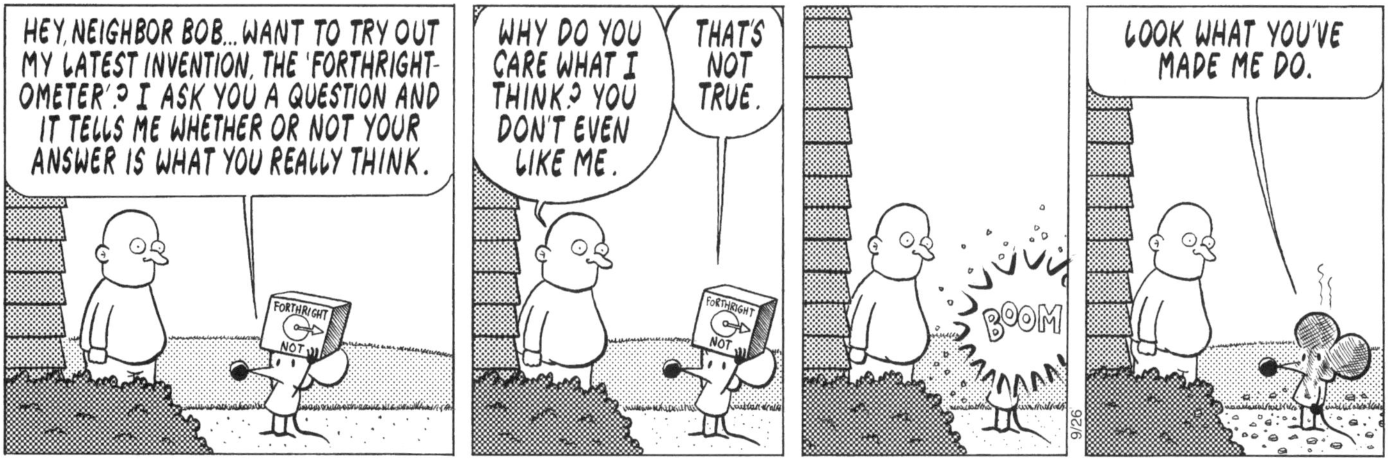
HEY, NEIGHBOR BOB... WANT TO TRY OUT MY LATEST INVENTION, THE 'FORTHRIGHT-OMETER'? I ASK YOU A QUESTION AND IT TELLS ME WHETHER OR NOT YOUR ANSWER IS WHAT YOU REALLY THINK.
FORTHRIGHT
NOT
WHY DO YOU CARE WHAT I THINK? YOU DON'T EVEN LIKE ME.
THAT'S NOT TRUE.
FORTHRIGHT
NOT
BOOM
9/26
LOOK WHAT YOU'VE MADE ME DO.

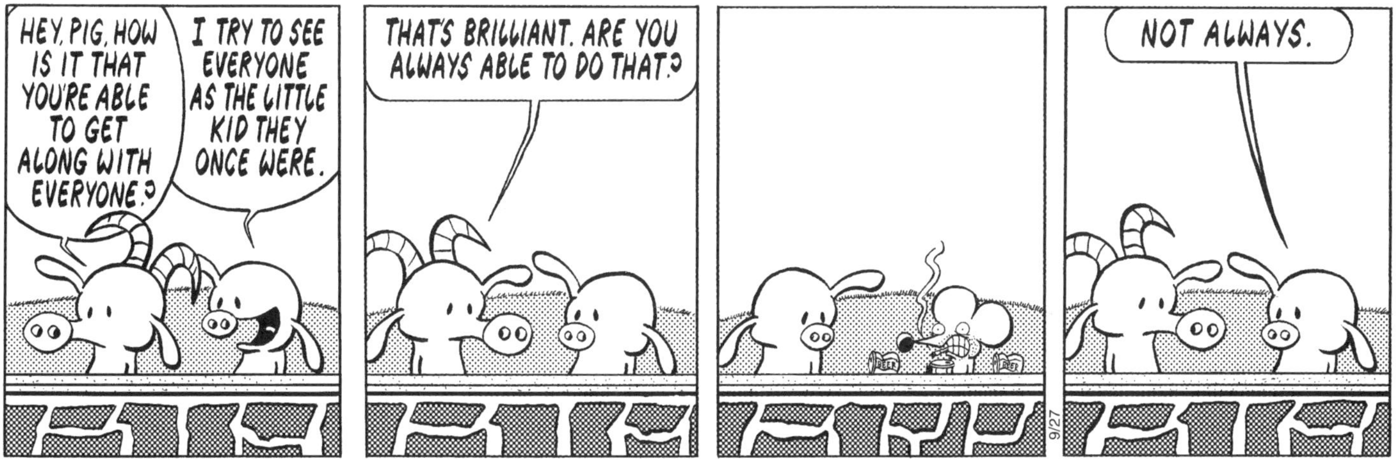
HEY, PIG, HOW IS IT THAT YOU'RE ABLE TO GET ALONG WITH EVERYONE?
I TRY TO SEE EVERYONE AS THE LITTLE KID THEY ONCE WERE.
THAT'S BRILLIANT. ARE YOU ALWAYS ABLE TO DO THAT?
9/27
NOT ALWAYS.

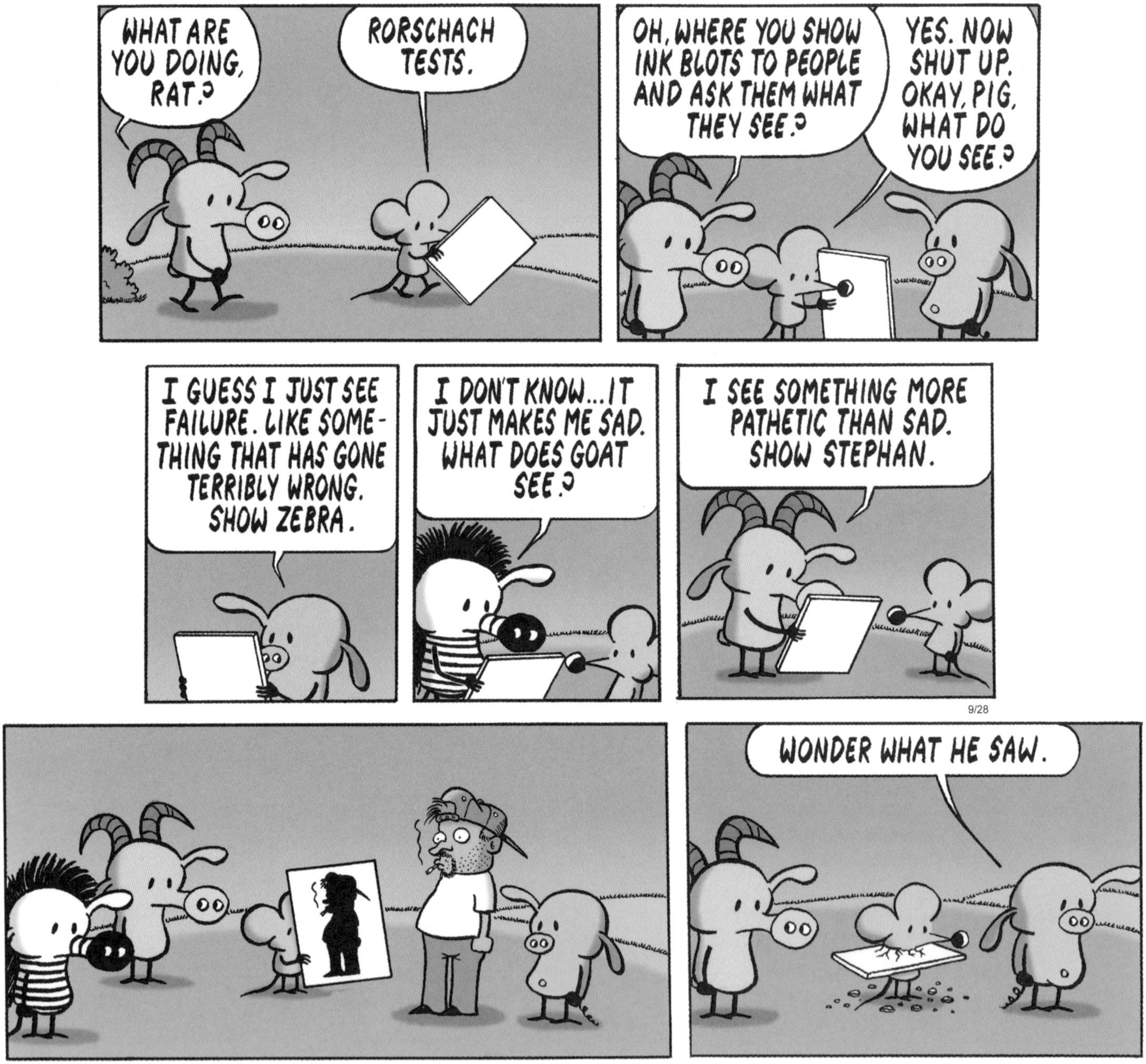
WHAT ARE YOU DOING, RAT?
RORSCHACH TESTS.
OH, WHERE YOU SHOW INK BLOTS TO PEOPLE AND ASK THEM WHAT THEY SEE?
YES. NOW SHUT UP. OKAY, PIG, WHAT DO YOU SEE?
I GUESS I JUST SEE FAILURE. LIKE SOMETHING THAT HAS GONE TERRIBLY WRONG. SHOW ZEBRA.
I DON'T KNOW... IT JUST MAKES ME SAD. WHAT DOES GOAT SEE?
I SEE SOMETHING MORE PATHETIC THAN SAD. SHOW STEPHAN.
9/28
WONDER WHAT HE SAW.

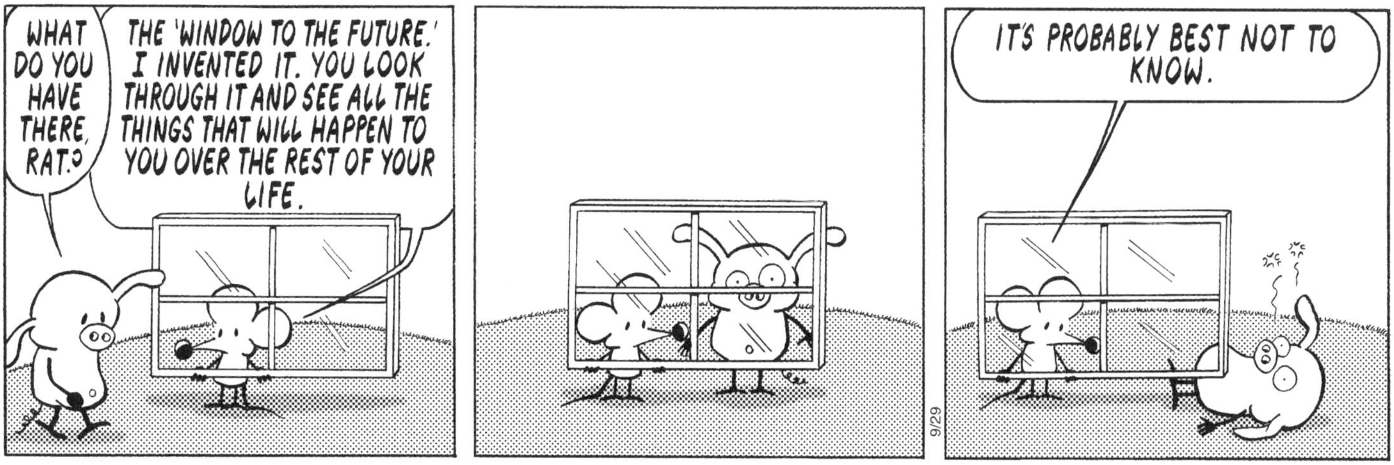
WHAT DO YOU HAVE THERE, RAT?
THE 'WINDOW TO THE FUTURE.' I INVENTED IT. YOU LOOK THROUGH IT AND SEE ALL THE THINGS THAT WILL HAPPEN TO YOU OVER THE REST OF YOUR LIFE.
IT'S PROBABLY BEST NOT TO KNOW.
9/29

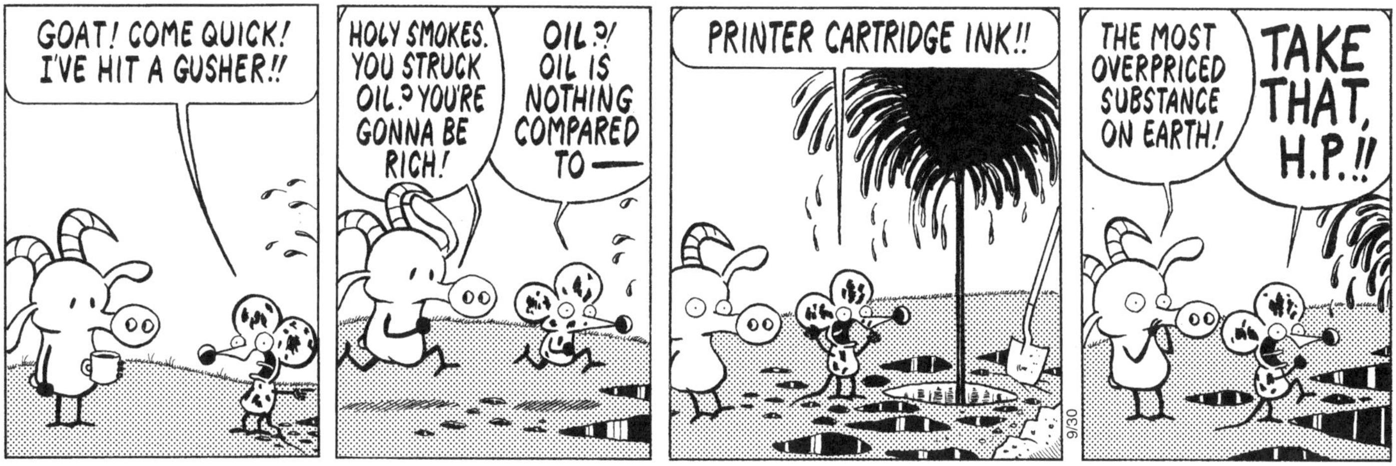
GOAT! COME QUICK! I'VE HIT A GUSHER!!
HOLY SMOKES. YOU STRUCK OIL? YOU'RE GONNA BE RICH!
OIL?! OIL IS NOTHING COMPARED TO —
PRINTER CARTRIDGE INK!!
THE MOST OVERPRICED SUBSTANCE ON EARTH!
TAKE THAT, H.P.!!
9/30

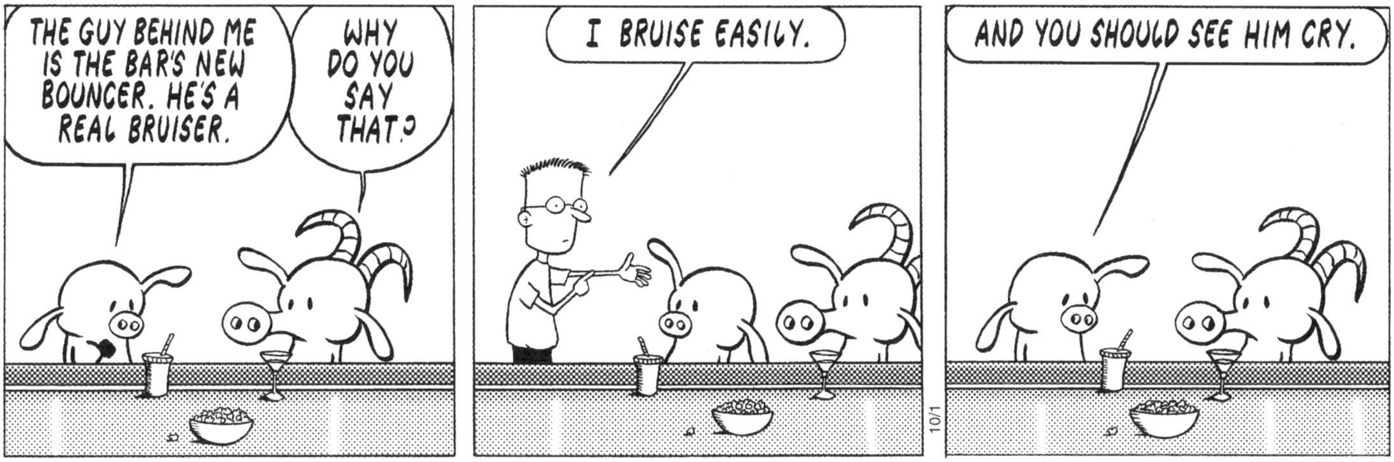
THE GUY BEHIND ME IS THE BAR'S NEW BOUNCER. HE'S A REAL BRUISER.
WHY DO YOU SAY THAT?
I BRUISE EASILY.
AND YOU SHOULD SEE HIM CRY.
10/1

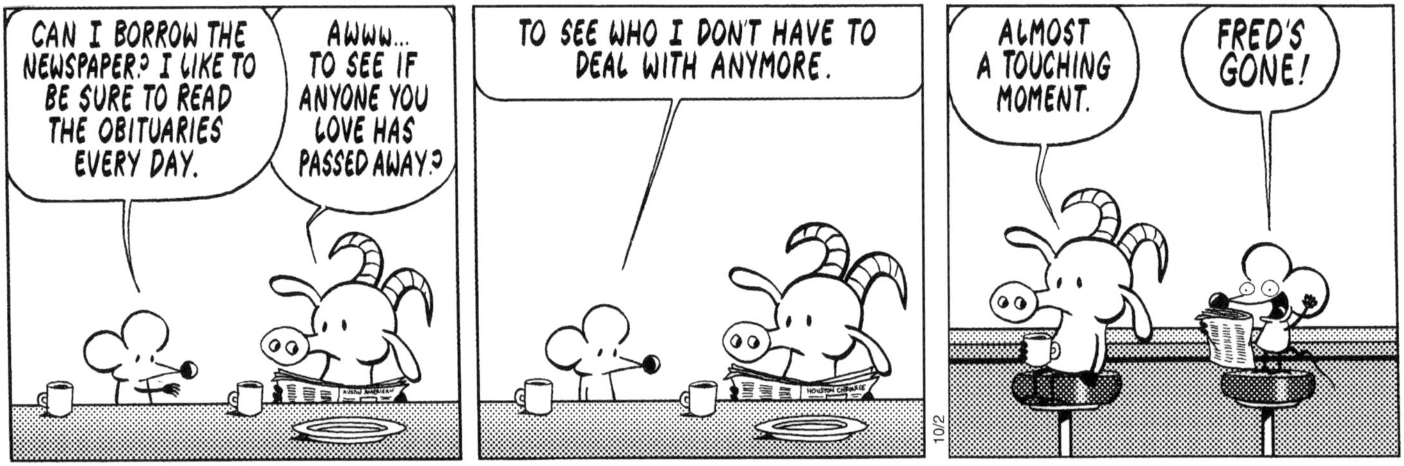
CAN I BORROW THE NEWSPAPER? I LIKE TO BE SURE TO READ THE OBITUARIES EVERY DAY.
AWWW... TO SEE IF ANYONE YOU LOVE HAS PASSED AWAY?
TO SEE WHO I DON'T HAVE TO DEAL WITH ANYMORE.
ALMOST A TOUCHING MOMENT.
FRED'S GONE!
10/2

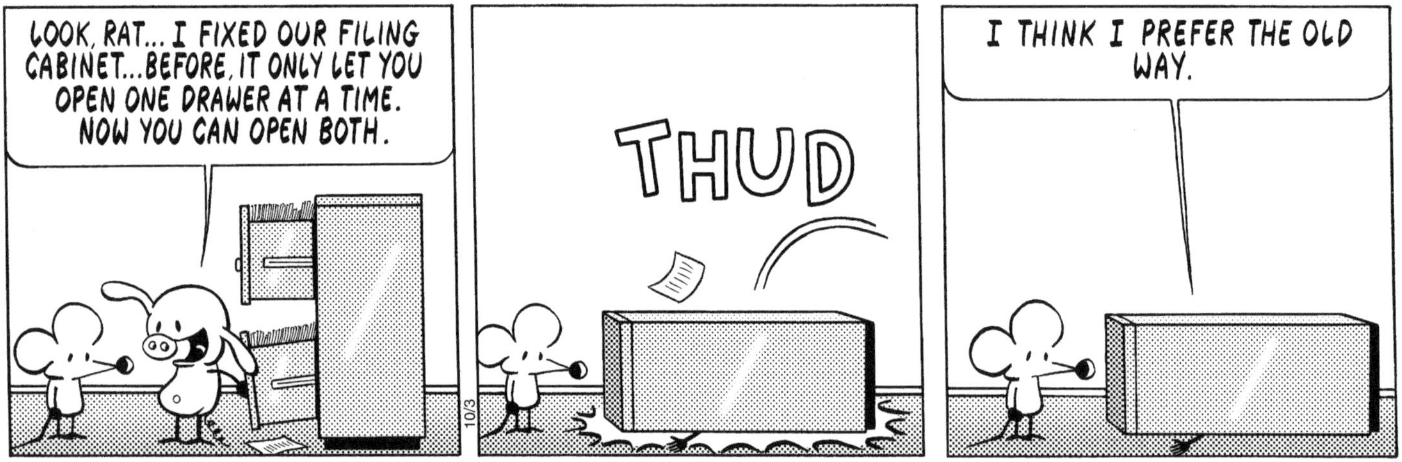
LOOK, RAT... I FIXED OUR FILING CABINET...BEFORE, IT ONLY LET YOU OPEN ONE DRAWER AT A TIME. NOW YOU CAN OPEN BOTH.
10/3
THUD
I THINK I PREFER THE OLD WAY.

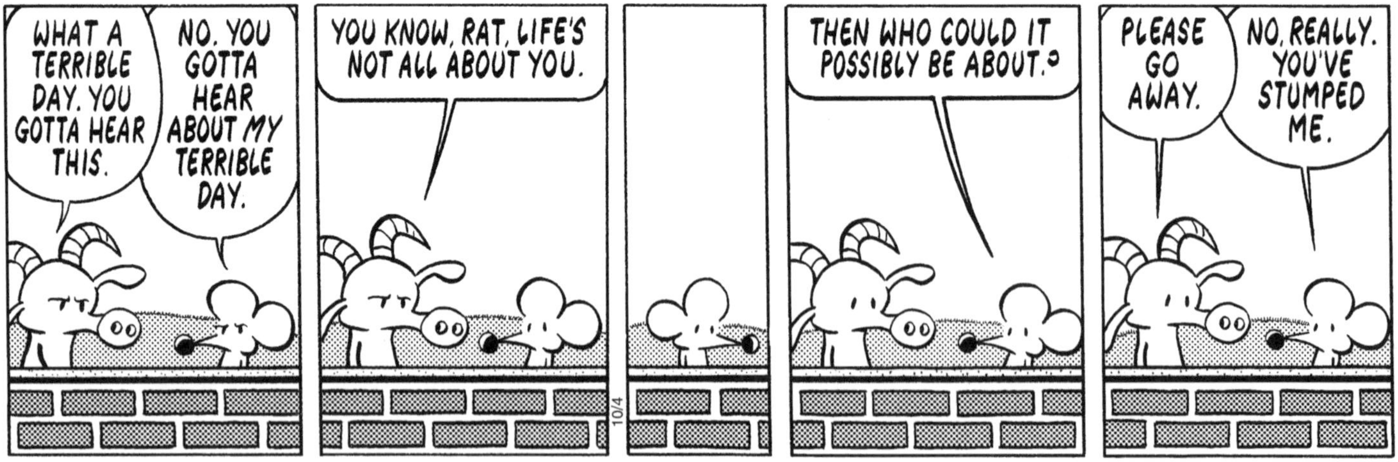
WHAT A TERRIBLE DAY. YOU GOTTA HEAR THIS.
NO. YOU GOTTA HEAR ABOUT MY TERRIBLE DAY.
YOU KNOW, RAT, LIFE'S NOT ALL ABOUT YOU.
10/4
THEN WHO COULD IT POSSIBLY BE ABOUT?
PLEASE GO AWAY.
NO, REALLY. YOU'VE STUMPED ME.

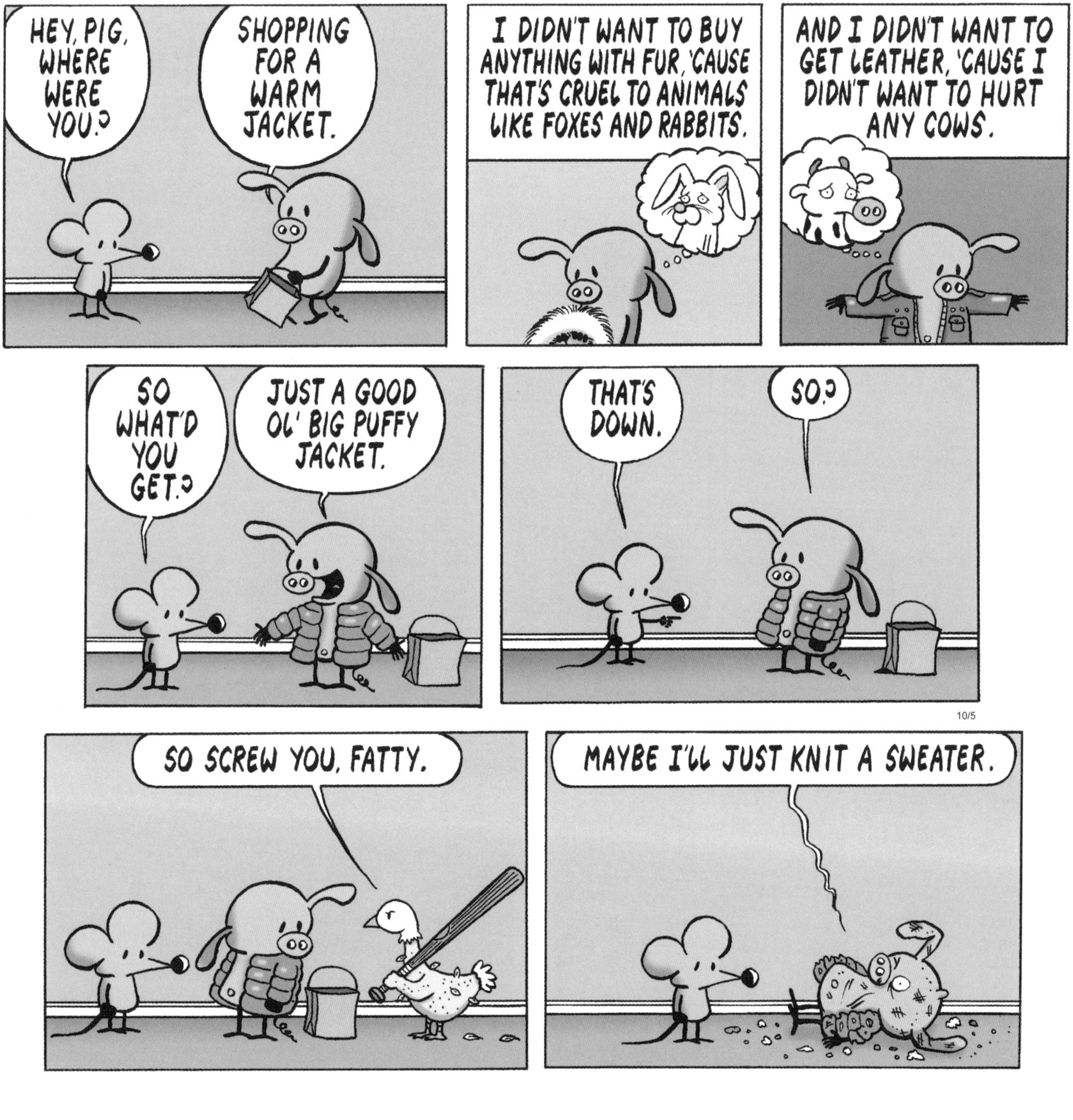
HEY, PIG, WHERE WERE YOU?
SHOPPING FOR A WARM JACKET.
I DIDN'T WANT TO BUY ANYTHING WITH FUR, 'CAUSE THAT'S CRUEL TO ANIMALS LIKE FOXES AND RABBITS.
AND I DIDN'T WANT TO GET LEATHER, 'CAUSE I DIDN'T WANT TO HURT ANY COWS.
SO WHAT'D YOU GET?
JUST A GOOD OL' BIG PUFFY JACKET.
THAT'S DOWN.
SO?
10/5
SO SCREW YOU, FATTY.
MAYBE I'LL JUST KNIT A SWEATER.

Panel 1:
HEY, GOAT, THIS IS MY FRIEND, FAT FINGERS.

OH, YEAH. I THINK I GOT A TEXT FROM HIM.

Panel 2:
askgjdsb w7n2m4 kmvkm g893k spplpl;,iojiuuhewr

Panel 3:
TEXTS ARE TOUGH FOR FAT FINGERS.

Panel 4:
IT TOOK ME AND FAT FINGERS FOREVER TO FIND A PARKING SPACE TODAY, BUT THEN I REMEMBERED HE HAS ONE OF THOSE DISABLED PLACARDS ON HIS CAR.

WHAT'S HIS DISABILITY?

Panel 5:
ads;lj vwqet gsfv

Panel 6:
YOU TRY TEXTING WITH FAT FINGERS.

Panel 7:
HEY, PIG. WHERE WERE YOU TODAY?

VISITING MY FRIEND, BOB. THE POOR GUY HAS A LOT OF SKELETONS IN HIS CLOSET.

Panel 8:
HE HAS A LOT OF SHAMEFUL PARTS OF HIS LIFE THAT HE DOESN'T WANT EXAMINED?

HE HAS A HALLOWEEN STORE THAT WENT OUT OF BUSINESS.

Panel 9:
YOU REALLY JUMP TO CONCLUSIONS.

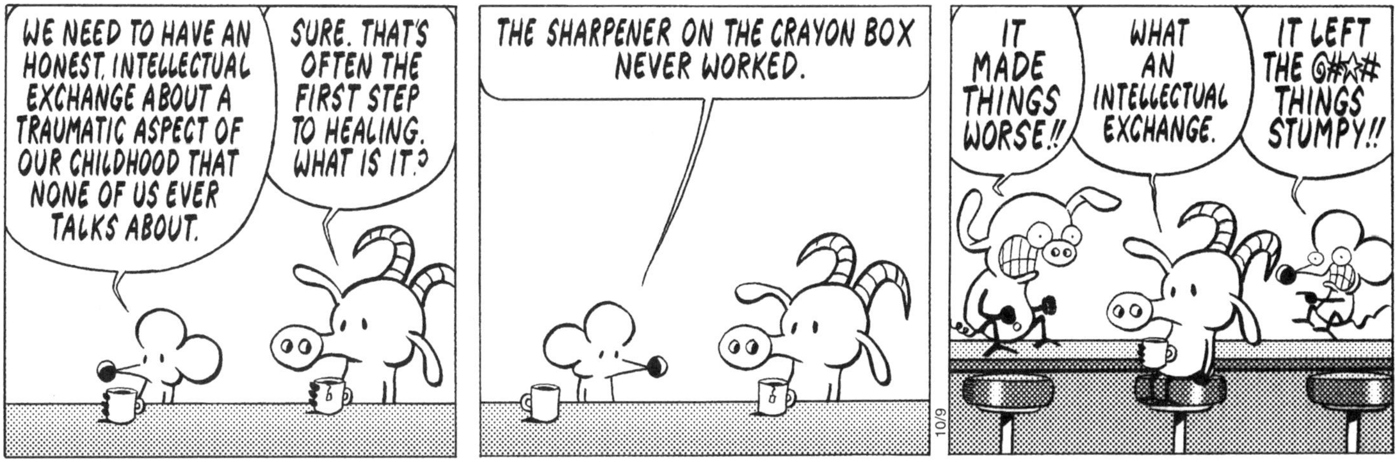
WE NEED TO HAVE AN HONEST, INTELLECTUAL EXCHANGE ABOUT A TRAUMATIC ASPECT OF OUR CHILDHOOD THAT NONE OF US EVER TALKS ABOUT.
SURE. THAT'S OFTEN THE FIRST STEP TO HEALING. WHAT IS IT?
THE SHARPENER ON THE CRAYON BOX NEVER WORKED.
10/9
IT MADE THINGS WORSE!!
WHAT AN INTELLECTUAL EXCHANGE.
IT LEFT THE @#☆# THINGS STUMPY!!

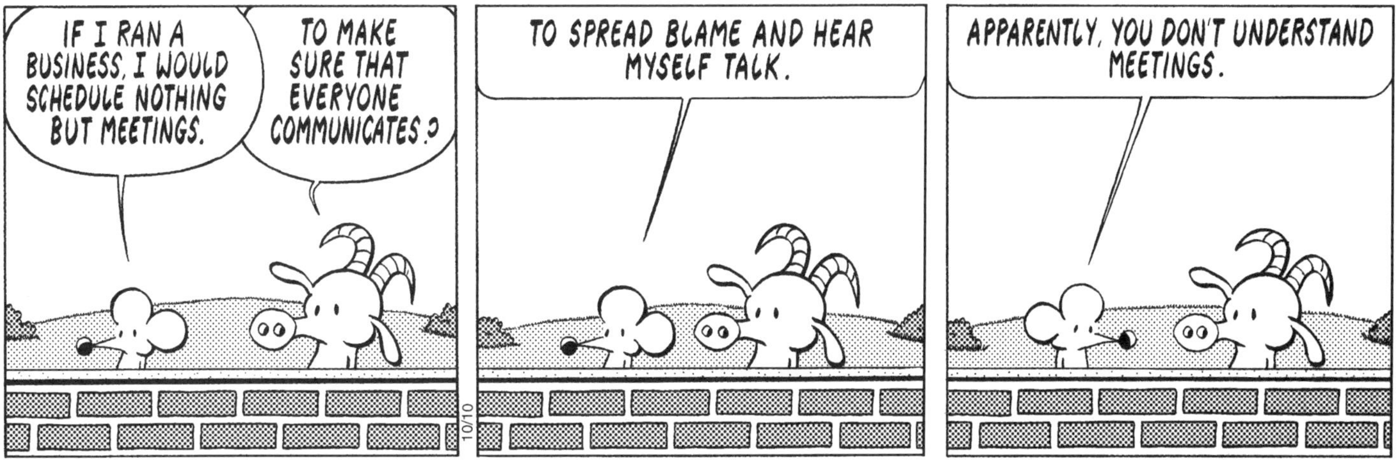
IF I RAN A BUSINESS, I WOULD SCHEDULE NOTHING BUT MEETINGS.
TO MAKE SURE THAT EVERYONE COMMUNICATES?
10/10
TO SPREAD BLAME AND HEAR MYSELF TALK.
APPARENTLY, YOU DON'T UNDERSTAND MEETINGS.

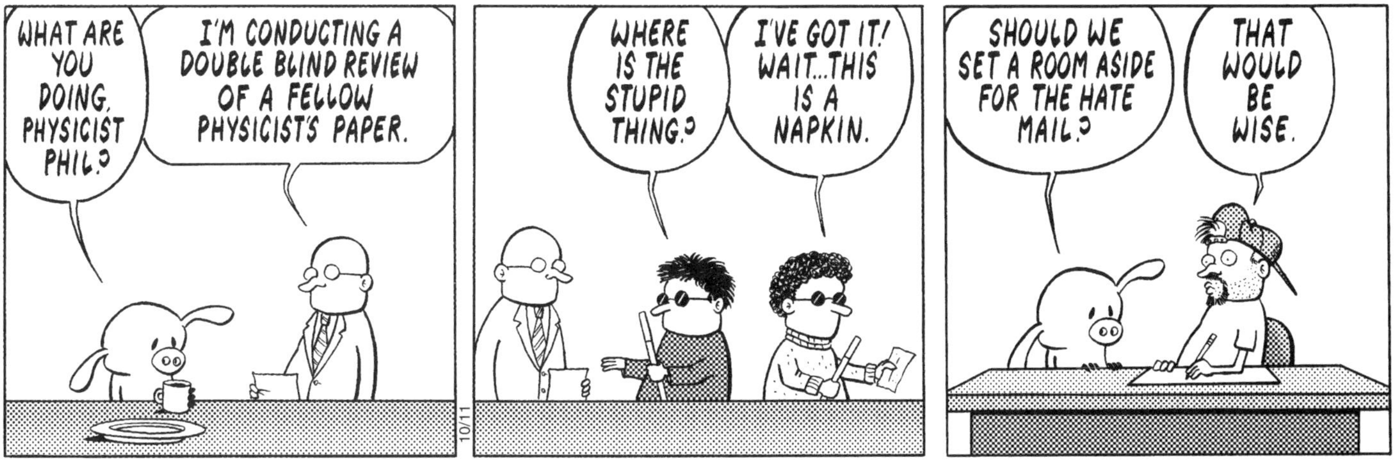
WHAT ARE YOU DOING, PHYSICIST PHIL?
I'M CONDUCTING A DOUBLE BLIND REVIEW OF A FELLOW PHYSICIST'S PAPER.
10/11
WHERE IS THE STUPID THING?
I'VE GOT IT! WAIT...THIS IS A NAPKIN.
SHOULD WE SET A ROOM ASIDE FOR THE HATE MAIL?
THAT WOULD BE WISE.

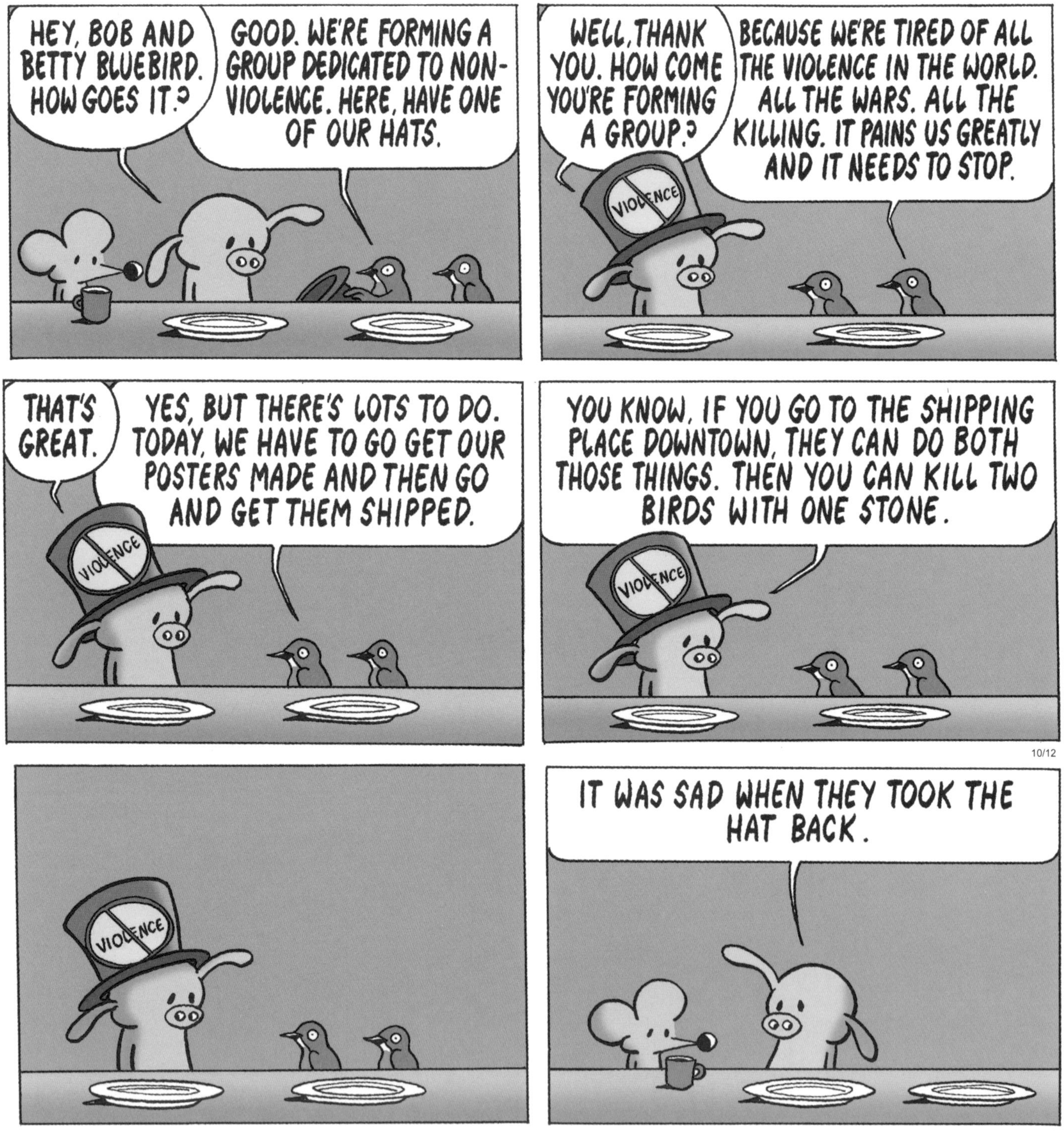
HEY, BOB AND BETTY BLUEBIRD. HOW GOES IT?
GOOD. WE'RE FORMING A GROUP DEDICATED TO NON-VIOLENCE. HERE, HAVE ONE OF OUR HATS.
VIOLENCE
WELL, THANK YOU. HOW COME YOU'RE FORMING A GROUP?
BECAUSE WE'RE TIRED OF ALL THE VIOLENCE IN THE WORLD. ALL THE WARS. ALL THE KILLING. IT PAINS US GREATLY AND IT NEEDS TO STOP.
THAT'S GREAT.
YES, BUT THERE'S LOTS TO DO. TODAY, WE HAVE TO GO GET OUR POSTERS MADE AND THEN GO AND GET THEM SHIPPED.
VIOLENCE
YOU KNOW, IF YOU GO TO THE SHIPPING PLACE DOWNTOWN, THEY CAN DO BOTH THOSE THINGS. THEN YOU CAN KILL TWO BIRDS WITH ONE STONE.
VIOLENCE
VIOLENCE
IT WAS SAD WHEN THEY TOOK THE HAT BACK.

10/12

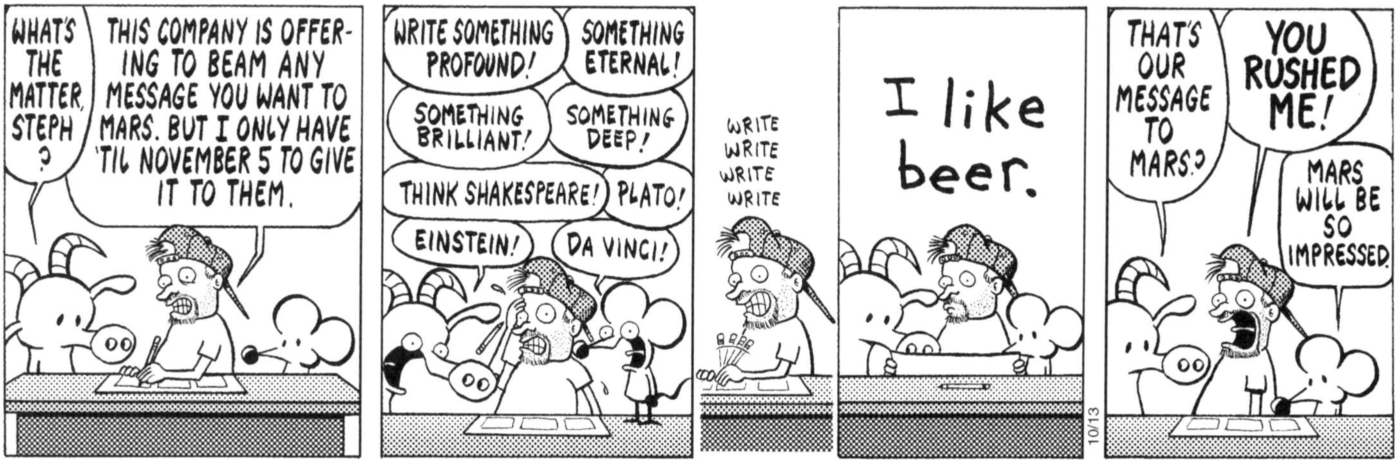
WHAT'S THE MATTER, STEPH?
THIS COMPANY IS OFFERING TO BEAM ANY MESSAGE YOU WANT TO MARS. BUT I ONLY HAVE 'TIL NOVEMBER 5 TO GIVE IT TO THEM.
WRITE SOMETHING PROFOUND!
SOMETHING ETERNAL!
SOMETHING BRILLIANT!
SOMETHING DEEP!
THINK SHAKESPEARE!
PLATO!
EINSTEIN!
DA VINCI!
WRITE WRITE WRITE WRITE
I like beer.
THAT'S OUR MESSAGE TO MARS?
YOU RUSHED ME!
MARS WILL BE SO IMPRESSED.
10/13

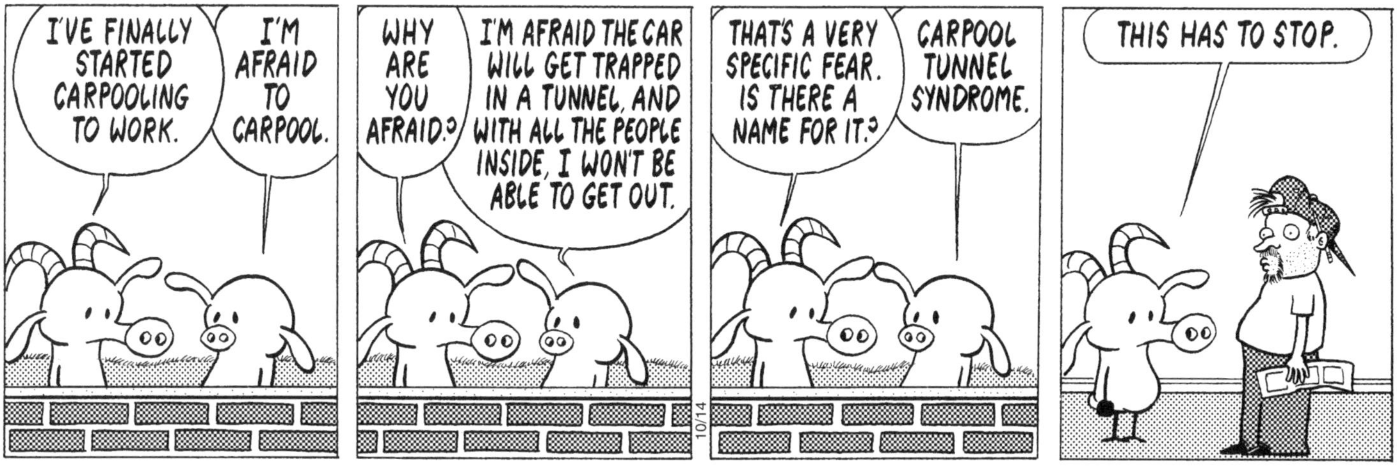
I'VE FINALLY STARTED CARPOOLING TO WORK.
I'M AFRAID TO CARPOOL.
WHY ARE YOU AFRAID?
I'M AFRAID THE CAR WILL GET TRAPPED IN A TUNNEL, AND WITH ALL THE PEOPLE INSIDE, I WON'T BE ABLE TO GET OUT.
10/14
THAT'S A VERY SPECIFIC FEAR. IS THERE A NAME FOR IT?
CARPOOL TUNNEL SYNDROME.
THIS HAS TO STOP.

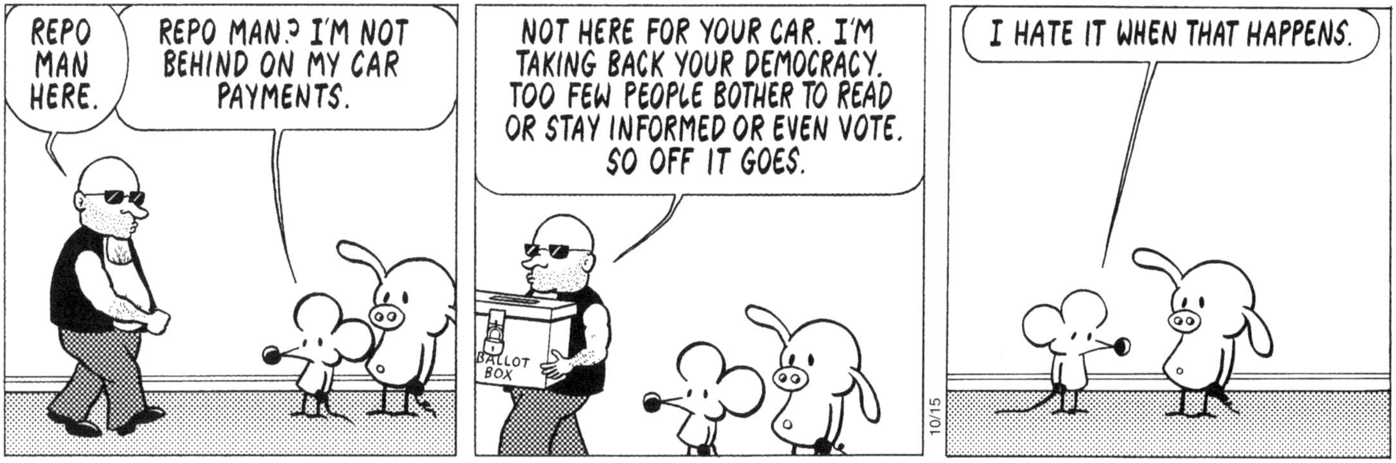
REPO MAN HERE.
REPO MAN? I'M NOT BEHIND ON MY CAR PAYMENTS.
NOT HERE FOR YOUR CAR. I'M TAKING BACK YOUR DEMOCRACY. TOO FEW PEOPLE BOTHER TO READ OR STAY INFORMED OR EVEN VOTE. SO OFF IT GOES.
BALLOT BOX
10/15
I HATE IT WHEN THAT HAPPENS.

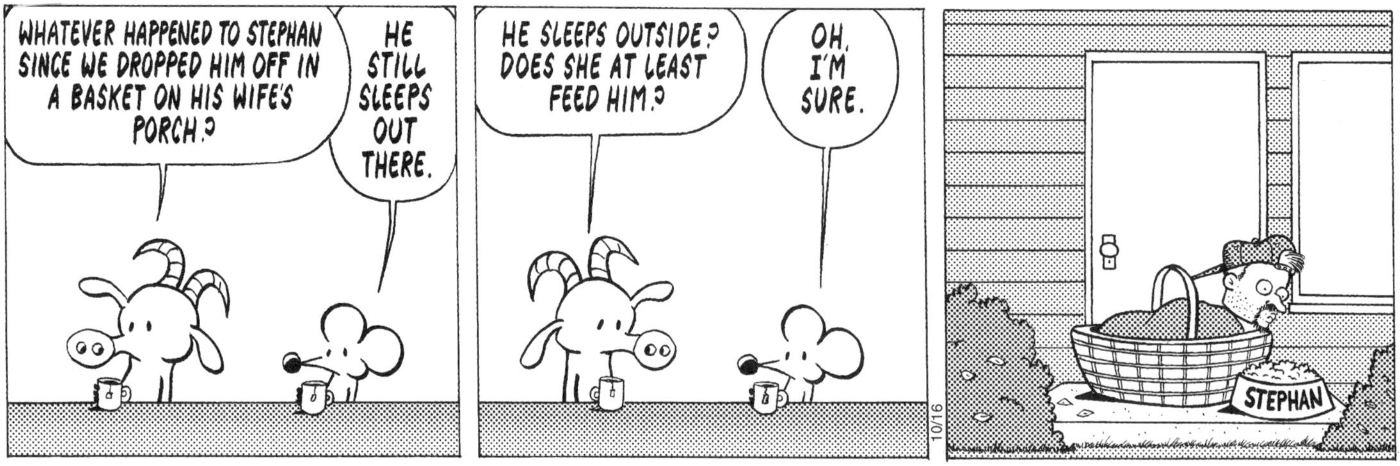
WHATEVER HAPPENED TO STEPHAN SINCE WE DROPPED HIM OFF IN A BASKET ON HIS WIFE'S PORCH?
HE STILL SLEEPS OUT THERE.
HE SLEEPS OUTSIDE? DOES SHE AT LEAST FEED HIM?
OH, I'M SURE.
STEPHAN
10/16

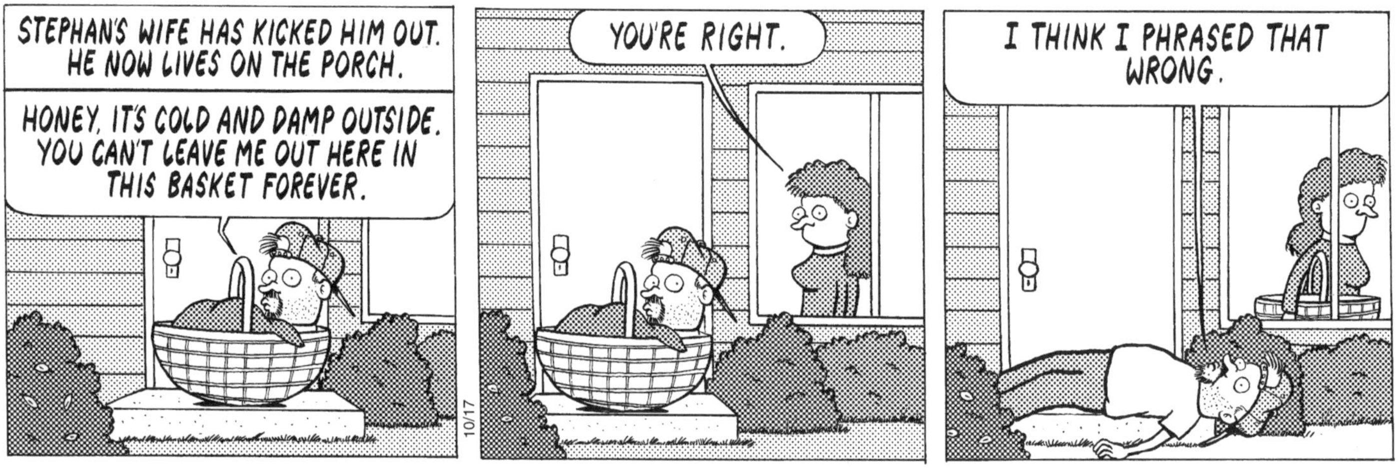
STEPHAN'S WIFE HAS KICKED HIM OUT. HE NOW LIVES ON THE PORCH.
HONEY, IT'S COLD AND DAMP OUTSIDE. YOU CAN'T LEAVE ME OUT HERE IN THIS BASKET FOREVER.
10/17
YOU'RE RIGHT.
I THINK I PHRASED THAT WRONG.

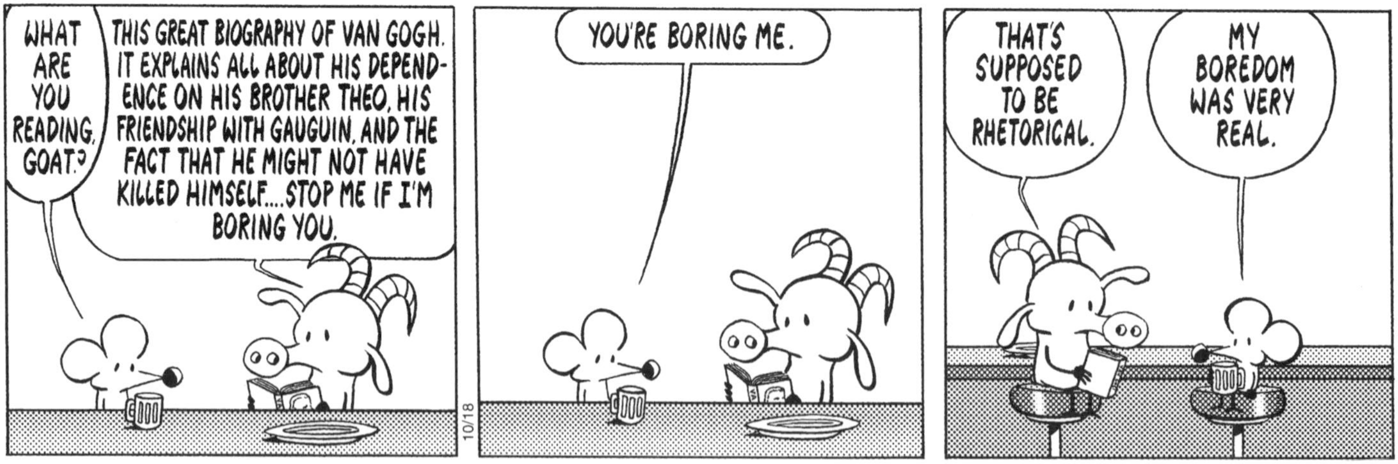
WHAT ARE YOU READING, GOAT?
THIS GREAT BIOGRAPHY OF VAN GOGH. IT EXPLAINS ALL ABOUT HIS DEPENDENCE ON HIS BROTHER THEO, HIS FRIENDSHIP WITH GAUGUIN, AND THE FACT THAT HE MIGHT NOT HAVE KILLED HIMSELF....STOP ME IF I'M BORING YOU.
10/18
YOU'RE BORING ME.
THAT'S SUPPOSED TO BE RHETORICAL.
MY BOREDOM WAS VERY REAL.

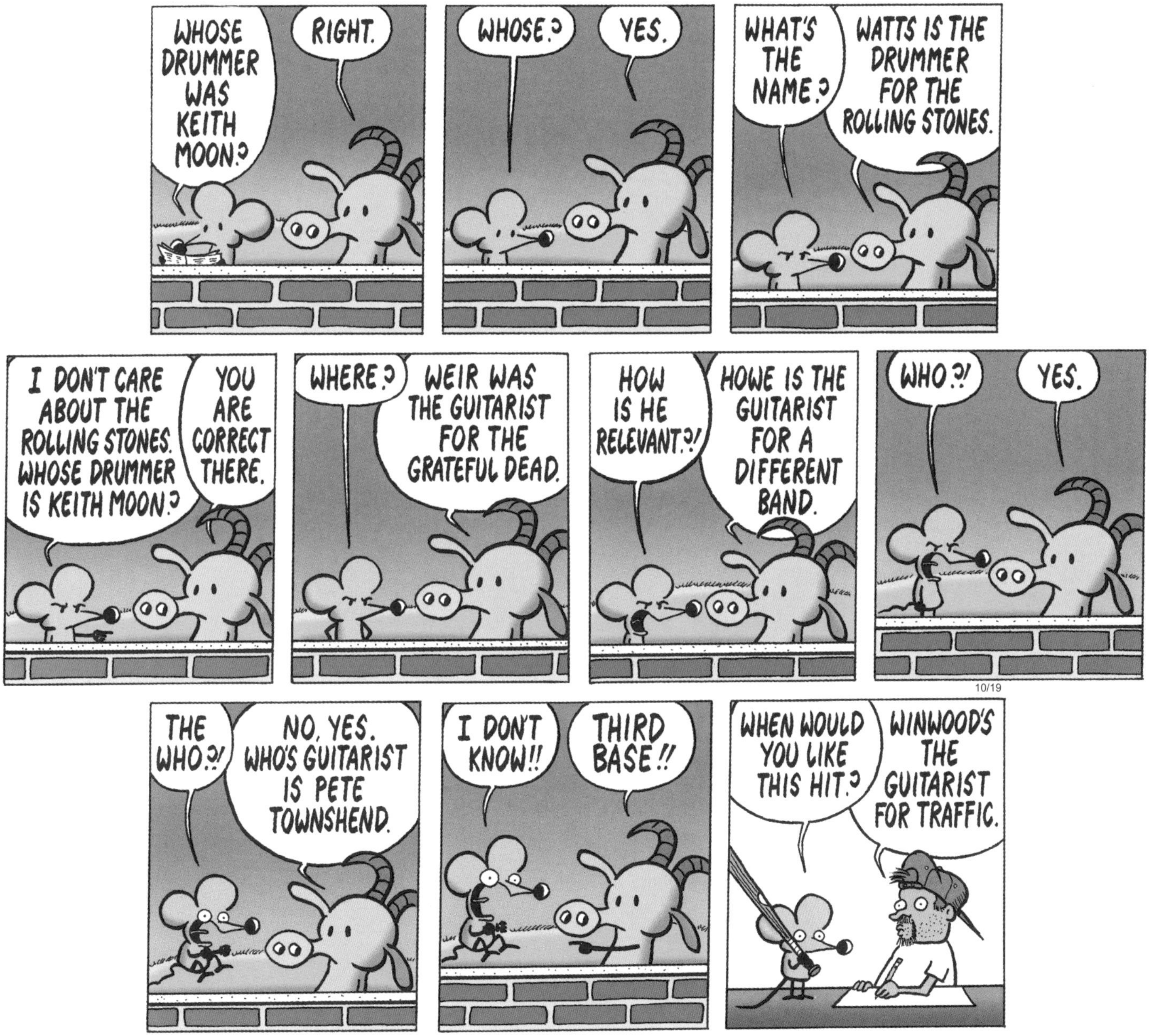
WHOSE DRUMMER WAS KEITH MOON?
RIGHT.
WHOSE?
YES.
WHAT'S THE NAME?
WATTS IS THE DRUMMER FOR THE ROLLING STONES.
I DON'T CARE ABOUT THE ROLLING STONES. WHOSE DRUMMER IS KEITH MOON?
YOU ARE CORRECT THERE.
WHERE?
WEIR WAS THE GUITARIST FOR THE GRATEFUL DEAD.
HOW IS HE RELEVANT?!
HOWE IS THE GUITARIST FOR A DIFFERENT BAND.
WHO?!
YES.
10/19
THE WHO?!
NO, YES. WHO'S GUITARIST IS PETE TOWNSHEND.
I DON'T KNOW!!
THIRD BASE!!
WHEN WOULD YOU LIKE THIS HIT?
WINWOOD'S THE GUITARIST FOR TRAFFIC.

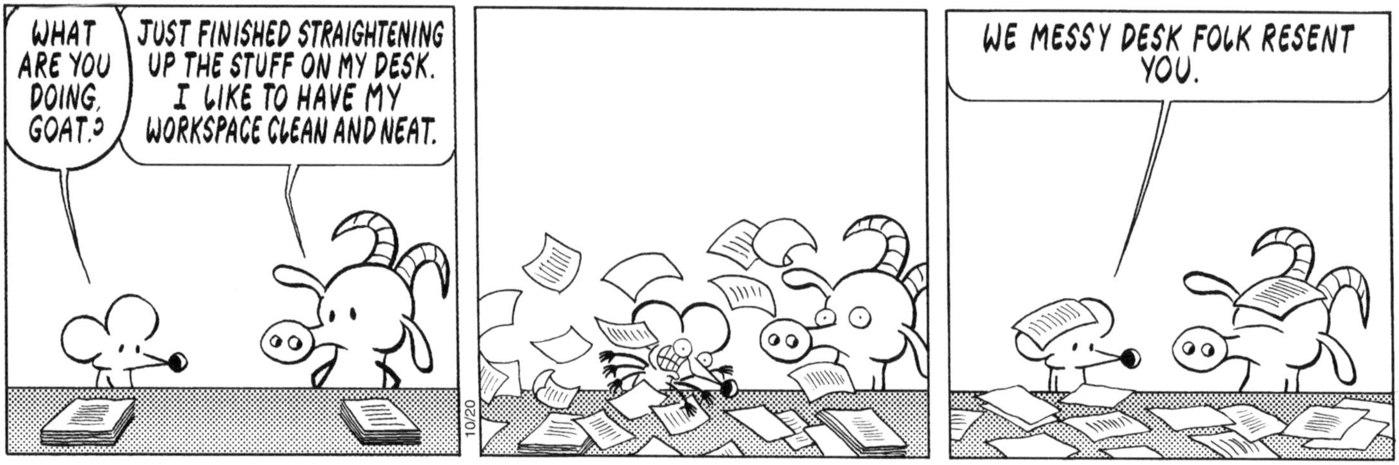
WHAT ARE YOU DOING, GOAT?
JUST FINISHED STRAIGHTENING UP THE STUFF ON MY DESK. I LIKE TO HAVE MY WORKSPACE CLEAN AND NEAT.
10/20
WE MESSY DESK FOLK RESENT YOU.

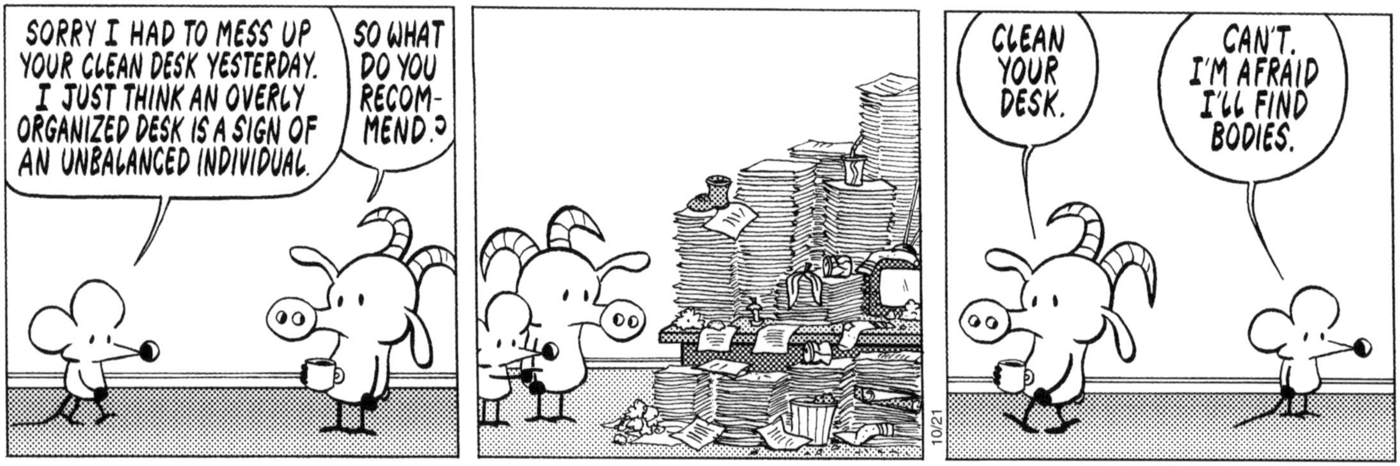
SORRY I HAD TO MESS UP YOUR CLEAN DESK YESTERDAY. I JUST THINK AN OVERLY ORGANIZED DESK IS A SIGN OF AN UNBALANCED INDIVIDUAL.
SO WHAT DO YOU RECOMMEND?
10/21
CLEAN YOUR DESK.
CAN'T. I'M AFRAID I'LL FIND BODIES.

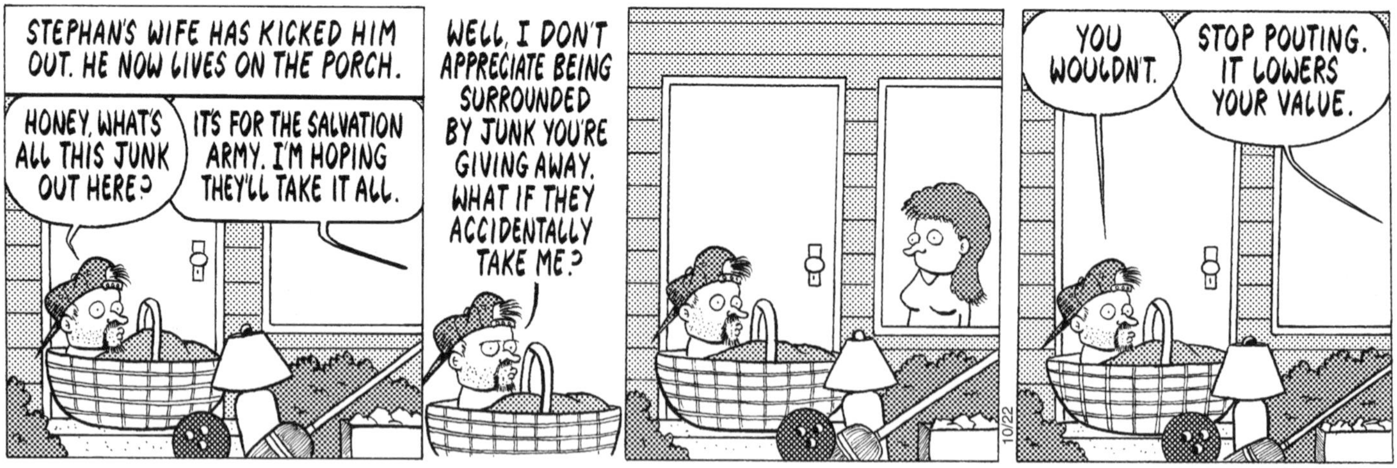
STEPHAN'S WIFE HAS KICKED HIM OUT. HE NOW LIVES ON THE PORCH.
HONEY, WHAT'S ALL THIS JUNK OUT HERE?
IT'S FOR THE SALVATION ARMY. I'M HOPING THEY'LL TAKE IT ALL.
WELL, I DON'T APPRECIATE BEING SURROUNDED BY JUNK YOU'RE GIVING AWAY. WHAT IF THEY ACCIDENTALLY TAKE ME?
10/22
YOU WOULDN'T.
STOP POUTING. IT LOWERS YOUR VALUE.

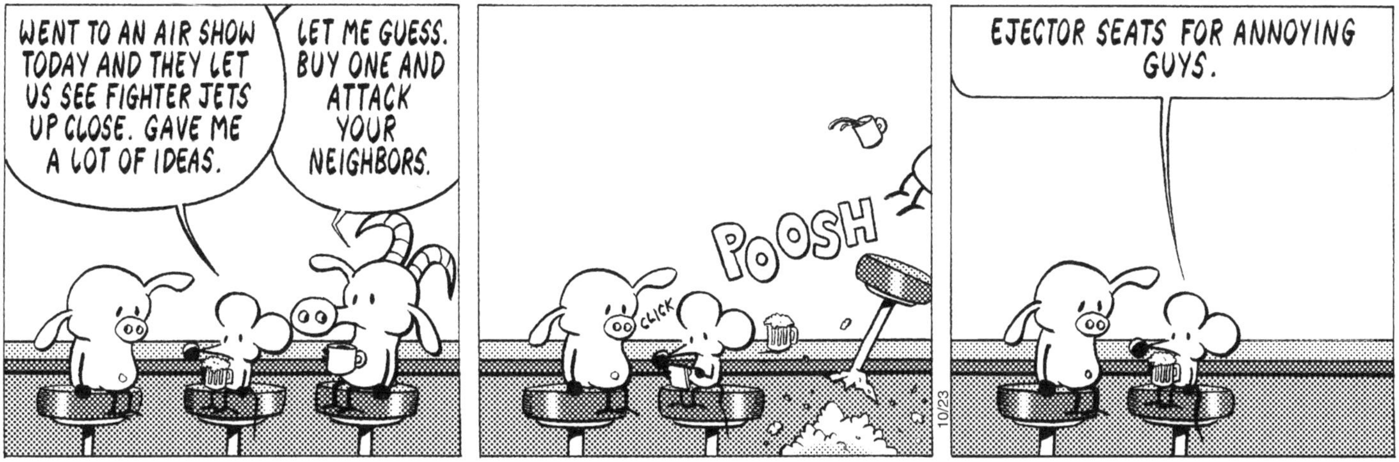
WENT TO AN AIR SHOW TODAY AND THEY LET US SEE FIGHTER JETS UP CLOSE. GAVE ME A LOT OF IDEAS.
LET ME GUESS. BUY ONE AND ATTACK YOUR NEIGHBORS.
CLICK
POOSH
EJECTOR SEATS FOR ANNOYING GUYS.
10/23

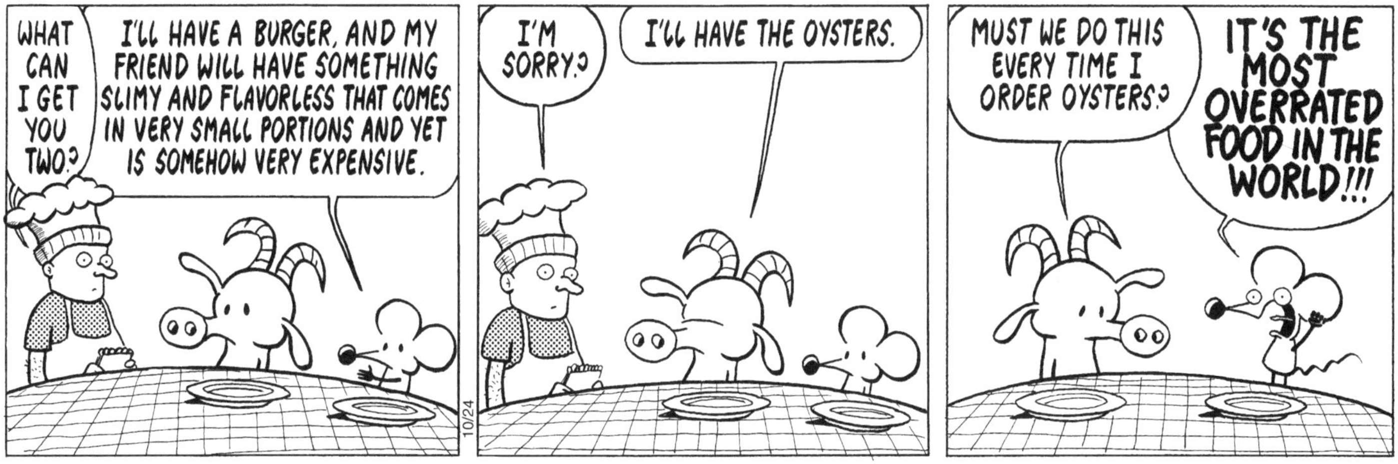
WHAT CAN I GET YOU TWO?
I'LL HAVE A BURGER, AND MY FRIEND WILL HAVE SOMETHING SLIMY AND FLAVORLESS THAT COMES IN VERY SMALL PORTIONS AND YET IS SOMEHOW VERY EXPENSIVE.
I'M SORRY?
I'LL HAVE THE OYSTERS.
MUST WE DO THIS EVERY TIME I ORDER OYSTERS?
IT'S THE MOST OVERRATED FOOD IN THE WORLD!!!
10/24

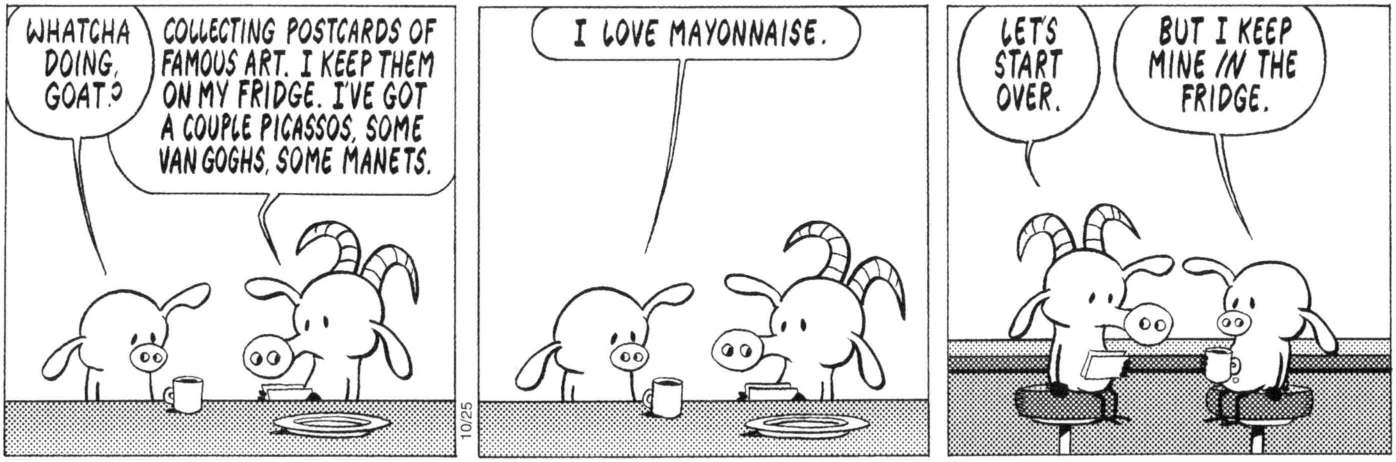
WHATCHA DOING, GOAT?
COLLECTING POSTCARDS OF FAMOUS ART. I KEEP THEM ON MY FRIDGE. I'VE GOT A COUPLE PICASSOS, SOME VAN GOGHS, SOME MANETS.
I LOVE MAYONNAISE.
LET'S START OVER.
BUT I KEEP MINE IN THE FRIDGE.
10/25

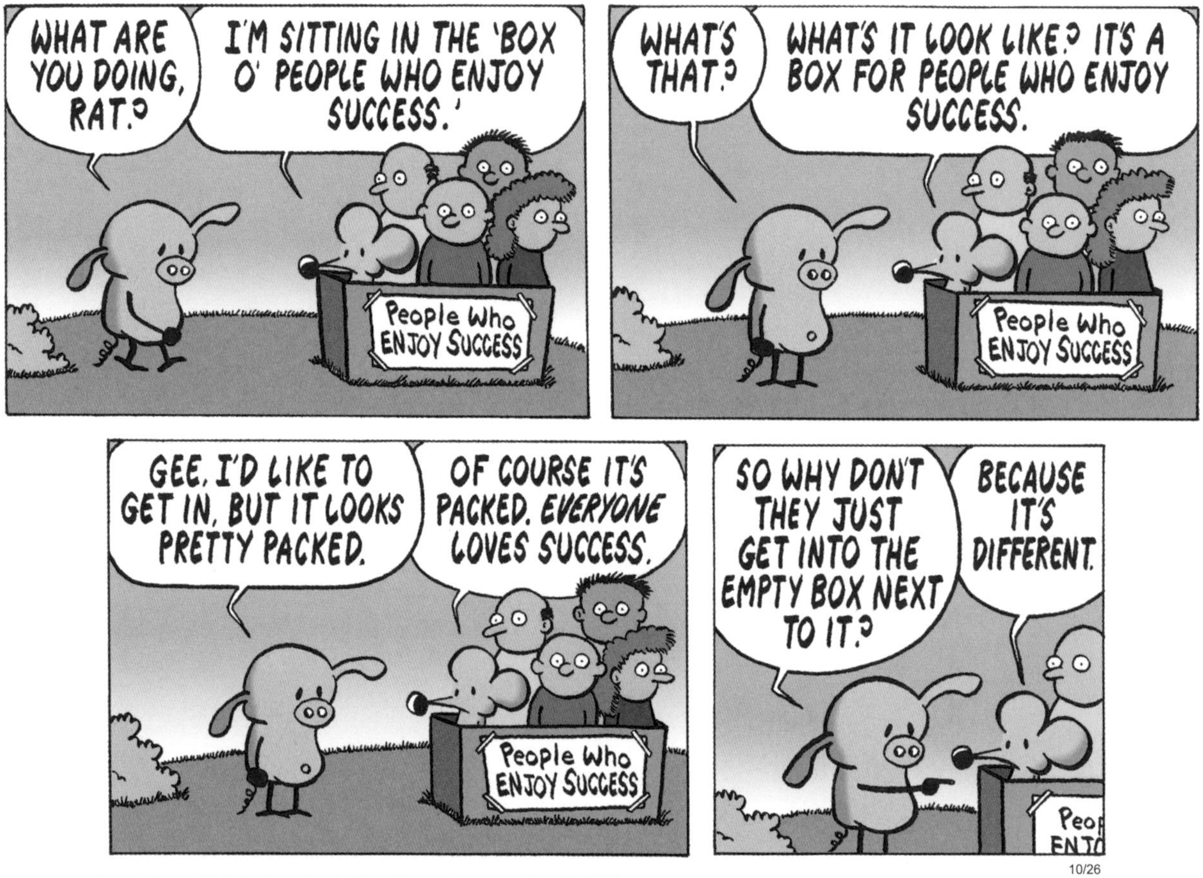
WHAT ARE YOU DOING, RAT?
I'M SITTING IN THE 'BOX O' PEOPLE WHO ENJOY SUCCESS.'
People Who ENJOY SUCCESS
WHAT'S THAT?
WHAT'S IT LOOK LIKE? IT'S A BOX FOR PEOPLE WHO ENJOY SUCCESS.
People Who ENJOY SUCCESS
GEE, I'D LIKE TO GET IN, BUT IT LOOKS PRETTY PACKED.
OF COURSE IT'S PACKED. *EVERYONE* LOVES SUCCESS.
People Who ENJOY SUCCESS
SO WHY DON'T THEY JUST GET INTO THE EMPTY BOX NEXT TO IT?
BECAUSE IT'S DIFFERENT.
10/26

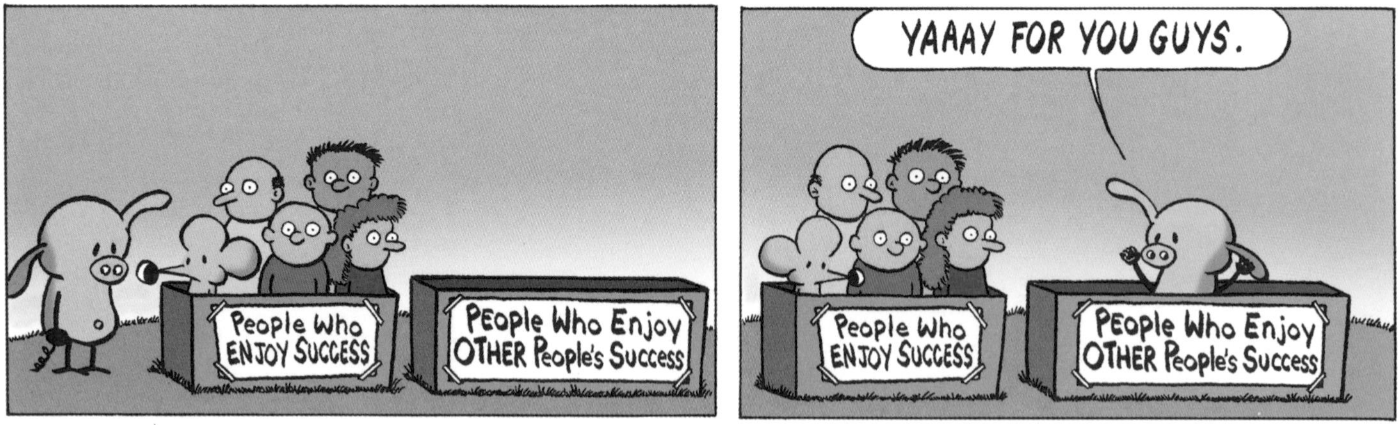
People Who ENJOY SUCCESS
PEOPLE Who Enjoy OTHER People's Success
YAAAY FOR YOU GUYS.
People Who ENJOY SUCCESS
PEOPLE Who Enjoy OTHER People's Success

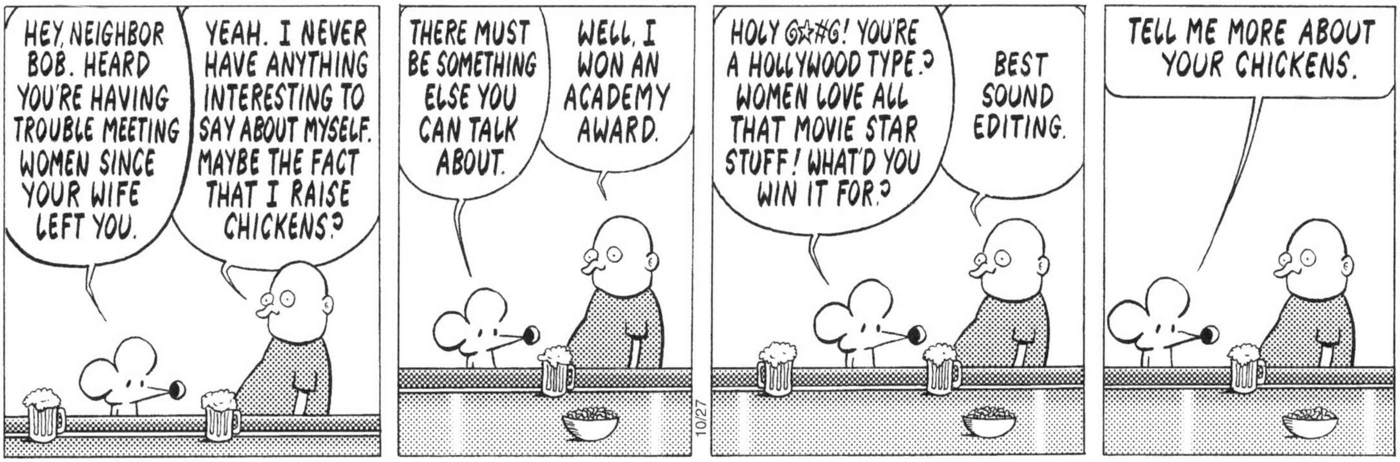
HEY, NEIGHBOR BOB. HEARD YOU'RE HAVING TROUBLE MEETING WOMEN SINCE YOUR WIFE LEFT YOU.
YEAH. I NEVER HAVE ANYTHING INTERESTING TO SAY ABOUT MYSELF. MAYBE THE FACT THAT I RAISE CHICKENS?
THERE MUST BE SOMETHING ELSE YOU CAN TALK ABOUT.
WELL, I WON AN ACADEMY AWARD.
10/27
HOLY @☆#@! YOU'RE A HOLLYWOOD TYPE? WOMEN LOVE ALL THAT MOVIE STAR STUFF! WHAT'D YOU WIN IT FOR?
BEST SOUND EDITING.
TELL ME MORE ABOUT YOUR CHICKENS.

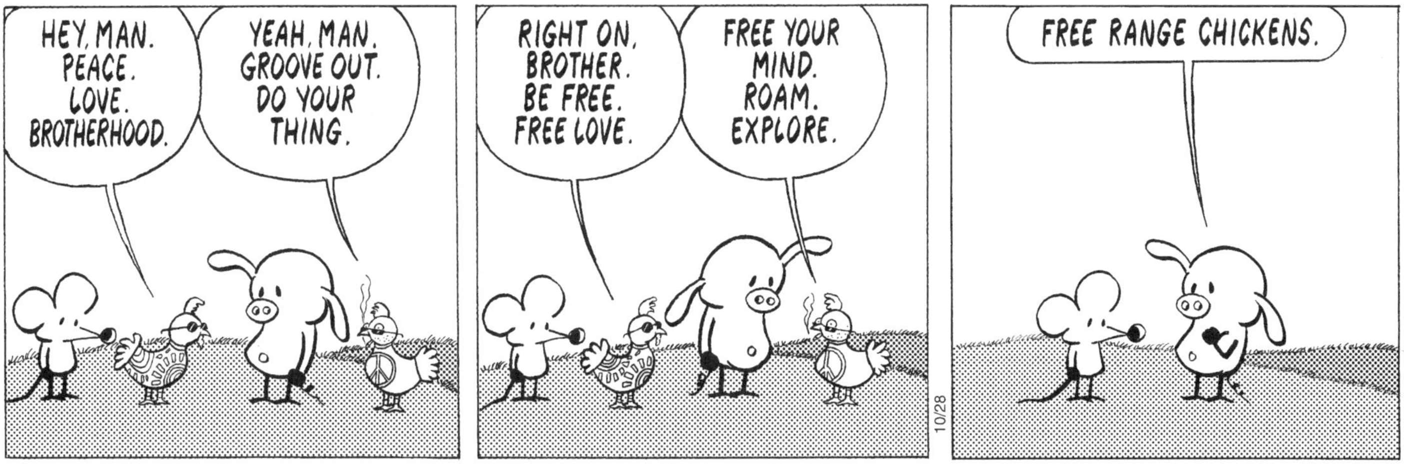
HEY, MAN. PEACE. LOVE. BROTHERHOOD.
YEAH, MAN. GROOVE OUT. DO YOUR THING.
RIGHT ON, BROTHER. BE FREE. FREE LOVE.
FREE YOUR MIND. ROAM. EXPLORE.
10/28
FREE RANGE CHICKENS.

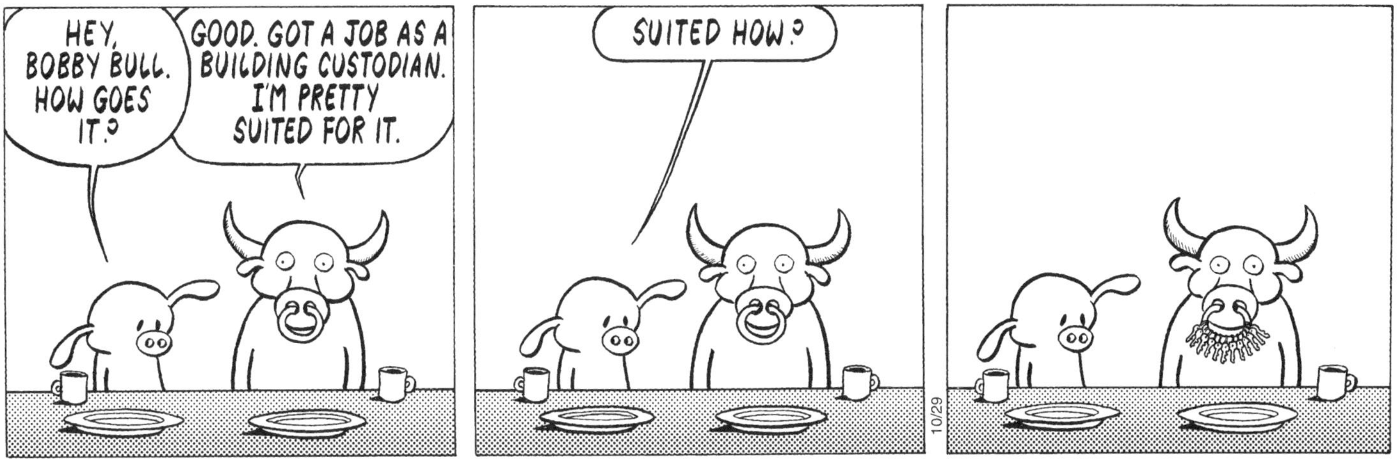
HEY, BOBBY BULL. HOW GOES IT?
GOOD. GOT A JOB AS A BUILDING CUSTODIAN. I'M PRETTY SUITED FOR IT.
SUITED HOW?
10/29

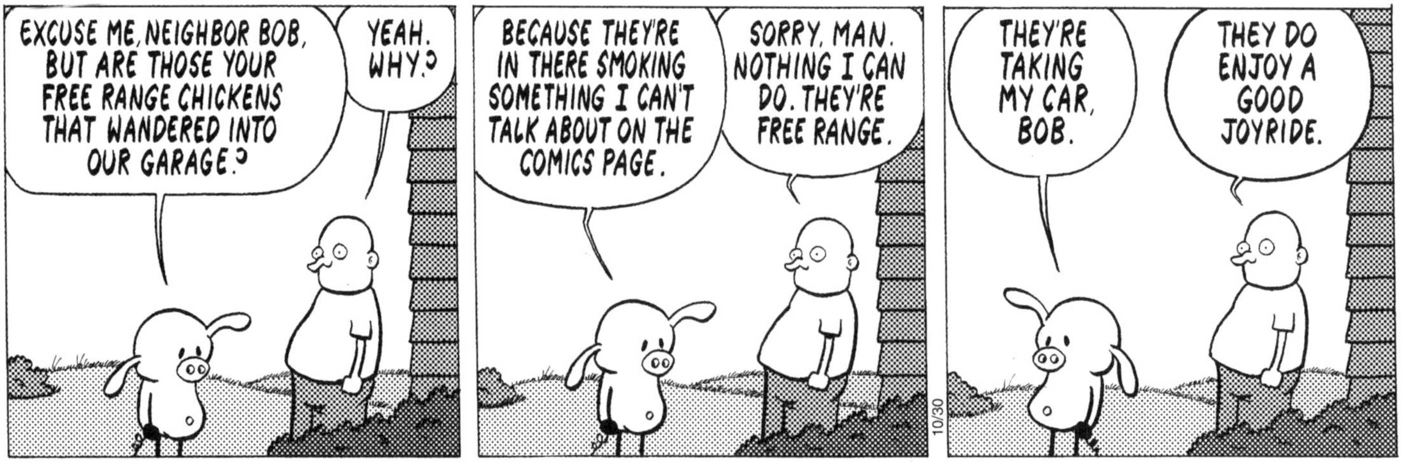
EXCUSE ME, NEIGHBOR BOB, BUT ARE THOSE YOUR FREE RANGE CHICKENS THAT WANDERED INTO OUR GARAGE?
YEAH. WHY?
BECAUSE THEY'RE IN THERE SMOKING SOMETHING I CAN'T TALK ABOUT ON THE COMICS PAGE.
SORRY, MAN. NOTHING I CAN DO. THEY'RE FREE RANGE.
10/30
THEY'RE TAKING MY CAR, BOB.
THEY DO ENJOY A GOOD JOYRIDE.

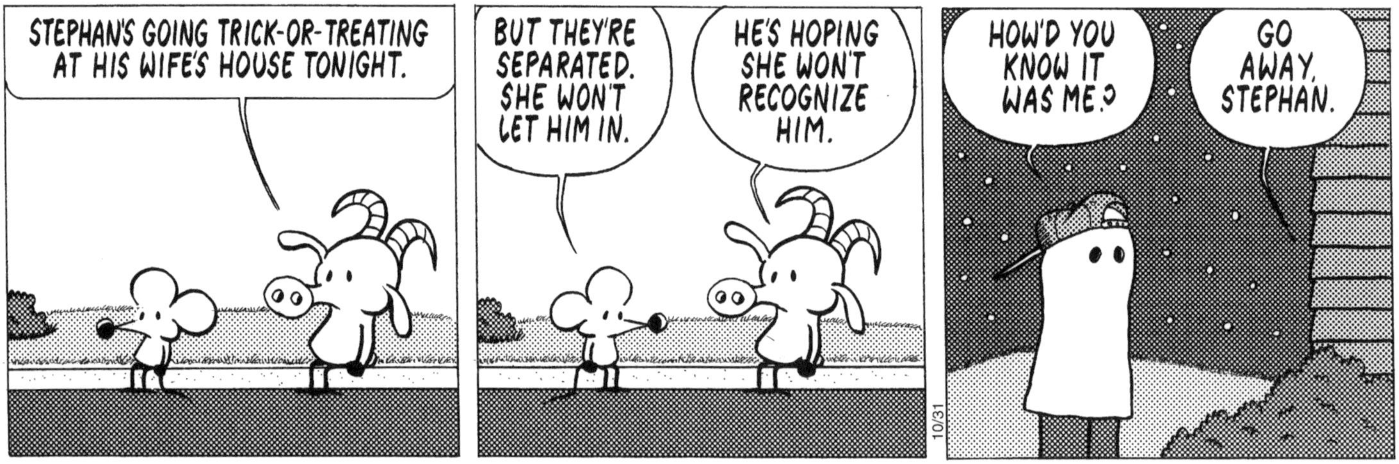
STEPHAN'S GOING TRICK-OR-TREATING AT HIS WIFE'S HOUSE TONIGHT.
BUT THEY'RE SEPARATED. SHE WON'T LET HIM IN.
HE'S HOPING SHE WON'T RECOGNIZE HIM.
10/31
HOW'D YOU KNOW IT WAS ME?
GO AWAY, STEPHAN.

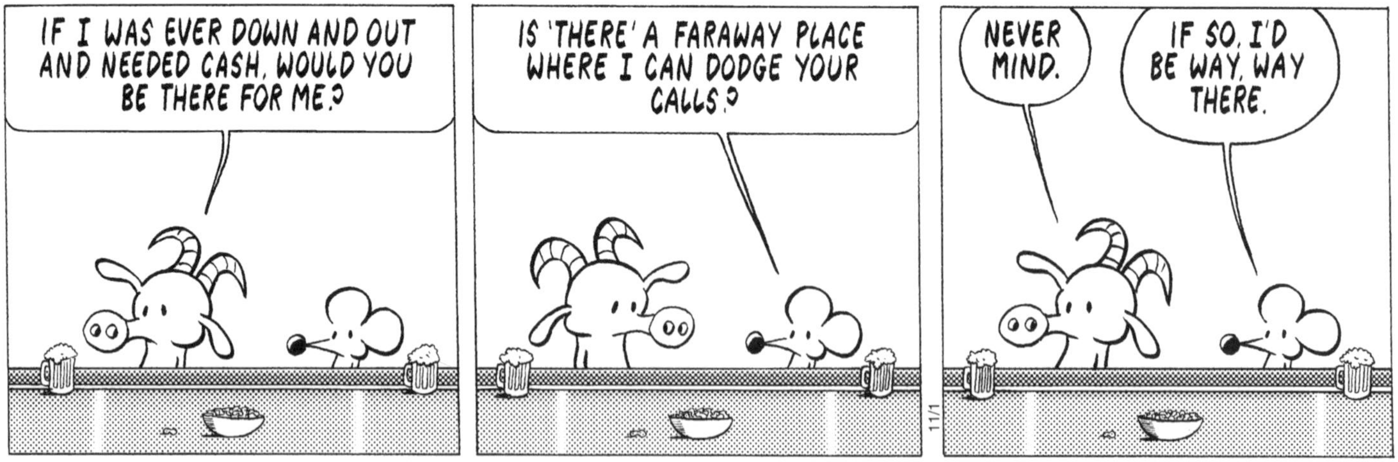
IF I WAS EVER DOWN AND OUT AND NEEDED CASH, WOULD YOU BE THERE FOR ME?
IS 'THERE' A FARAWAY PLACE WHERE I CAN DODGE YOUR CALLS?
11/1
NEVER MIND.
IF SO, I'D BE WAY, WAY THERE.

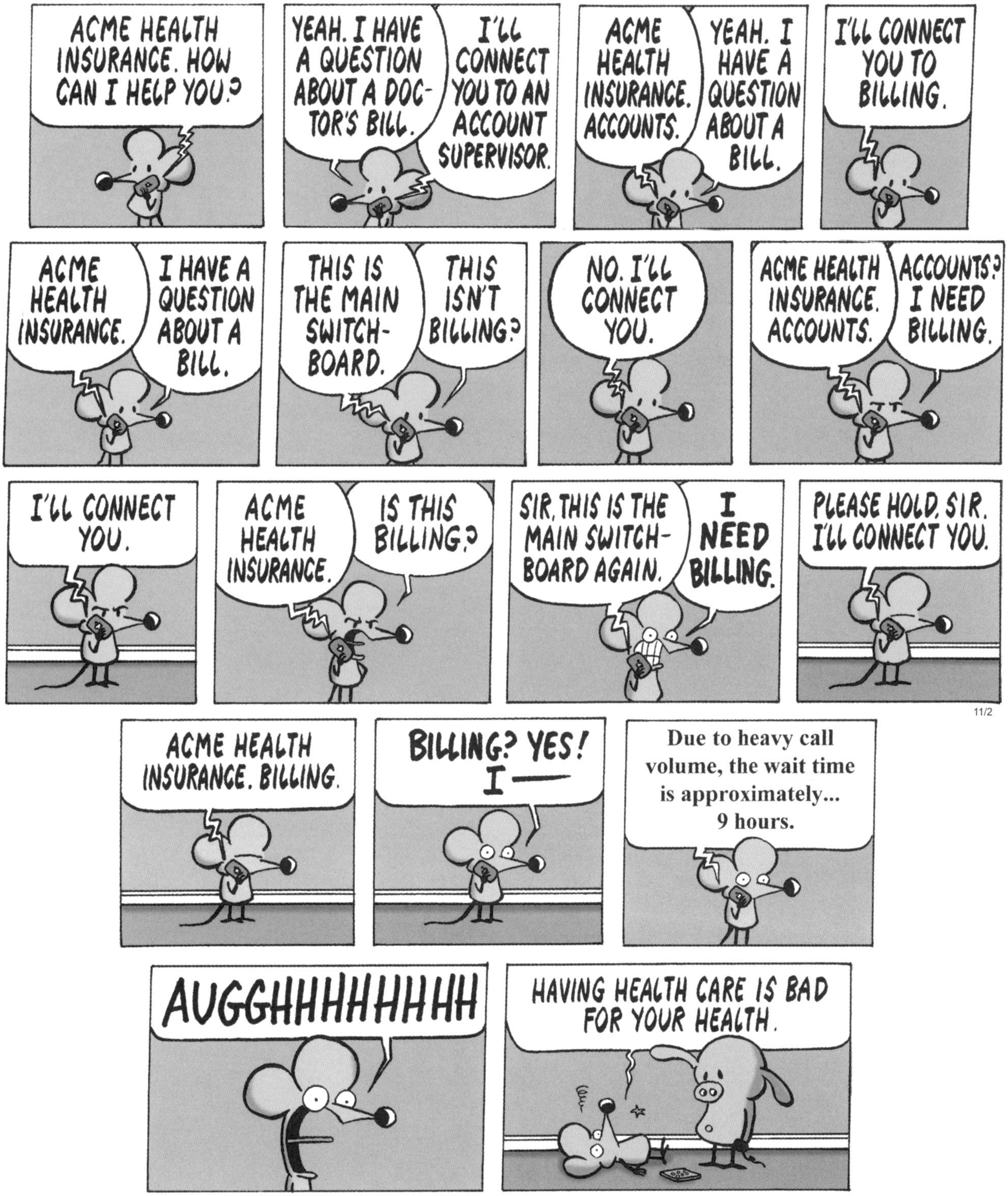

ACME HEALTH INSURANCE. HOW CAN I HELP YOU?
YEAH. I HAVE A QUESTION ABOUT A DOCTOR'S BILL.
I'LL CONNECT YOU TO AN ACCOUNT SUPERVISOR.
ACME HEALTH INSURANCE. ACCOUNTS.
YEAH. I HAVE A QUESTION ABOUT A BILL.
I'LL CONNECT YOU TO BILLING.
ACME HEALTH INSURANCE.
I HAVE A QUESTION ABOUT A BILL.
THIS IS THE MAIN SWITCHBOARD.
THIS ISN'T BILLING?
NO. I'LL CONNECT YOU.
ACME HEALTH INSURANCE. ACCOUNTS.
ACCOUNTS? I NEED BILLING.
I'LL CONNECT YOU.
ACME HEALTH INSURANCE.
IS THIS BILLING?
SIR, THIS IS THE MAIN SWITCHBOARD AGAIN.
I NEED BILLING.
PLEASE HOLD, SIR. I'LL CONNECT YOU.
11/2
ACME HEALTH INSURANCE. BILLING.
BILLING? YES! I—
Due to heavy call volume, the wait time is approximately... 9 hours.
AUGGHHHHHHHH
HAVING HEALTH CARE IS BAD FOR YOUR HEALTH.

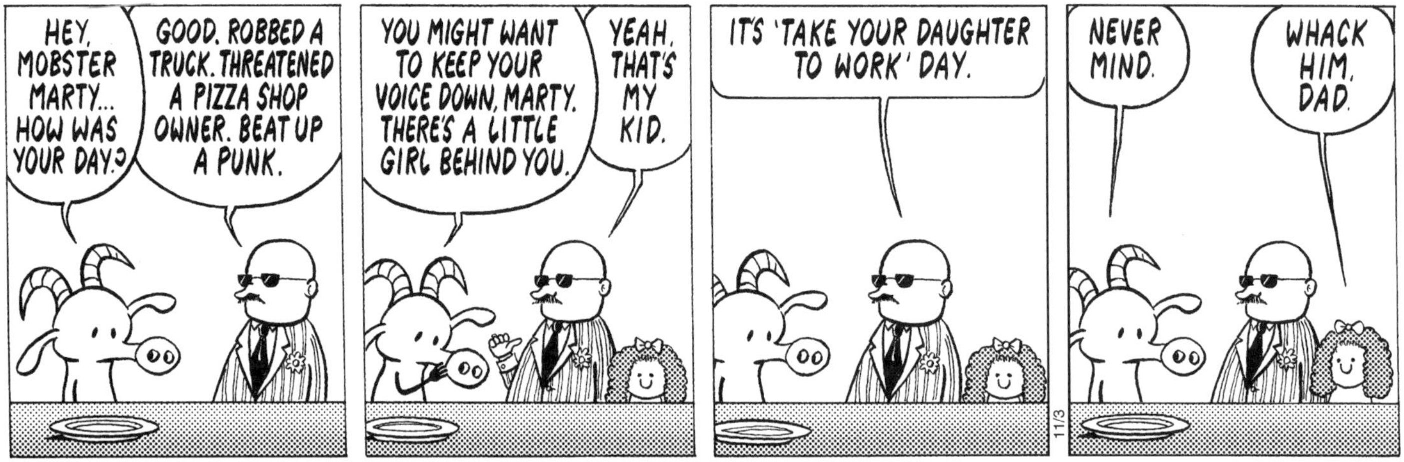
HEY, MOBSTER MARTY... HOW WAS YOUR DAY?
GOOD. ROBBED A TRUCK. THREATENED A PIZZA SHOP OWNER. BEAT UP A PUNK.
YOU MIGHT WANT TO KEEP YOUR VOICE DOWN, MARTY. THERE'S A LITTLE GIRL BEHIND YOU.
YEAH, THAT'S MY KID.
IT'S 'TAKE YOUR DAUGHTER TO WORK' DAY.
11/3
NEVER MIND.
WHACK HIM, DAD.

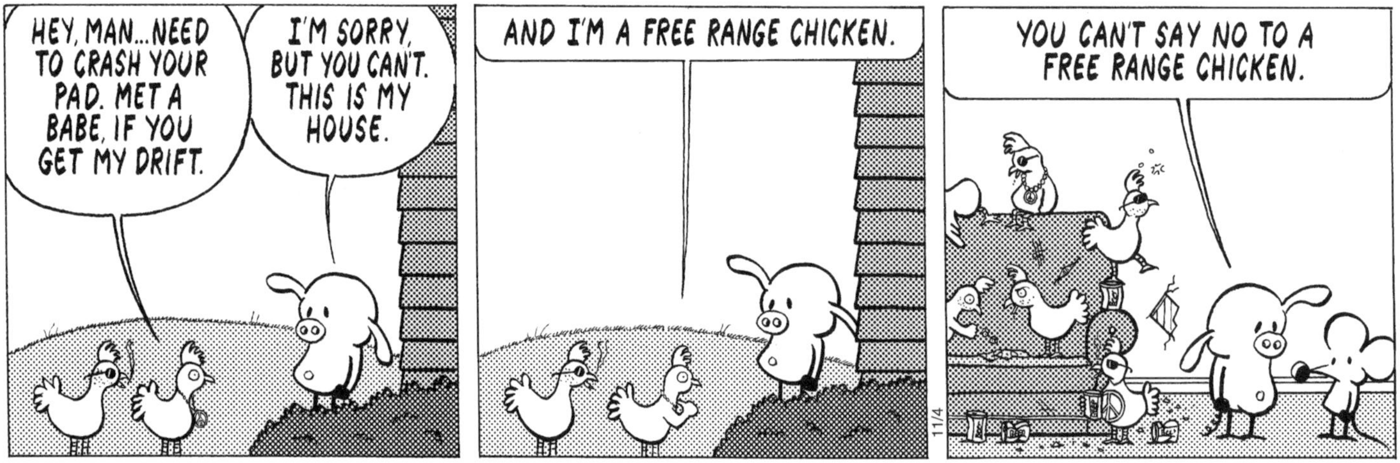
HEY, MAN...NEED TO CRASH YOUR PAD. MET A BABE, IF YOU GET MY DRIFT.
I'M SORRY, BUT YOU CAN'T. THIS IS MY HOUSE.
AND I'M A FREE RANGE CHICKEN.
11/4
YOU CAN'T SAY NO TO A FREE RANGE CHICKEN.

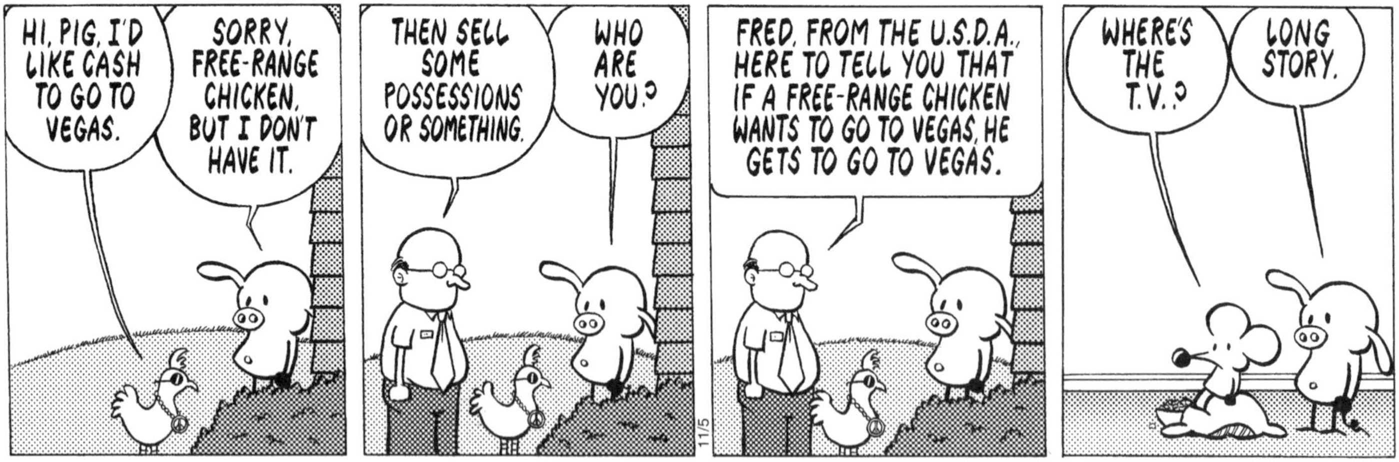
HI, PIG, I'D LIKE CASH TO GO TO VEGAS.
SORRY, FREE-RANGE CHICKEN, BUT I DON'T HAVE IT.
THEN SELL SOME POSSESSIONS OR SOMETHING.
WHO ARE YOU?
FRED, FROM THE U.S.D.A., HERE TO TELL YOU THAT IF A FREE-RANGE CHICKEN WANTS TO GO TO VEGAS, HE GETS TO GO TO VEGAS.
11/5
WHERE'S THE T.V.?
LONG STORY.

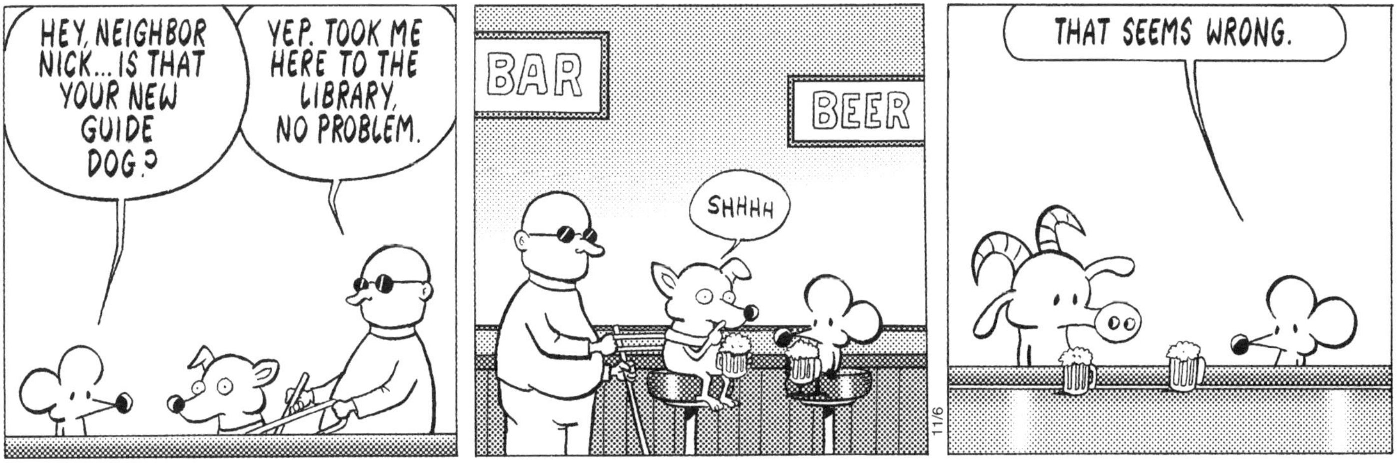
HEY, NEIGHBOR NICK... IS THAT YOUR NEW GUIDE DOG?
YEP. TOOK ME HERE TO THE LIBRARY, NO PROBLEM.
BAR
BEER
SHHHH
11/6
THAT SEEMS WRONG.

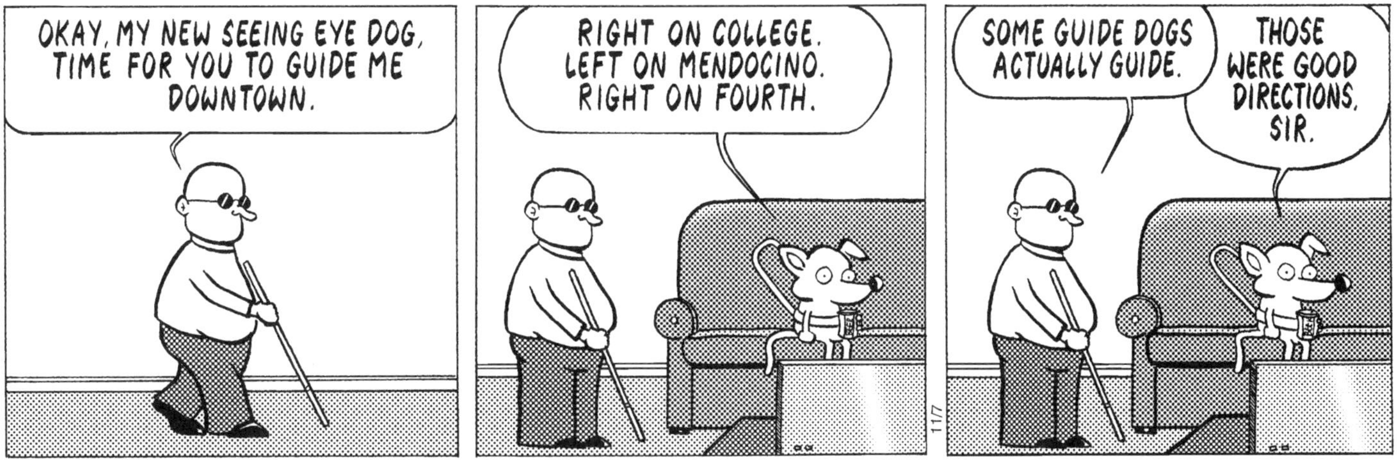
OKAY, MY NEW SEEING EYE DOG, TIME FOR YOU TO GUIDE ME DOWNTOWN.
RIGHT ON COLLEGE. LEFT ON MENDOCINO. RIGHT ON FOURTH.
11/7
SOME GUIDE DOGS ACTUALLY GUIDE.
THOSE WERE GOOD DIRECTIONS, SIR.

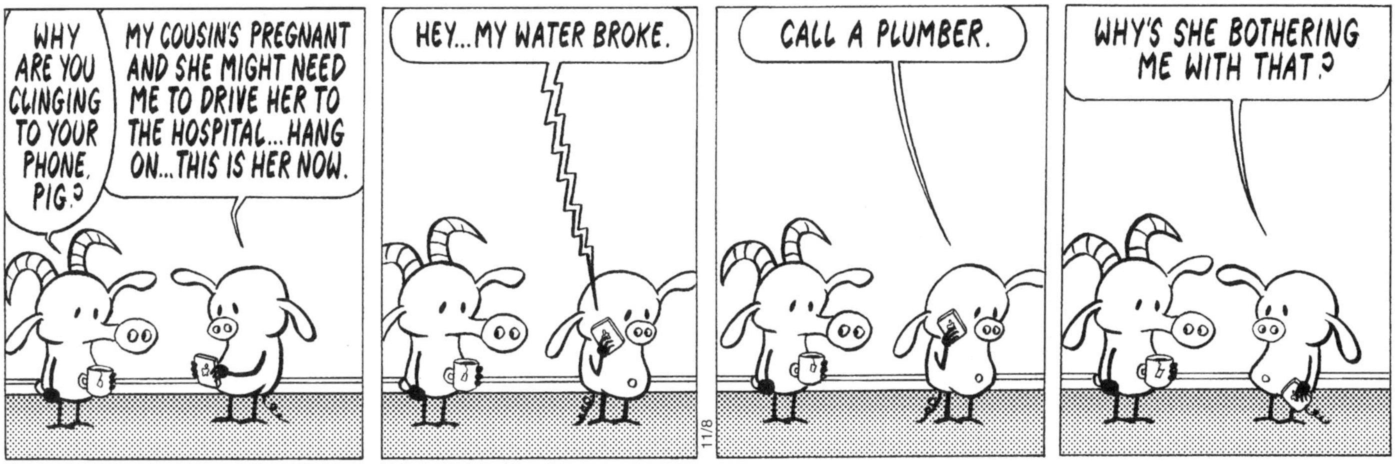
WHY ARE YOU CLINGING TO YOUR PHONE, PIG?
MY COUSIN'S PREGNANT AND SHE MIGHT NEED ME TO DRIVE HER TO THE HOSPITAL... HANG ON... THIS IS HER NOW.
HEY... MY WATER BROKE.
11/8
CALL A PLUMBER.
WHY'S SHE BOTHERING ME WITH THAT?

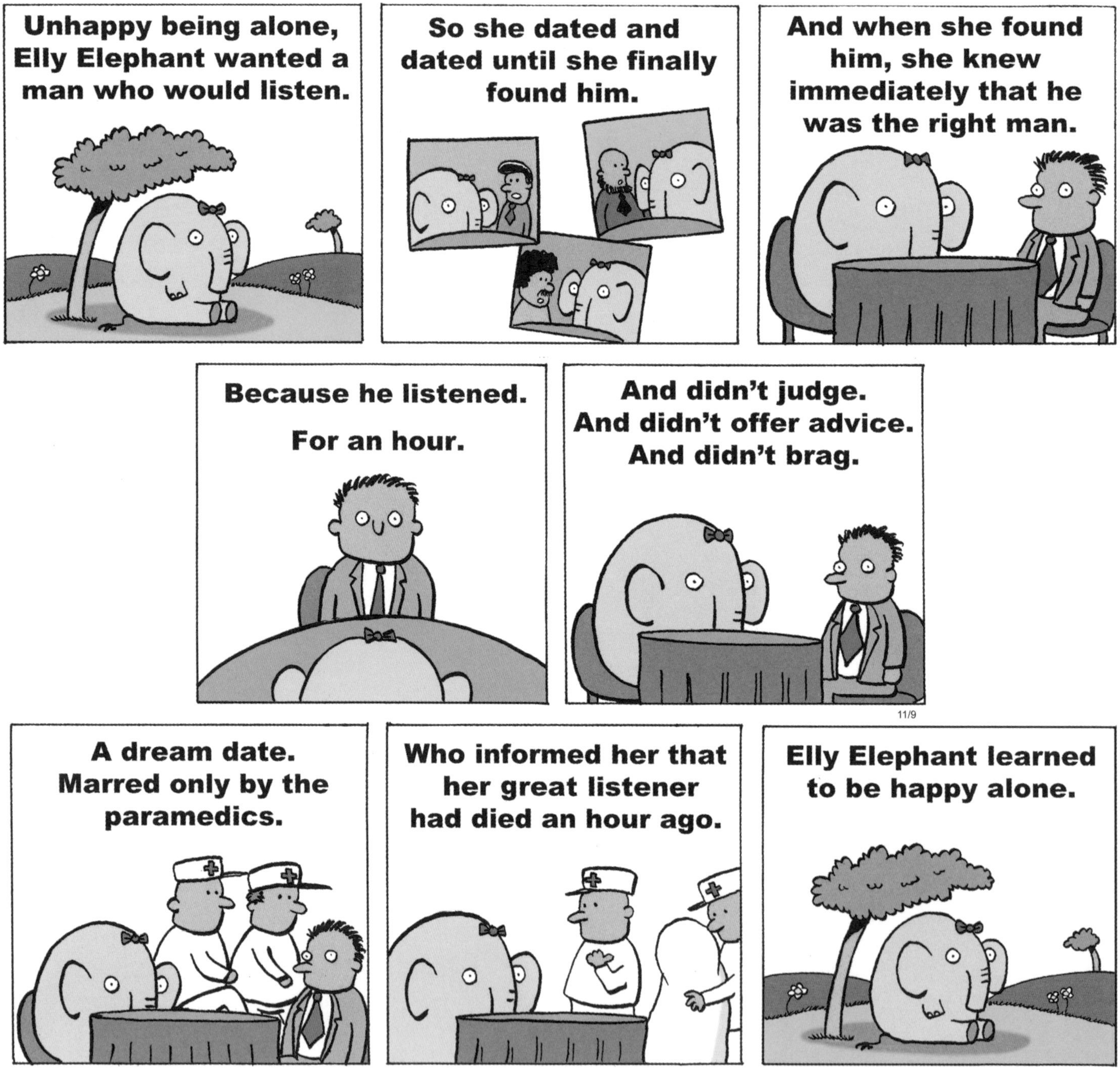
Unhappy being alone, Elly Elephant wanted a man who would listen.
So she dated and dated until she finally found him.
And when she found him, she knew immediately that he was the right man.
Because he listened.
For an hour.
And didn't judge.
And didn't offer advice.
And didn't brag.
11/9
A dream date.
Marred only by the paramedics.
Who informed her that her great listener had died an hour ago.
Elly Elephant learned to be happy alone.

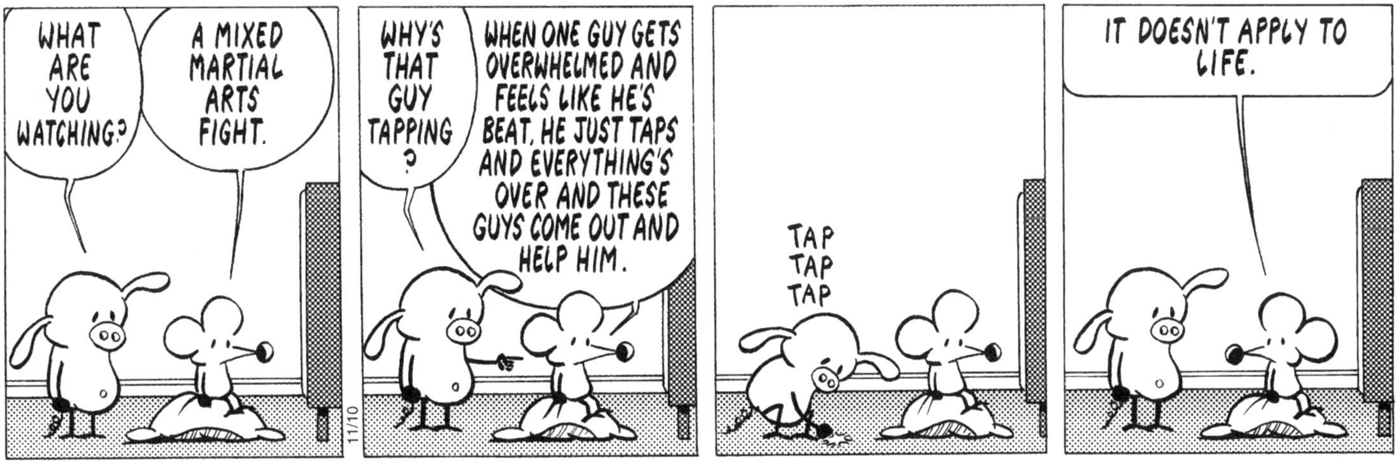
WHAT ARE YOU WATCHING?
A MIXED MARTIAL ARTS FIGHT.
11/10
WHY'S THAT GUY TAPPING?
WHEN ONE GUY GETS OVERWHELMED AND FEELS LIKE HE'S BEAT, HE JUST TAPS AND EVERYTHING'S OVER AND THESE GUYS COME OUT AND HELP HIM.
TAP TAP TAP
IT DOESN'T APPLY TO LIFE.

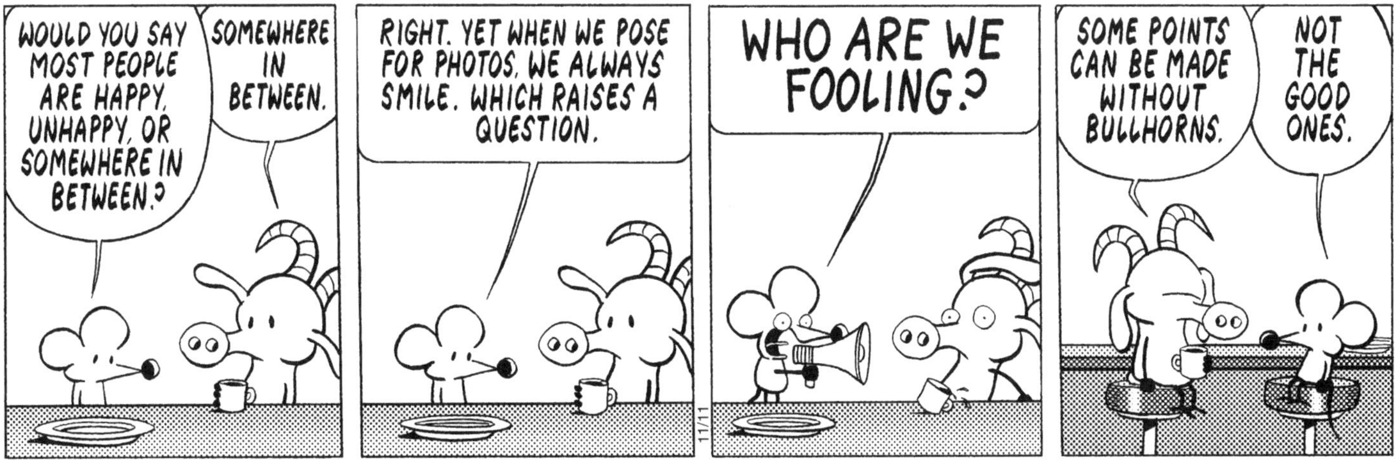
WOULD YOU SAY MOST PEOPLE ARE HAPPY, UNHAPPY, OR SOMEWHERE IN BETWEEN?
SOMEWHERE IN BETWEEN.
RIGHT. YET WHEN WE POSE FOR PHOTOS, WE ALWAYS SMILE. WHICH RAISES A QUESTION.
11/11
WHO ARE WE FOOLING?
SOME POINTS CAN BE MADE WITHOUT BULLHORNS.
NOT THE GOOD ONES.

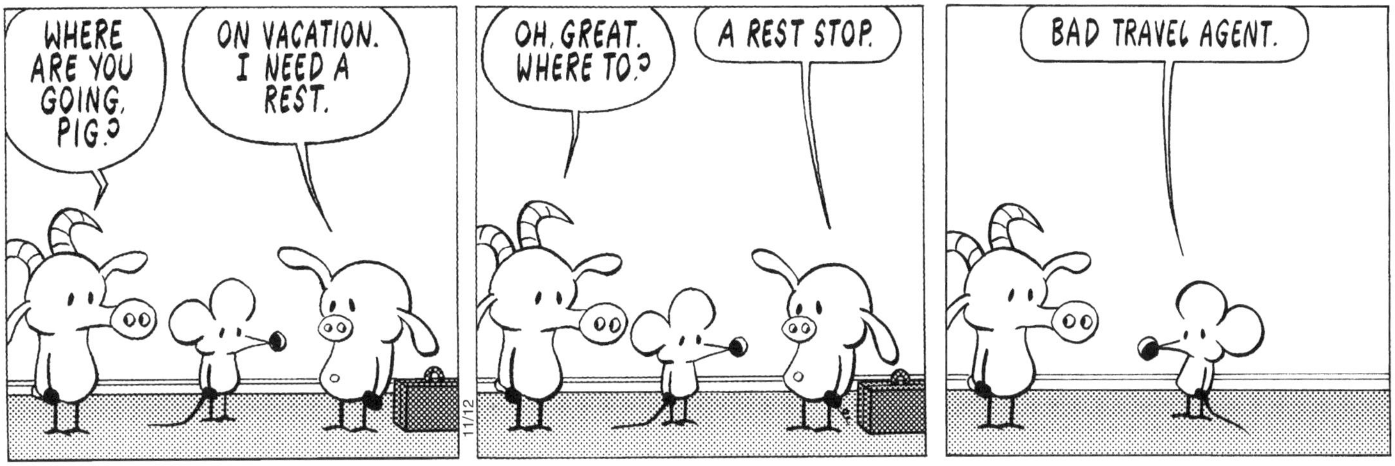
WHERE ARE YOU GOING, PIG?
ON VACATION. I NEED A REST.
11/12
OH, GREAT. WHERE TO?
A REST STOP.
BAD TRAVEL AGENT.

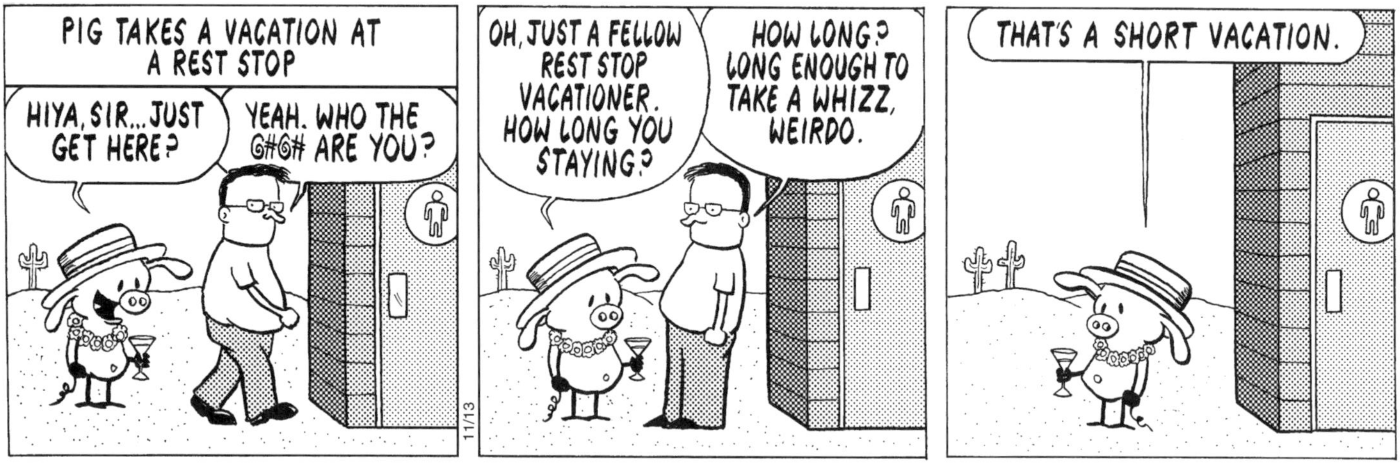
PIG TAKES A VACATION AT A REST STOP
HIYA, SIR...JUST GET HERE?
YEAH. WHO THE G#@# ARE YOU?
11/13
OH, JUST A FELLOW REST STOP VACATIONER. HOW LONG YOU STAYING?
HOW LONG? LONG ENOUGH TO TAKE A WHIZZ, WEIRDO.
THAT'S A SHORT VACATION.

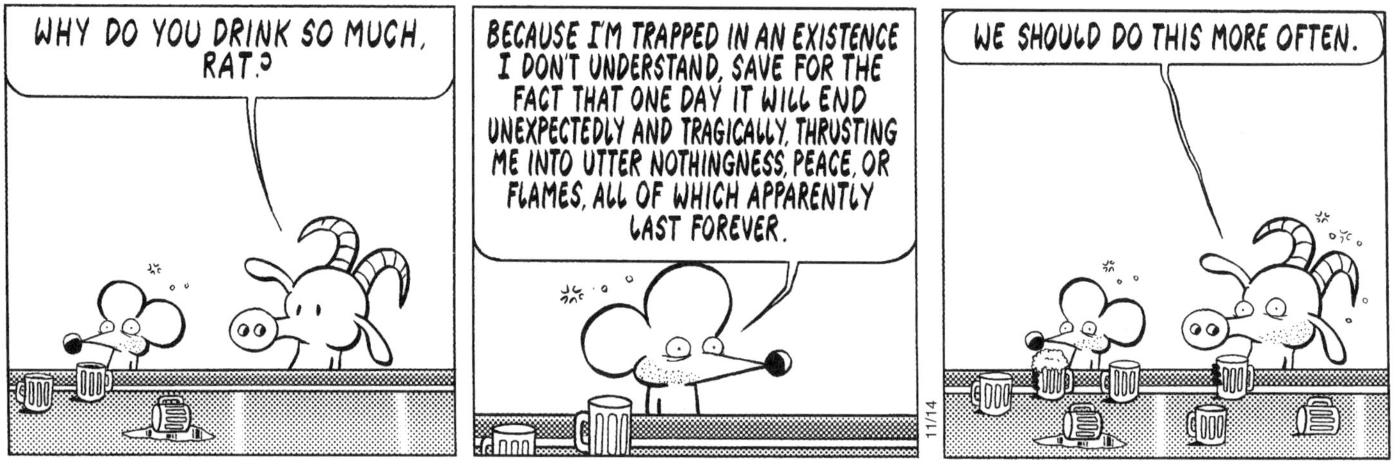
WHY DO YOU DRINK SO MUCH, RAT?
BECAUSE I'M TRAPPED IN AN EXISTENCE I DON'T UNDERSTAND, SAVE FOR THE FACT THAT ONE DAY IT WILL END UNEXPECTEDLY AND TRAGICALLY, THRUSTING ME INTO UTTER NOTHINGNESS, PEACE, OR FLAMES, ALL OF WHICH APPARENTLY LAST FOREVER.
11/14
WE SHOULD DO THIS MORE OFTEN.

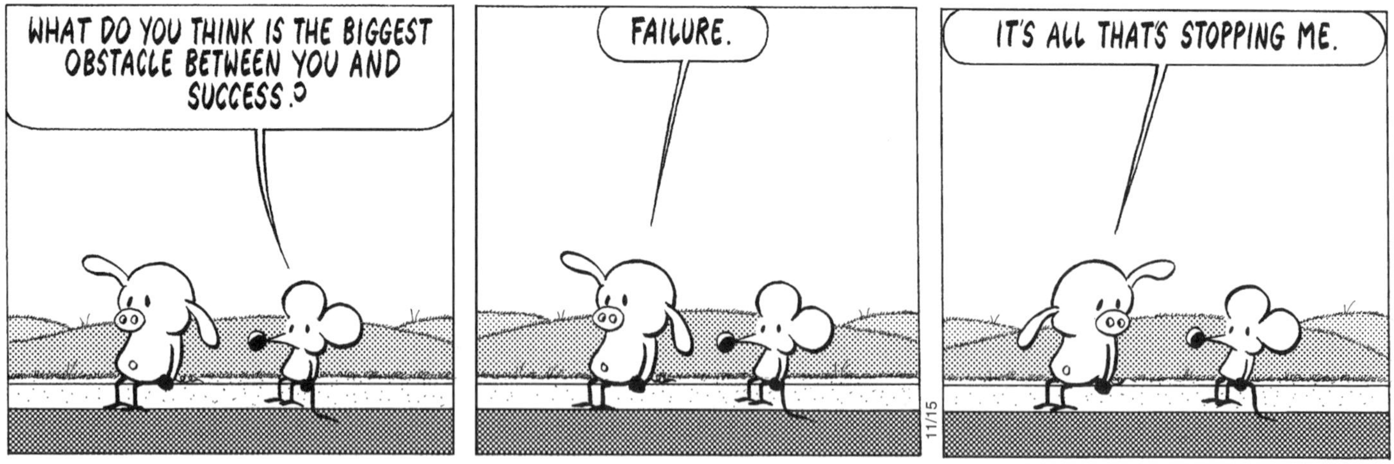
WHAT DO YOU THINK IS THE BIGGEST OBSTACLE BETWEEN YOU AND SUCCESS?
FAILURE.
11/15
IT'S ALL THAT'S STOPPING ME.

HI, MY NAME'S BOB, FROM ACME TIMESHARE...HOPE I'M NOT DISTURBING YOU...JUST CALLING TO TELL YOU ABOUT SOME EXCITING TIMESHARE OPPORTUNITIES....

WAIT... WHAT'S YOUR LAST NAME, BOB?

HIGGIN-BOTTOM. WHY?

HEY, RAT...YOU'RE UP FROM YOUR NAP EARLY.

VROOOOOOOOM...

11/16

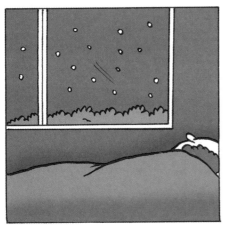

BBRRRRR

I FOUND A WAY TO DISCOURAGE TELEMARKETERS.

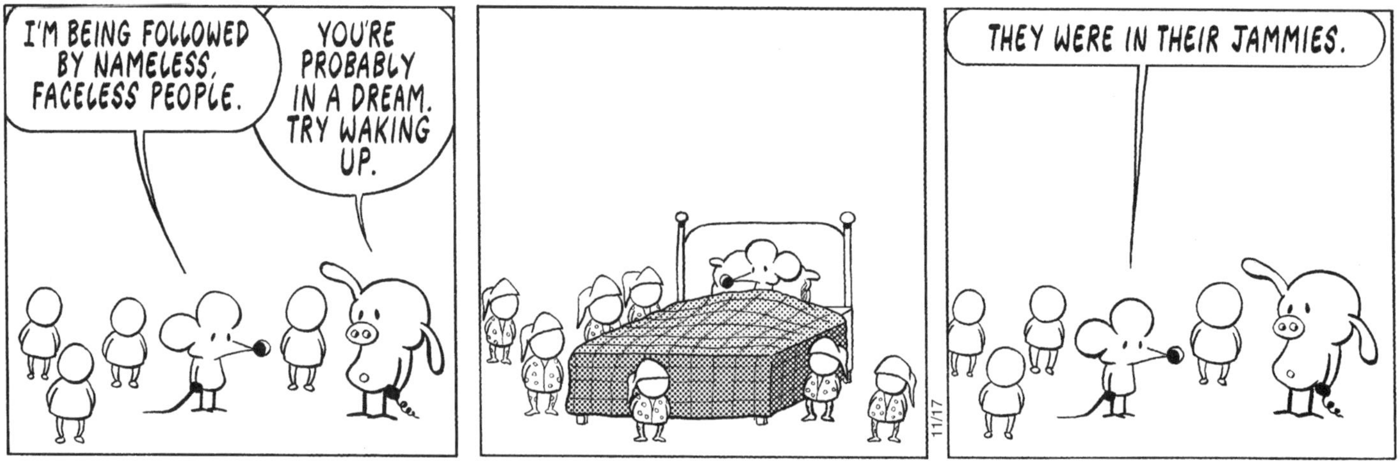
I'M BEING FOLLOWED BY NAMELESS, FACELESS PEOPLE.
YOU'RE PROBABLY IN A DREAM. TRY WAKING UP.
11/17
THEY WERE IN THEIR JAMMIES.

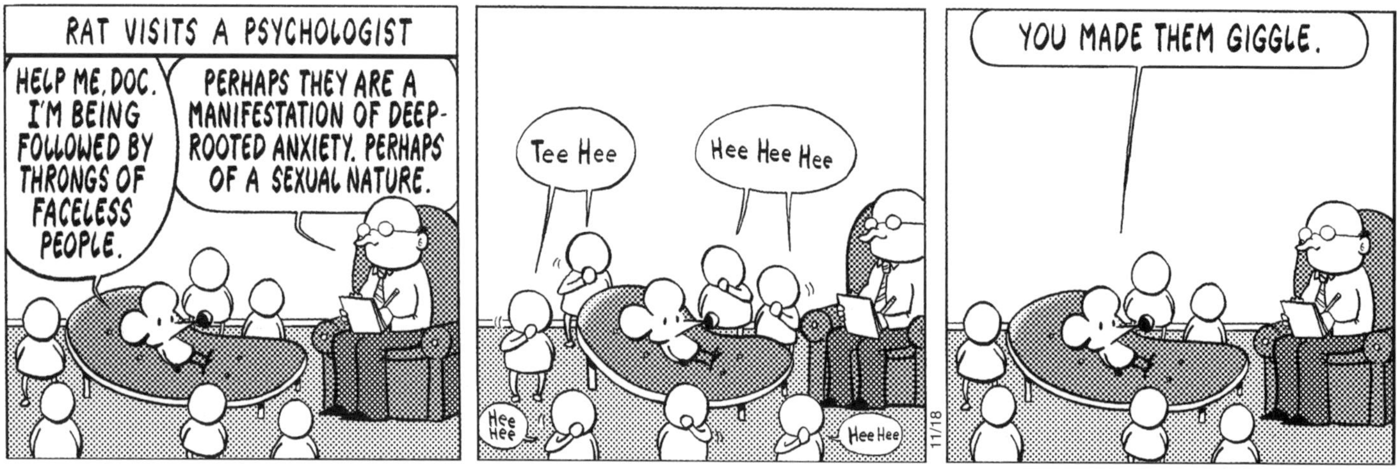
RAT VISITS A PSYCHOLOGIST
HELP ME, DOC. I'M BEING FOLLOWED BY THRONGS OF FACELESS PEOPLE.
PERHAPS THEY ARE A MANIFESTATION OF DEEP-ROOTED ANXIETY. PERHAPS OF A SEXUAL NATURE.
Tee Hee
Hee Hee Hee
Hee Hee
Hee Hee
11/18
YOU MADE THEM GIGGLE.

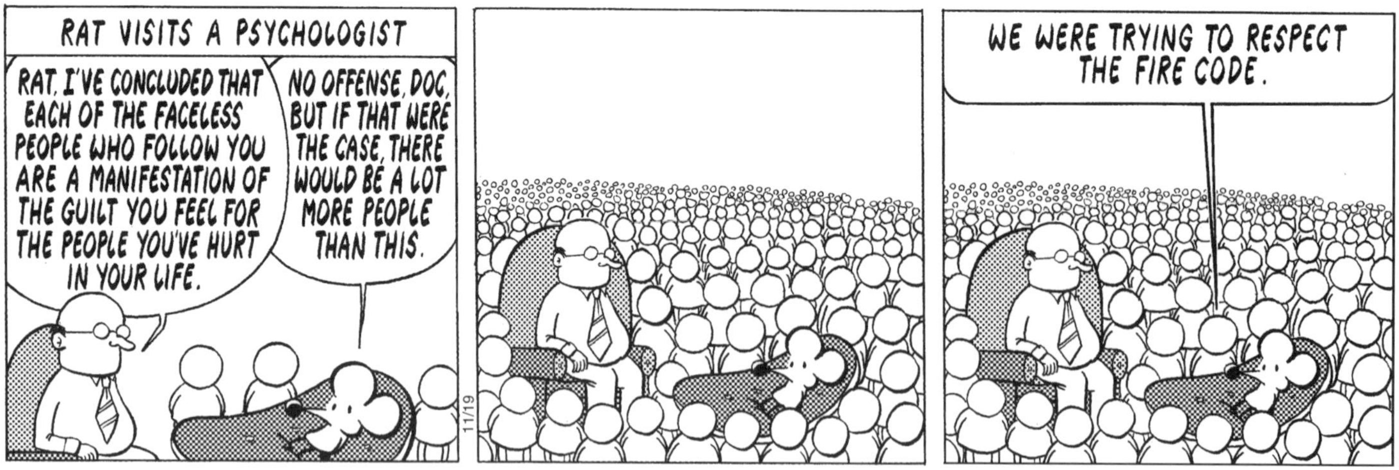
RAT VISITS A PSYCHOLOGIST
RAT, I'VE CONCLUDED THAT EACH OF THE FACELESS PEOPLE WHO FOLLOW YOU ARE A MANIFESTATION OF THE GUILT YOU FEEL FOR THE PEOPLE YOU'VE HURT IN YOUR LIFE.
NO OFFENSE, DOC, BUT IF THAT WERE THE CASE, THERE WOULD BE A LOT MORE PEOPLE THAN THIS.
11/19
WE WERE TRYING TO RESPECT THE FIRE CODE.

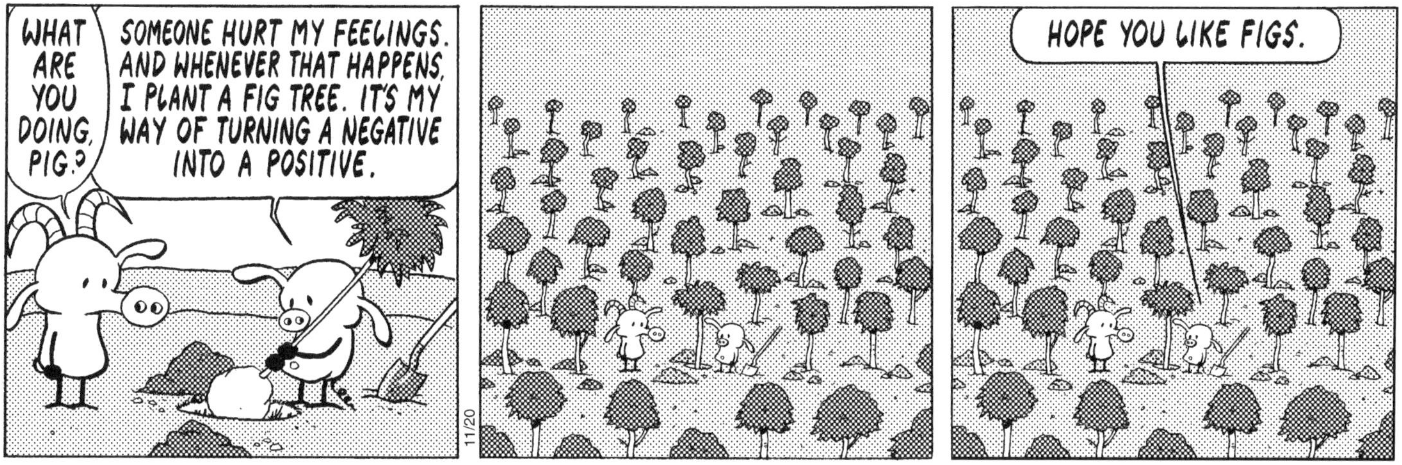
WHAT ARE YOU DOING, PIG?
SOMEONE HURT MY FEELINGS. AND WHENEVER THAT HAPPENS, I PLANT A FIG TREE. IT'S MY WAY OF TURNING A NEGATIVE INTO A POSITIVE.
HOPE YOU LIKE FIGS.
11/20

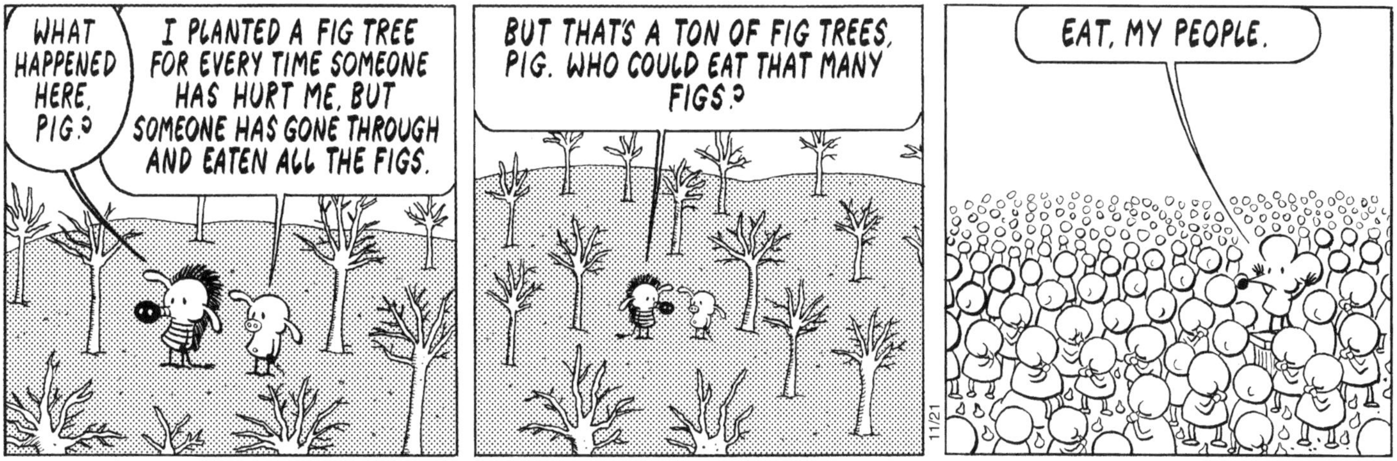
WHAT HAPPENED HERE, PIG?
I PLANTED A FIG TREE FOR EVERY TIME SOMEONE HAS HURT ME, BUT SOMEONE HAS GONE THROUGH AND EATEN ALL THE FIGS.
BUT THAT'S A TON OF FIG TREES, PIG. WHO COULD EAT THAT MANY FIGS?
EAT, MY PEOPLE.
11/21

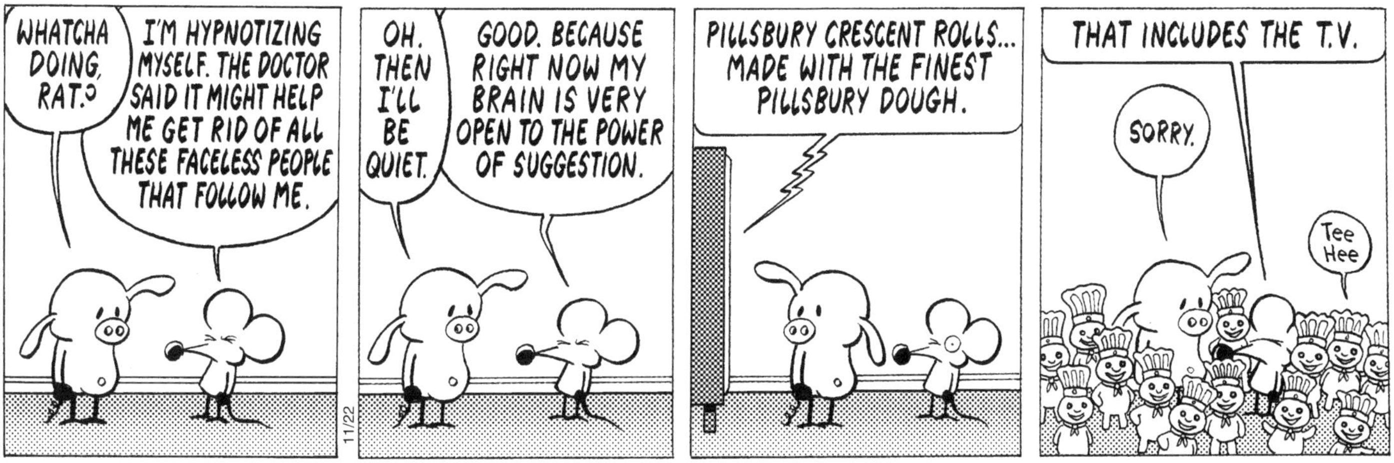
WHATCHA DOING, RAT?
I'M HYPNOTIZING MYSELF. THE DOCTOR SAID IT MIGHT HELP ME GET RID OF ALL THESE FACELESS PEOPLE THAT FOLLOW ME.
OH. THEN I'LL BE QUIET.
GOOD. BECAUSE RIGHT NOW MY BRAIN IS VERY OPEN TO THE POWER OF SUGGESTION.
PILLSBURY CRESCENT ROLLS... MADE WITH THE FINEST PILLSBURY DOUGH.
THAT INCLUDES THE T.V.
SORRY.
Tee Hee
11/22

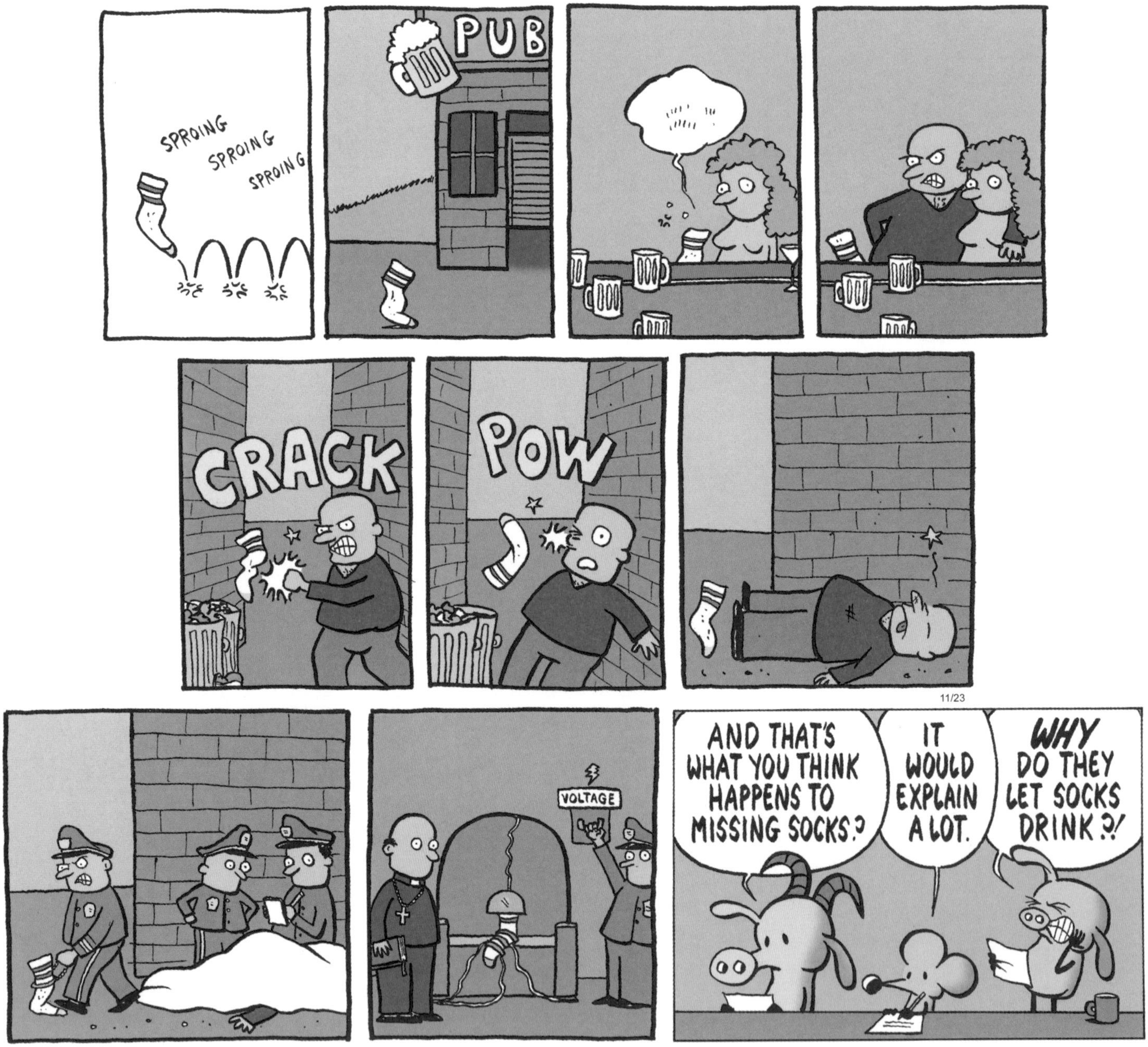
SPROING
SPROING
SPROING
PUB
CRACK
POW
11/23
VOLTAGE
AND THAT'S WHAT YOU THINK HAPPENS TO MISSING SOCKS?
IT WOULD EXPLAIN A LOT.
WHY DO THEY LET SOCKS DRINK?!

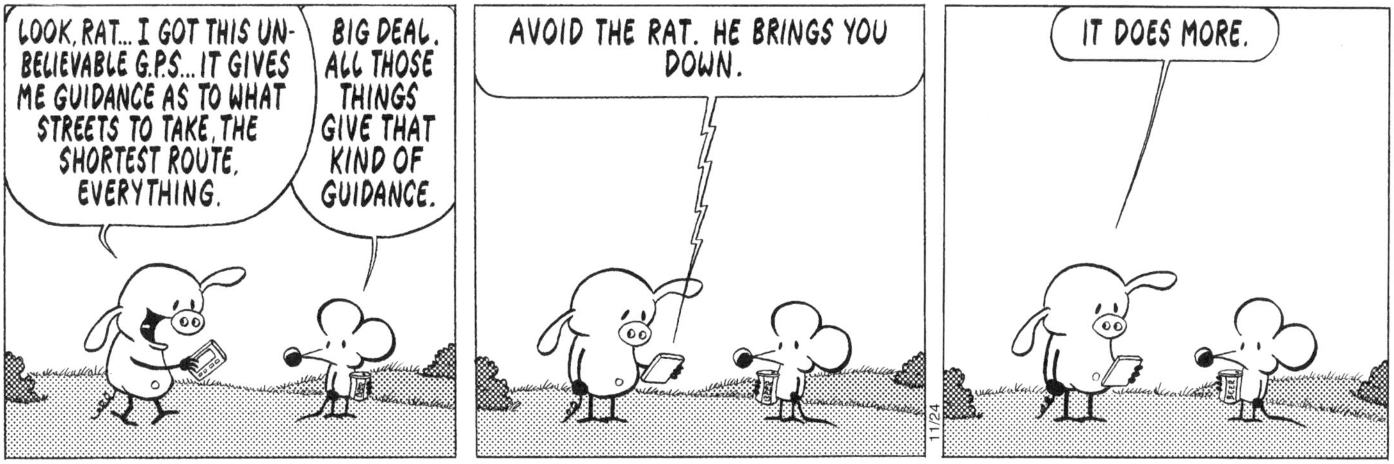
LOOK, RAT... I GOT THIS UNBELIEVABLE G.P.S... IT GIVES ME GUIDANCE AS TO WHAT STREETS TO TAKE, THE SHORTEST ROUTE, EVERYTHING.
BIG DEAL. ALL THOSE THINGS GIVE THAT KIND OF GUIDANCE.
AVOID THE RAT. HE BRINGS YOU DOWN.
11/24
IT DOES MORE.

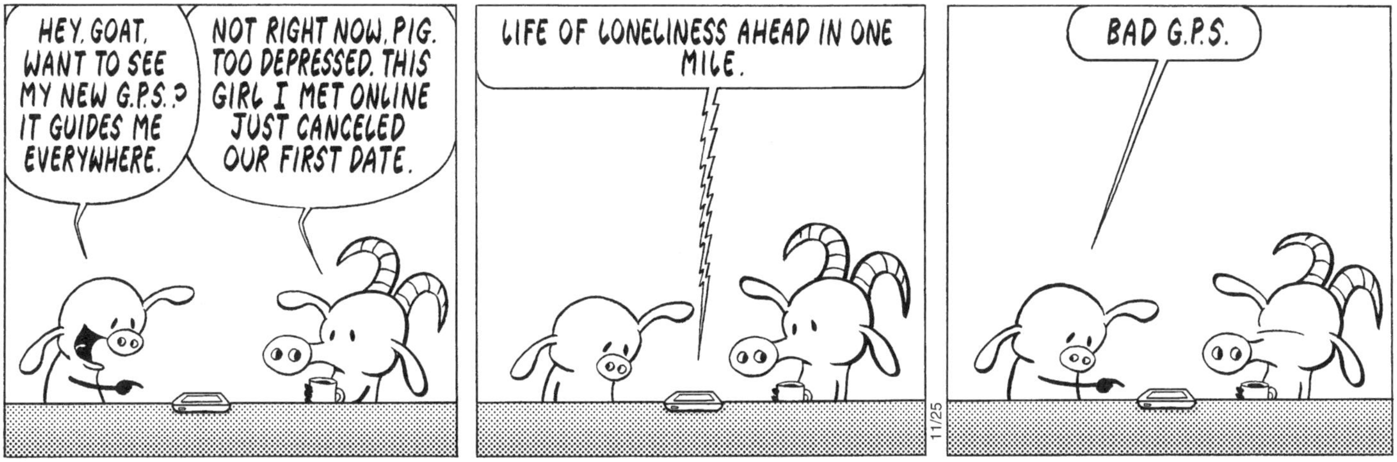
HEY, GOAT, WANT TO SEE MY NEW G.P.S.? IT GUIDES ME EVERYWHERE.
NOT RIGHT NOW, PIG. TOO DEPRESSED. THIS GIRL I MET ONLINE JUST CANCELED OUR FIRST DATE.
LIFE OF LONELINESS AHEAD IN ONE MILE.
11/25
BAD G.P.S.

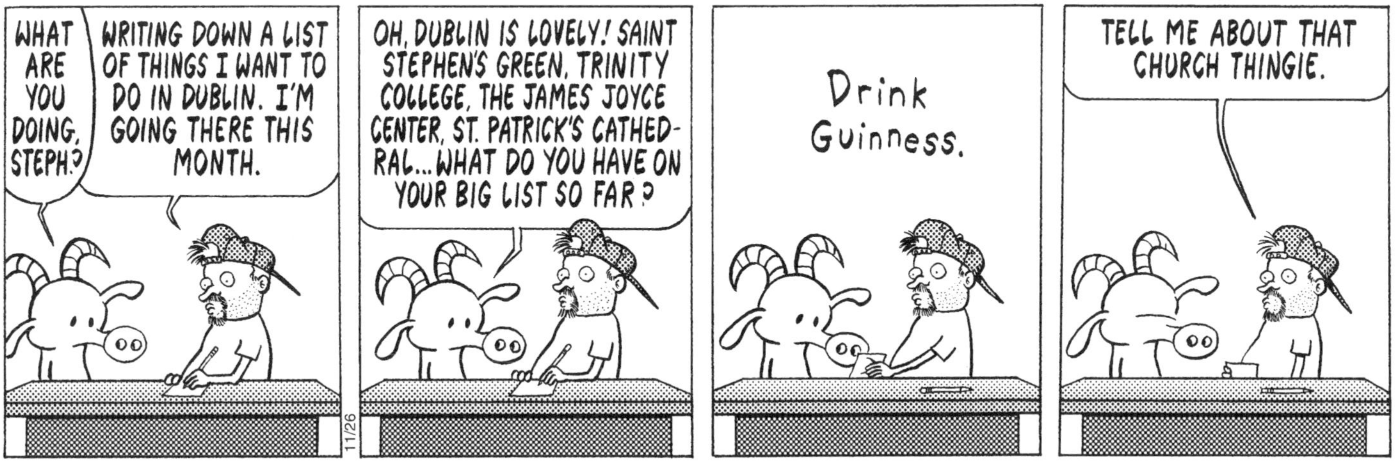
WHAT ARE YOU DOING, STEPH?
WRITING DOWN A LIST OF THINGS I WANT TO DO IN DUBLIN. I'M GOING THERE THIS MONTH.
11/26
OH, DUBLIN IS LOVELY! SAINT STEPHEN'S GREEN, TRINITY COLLEGE, THE JAMES JOYCE CENTER, ST. PATRICK'S CATHEDRAL... WHAT DO YOU HAVE ON YOUR BIG LIST SO FAR?
Drink Guinness.
TELL ME ABOUT THAT CHURCH THINGIE.

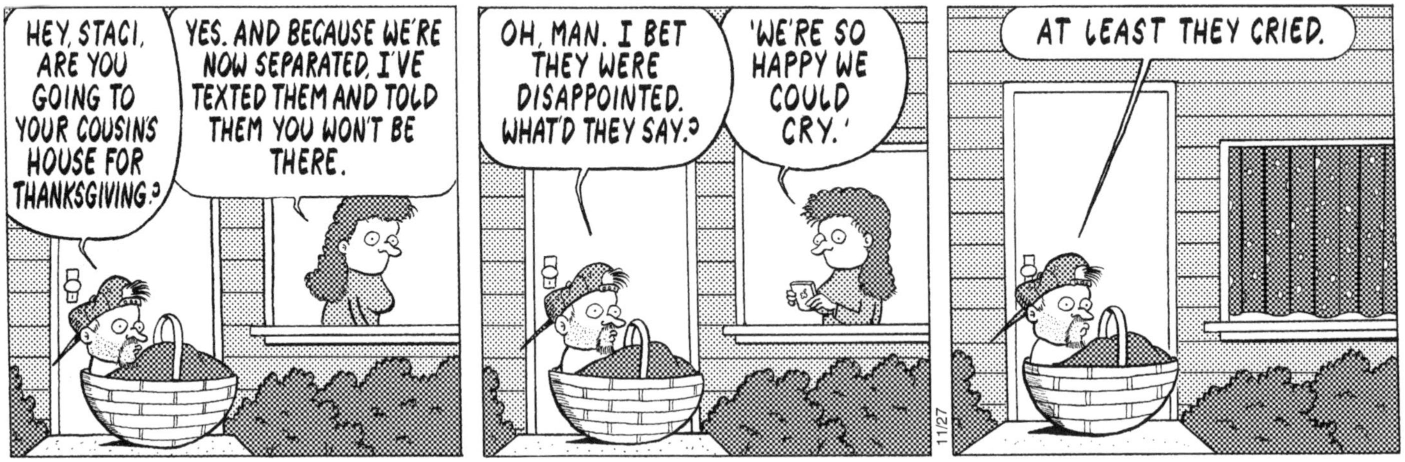
HEY, STACI, ARE YOU GOING TO YOUR COUSIN'S HOUSE FOR THANKSGIVING?
YES. AND BECAUSE WE'RE NOW SEPARATED, I'VE TEXTED THEM AND TOLD THEM YOU WON'T BE THERE.
OH, MAN. I BET THEY WERE DISAPPOINTED. WHAT'D THEY SAY?
'WE'RE SO HAPPY WE COULD CRY.'
AT LEAST THEY CRIED.
11/27

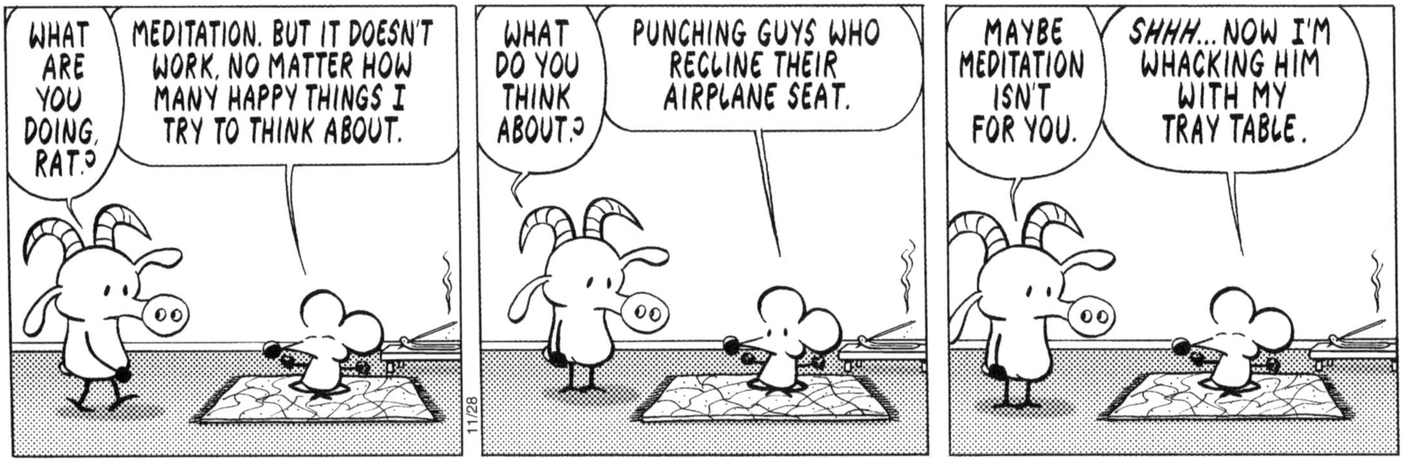
WHAT ARE YOU DOING, RAT?
MEDITATION. BUT IT DOESN'T WORK, NO MATTER HOW MANY HAPPY THINGS I TRY TO THINK ABOUT.
11/28
WHAT DO YOU THINK ABOUT?
PUNCHING GUYS WHO RECLINE THEIR AIRPLANE SEAT.
MAYBE MEDITATION ISN'T FOR YOU.
SHHH... NOW I'M WHACKING HIM WITH MY TRAY TABLE.

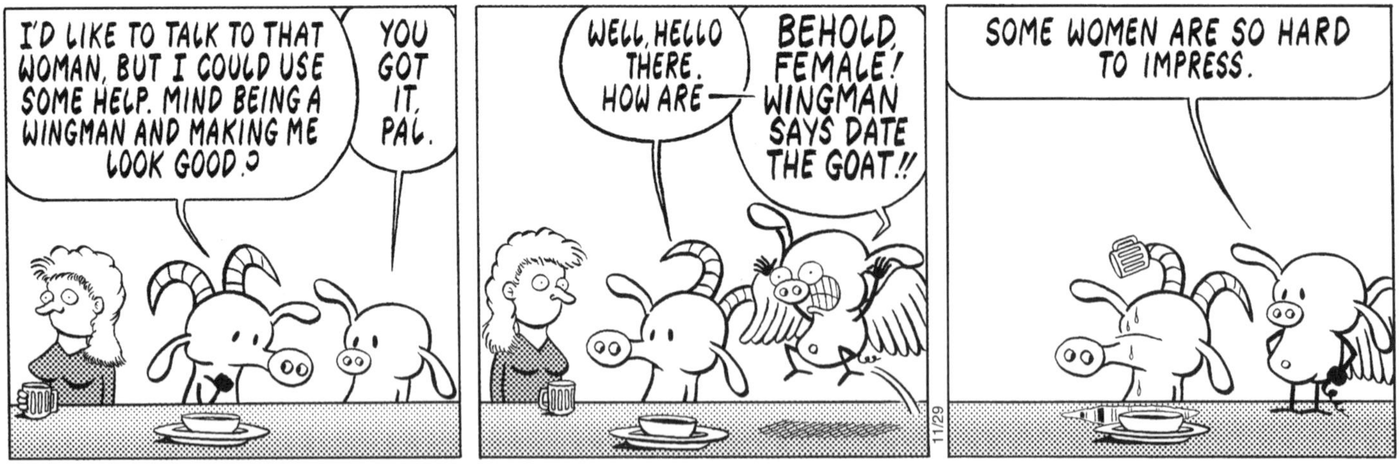
I'D LIKE TO TALK TO THAT WOMAN, BUT I COULD USE SOME HELP. MIND BEING A WINGMAN AND MAKING ME LOOK GOOD?
YOU GOT IT, PAL.
WELL, HELLO THERE. HOW ARE—
BEHOLD, FEMALE! WINGMAN SAYS DATE THE GOAT!!
11/29
SOME WOMEN ARE SO HARD TO IMPRESS.

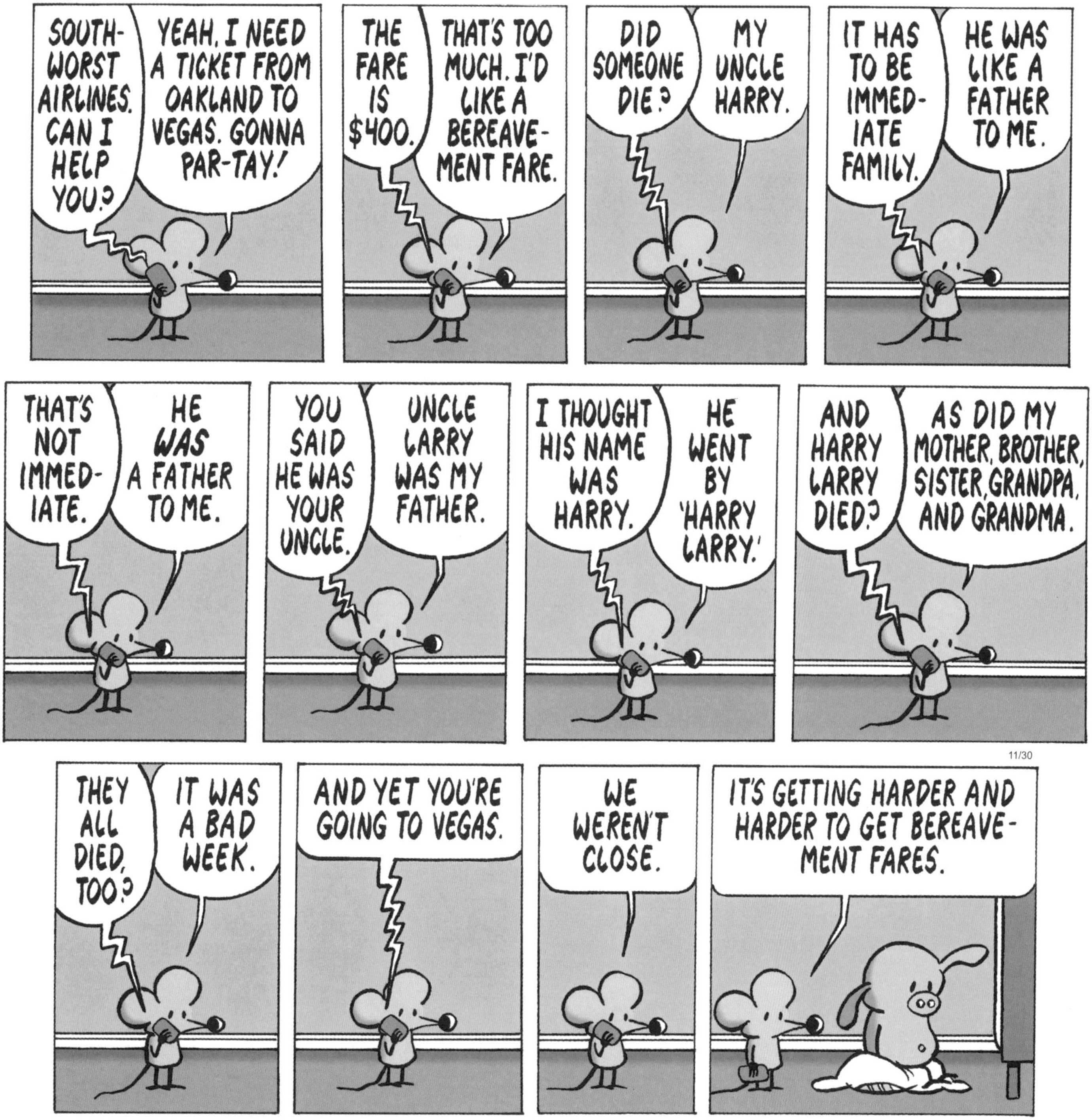
SOUTH-WORST AIRLINES. CAN I HELP YOU?
YEAH, I NEED A TICKET FROM OAKLAND TO VEGAS. GONNA PAR-TAY!
THE FARE IS $400.
THAT'S TOO MUCH. I'D LIKE A BEREAVEMENT FARE.
DID SOMEONE DIE?
MY UNCLE HARRY.
IT HAS TO BE IMMEDIATE FAMILY.
HE WAS LIKE A FATHER TO ME.
THAT'S NOT IMMEDIATE.
HE *WAS* A FATHER TO ME.
YOU SAID HE WAS YOUR UNCLE.
UNCLE LARRY WAS MY FATHER.
I THOUGHT HIS NAME WAS HARRY.
HE WENT BY 'HARRY LARRY.'
AND HARRY LARRY DIED?
AS DID MY MOTHER, BROTHER, SISTER, GRANDPA, AND GRANDMA.
11/30
THEY ALL DIED, TOO?
IT WAS A BAD WEEK.
AND YET YOU'RE GOING TO VEGAS.
WE WEREN'T CLOSE.
IT'S GETTING HARDER AND HARDER TO GET BEREAVEMENT FARES.

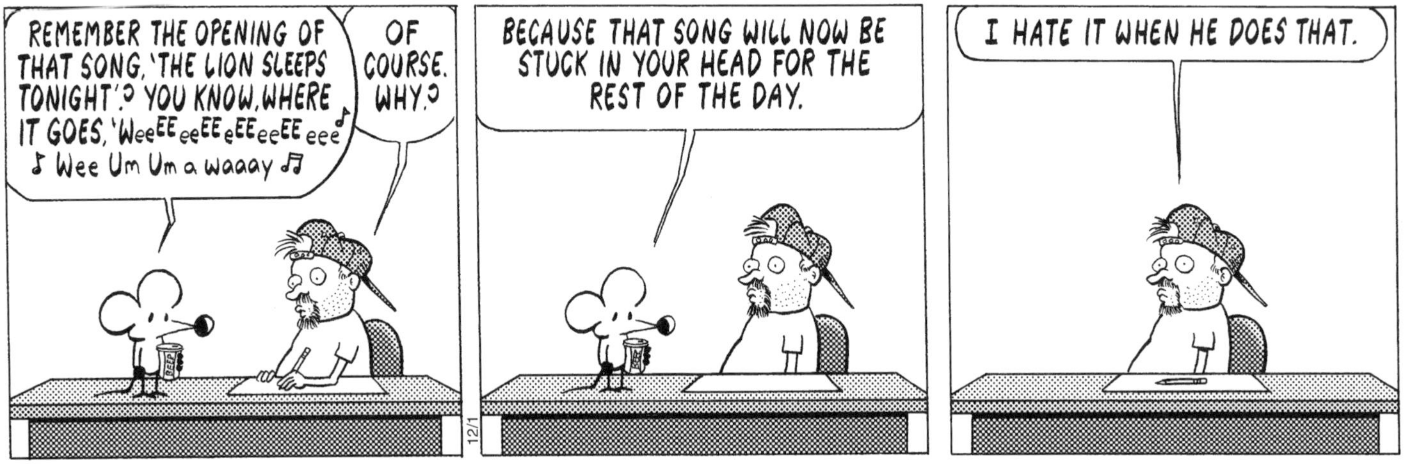
REMEMBER THE OPENING OF THAT SONG, 'THE LION SLEEPS TONIGHT'? YOU KNOW, WHERE IT GOES, 'WeeEEeeEEeEEeeEE eee ♪ Wee Um Um a waaay ♫
OF COURSE. WHY?
BECAUSE THAT SONG WILL NOW BE STUCK IN YOUR HEAD FOR THE REST OF THE DAY.
I HATE IT WHEN HE DOES THAT.
12/1

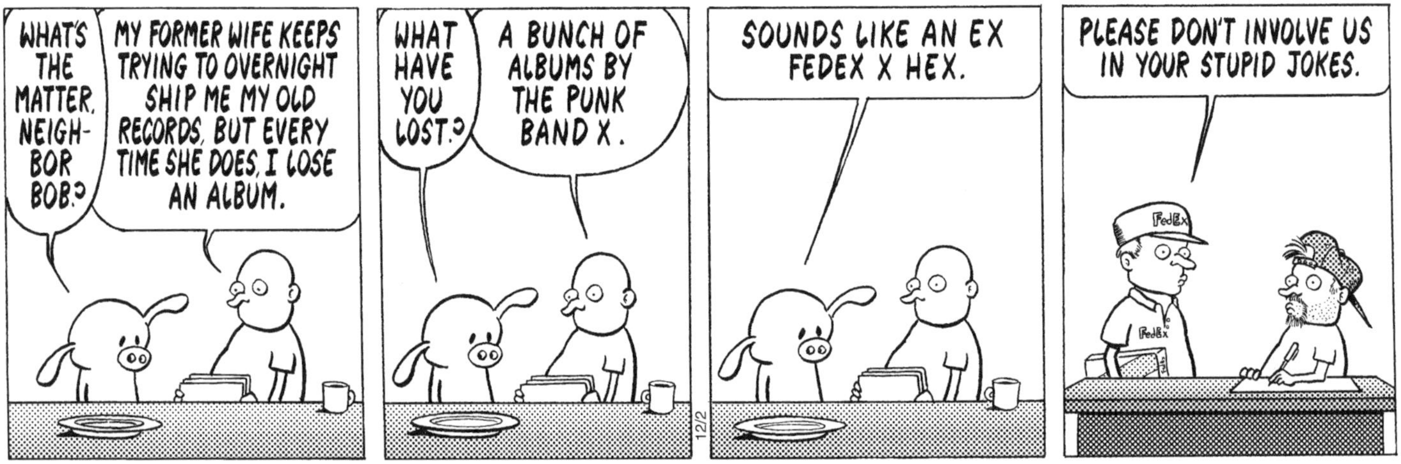
WHAT'S THE MATTER, NEIGHBOR BOB?
MY FORMER WIFE KEEPS TRYING TO OVERNIGHT SHIP ME MY OLD RECORDS, BUT EVERY TIME SHE DOES, I LOSE AN ALBUM.
WHAT HAVE YOU LOST?
A BUNCH OF ALBUMS BY THE PUNK BAND X.
SOUNDS LIKE AN EX FEDEX X HEX.
PLEASE DON'T INVOLVE US IN YOUR STUPID JOKES.
12/2

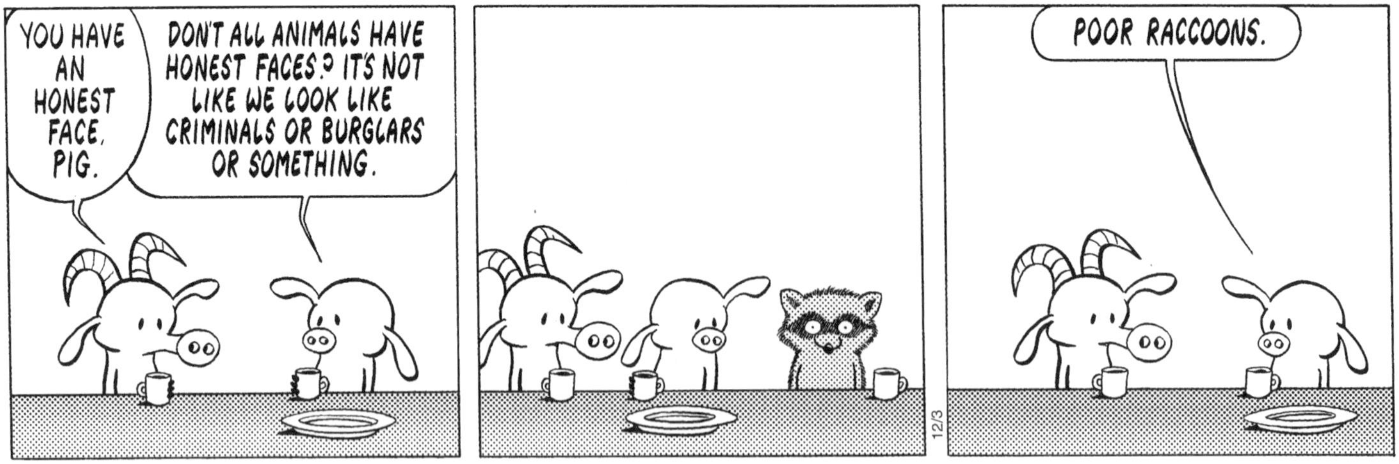
YOU HAVE AN HONEST FACE, PIG.
DON'T ALL ANIMALS HAVE HONEST FACES? IT'S NOT LIKE WE LOOK LIKE CRIMINALS OR BURGLARS OR SOMETHING.
POOR RACCOONS.
12/3

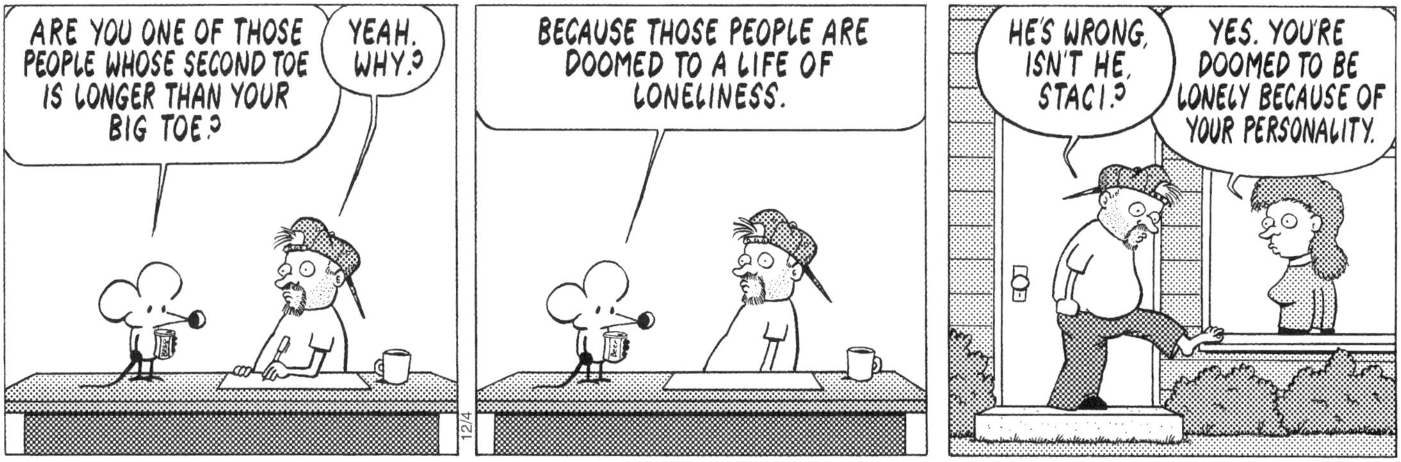
ARE YOU ONE OF THOSE PEOPLE WHOSE SECOND TOE IS LONGER THAN YOUR BIG TOE?
YEAH. WHY?
12/4
BECAUSE THOSE PEOPLE ARE DOOMED TO A LIFE OF LONELINESS.
HE'S WRONG, ISN'T HE, STACI?
YES. YOU'RE DOOMED TO BE LONELY BECAUSE OF YOUR PERSONALITY.

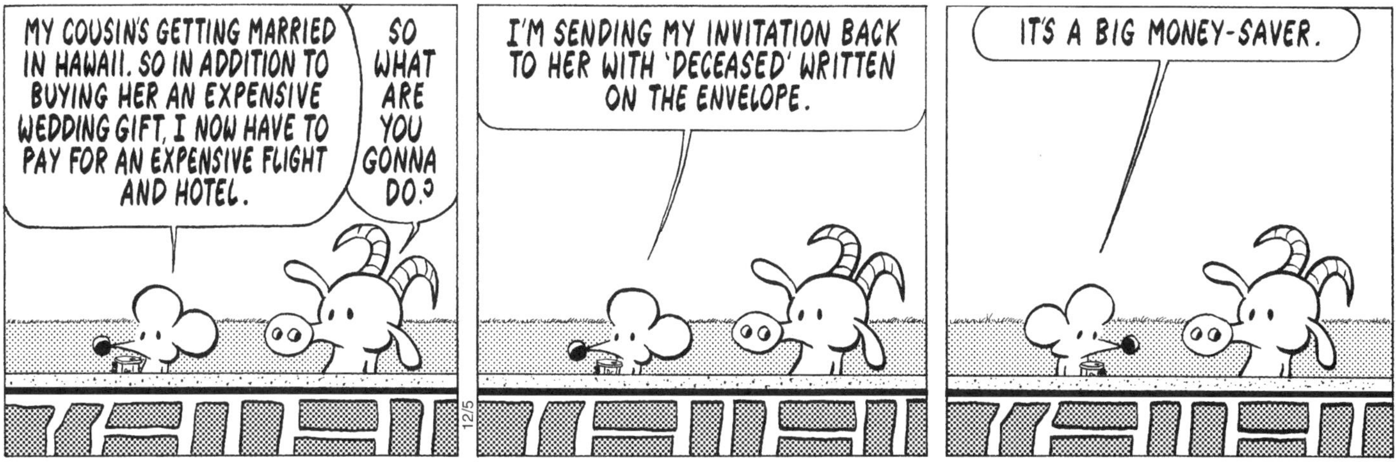
MY COUSIN'S GETTING MARRIED IN HAWAII. SO IN ADDITION TO BUYING HER AN EXPENSIVE WEDDING GIFT, I NOW HAVE TO PAY FOR AN EXPENSIVE FLIGHT AND HOTEL.
SO WHAT ARE YOU GONNA DO?
12/5
I'M SENDING MY INVITATION BACK TO HER WITH 'DECEASED' WRITTEN ON THE ENVELOPE.
IT'S A BIG MONEY-SAVER.

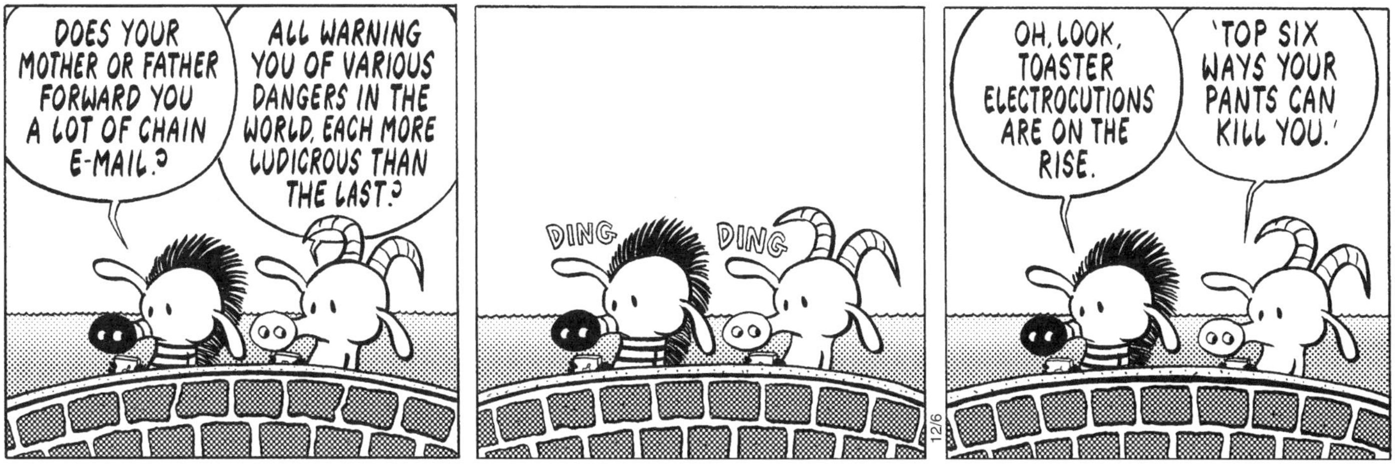
DOES YOUR MOTHER OR FATHER FORWARD YOU A LOT OF CHAIN E-MAIL?
ALL WARNING YOU OF VARIOUS DANGERS IN THE WORLD, EACH MORE LUDICROUS THAN THE LAST?
DING
DING
12/6
OH, LOOK, TOASTER ELECTROCUTIONS ARE ON THE RISE.
'TOP SIX WAYS YOUR PANTS CAN KILL YOU.'

Pearls Before Swine is distributed internationally by Universal Uclick.

I'm Only in This for Me copyright © 2016 by Stephan Pastis. All rights reserved. Printed in China. No part of this book may be used or reproduced in any manner whatsoever without written permission except in the case of reprints in the context of reviews.

Andrews McMeel Publishing
a division of Andrews McMeel Universal
1130 Walnut Street, Kansas City, Missouri 64106

www.andrewsmcmeel.com

16 17 18 19 20 SDB 10 9 8 7 6 5 4 3 2 1

ISBN: 978-1-4494-7626-7

Library of Congress Control Number: 2015955662

Pearls Before Swine can be viewed on the Internet at
www.pearlscomic.com

These strips appeared in newspapers from March 3, 2014 to December 6, 2014.